Othello

4

Satomi Ikezawa

TRANSLATED AND ADAPTED BY
William Flanagan

LETTERED BY
Michaelis/Carpelis Design

tanoshimi

LONDON

Published in the United Kingdom by Tanoshimi in 2007

1 3 5 7 9 10 8 6 4 2

Othello Volume 4 is a work of fiction. Names, characters, places and incidents are the products of the
author's imagination or are used fictitiously. Any resemblance to actual events, locales, or
persons, living or dead, is entirely coincidental.

This book is sold subject to the condition that it shall not, by way of trade or otherwise, be lent,
resold, hired out, or otherwise circulated without the publisher's prior consent in any form of
binding or cover other than that in which it is published and without a similar condition including
this condition being imposed on the subsequent purchaser.

First published in Japan in 2003 by Kodansha Ltd., Tokyo

Published by arrangement with Kodansha Ltd., Tokyo and with Del Rey,
an imprint of Random House Inc., New York

Tanoshimi
Random House, 20 Vauxhall Bridge Road,
London, SW1V 2SA

www.tanoshimi.tv
www.randomhouse.co.uk

Addresses for companies within The Random House Group Limited can be found at:
www.randomhouse.co.uk/offices.htm

The Random House Group Limited Reg. No. 954009

A CIP catalogue record for this book is available from the British Library

ISBN 9780099506690

The Random House Group Limited makes every effort to ensure that the papers used in its books are made
from trees that have been legally sourced from well-managed and credibly certified forests. Our paper pro-
curement policy can be found at: www.randomhouse.co.uk/paper.htm

Printed and bound in Germany by GGP Media GmbH, Pößneck

Translator and adaptor – William Flanagan
Lettering – Michaelis/Carpelis Design

Contents

Honorifics

Throughout the Tanoshimi Manga books, you will find Japanese honorifics left intact in the translations. For those not familiar with how the Japanese use honorifics and, more importantly, how they differ from English honorifics, we present this brief overview.

Politeness has always been a critical facet of Japanese culture. Ever since the feudal era, when Japan was a highly stratified society, use of honorifics—which can be defined as polite speech that indicates relationship or status—has played an essential role in the Japanese language. When addressing someone in Japanese, an honorific usually takes the form of a suffix attached to one's name (example: "Asuna-san"), or as a title at the end of one's name or in place of the name itself (example: "Negi-sensei," or simply "Sensei!").

Honorifics can be expressions of respect or endearment. In the context of manga and anime, honorifics give insight into the nature of the relationship between characters. Many translations into English leave out these important honorifics, and therefore distort the "feel" of the original Japanese. Because Japanese honorifics contain nuances that English honorifics lack, it is our policy at Tanoshimi not to translate them. Here, instead, is a guide to some of the honorifics you may encounter in Tanoshimi Manga.

-san: This is the most common honorific and is equivalent to Mr., Miss, Ms., or Mrs. It is the all-purpose honorific and can be used in any situation where politeness is required.

-sama: This is one level higher than "-san" It is used to confer great respect.

-dono: This comes from the word "tono," which means "lord." It is an even higher level than "-sama" and confers utmost respect.

-kun: This suffix is used at the end of boys' names to express familiarity or endearment. It is also sometimes used by men among friends, or when addressing someone younger or of a lower station.

-chan: This is used to express endearment, mostly toward girls. It is also used for little boys, pets, and even among lovers. It gives a sense of childish cuteness.

Bozu: This is an informal way to refer to a boy, similar to the English term "kid".

Sempai: This title suggests that the addressee is one's senior in a group or organization. It is most often used in a school setting, where underclassmen refer to their upperclassmen as "sempai." It can also be used in the workplace, such as when a newer employee addresses an employee who has seniority in the company.

Kohai: This is the opposite of "sempai" and is used toward underclassmen in school or newcomers in the workplace. It connotes that the addressee is of a lower station.

Sensei: Literally meaning "one who has come before," this title is used for teachers, doctors, or masters of any profession or art.

[blank]: Usually forgotten in these lists, but perhaps the most significant difference between Japanese and English. The lack of honorific means that the speaker has permission to address the person in a very intimate way. Usually, only family, spouses, or very close friends have this kind of permission. Known as *yobisute,* it can be gratifying when someone who has earned the intimacy starts to call one by one's name without an honorific. But when that intimacy hasn't been earned, it can also be very insulting.

A Note from the Author

My father once said to me, "You're an analog girl." But for the past several years, I've lived my life relying heavily on my personal computer. At work, I use it for checking my facts and doing image processing for my manga pages. In my personal life, I use it for e-mail and the net (shopping, almost exclusively). Recently, I've developed a hobby—to upgrade and improve my computer! It's sooo fun!

OTHELLO
オセロ。

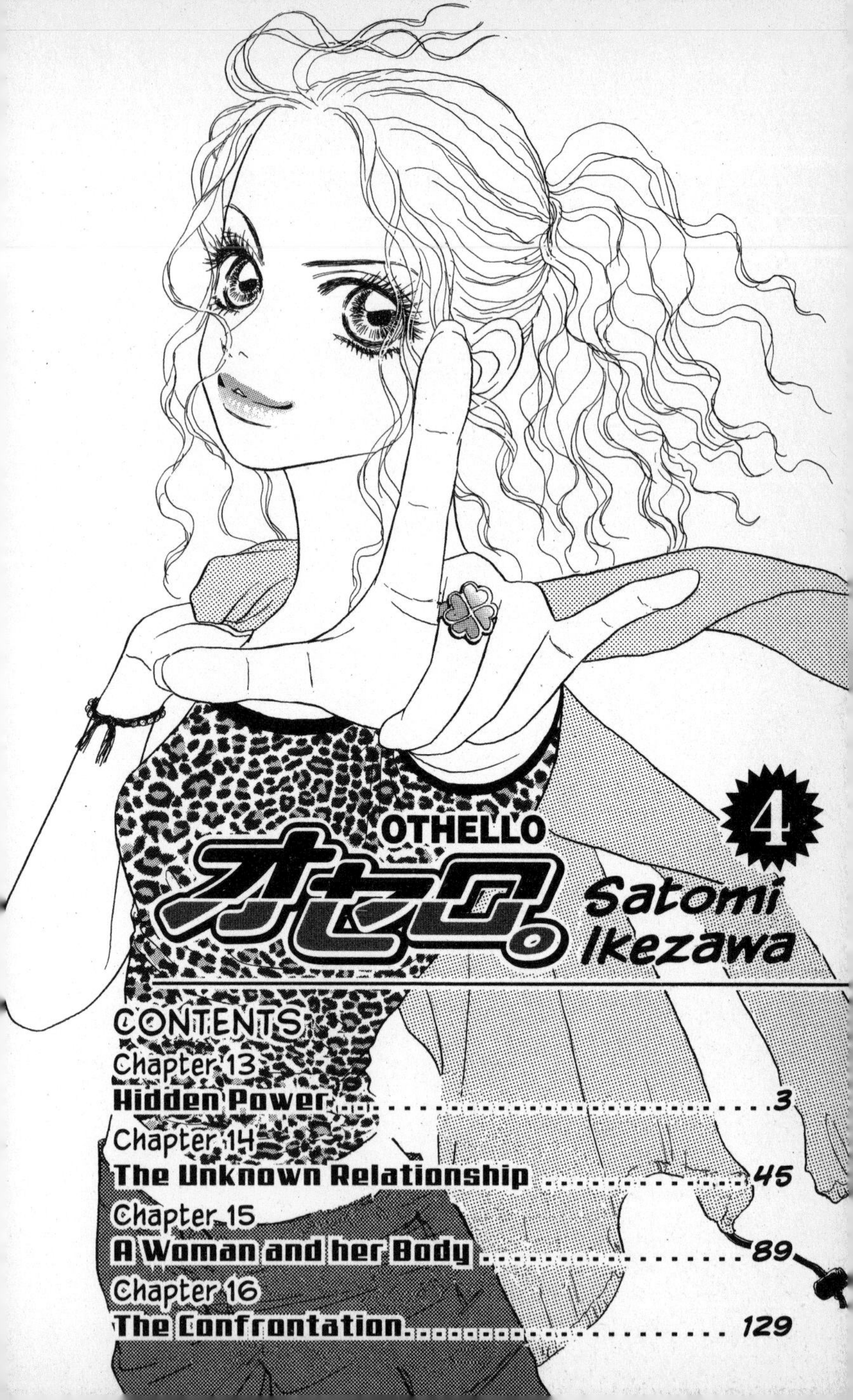

OTHELLO オセロ。 4

Satomi Ikezawa

CONTENTS

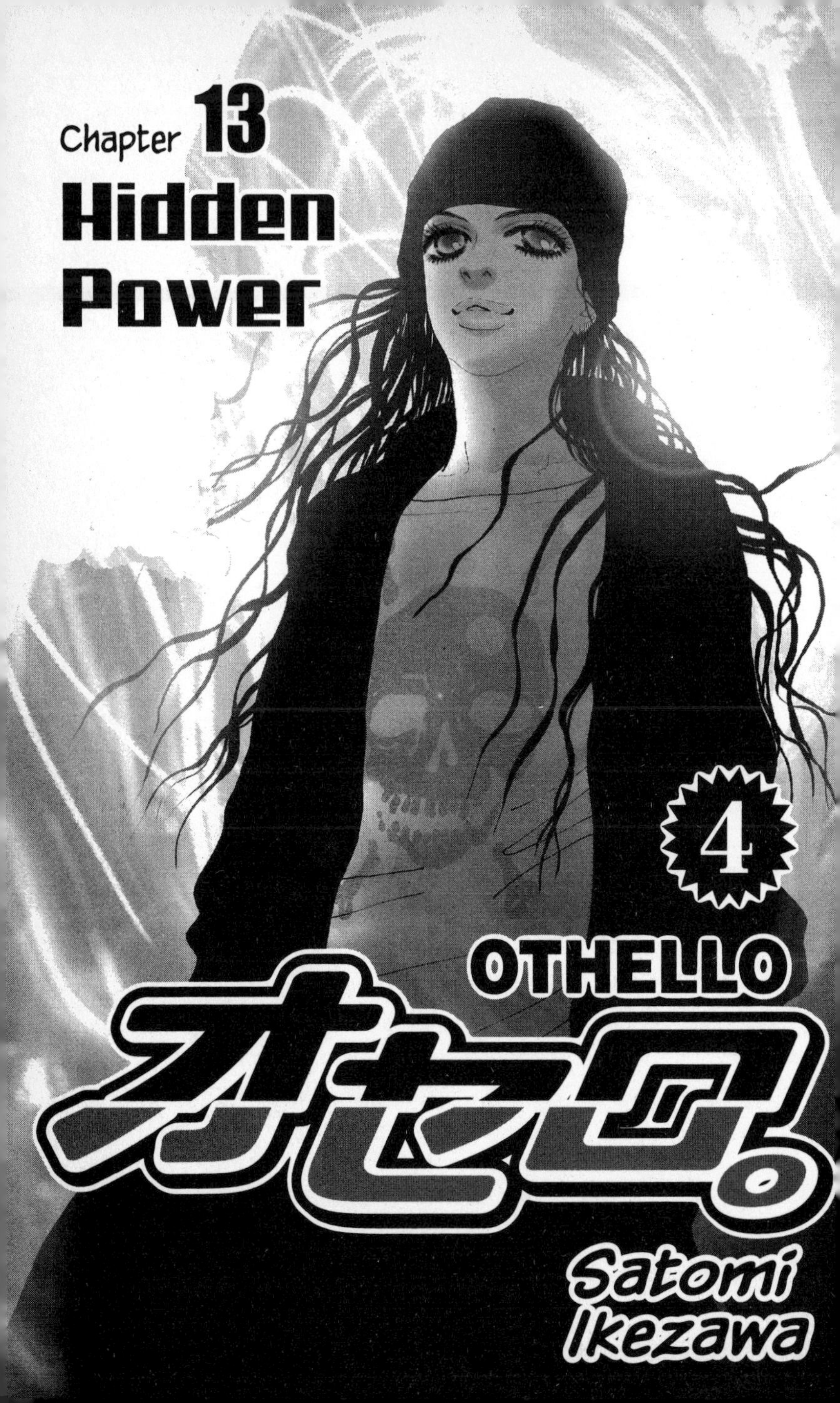

Chapter 13
Hidden Power
4
OTHELLO
オセロ
Satomi Ikezawa

OTHELLO

オセロ。

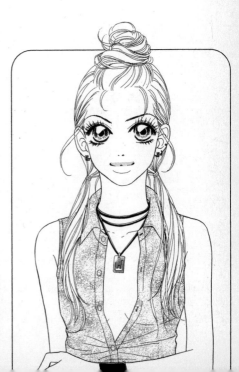

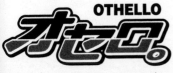

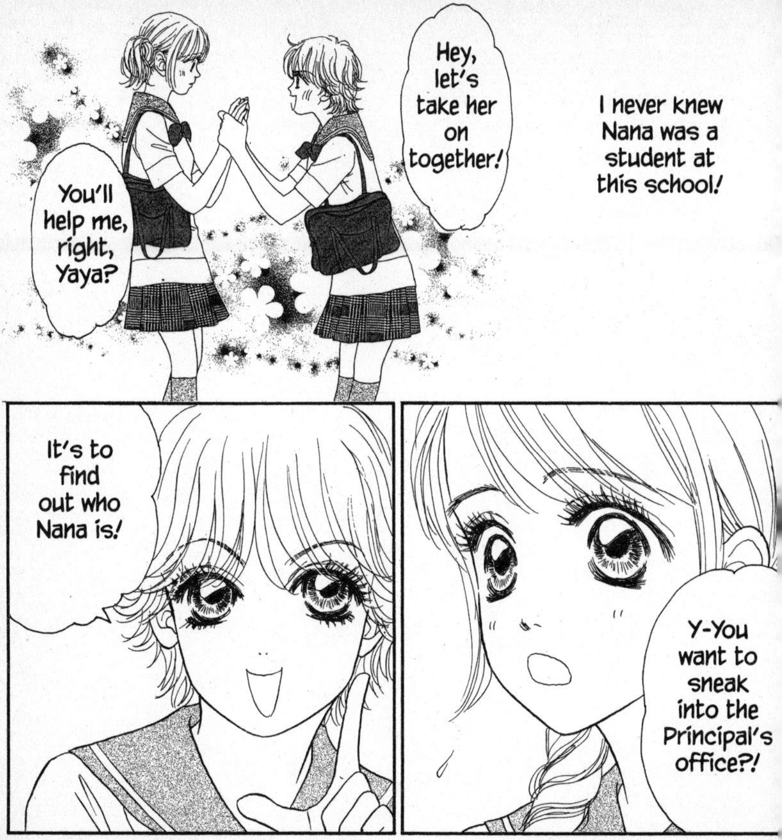
I never knew Nana was a student at this school!
Hey, let's take her on together!
You'll help me, right, Yaya?
Y-You want to sneak into the Principal's office?!
It's to find out who Nana is!

Nana's on a rampage, and Yaya doesn't know!!

オセロ。

The Story Thus Far

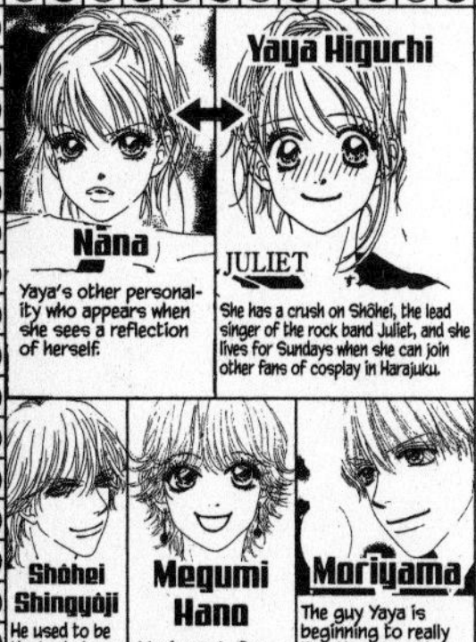
Yaya Higuchi
JULIET
Nana
Yaya's other personality who appears when she sees a reflection of herself.
She has a crush on Shōhei, the lead singer of the rock band Juliet, and she lives for Sundays when she can join other fans of cosplay in Harajuku.
Shōhei Shingyōji
He used to be the lead singer, Shōhei from Juliet.
Megumi Hano
Moriyama's fan and an enemy to Nana.
Moriyama
The guy Yaya is beginning to really like. He knows that Yaya and Nana are the same person.

♪ Nana performed live as a guest during a gig with Moriyama's band Black Dog, but soon she was subjected to a slap in the face by Moriyama's fan, Megumi Hano. Afterwards, "Hano-chan" transferred into their school hoping to capture Moriyama's attention.

♪ At school, Hano-chan noticed just how friendly Moriyama and Yaya were getting. She feigned friendship with Yaya, and with words as sharp as carving knives, she verbally stabbed Yaya dozens of times. When the words began hurting to the point where Yaya couldn't take it any more, that's when Nana made her entrance! She caught up with Hano-chan, and made sure that justice was done!

♪ But that let Hano-chan know that Nana was a student at her school, and now she's trying to enlist Yaya's aid in her plan to get revenge on Nana...

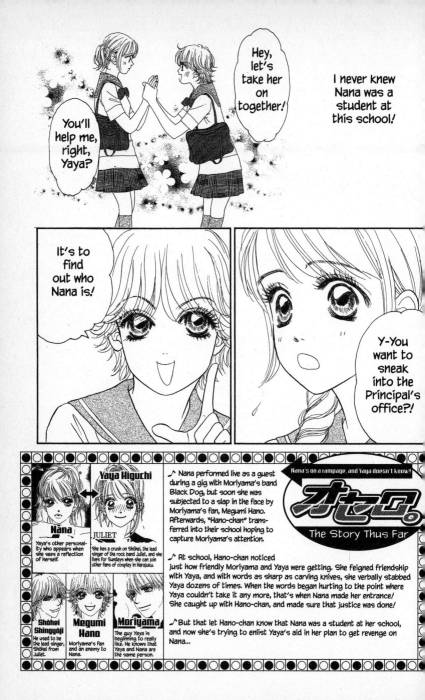

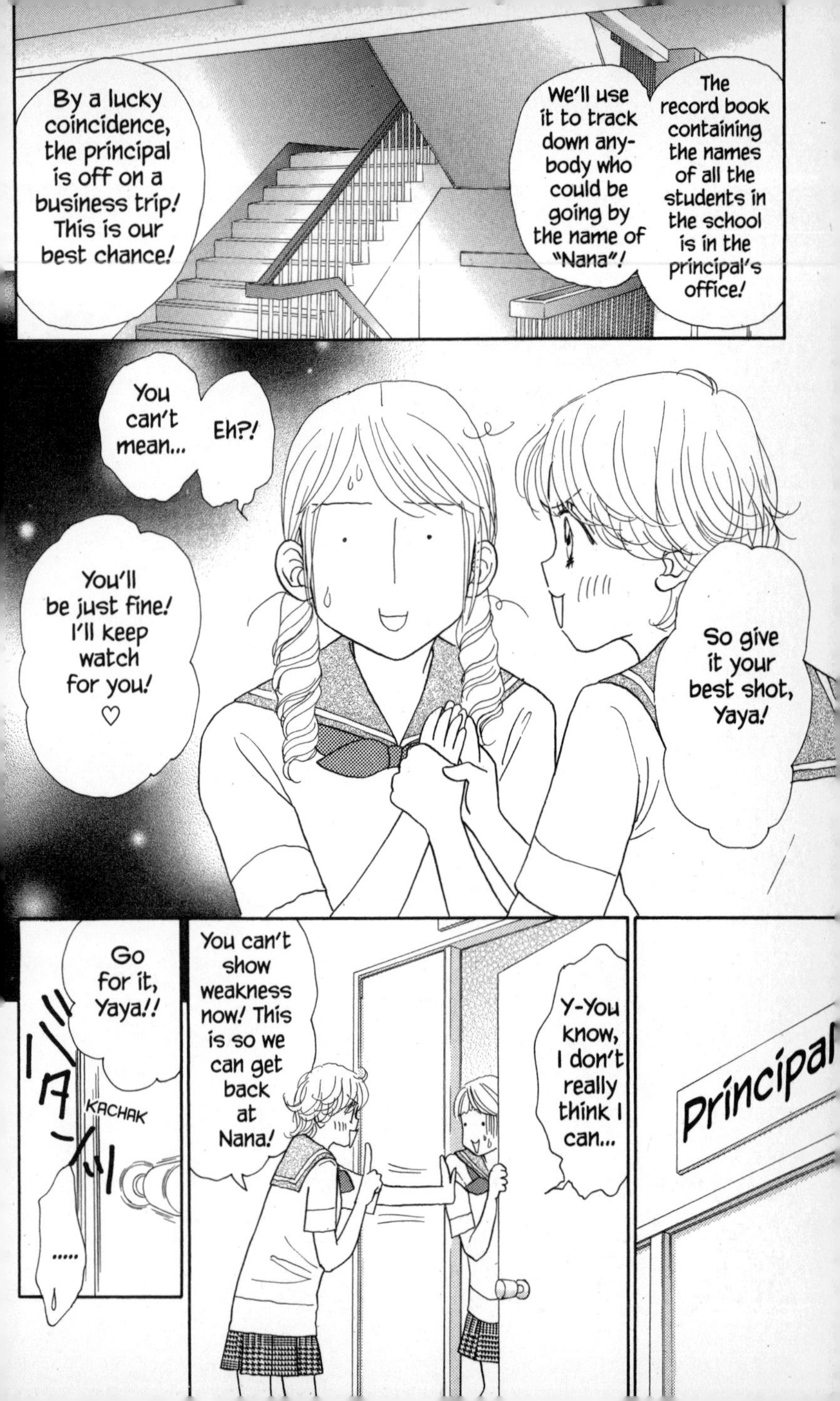
The record book containing the names of all the students in the school is in the principal's office!
We'll use it to track down any-body who could be going by the name of "Nana"!
By a lucky coincidence, the principal is off on a business trip! This is our best chance!
So give it your best shot, Yaya!
Eh?!
You can't mean...
You'll be just fine! I'll keep watch for you! ♡
Principal
Y-You know, I don't really think I can...
You can't show weakness now! This is so we can get back at Nana!
Go for it, Yaya!!
KACHAK
.....

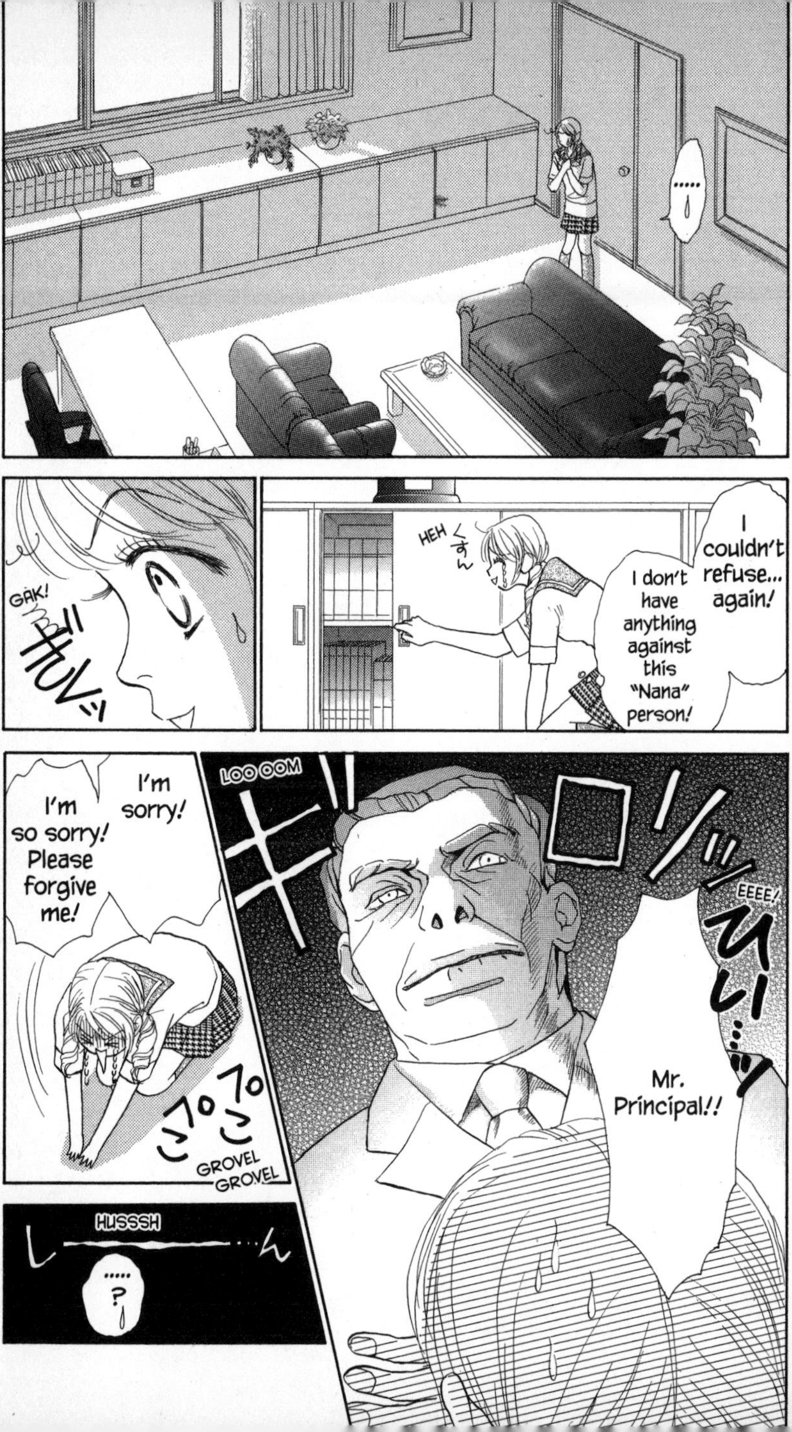
......
!
I couldn't refuse... again!
I don't have anything against this "Nana" person!
HEH
くすん
GAK!
ギクッ
LOO OOM
ギロッ
EEEE!
ひい…ッ
Mr. Principal!!
I'm sorry!
I'm so sorry! Please forgive me!
GROVEL GROVEL
ぺこぺこ
HUSSSH
し――…ん
......
?

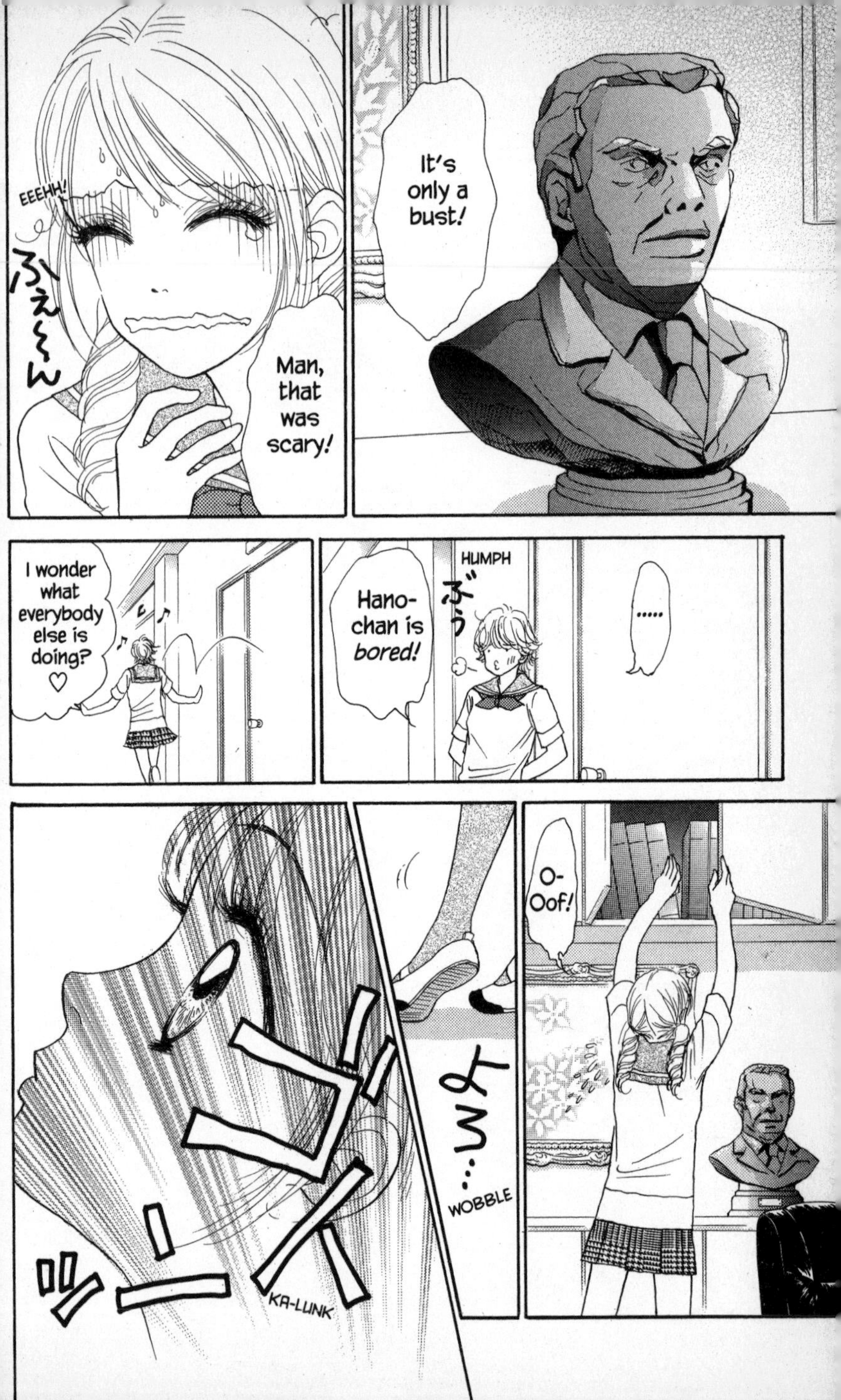
It's only a bust!
EEEHH!
ふぇ〜ん
Man, that was scary!
.....
HUMPH
ぶぅ
Hano-chan is bored!
I wonder what everybody else is doing? ♡
O-Oof!
よろ…
WOBBLE
ゴツーン
KA-LUNK

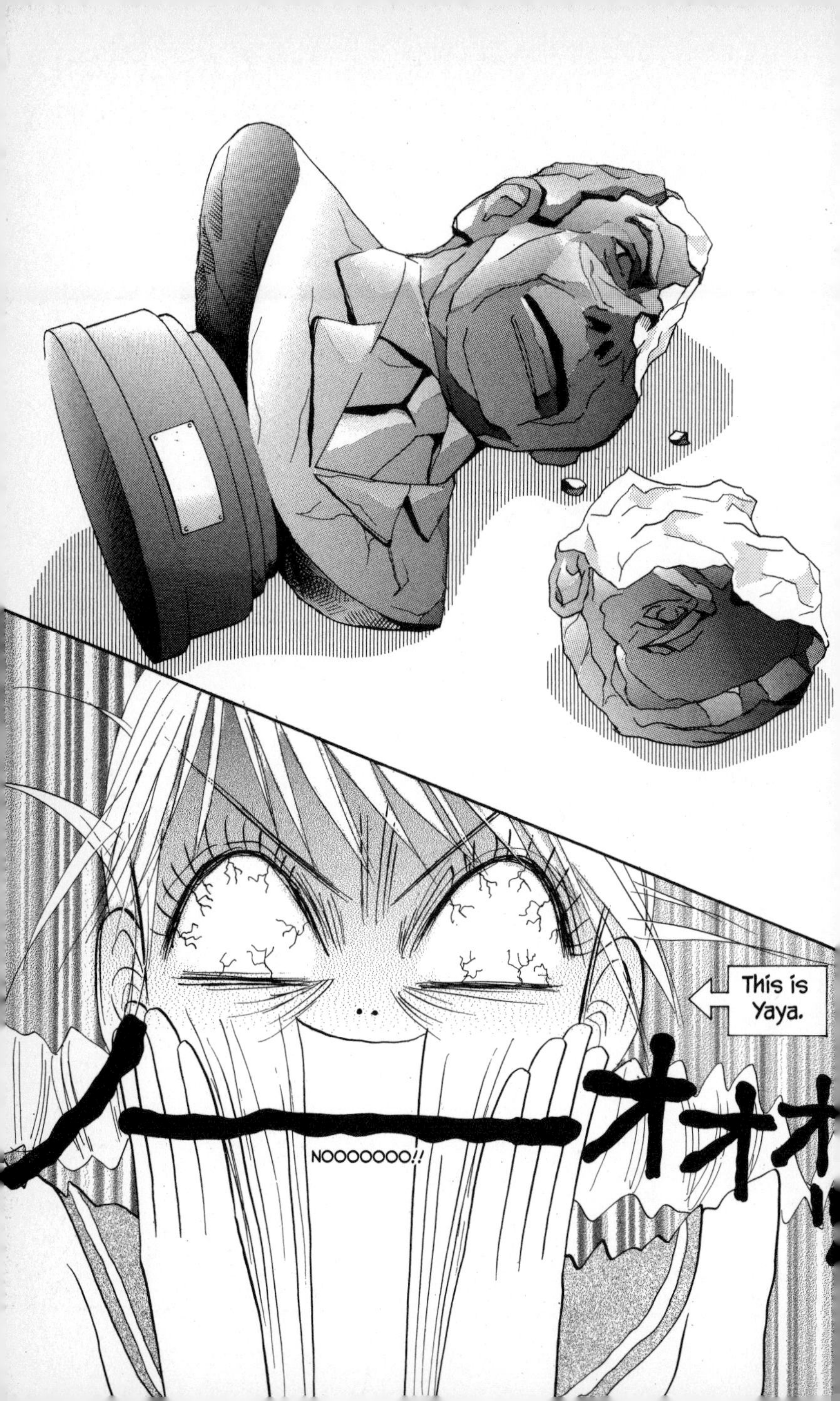
This is Yaya.
イーーーーオオオ!!
NOOOOOOO!!

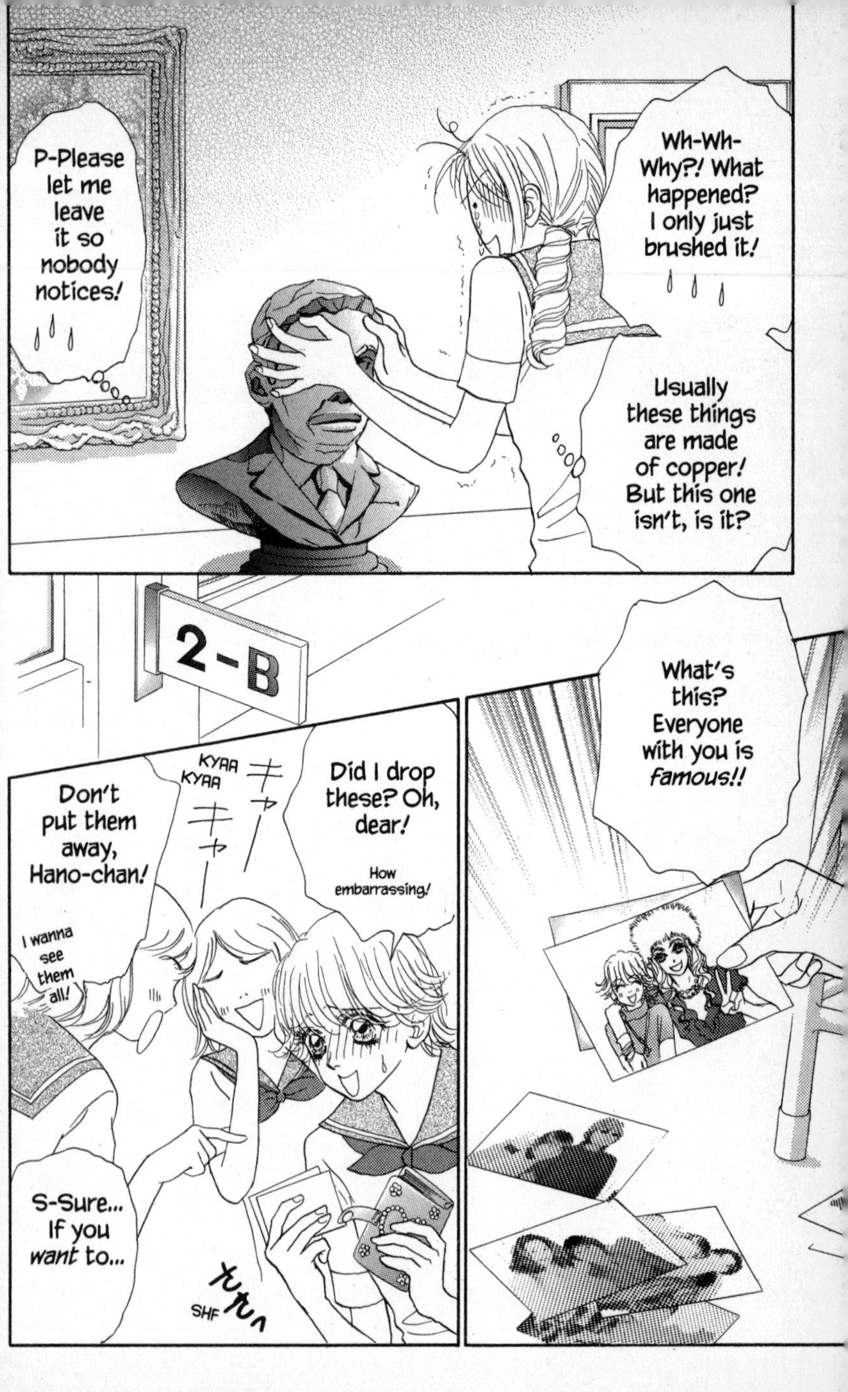

Wh-Wh-Why?! What happened? I only just brushed it!
Usually these things are made of copper! But this one isn't, is it?
P-Please let me leave it so nobody notices!
2-B
What's this? Everyone with you is *famous!!*
Did I drop these? Oh, dear!
How embarrassing!
KYAA KYAA
Don't put them away, Hano-chan!
I wanna see them all!
S-Sure... If you *want* to...
SHF

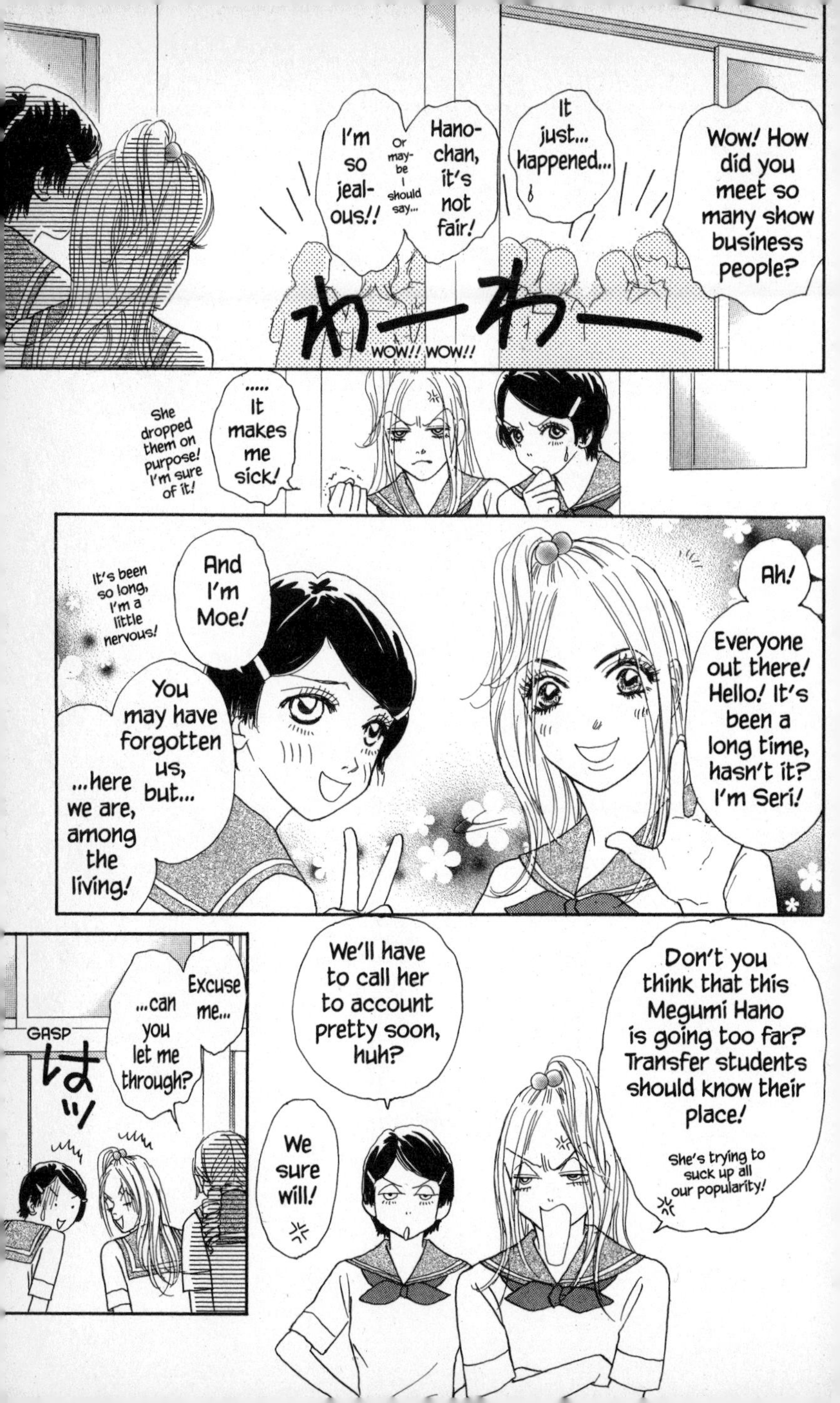

Wow! How did you meet so many show business people?
It just... happened...
Hano-chan, it's not fair!
Or may-be I should say...
I'm so jeal-ous!!
わーわー
WOW!! WOW!!
..... It makes me sick!
She dropped them on purpose! I'm sure of it!
Ah!
Everyone out there! Hello! It's been a long time, hasn't it? I'm Seri!
And I'm Moe!
It's been so long, I'm a little nervous!
You may have forgotten us, but...
...here we are, among the living!
Don't you think that this Megumi Hano is going too far? Transfer students should know their place!
She's trying to suck up all our popularity!
We'll have to call her to account pretty soon, huh?
We sure will!
Excuse me...
...can you let me through?
はッ
GASP

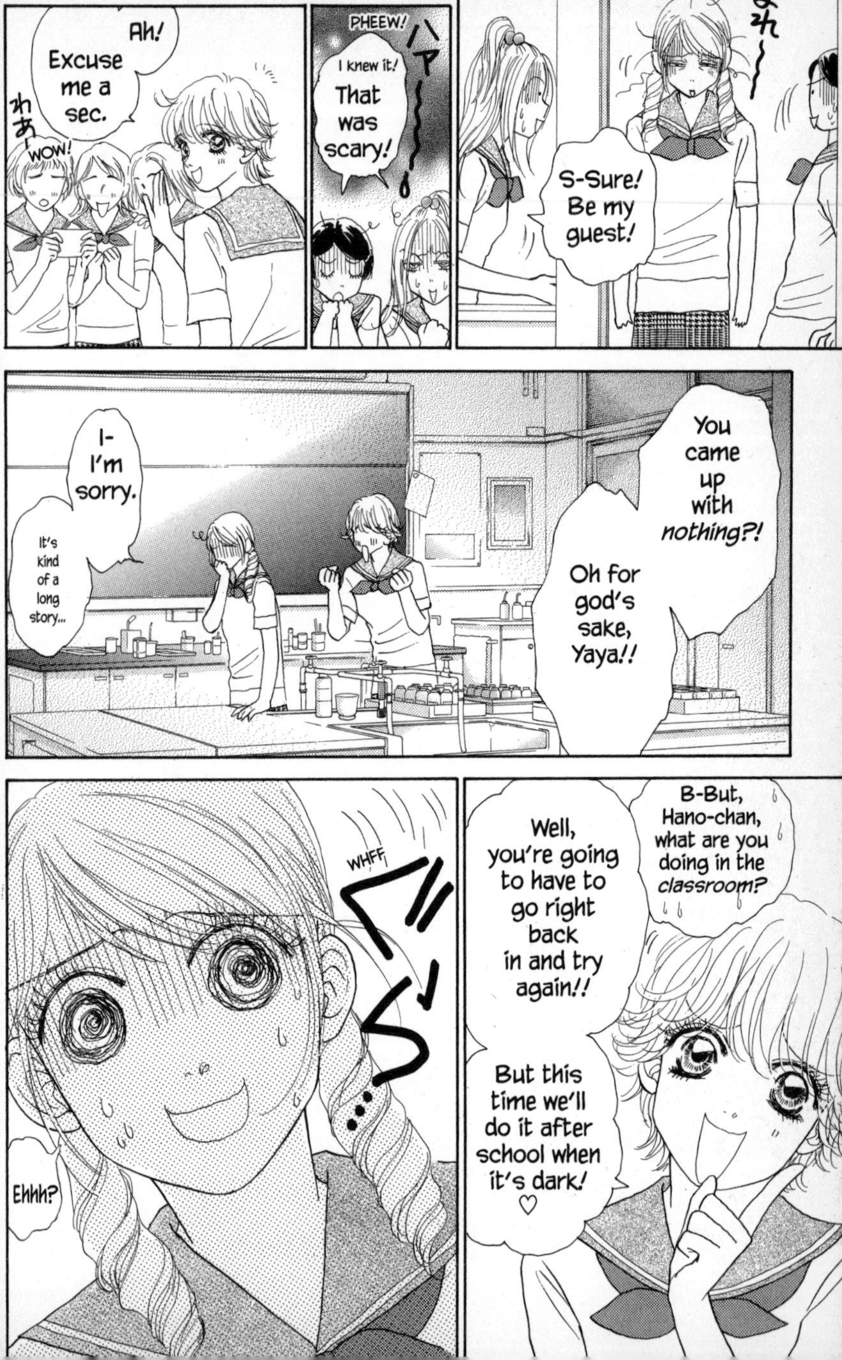

WOBBLE
よれ~
S-Sure! Be my guest!
PHEEW!
ハア~
I knew it! That was scary!
Ah! Excuse me a sec.
わあ
WOW!
You came up with *nothing?!*
Oh for god's sake, Yaya!!
I- I'm sorry.
It's kind of a long story...
B-But, Hano-chan, what are you doing in the *classroom?*
Well, you're going to have to go right back in and try again!!
But this time we'll do it after school when it's dark! ♡
WHFF
Ehhh?

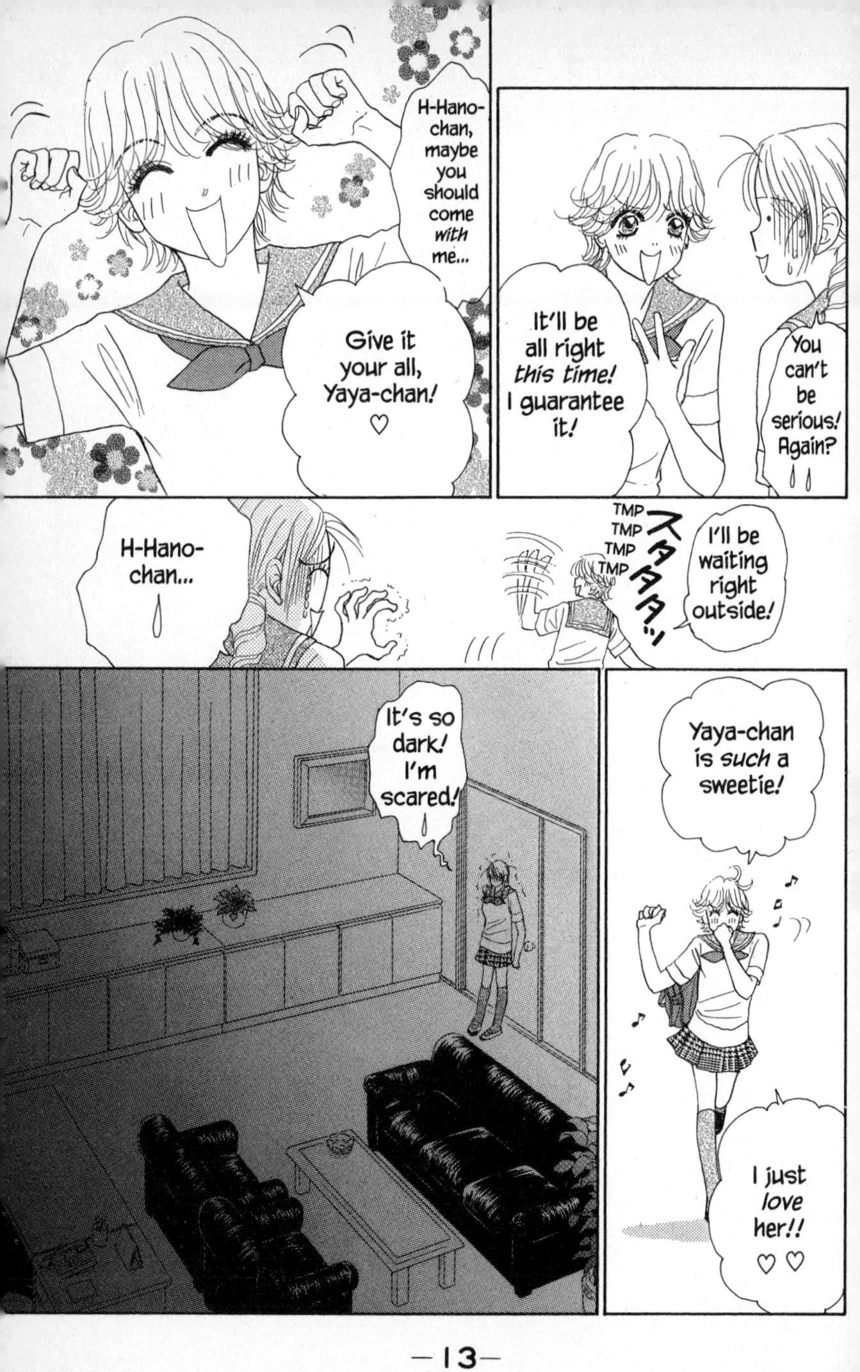
You can't be serious! Again?
It'll be all right *this time!* I guarantee it!
H-Hano-chan, maybe you should come *with* me...
Give it your all, Yaya-chan! ♡
I'll be waiting right outside!
TMP TMP TMP TMP
スタタタッ
H-Hano-chan...
Yaya-chan is *such* a sweetie!
I just *love* her!! ♡♡
It's so dark! I'm scared!

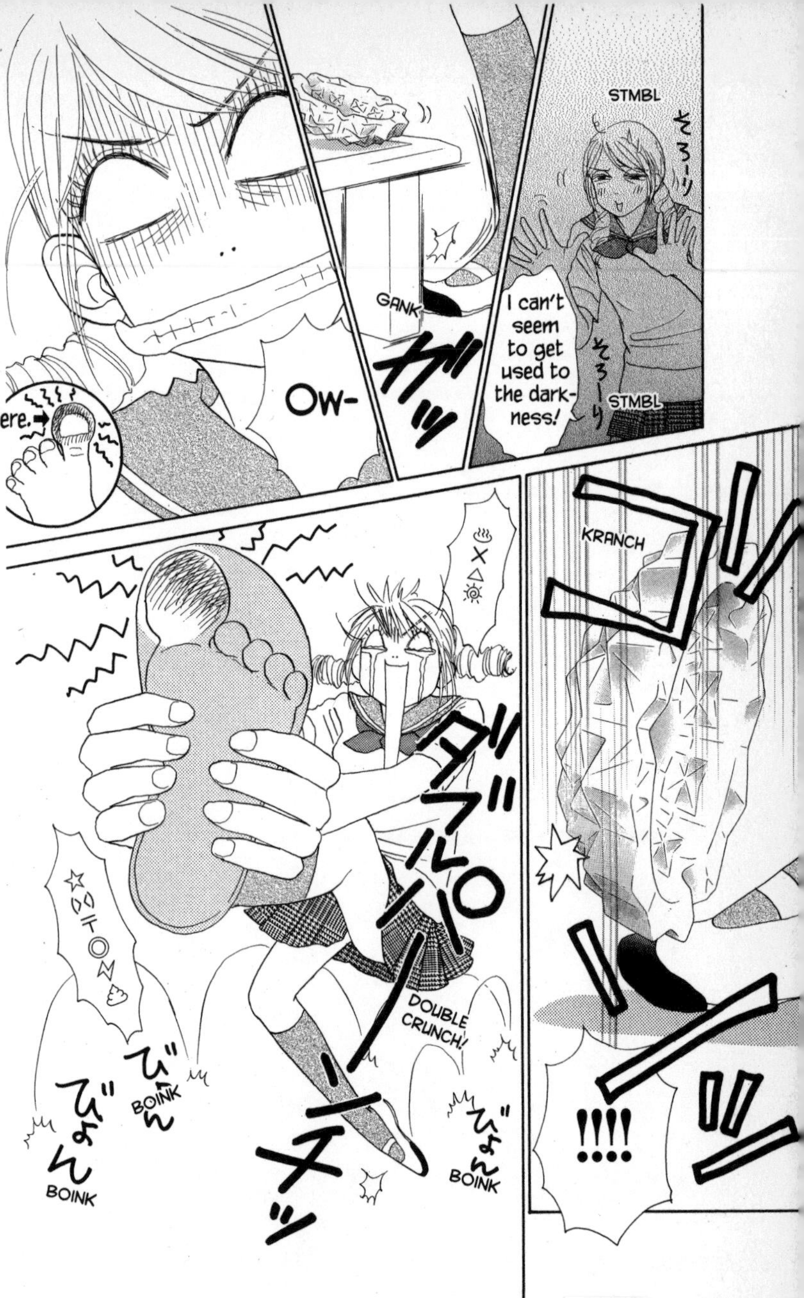
STMBL
そろーり
I can't seem to get used to the darkness!
STMBL
そろーり
GANK
ガッ
OW-
Here.
KRANCH
ゴッ
!!!!
DOUBLE CRUNCH!
ダブルパーンチッ
BOINK
びょん
BOINK
びょん
BOINK
びょん

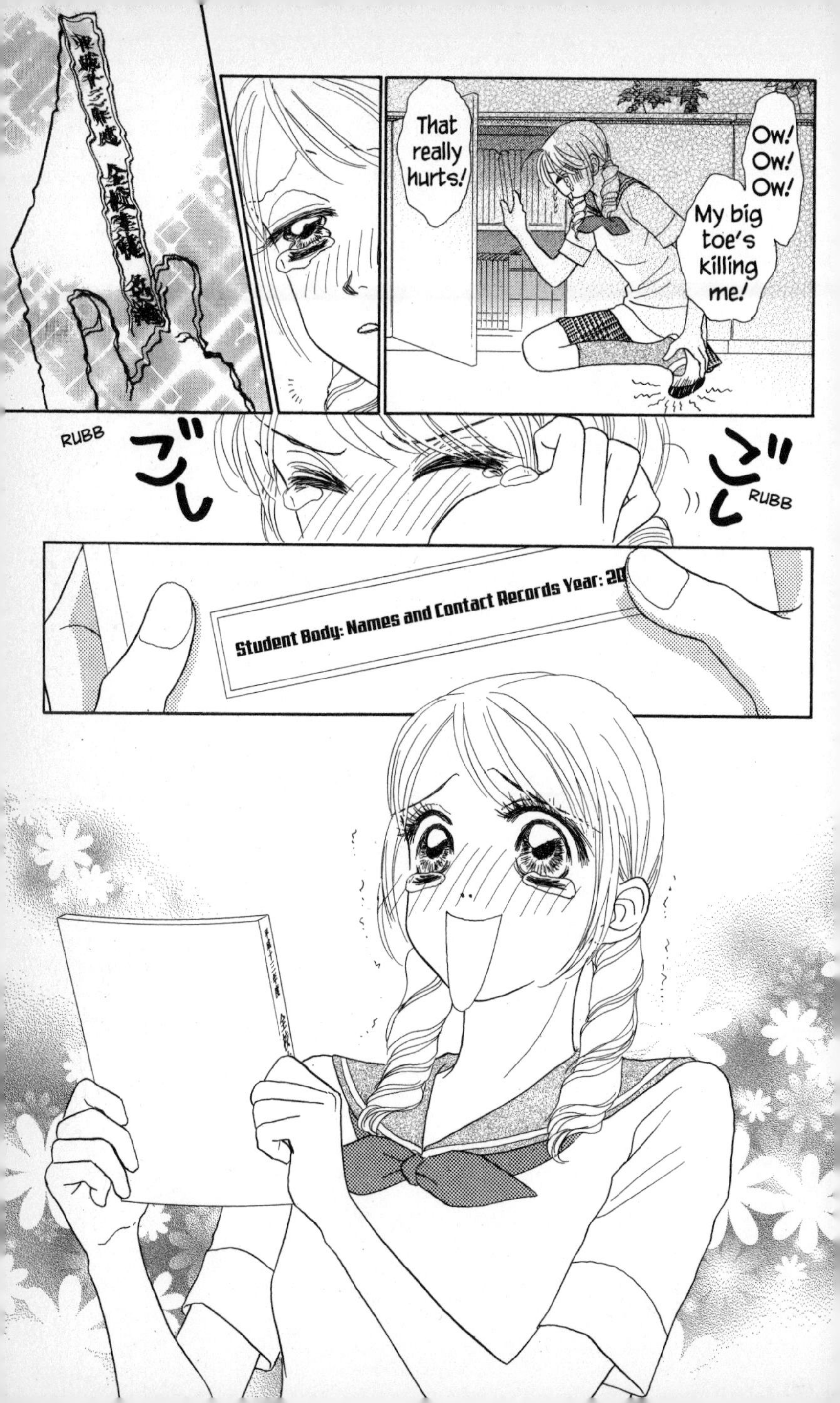
Ow!
Ow!
Ow!
My big toe's killing me!
That really hurts!
RUBB
RUBB
Student Body: Names and Contact Records Year: 20

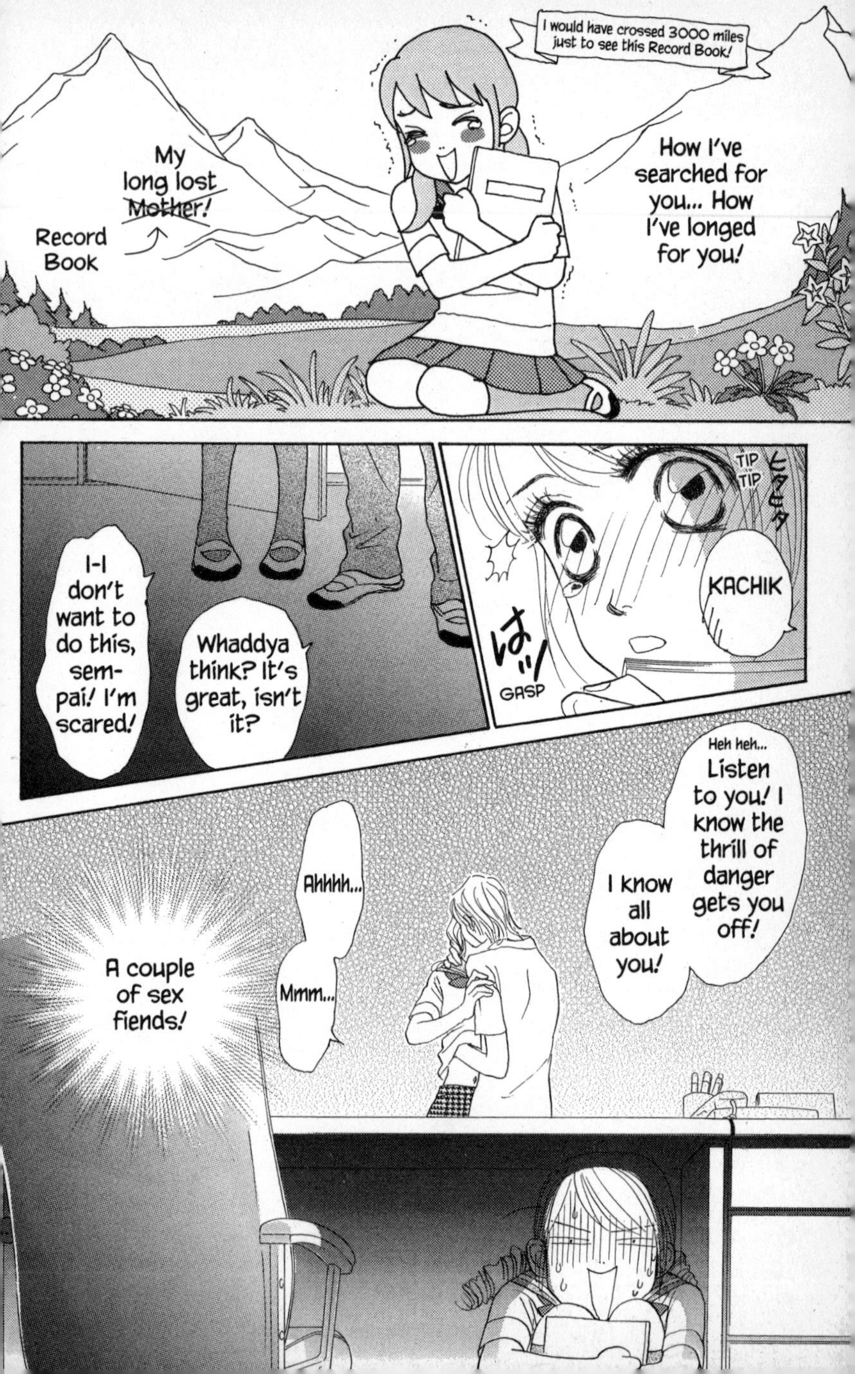
I would have crossed 3000 miles just to see this Record Book!
How I've searched for you... How I've longed for you!
My long lost Mother!
Record Book
ヒタヒタ
TIP TIP
KACHIK
はッ
GASP
Whaddya think? It's great, isn't it?
I-I don't want to do this, sem-pai! I'm scared!
Heh heh... Listen to you! I know the thrill of danger gets you off!
I know all about you!
Ahhhh...
Mmm...
A couple of sex fiends!

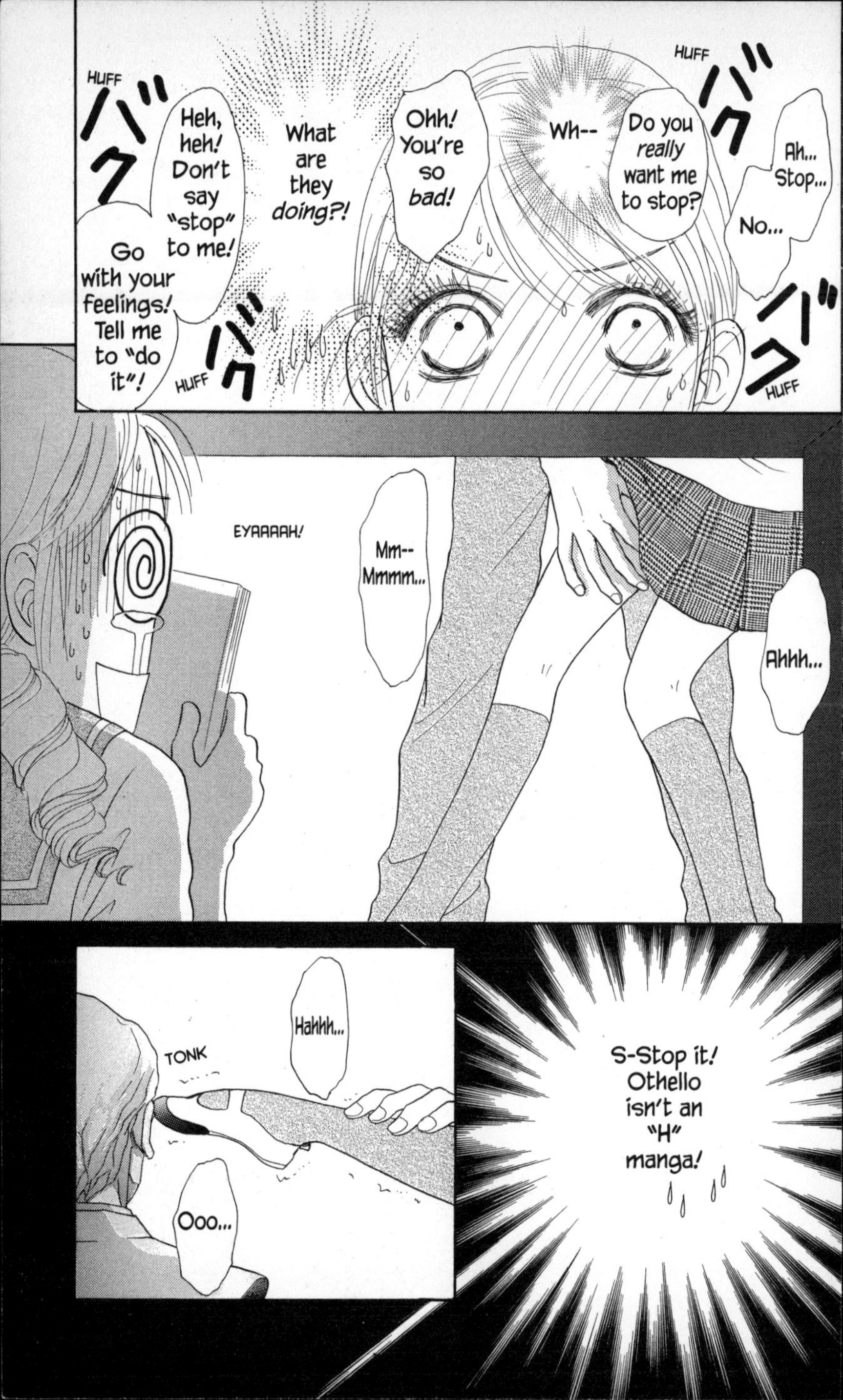
HUFF
Ah... Stop... No...
HUFF
Do you really want me to stop?
Wh--
Ohh! You're so bad!
What are they doing?!
Heh, heh! Don't say "stop" to me!
Go with your feelings! Tell me to "do it"!
HUFF
HUFF
Ahhh...
Mm-- Mmmm...
EYAAAAH!
Hahhh...
TONK
Ooo...
S-Stop it! Othello isn't an "H" manga!

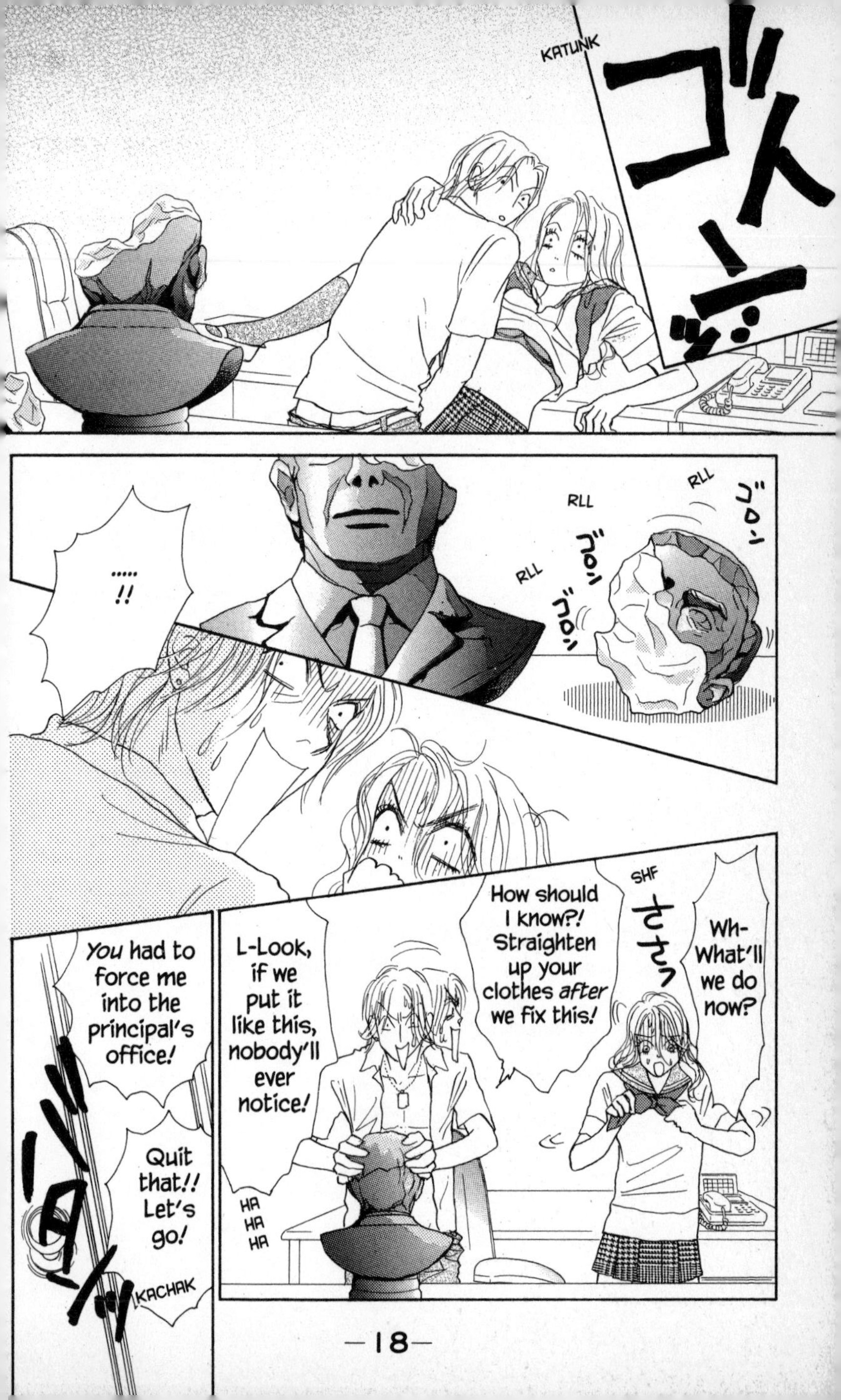
KATUNK
ゴトンッ
RLL
ゴロン
RLL
ゴロン
RLL
ゴロン
.....!!
Wh- What'll we do now?
SHF
ささっ
How should I know?! Straighten up your clothes *after* we fix this!
L-Look, if we put it like this, nobody'll ever notice!
HA HA HA
You had to force me into the principal's office!
Quit that!! Let's go!
KACHAK

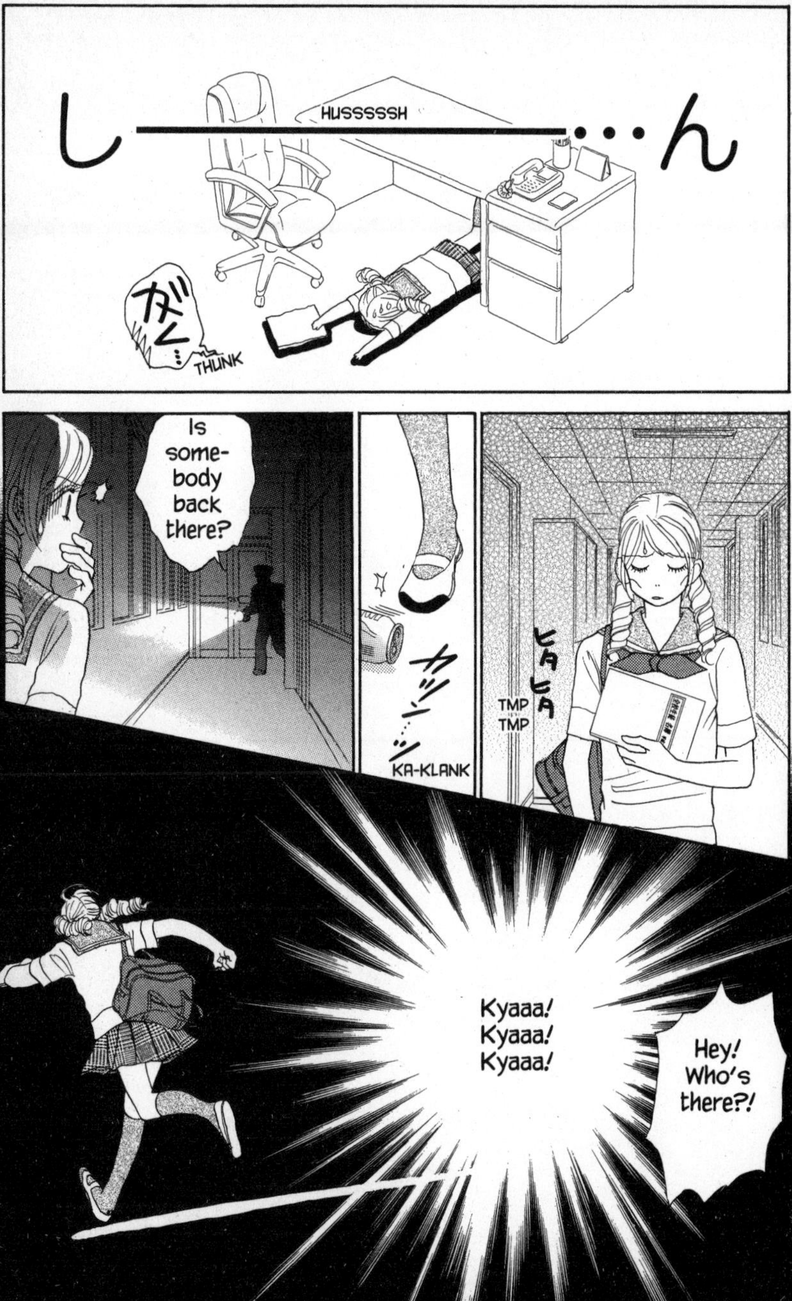
し————…ん
HUSSSSSH
がく…
THUNK
Is somebody back there?
カッン…ッ
KA-KLANK
ヒタ ヒタ
TMP TMP
Kyaaa! Kyaaa! Kyaaa!
Hey! Who's there?!

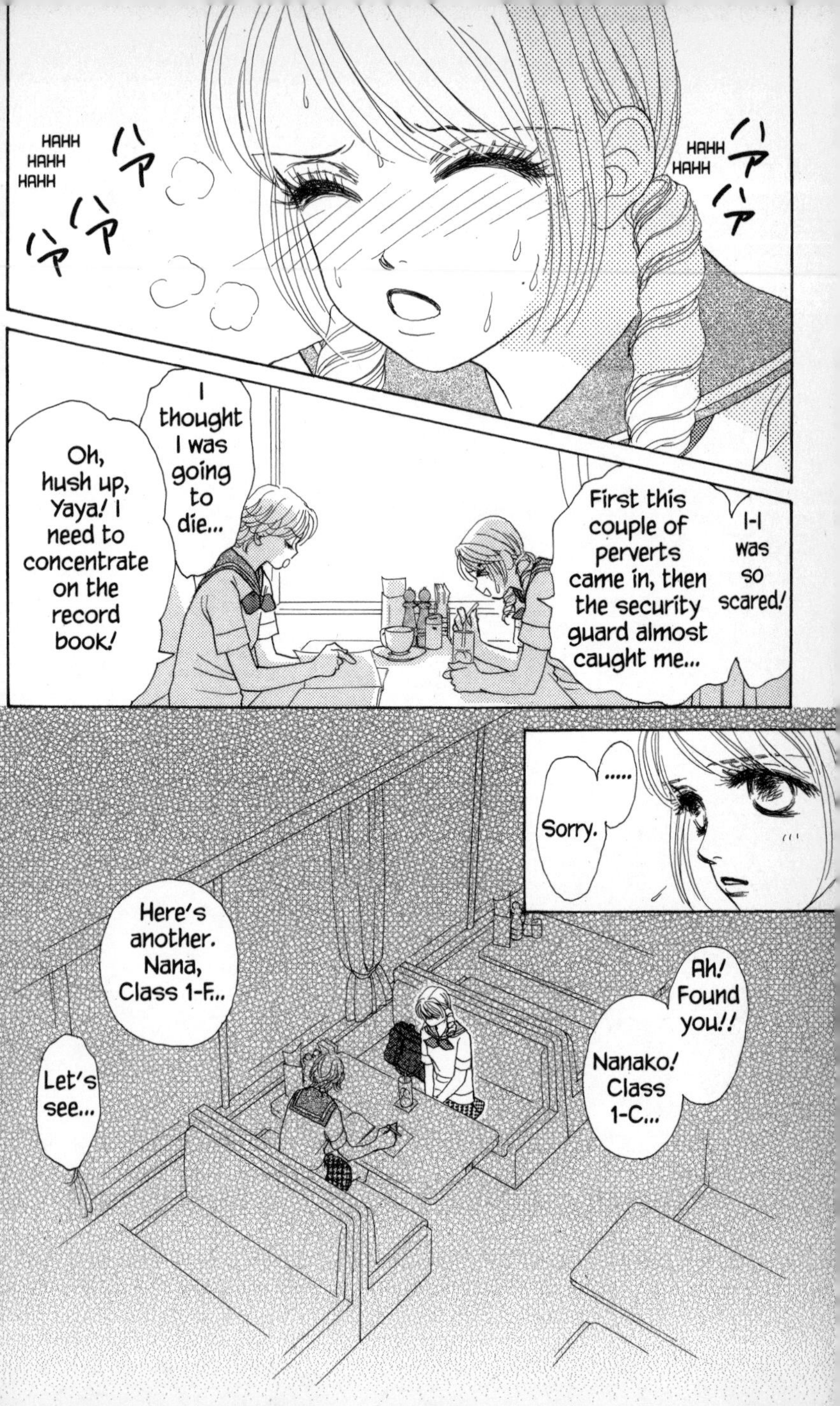
HAHH HAHH
HAHH HAHH HAHH
I-I was so scared!
First this couple of perverts came in, then the security guard almost caught me...
I thought I was going to die...
Oh, hush up, Yaya! I need to concentrate on the record book!
......
Sorry.
Ah! Found you!!
Nanako! Class 1-C...
Here's another. Nana, Class 1-F...
Let's see...

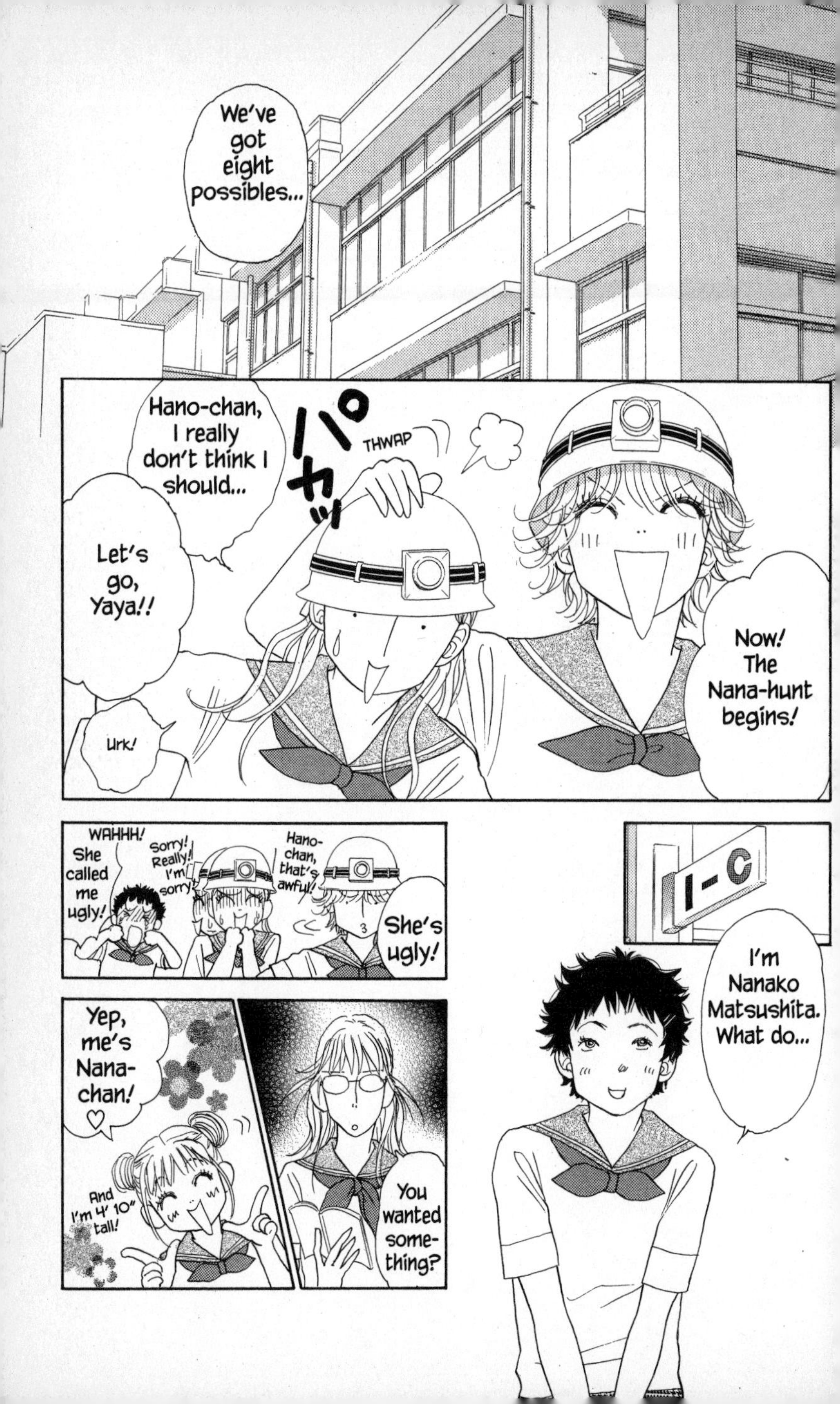
We've got eight possibles...
Now! The Nana-hunt begins!
パヤッ
THWAP
Hano-chan, I really don't think I should...
Let's go, Yaya!!
Urk!
I-C
I'm Nanako Matsushita. What do...
She's ugly!
Hano-chan, that's awful!
Sorry! Really! I'm sorry!
WAHHH! She called me ugly!
You wanted something?
Yep, me's Nana-chan! ♡
And I'm 4' 10" tall!

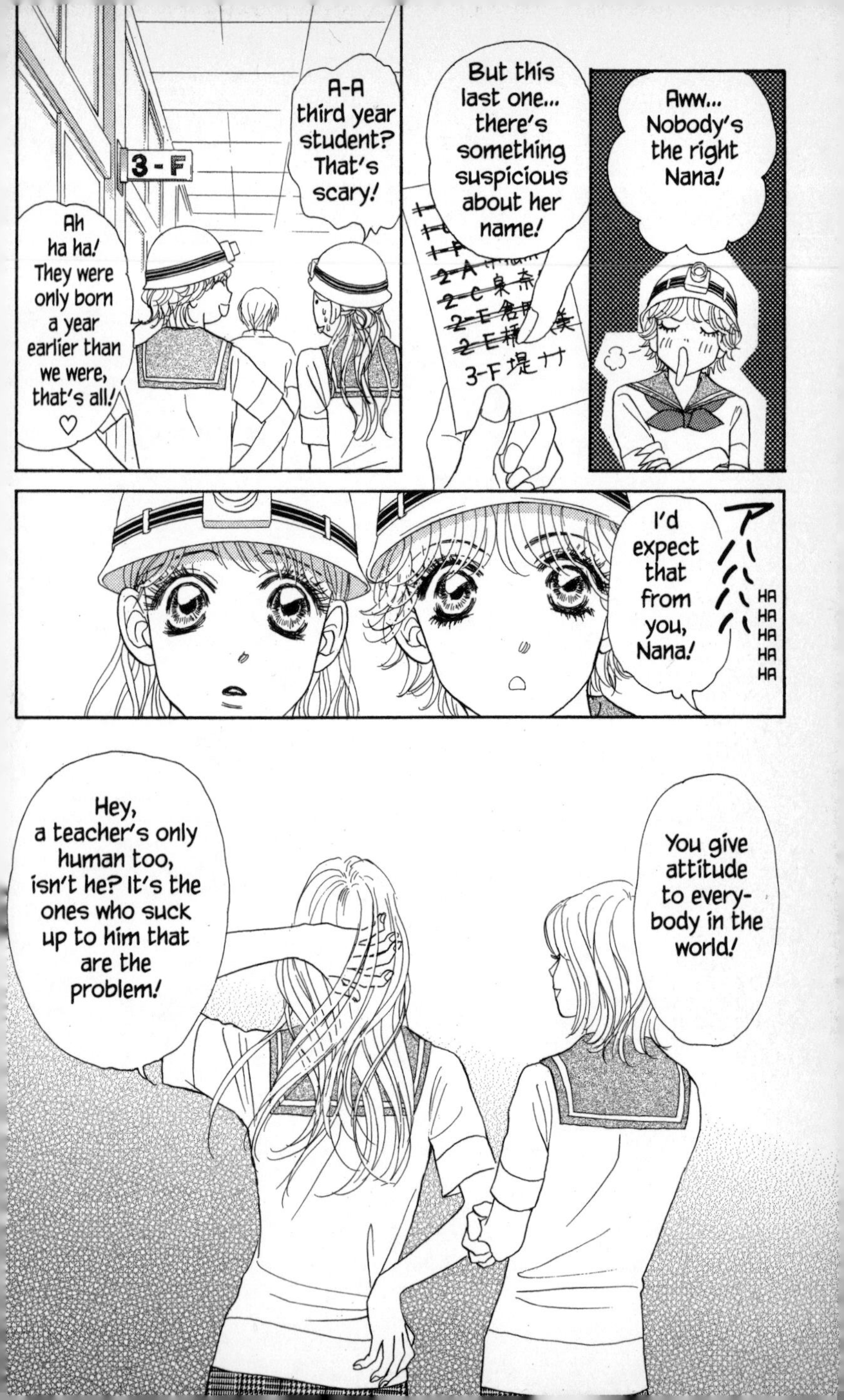
Aww... Nobody's the right Nana!
But this last one... there's something suspicious about her name!
3-F 堤ナナ
A-A third year student? That's scary!
3 - F
Ah ha ha! They were only born a year earlier than we were, that's all! ♡
アハハハハ
HA HA HA HA HA
I'd expect that from you, Nana!
You give attitude to every-body in the world!
Hey, a teacher's only human too, isn't he? It's the ones who suck up to him that are the problem!

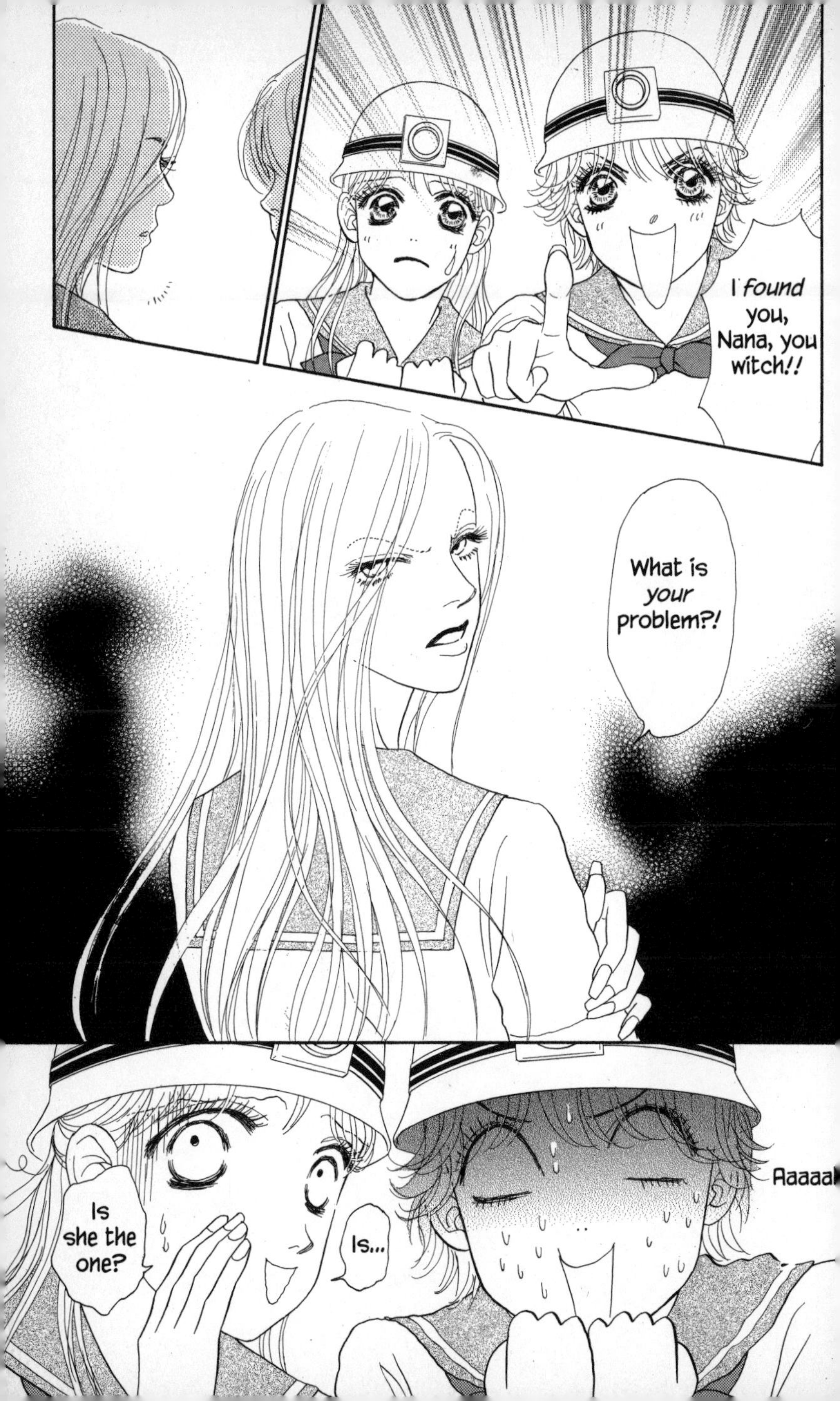
I found you, Nana, you witch!!
What is your problem?!
Aaaaa
Is...
Is she the one?

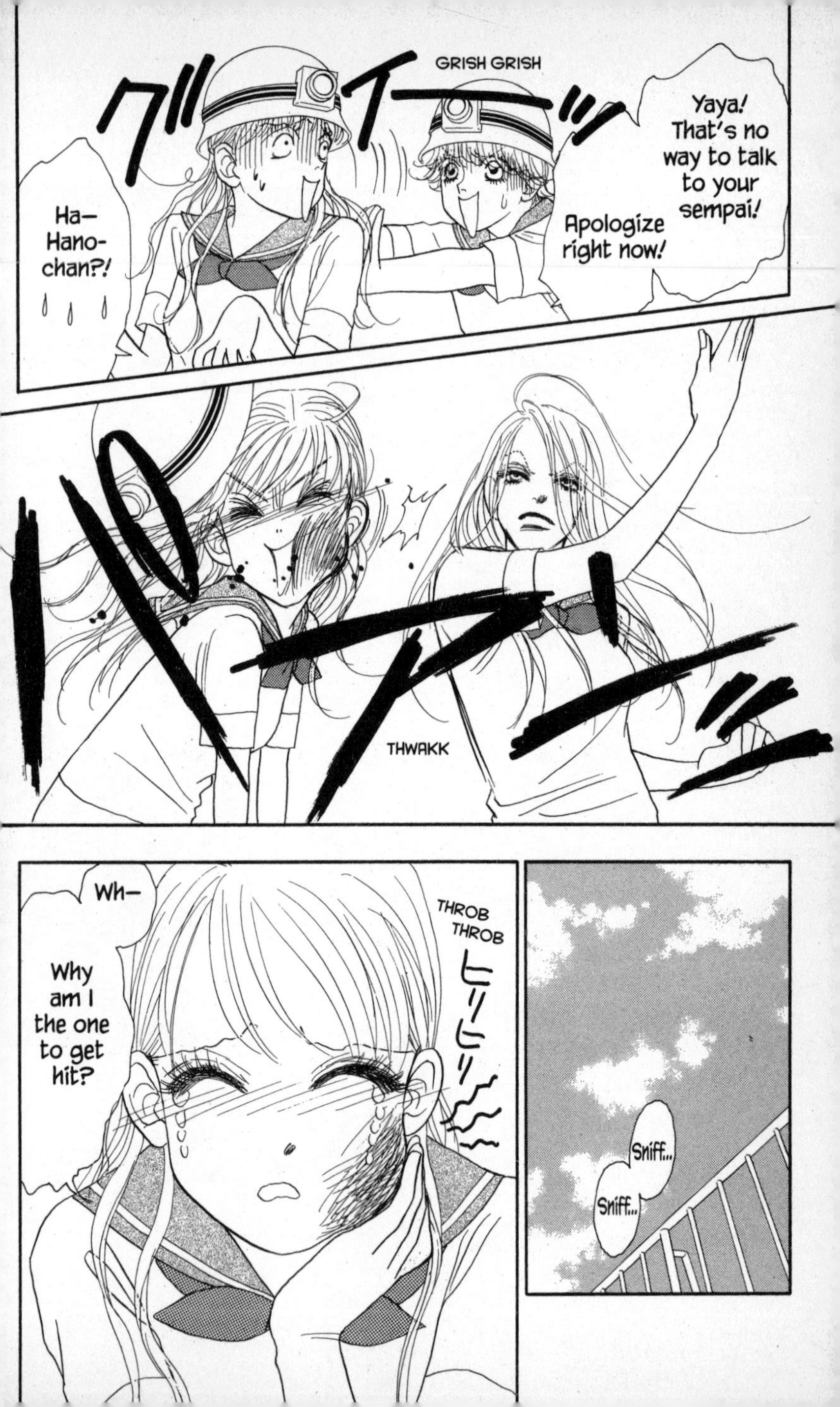

GRISH GRISH
グイーッ
Yaya! That's no way to talk to your sempai!
Apologize right now!
Ha- Hano-chan?!
パァン
THWAKK
Wh-
Why am I the one to get hit?
THROB THROB
ヒリヒリ
Sniff...
Sniff...

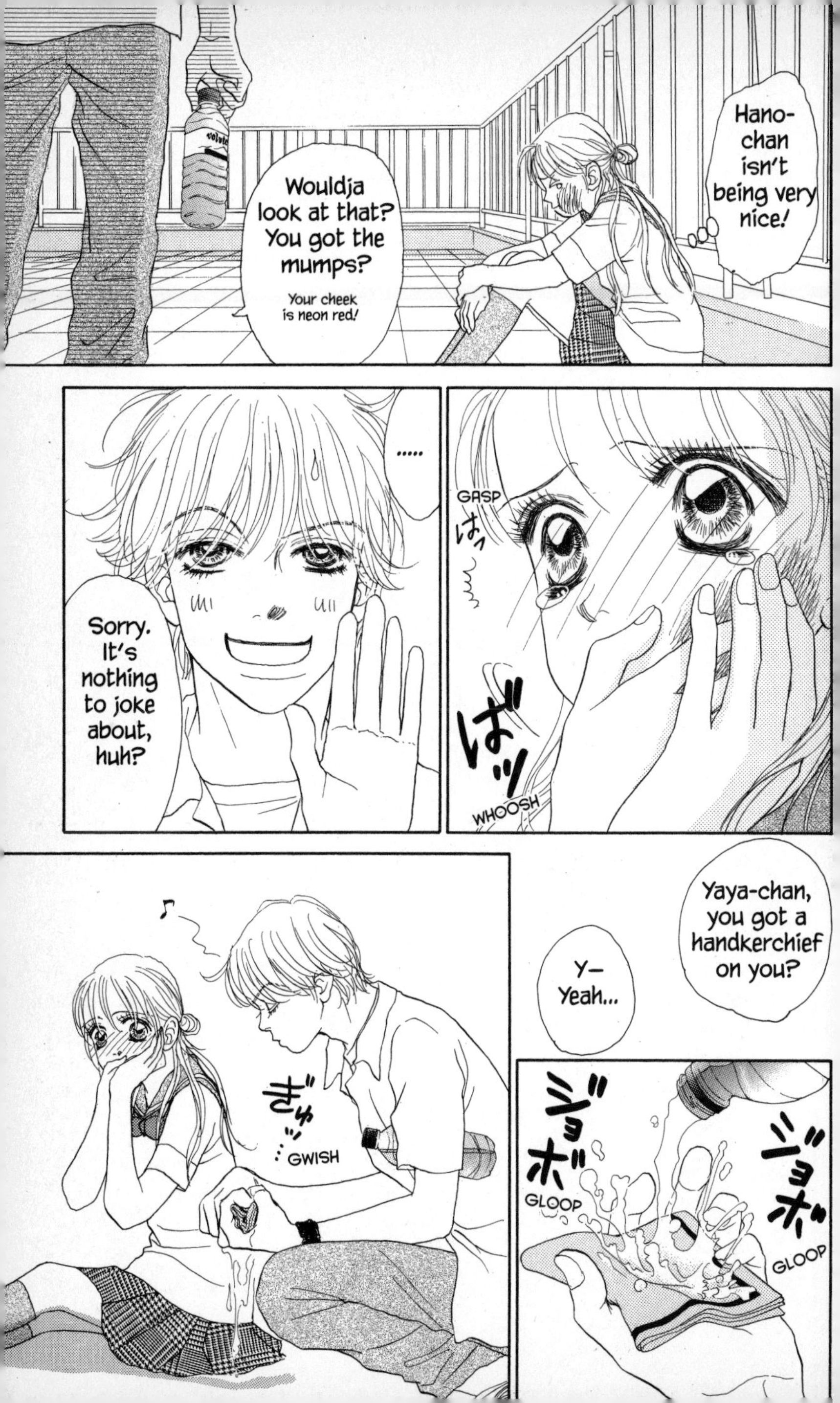
Hano-chan isn't being very nice!
Wouldja look at that? You got the mumps?
Your cheek is neon red!
GASP
はっ
ばッ
WHOOSH
......
Sorry. It's nothing to joke about, huh?
Yaya-chan, you got a handkerchief on you?
Y— Yeah...
ジョボ
GLOOP
ジョボ
GLOOP
ぎゅッ
GWISH

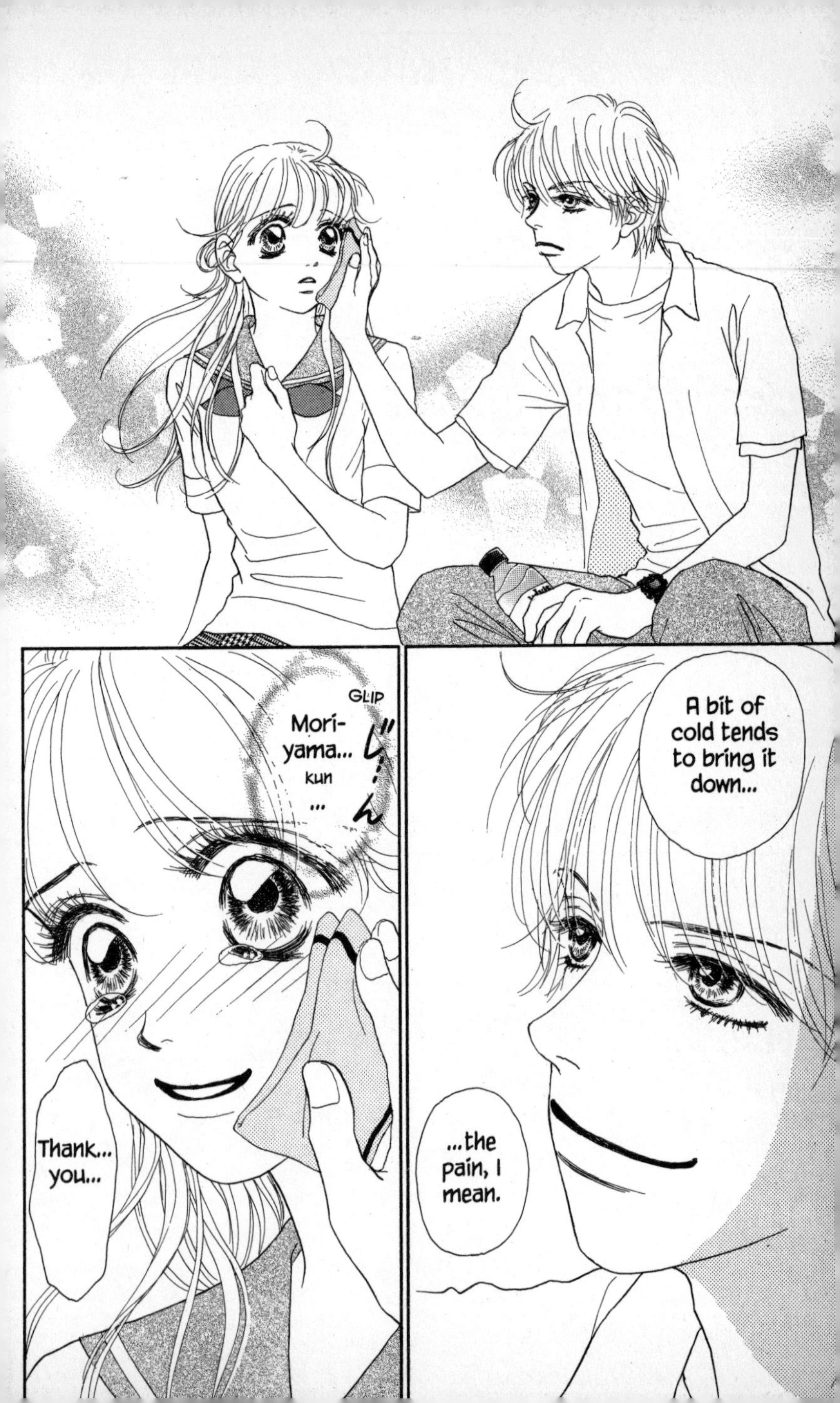

A bit of cold tends to bring it down...
...the pain, I mean.
GLIP
Mori-yama... kun ...
Thank... you...

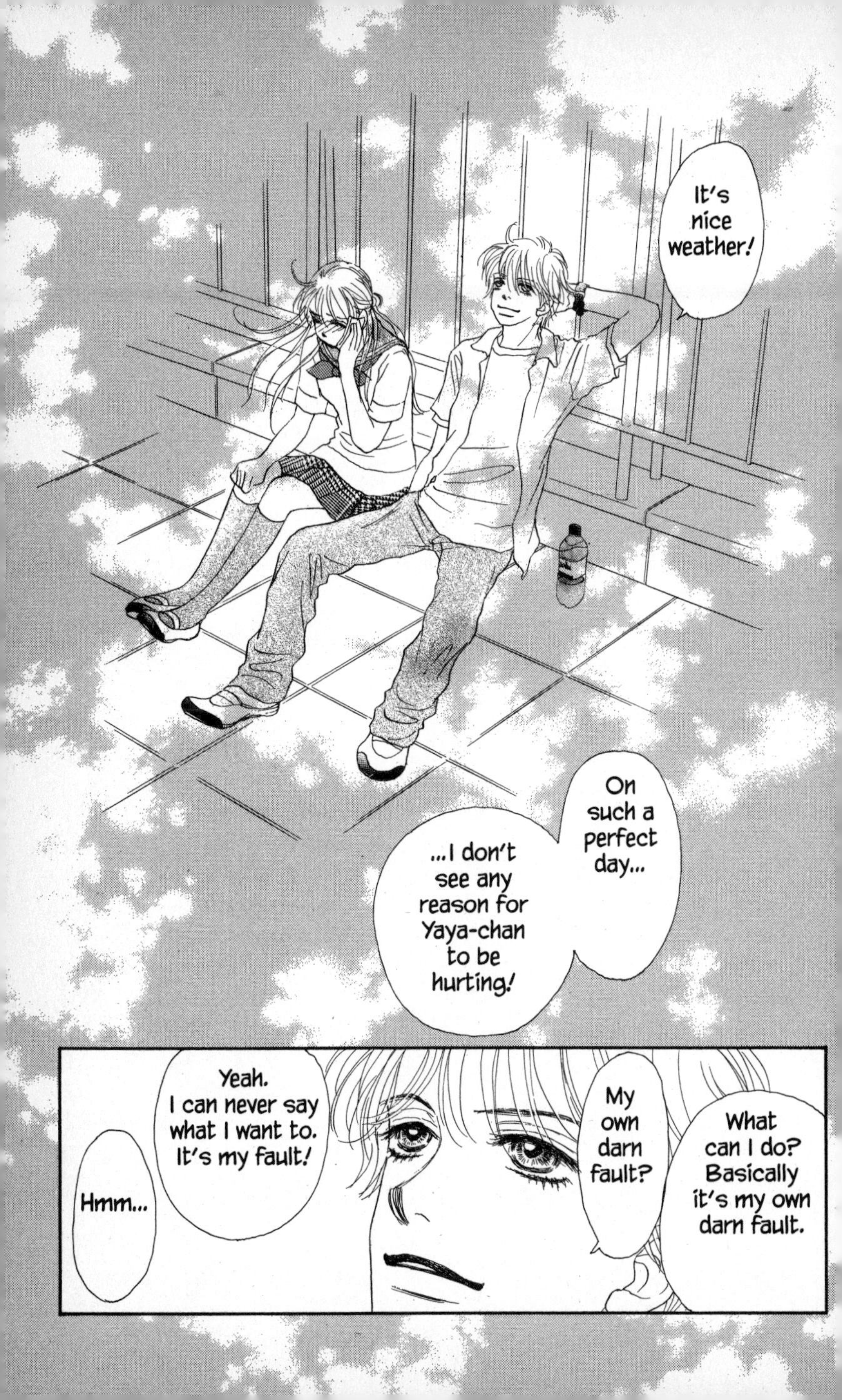
It's nice weather!
On such a perfect day...
...I don't see any reason for Yaya-chan to be hurting!
What can I do? Basically it's my own darn fault.
My own darn fault?
Yeah. I can never say what I want to. It's my fault!
Hmm...

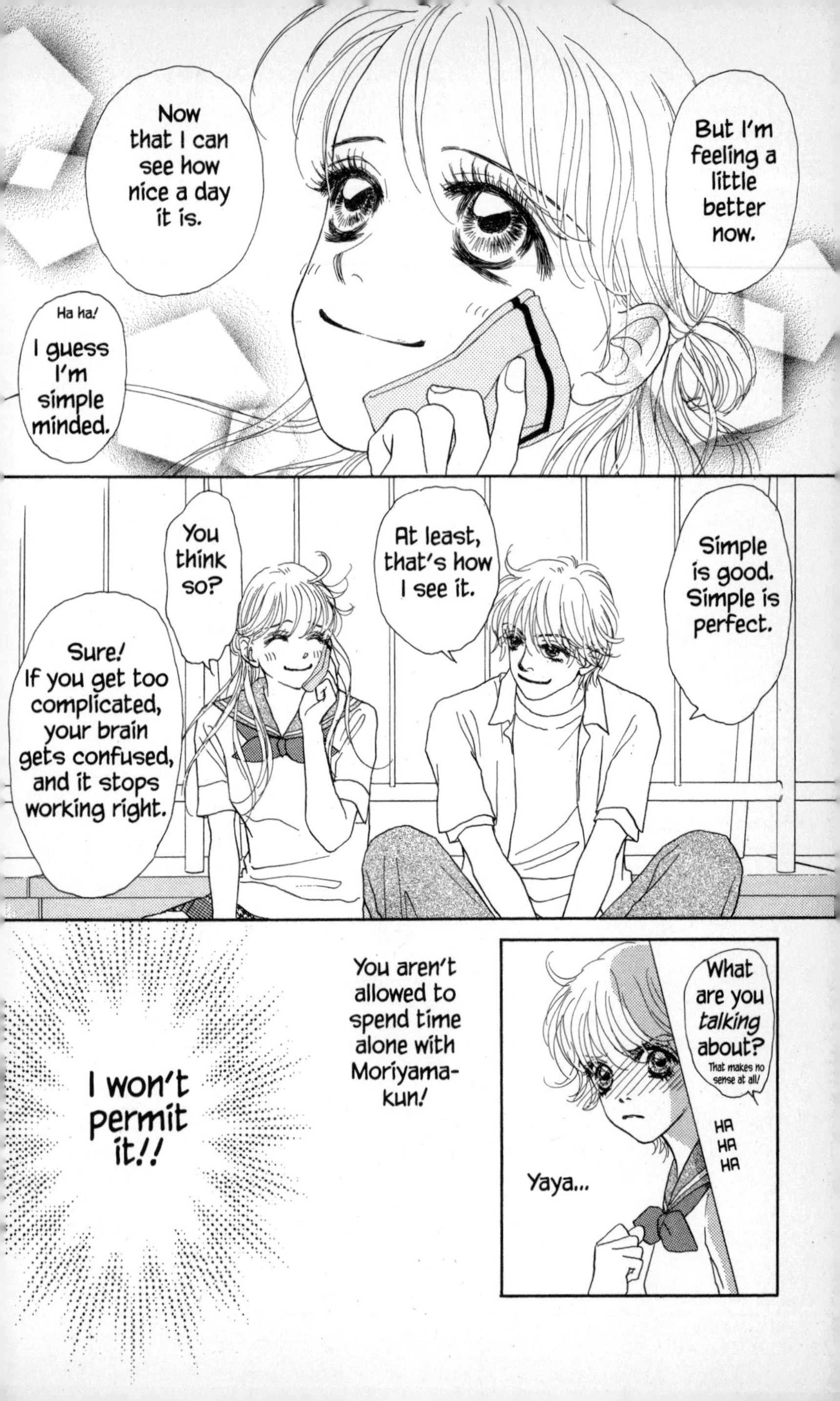

But I'm feeling a little better now.
Now that I can see how nice a day it is.
Ha ha!
I guess I'm simple minded.
Simple is good. Simple is perfect.
At least, that's how I see it.
You think so?
Sure! If you get too complicated, your brain gets confused, and it stops working right.
What are you *talking* about?
That makes no sense at all!
HA HA HA
Yaya...
You aren't allowed to spend time alone with Moriyama-kun!
I won't permit it!!

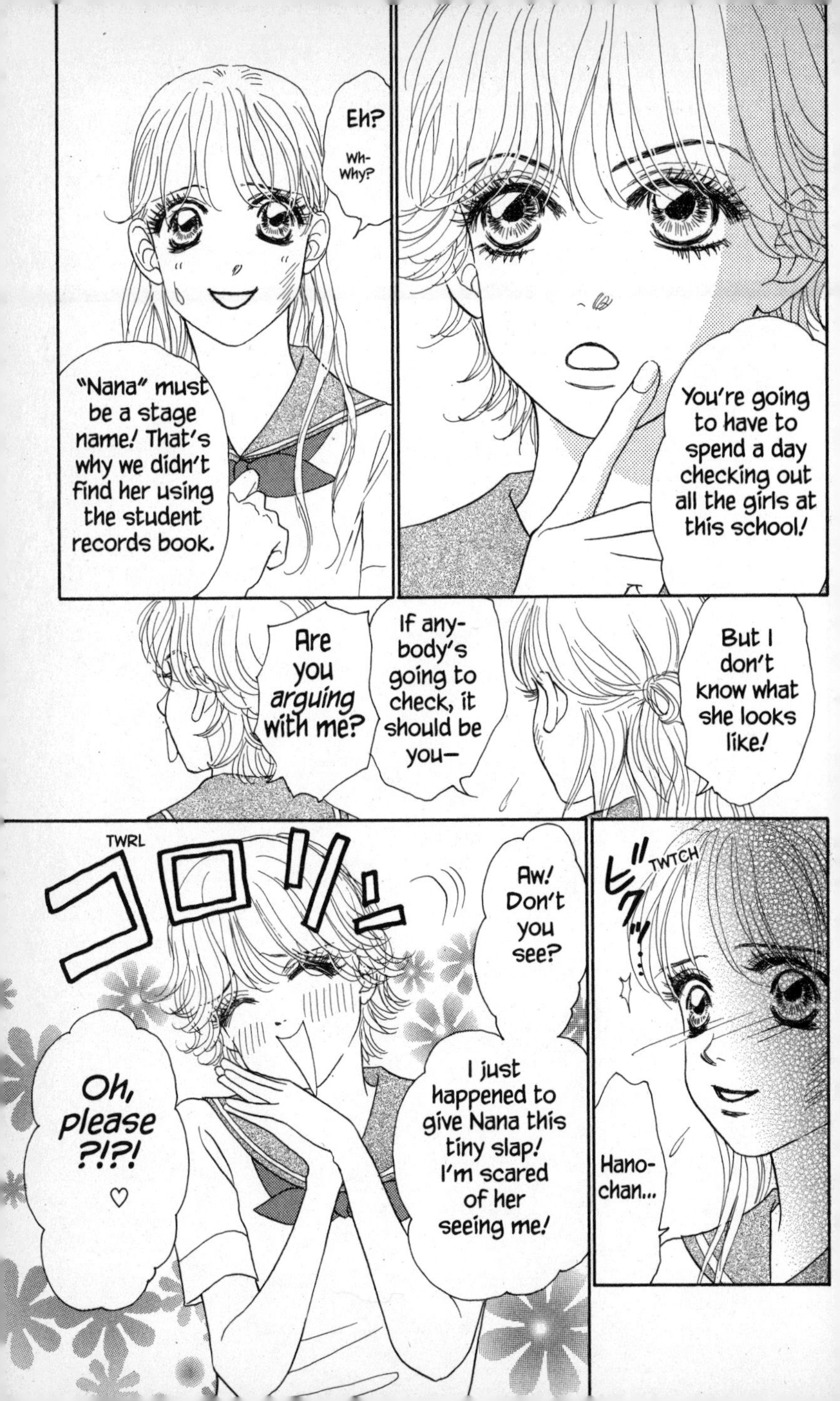

You're going to have to spend a day checking out all the girls at this school!
Eh?
Wh-Why?
"Nana" must be a stage name! That's why we didn't find her using the student records book.
But I don't know what she looks like!
If anybody's going to check, it should be you—
Are you arguing with me?
TWTCH
Hano-chan...
Aw! Don't you see?
I just happened to give Nana this tiny slap! I'm scared of her seeing me!
TWRL
Oh, please?!?! ♡

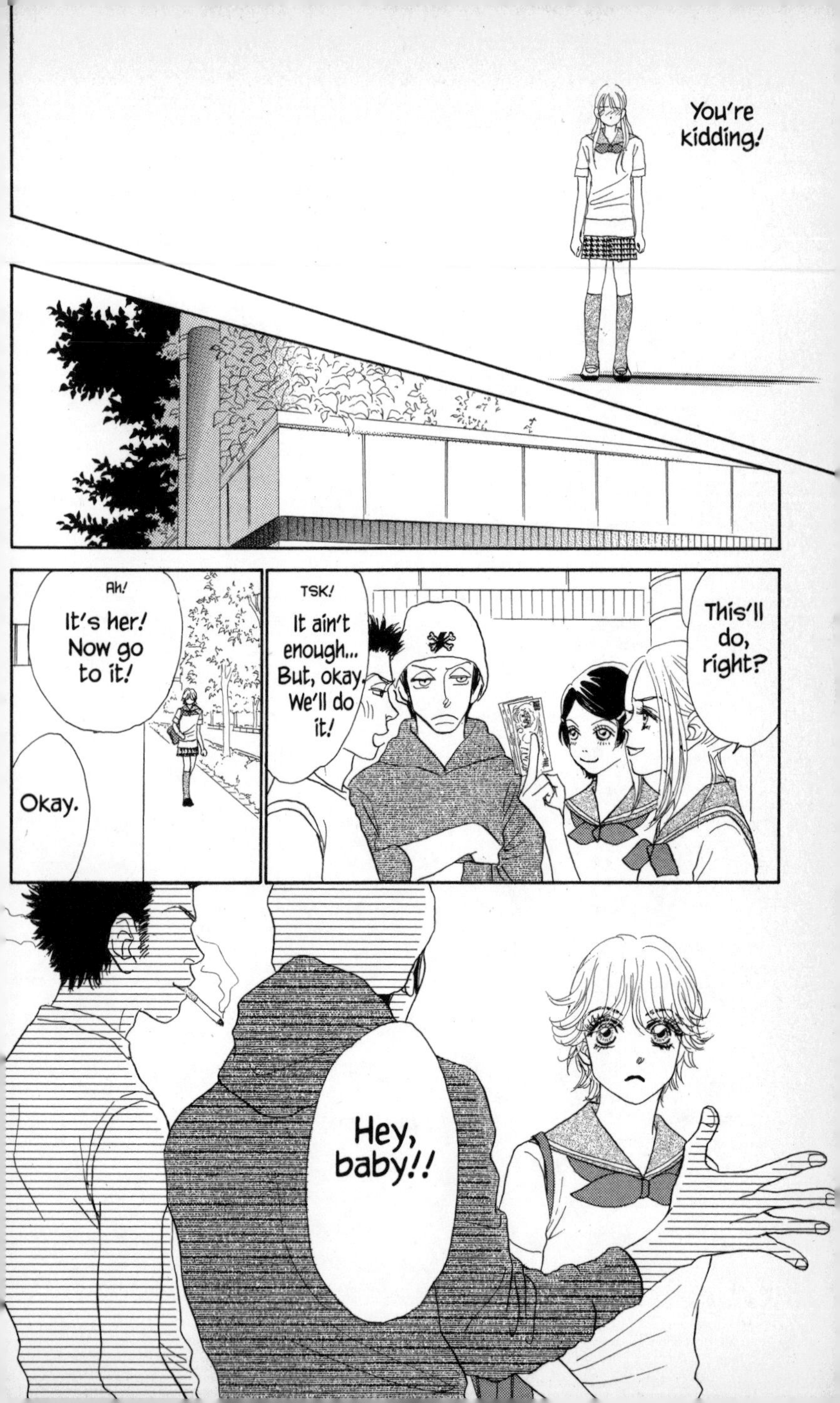

You're kidding!
Ah!
It's her! Now go to it!
Okay.
This'll do, right?
TSK!
It ain't enough... But, okay. We'll do it!
Hey, baby!!

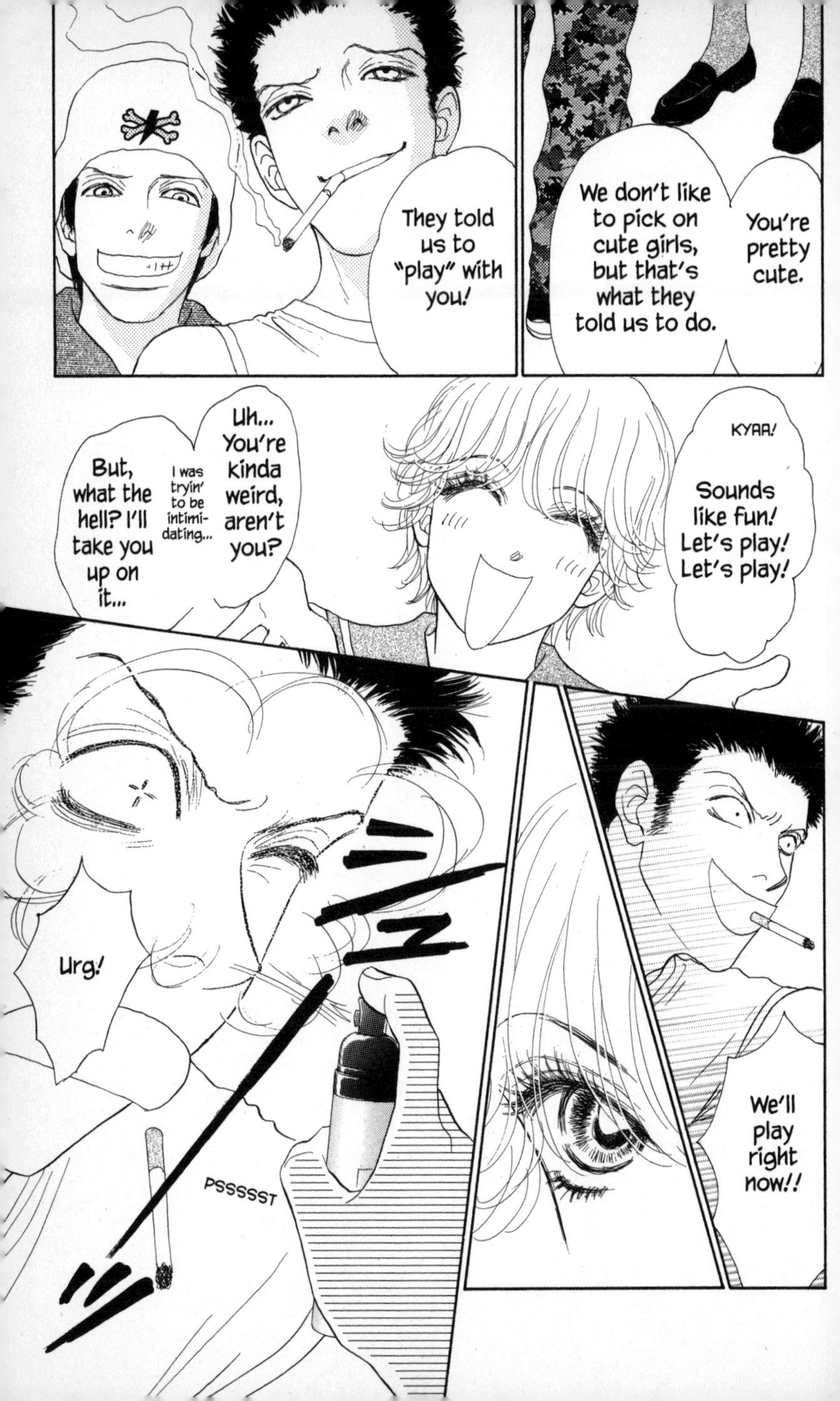
You're pretty cute.
We don't like to pick on cute girls, but that's what they told us to do.
They told us to "play" with you!
KYAA!
Sounds like fun! Let's play! Let's play!
Uh... You're kinda weird, aren't you?
I was tryin' to be intimi-dating...
But, what the hell? I'll take you up on it...
We'll play right now!!
PSSSSST
Urg!

His real name is Teruo.

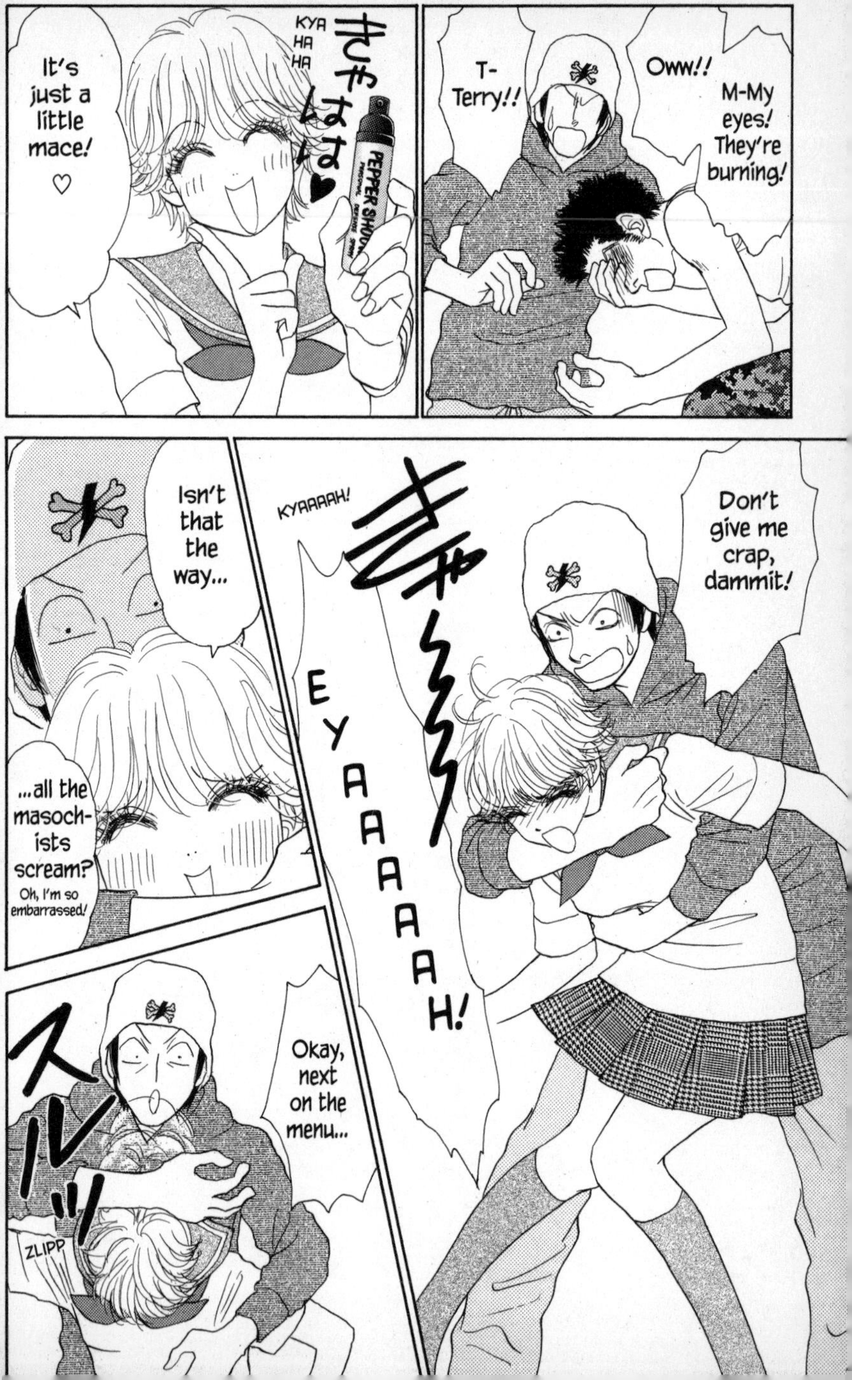
Oww!!
M-My eyes! They're burning!
T-Terry!!
It's just a little mace! ♡
KYA HA HA
PEPPER SHOUT
Don't give me crap, dammit!
KYAAAAH!
EYAAAAAAH!
Isn't that the way...
...all the masochists scream?
Oh, I'm so embarrassed!
Okay, next on the menu...
ZLIPP

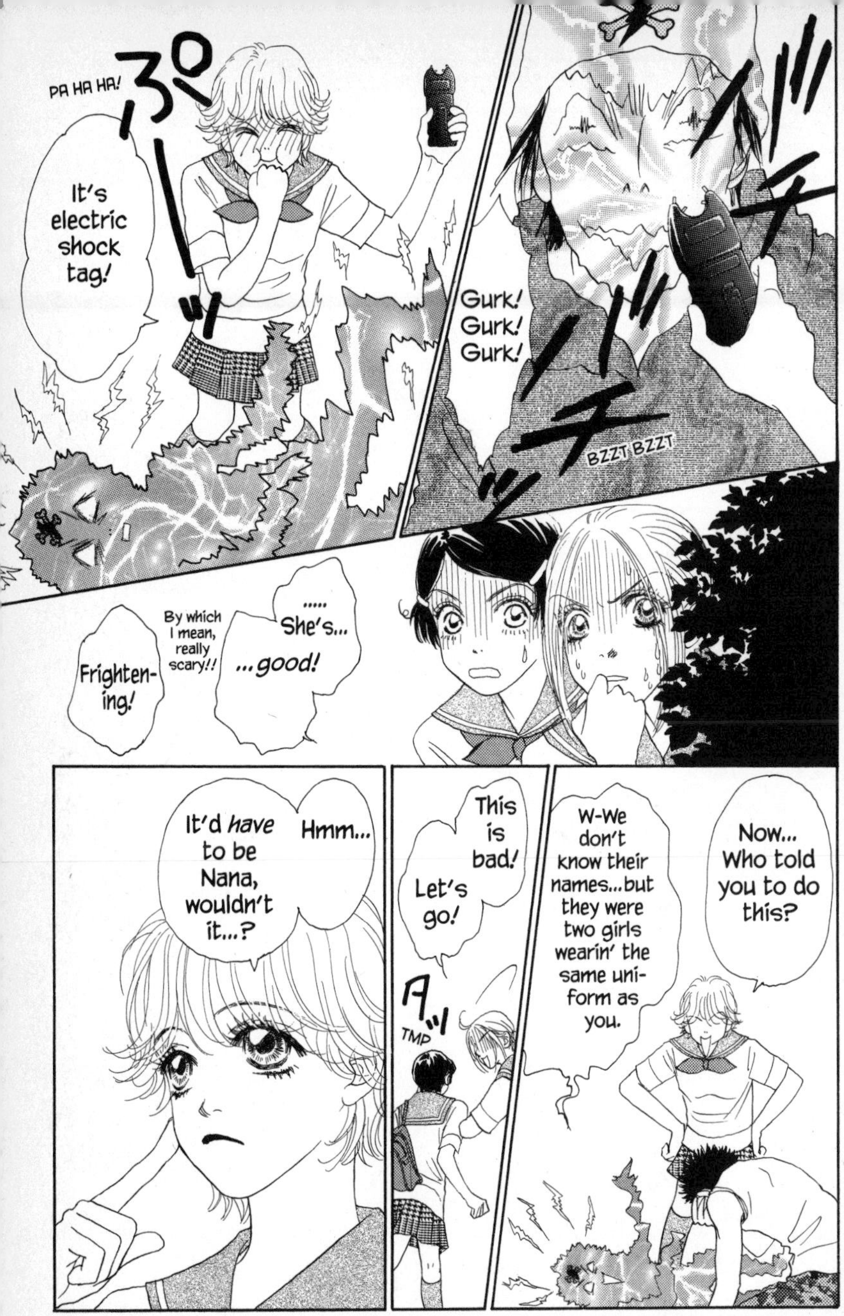
Gurk! Gurk! Gurk!
BZZT BZZT
PA HA HA!
It's electric shock tag!
..... She's... ...good!
Frighten-ing!
By which I mean, really scary!!
Now... Who told you to do this?
W-We don't know their names...but they were two girls wearin' the same uni-form as you.
This is bad!
Let's go!
TMP
Hmm...
It'd *have* to be Nana, wouldn't it...?

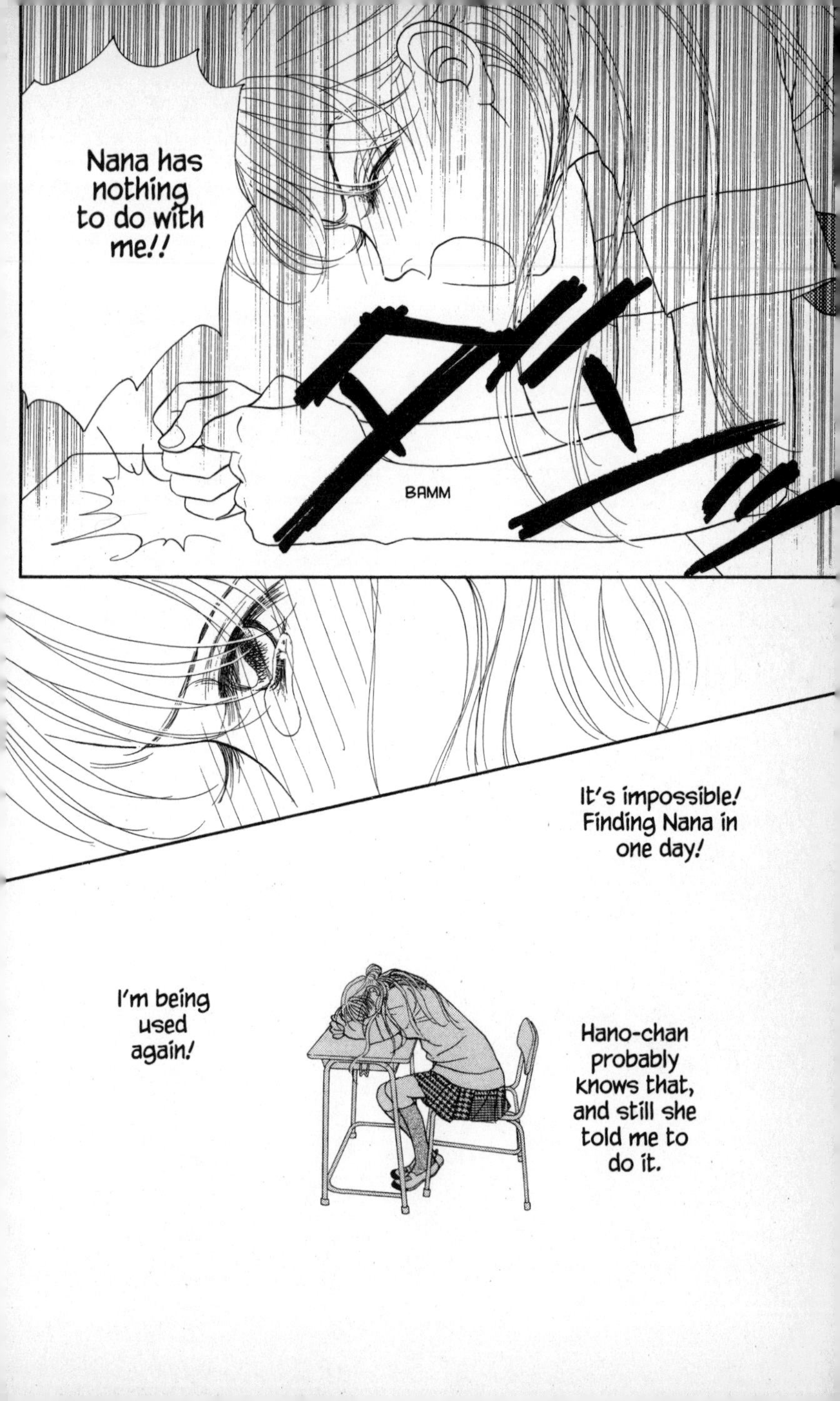

Nana has nothing to do with me!!
BAMM
It's impossible! Finding Nana in one day!
Hano-chan probably knows that, and still she told me to do it.
I'm being used again!

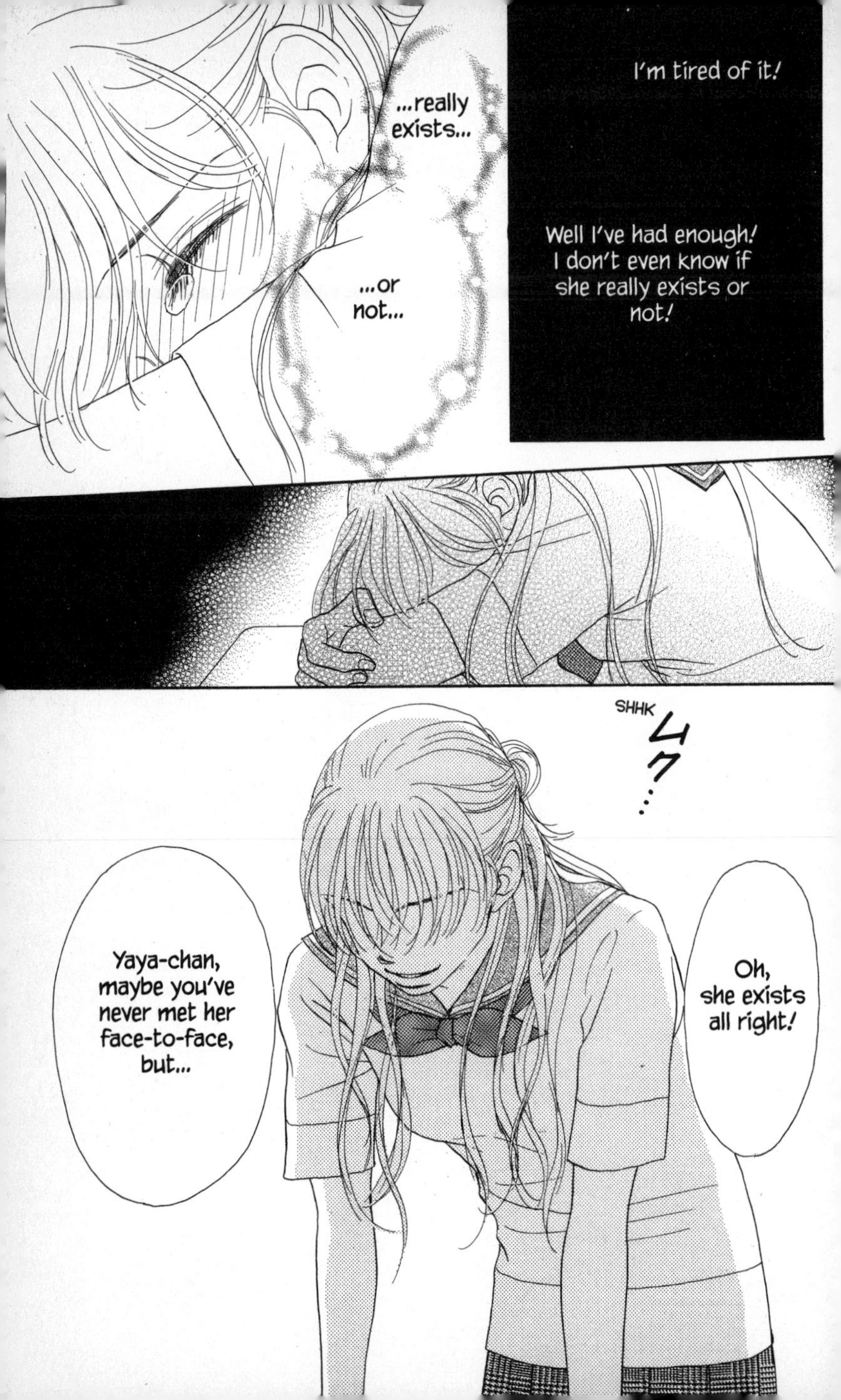
I'm tired of it!
Well I've had enough! I don't even know if she really exists or not!
...really exists...
...or not...
SHHK
Oh, she exists all right!
Yaya-chan, maybe you've never met her face-to-face, but...

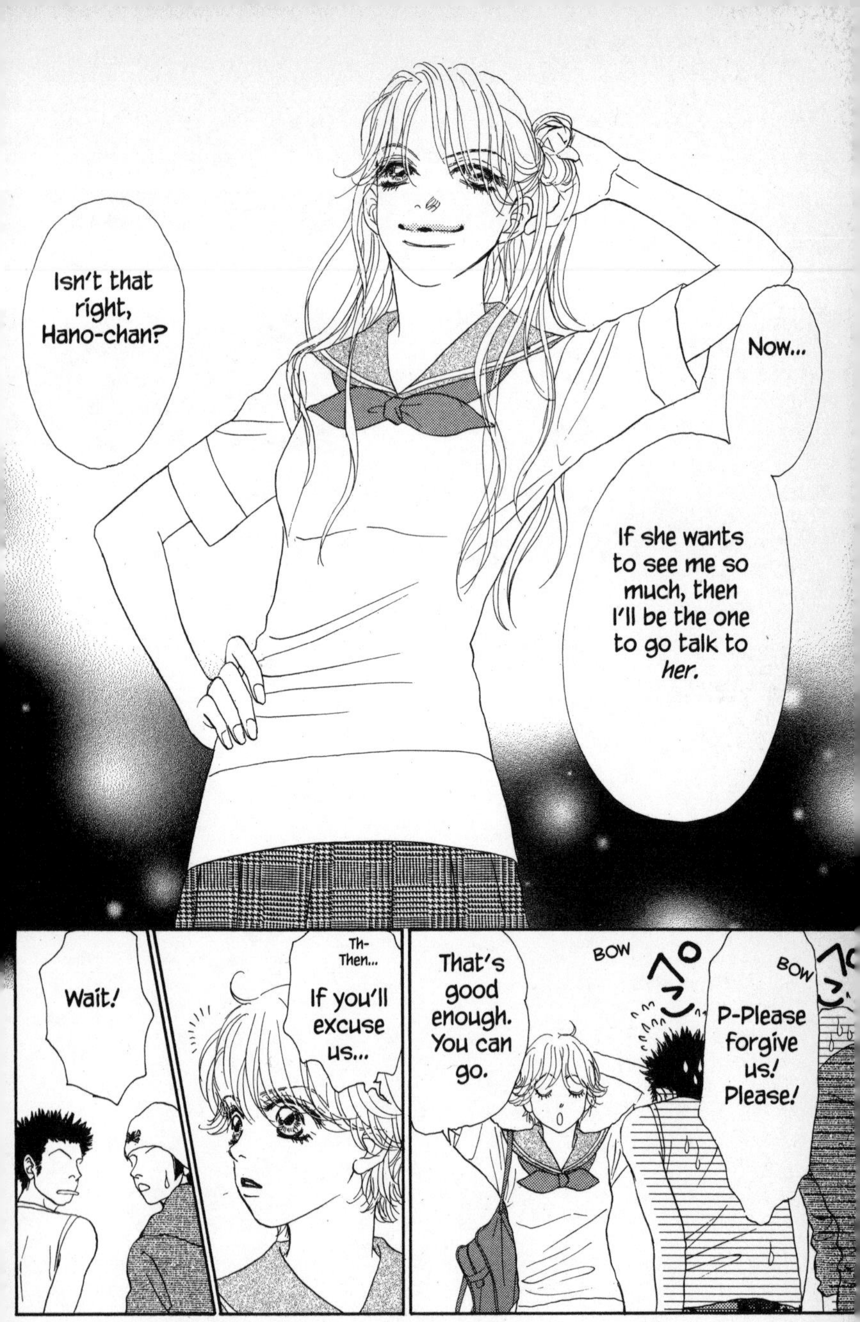
Now...
If she wants to see me so much, then I'll be the one to go talk to *her*.
Isn't that right, Hano-chan?
BOW
BOW
P-Please forgive us! Please!
That's good enough. You can go.
Th- Then...
If you'll excuse us...
Wait!

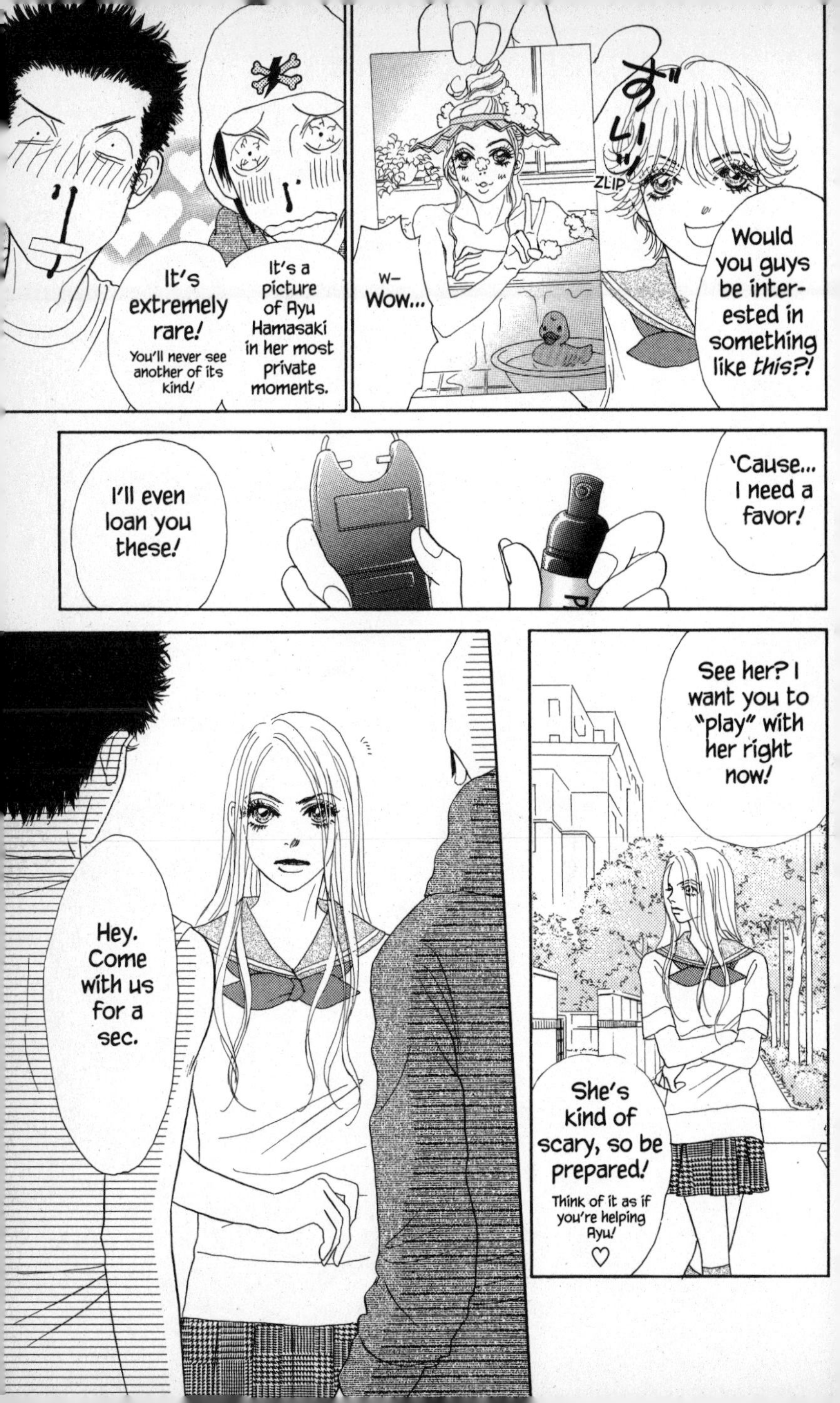
ZLIP
Would you guys be interested in something like this?!
W— Wow...
It's a picture of Ayu Hamasaki in her most private moments.
It's extremely rare!
You'll never see another of its kind!
'Cause... I need a favor!
I'll even loan you these!
See her? I want you to "play" with her right now!
She's kind of scary, so be prepared!
Think of it as if you're helping Ayu! ♡
Hey. Come with us for a sec.

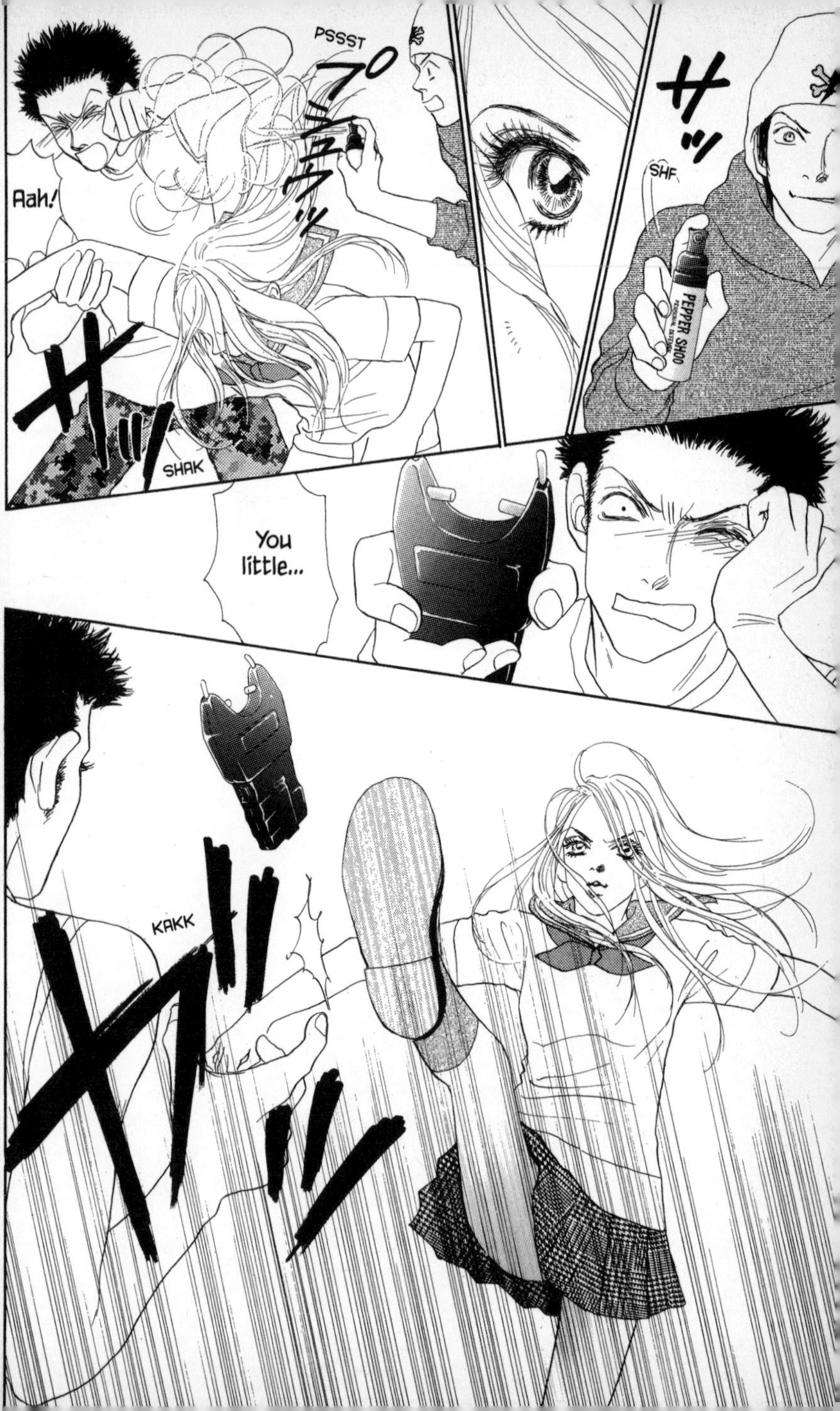
サッ
SHF
PEPPER SHOO
PSSST
プシュウッ
Aah!
ザッ
SHAK
You little...
KAKK
ガッ

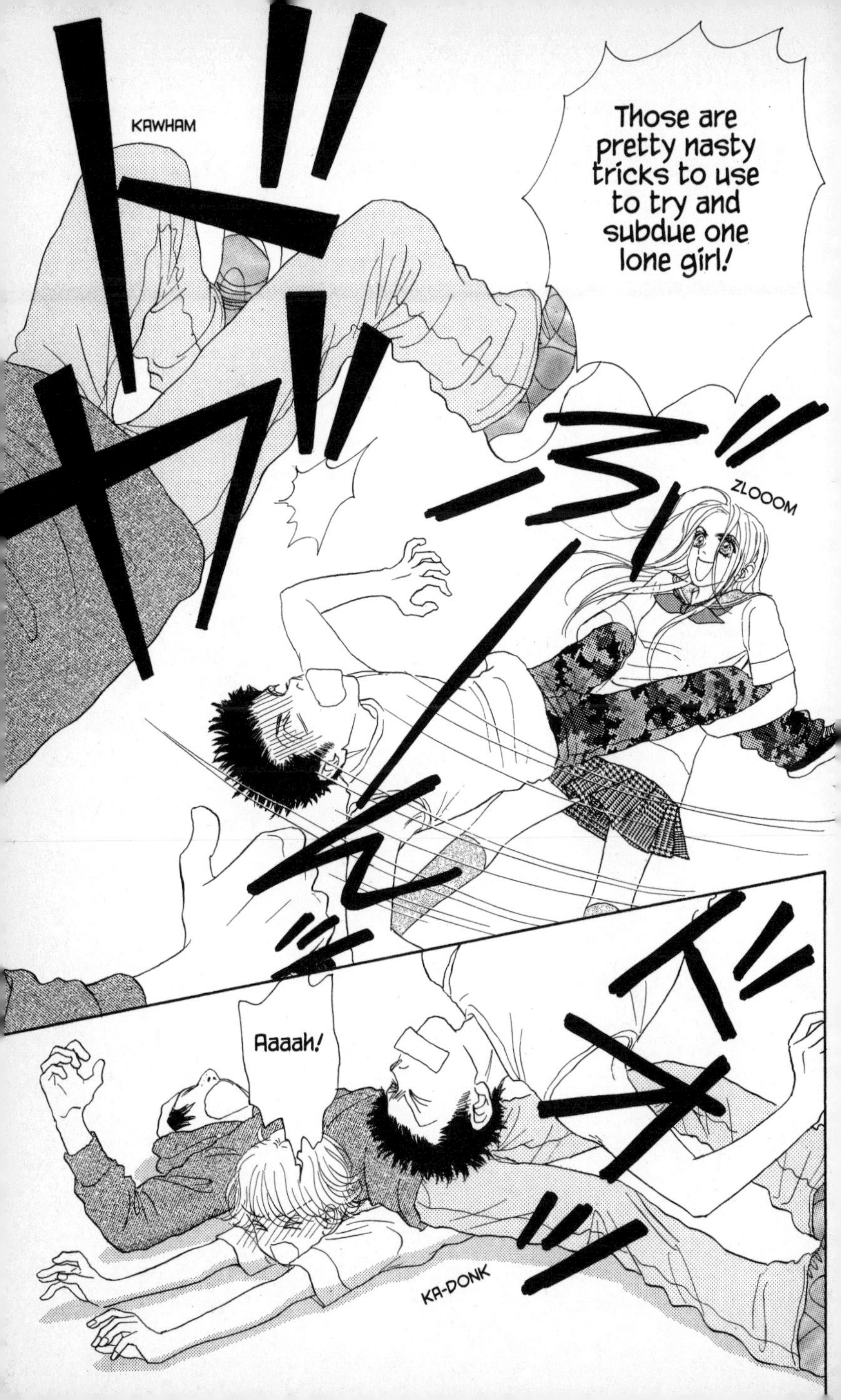
Those are pretty nasty tricks to use to try and subdue one lone girl!
KAWHAM
ZLOOOM
Aaaah!
KA-DONK

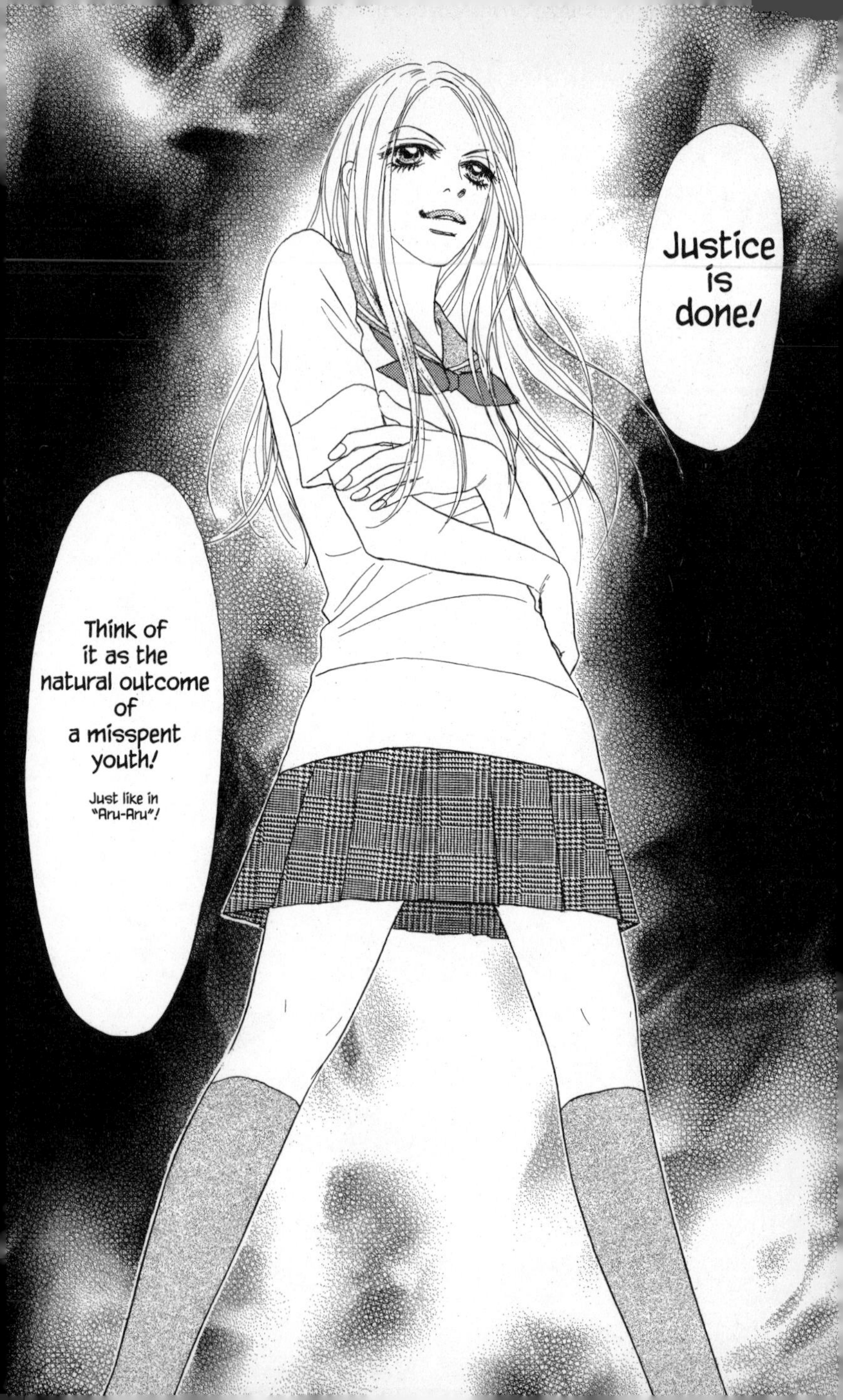
Justice is done!
Think of it as the natural outcome of a misspent youth!
Just like in "Aru-Aru"!

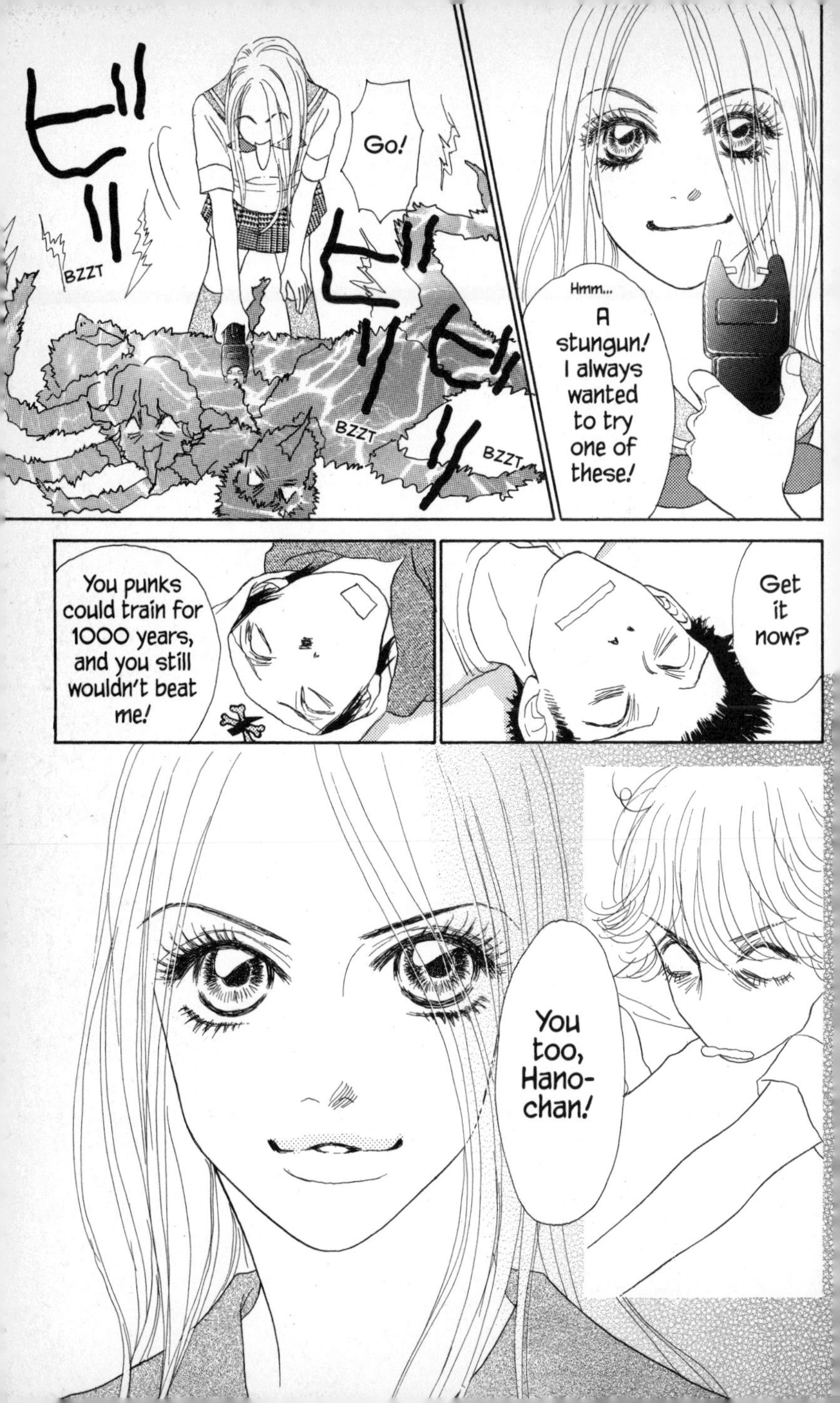
Hmm...
A stungun! I always wanted to try one of these!
Go!
BZZT
BZZT
BZZT
Get it now?
You punks could train for 1000 years, and you still wouldn't beat me!
You too, Hano-chan!

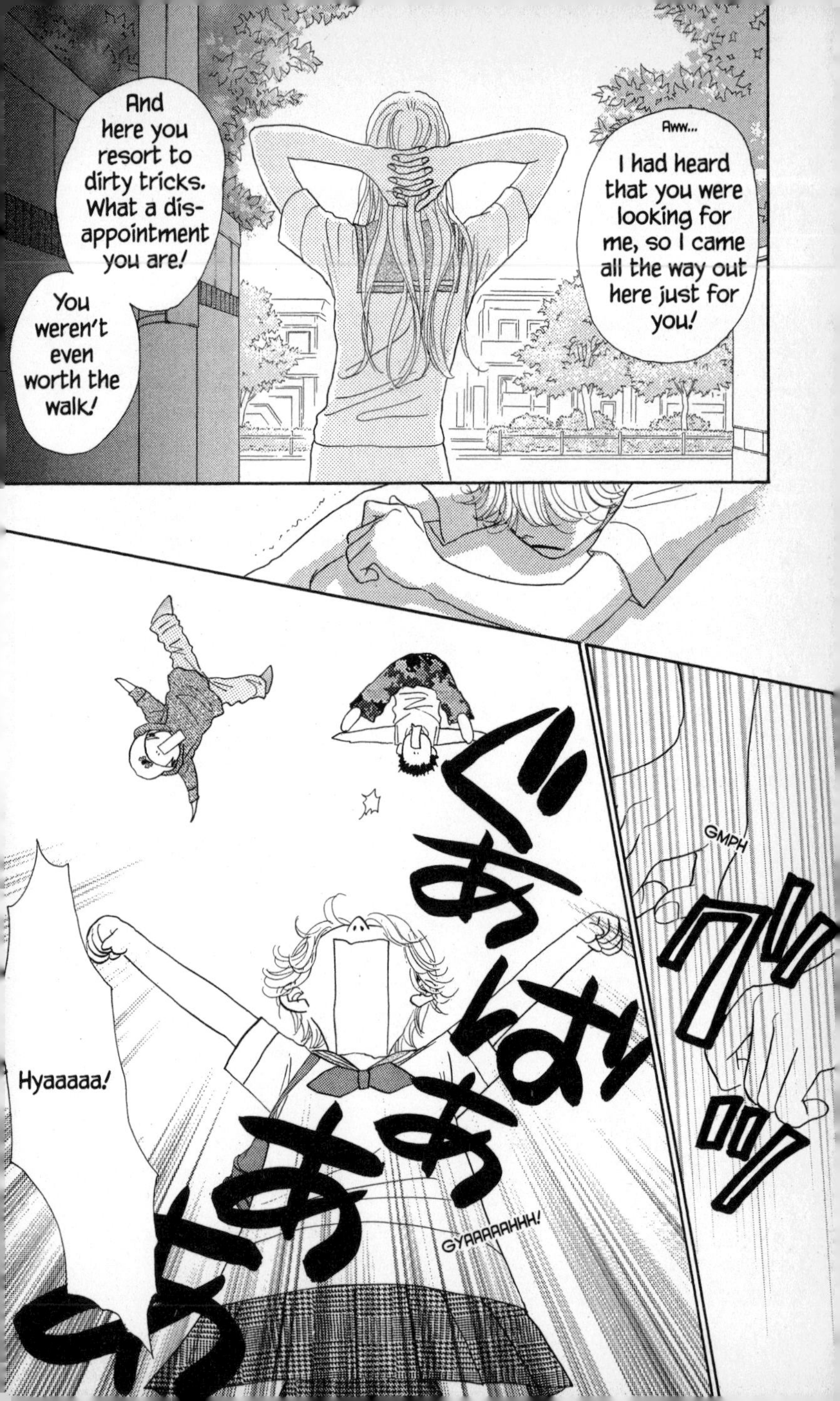
Aww...
I had heard that you were looking for me, so I came all the way out here just for you!
And here you resort to dirty tricks. What a dis-appointment you are!
You weren't even worth the walk!
GMPH
GYAAAAHHH!
Hyaaaaa!

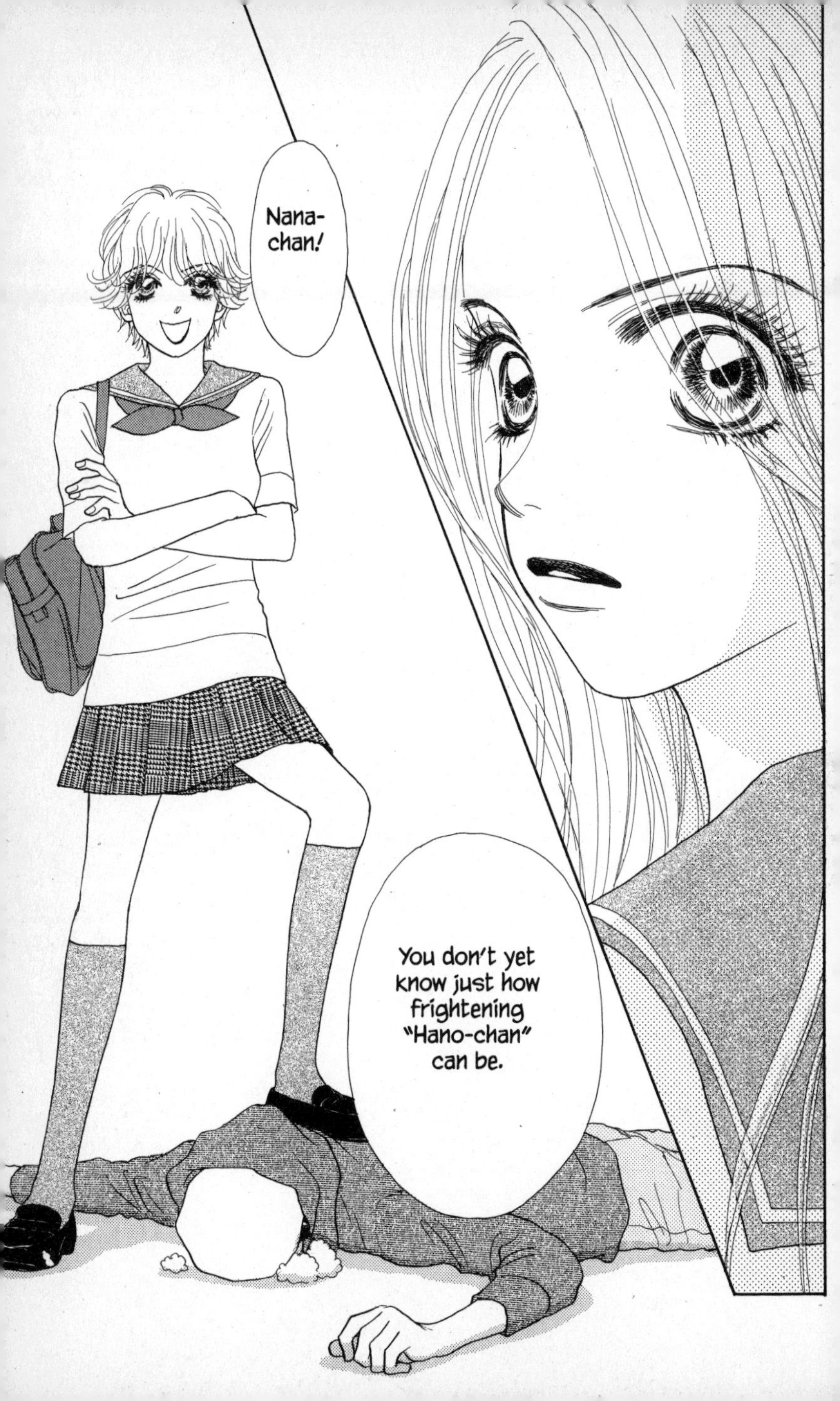
Nana-chan!
You don't yet know just how frightening "Hano-chan" can be.

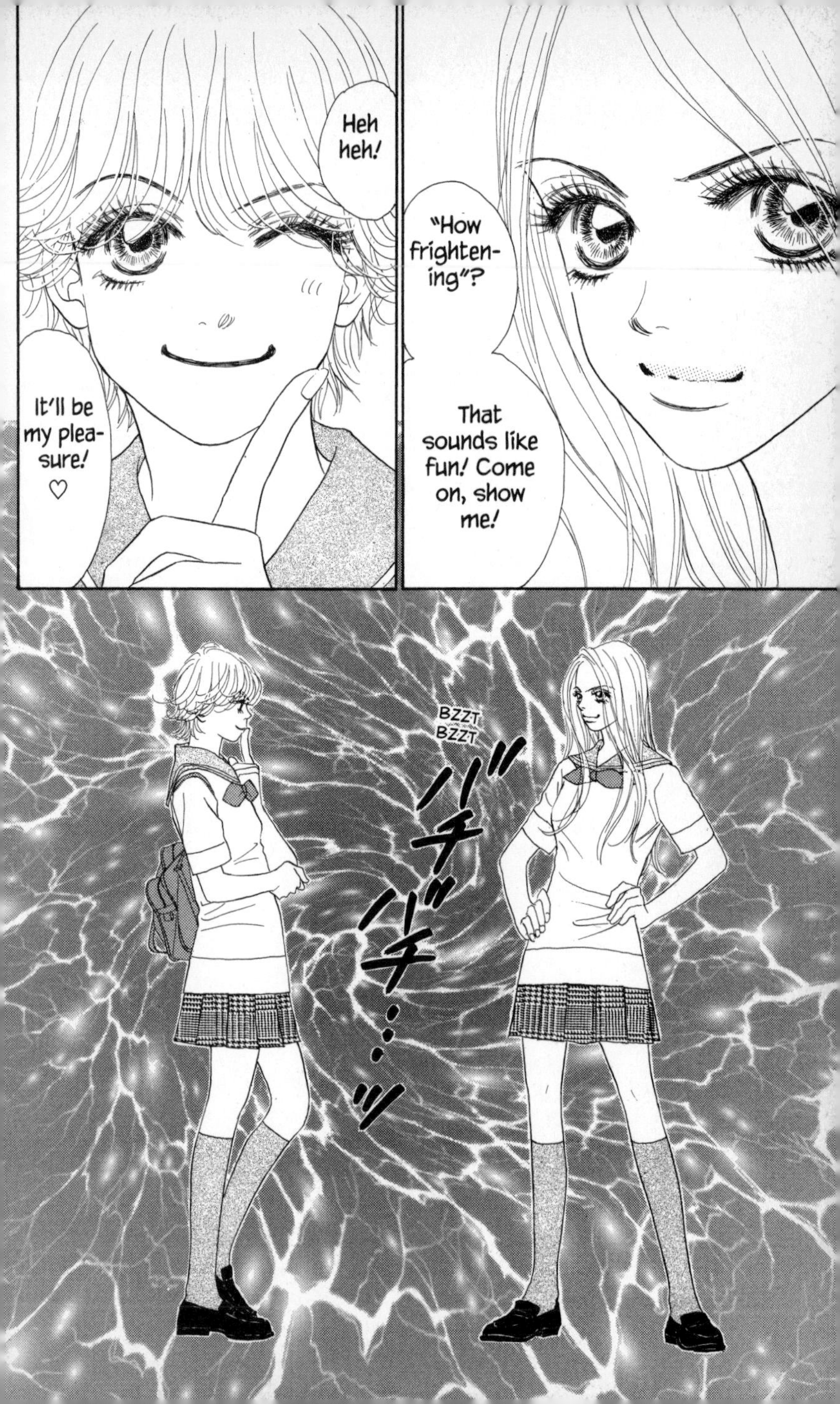
"How frightening"?
That sounds like fun! Come on, show me!
Heh heh!
It'll be my pleasure! ♡
BZZT BZZT
バチバチ……ッ

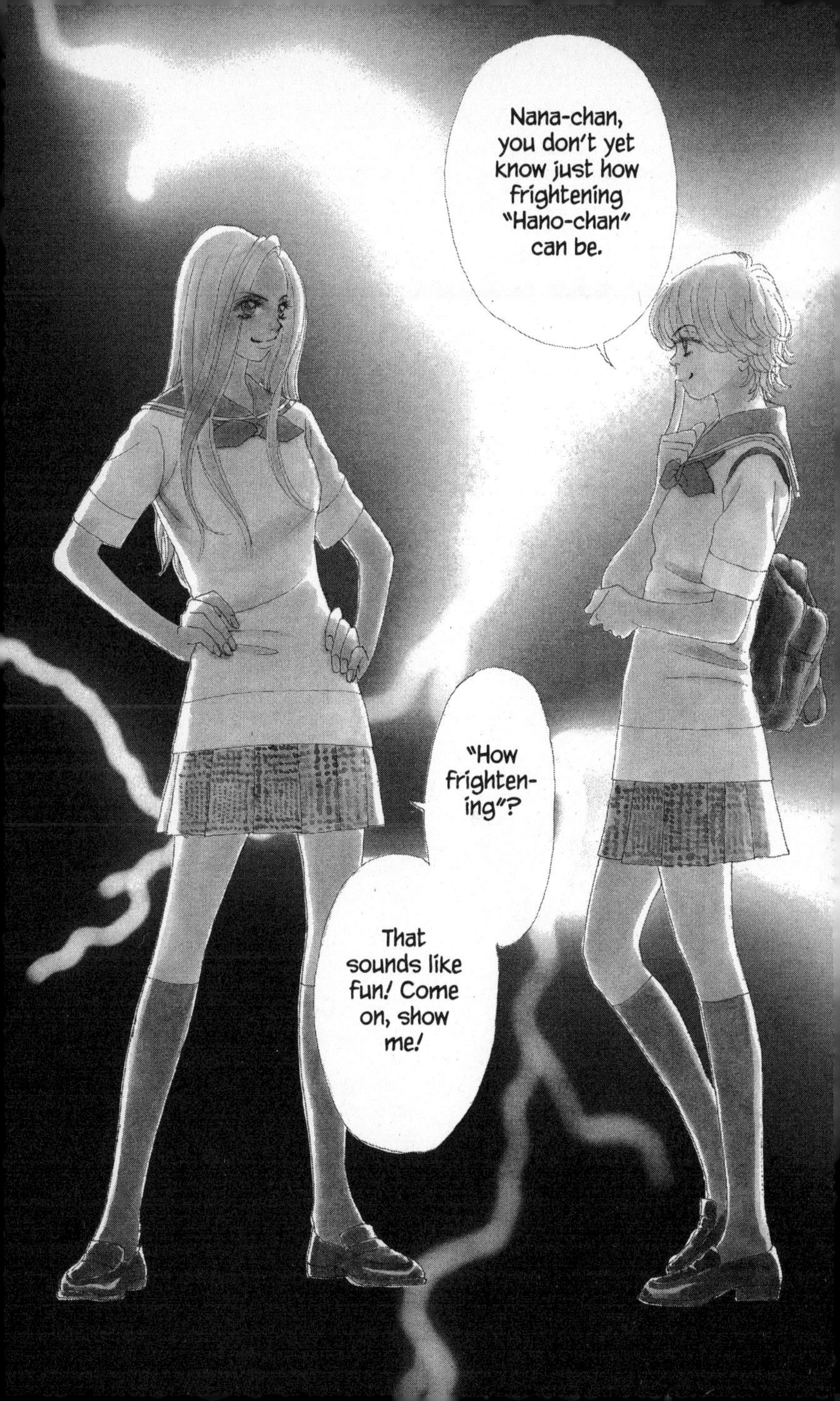
Nana-chan, you don't yet know just how frightening "Hano-chan" can be.
"How frighten-ing"?
That sounds like fun! Come on, show me!

Chapter 14
The Unknown Relationship

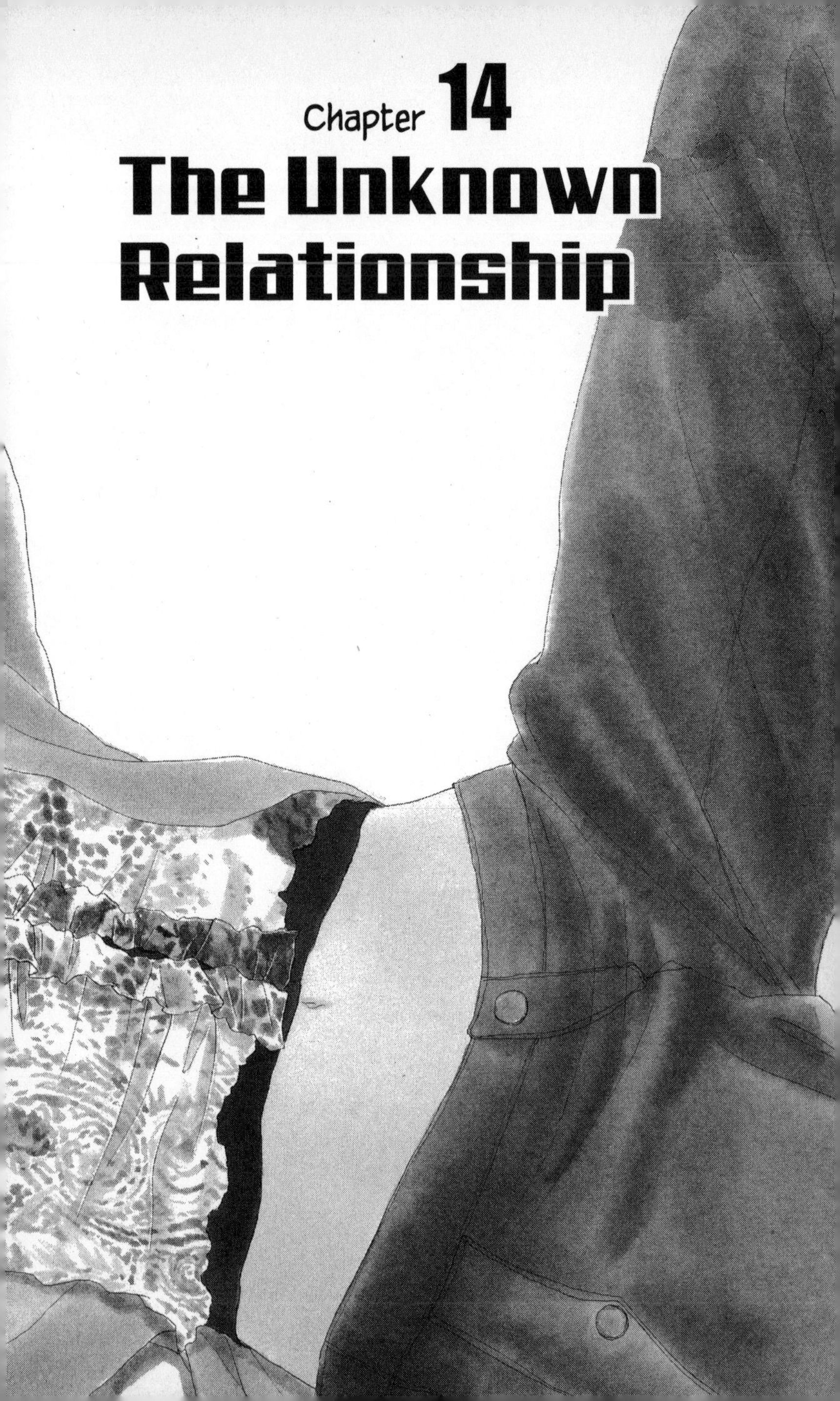

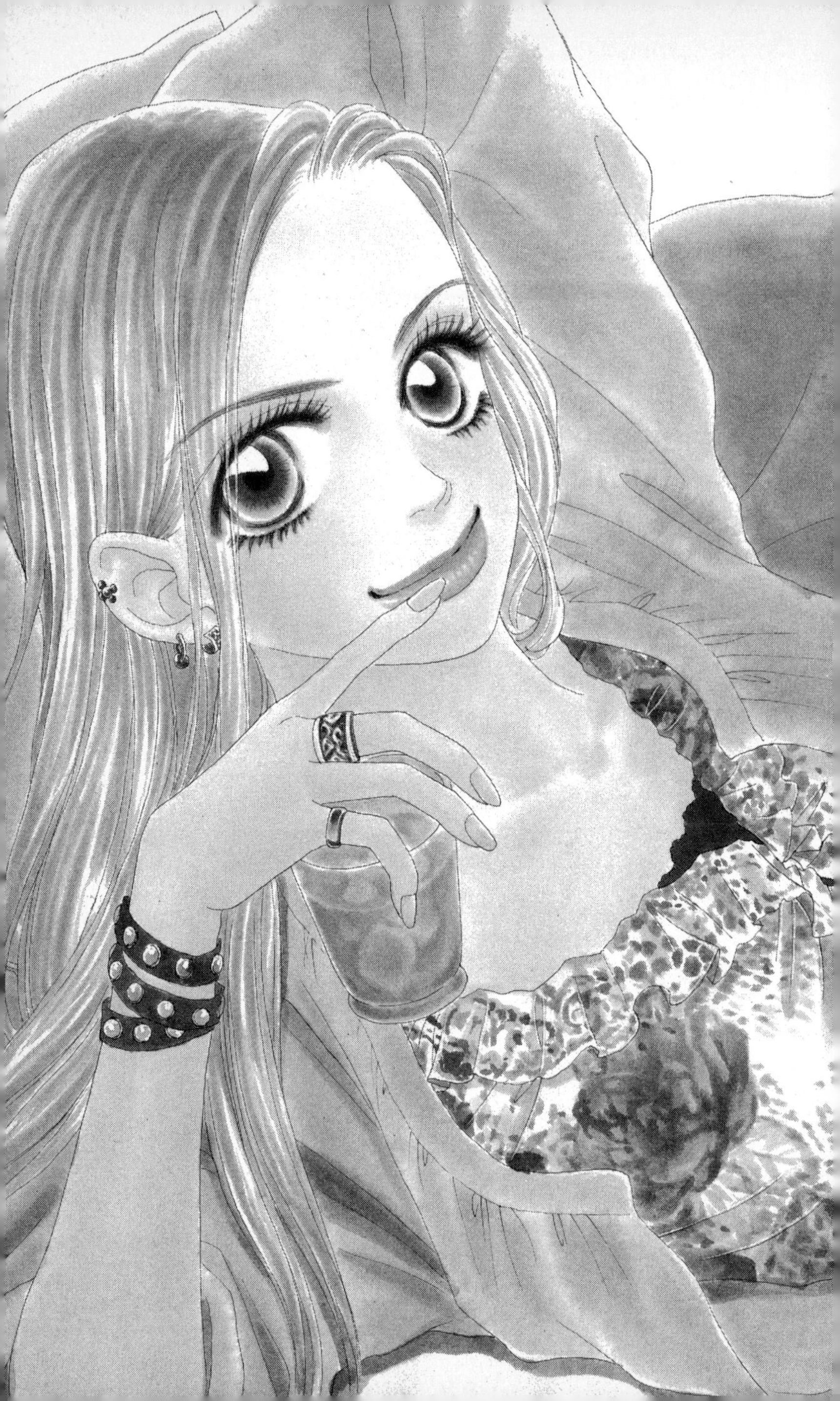

OTHELLO

オセロ。

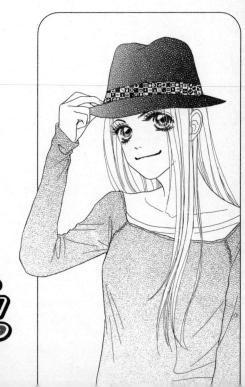

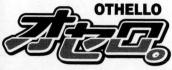

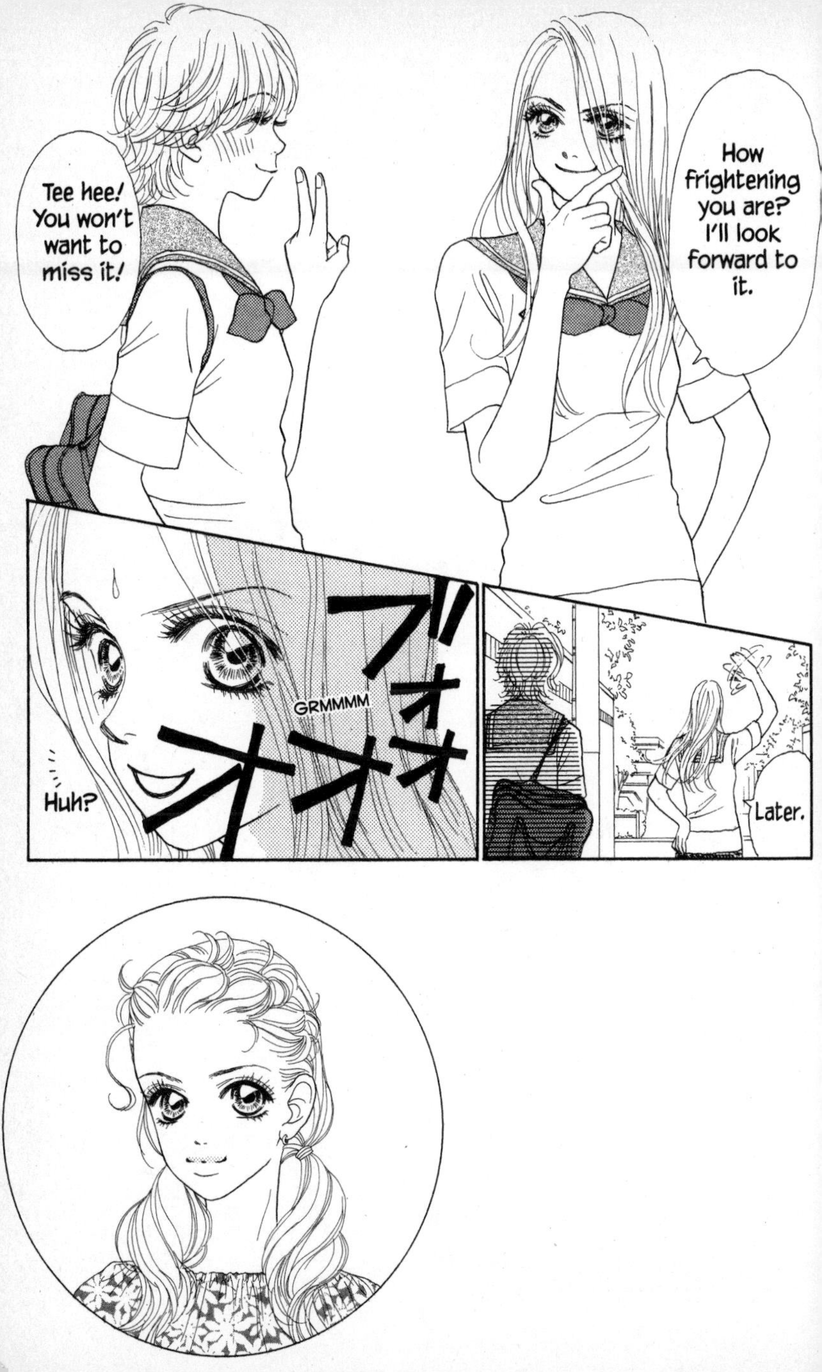

How frightening you are? I'll look forward to it.
Tee hee! You won't want to miss it!
Later.
ブオオオ
GRMMMM
Huh?

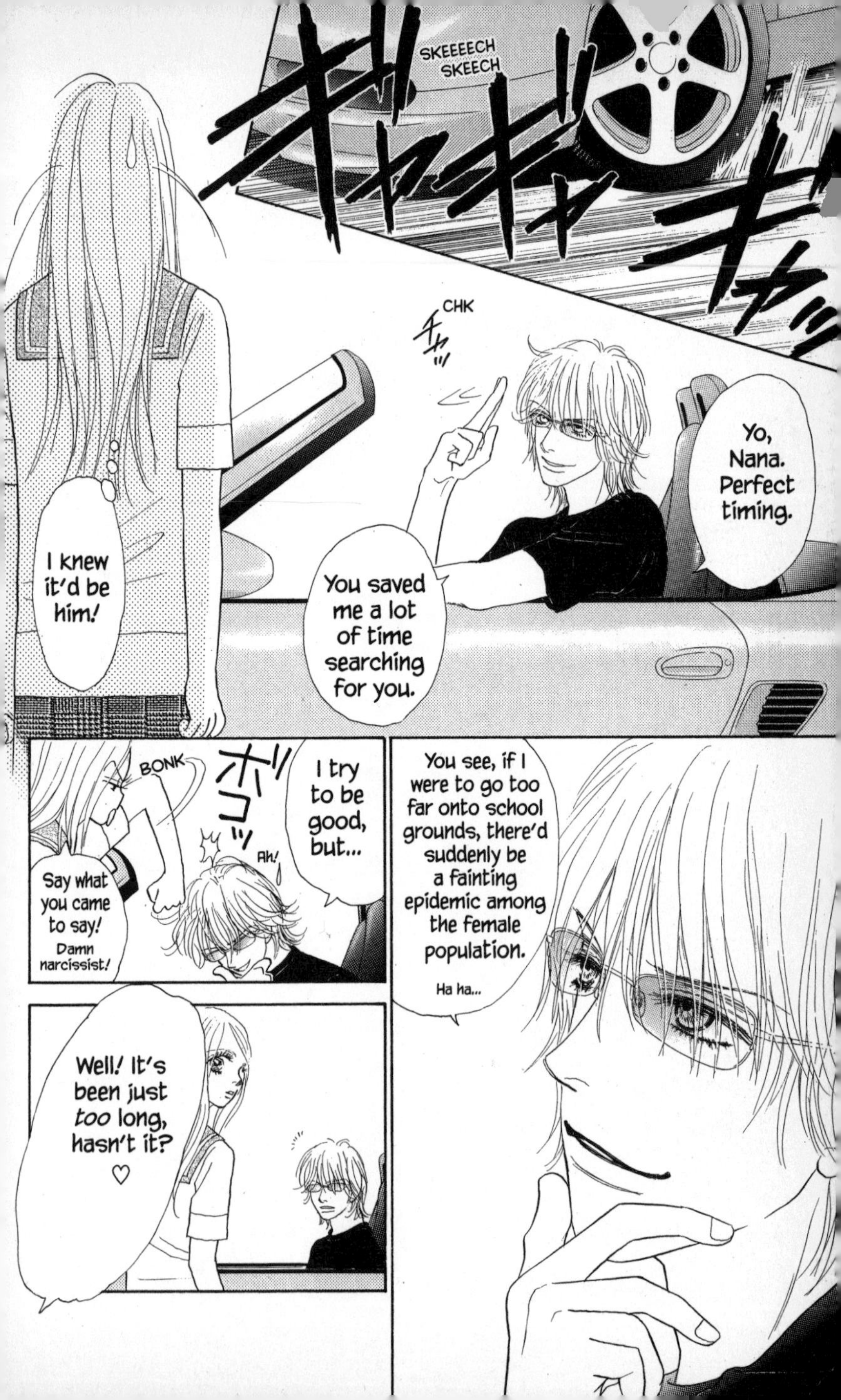
SKEEEECH
SKEECH
CHK
Yo, Nana. Perfect timing.
You saved me a lot of time searching for you.
I knew it'd be him!
You see, if I were to go too far onto school grounds, there'd suddenly be a fainting epidemic among the female population.
Ha ha...
I try to be good, but...
BONK
Ah!
Say what you came to say!
Damn narcissist!
Well! It's been just too long, hasn't it? ♡

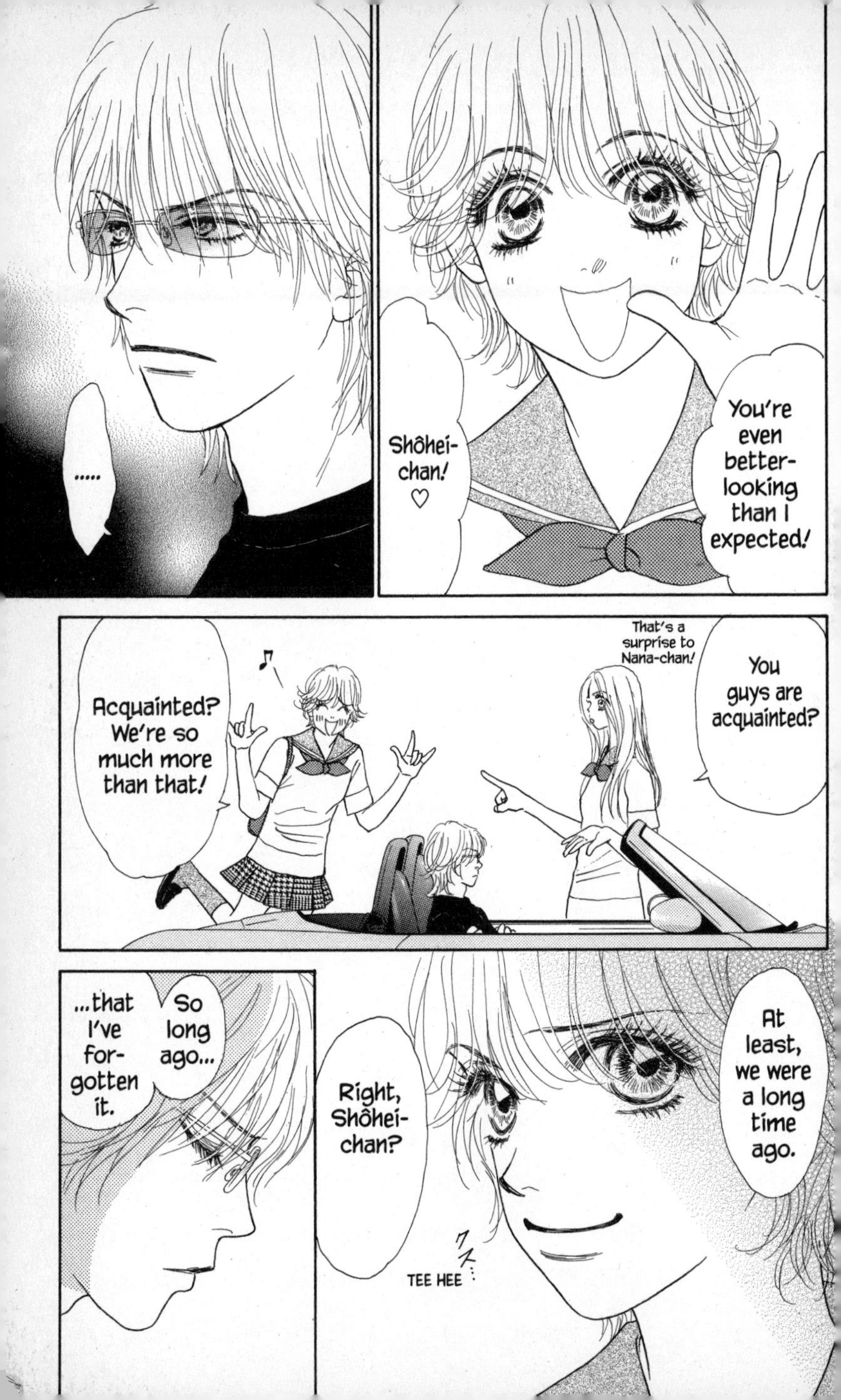
You're even better-looking than I expected!
Shôhei-chan! ♡
.....
You guys are acquainted?
That's a surprise to Nana-chan!
Acquainted? We're so much more than that!
At least, we were a long time ago.
Right, Shôhei-chan?
TEE HEE
So long ago...
...that I've for-gotten it.

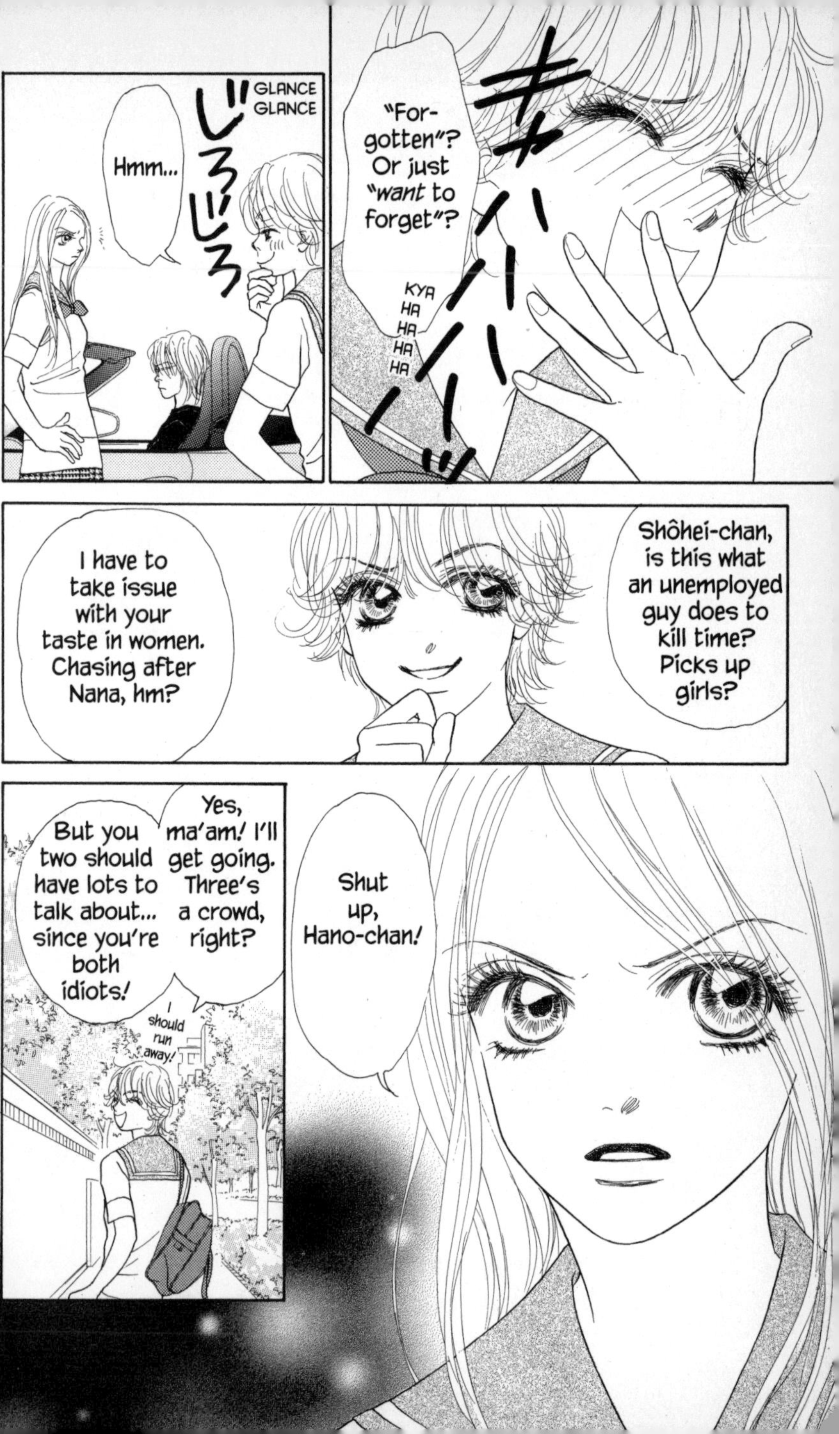

"For-gotten"? Or just "*want* to forget"?
KYA HA HA HA HA
GLANCE GLANCE
じろじろ
Hmm...
Shôhei-chan, is this what an unemployed guy does to kill time? Picks up girls?
I have to take issue with your taste in women. Chasing after Nana, hm?
Shut up, Hano-chan!
Yes, ma'am! I'll get going. Three's a crowd, right?
But you two should have lots to talk about... since you're both idiots!
I should run away!

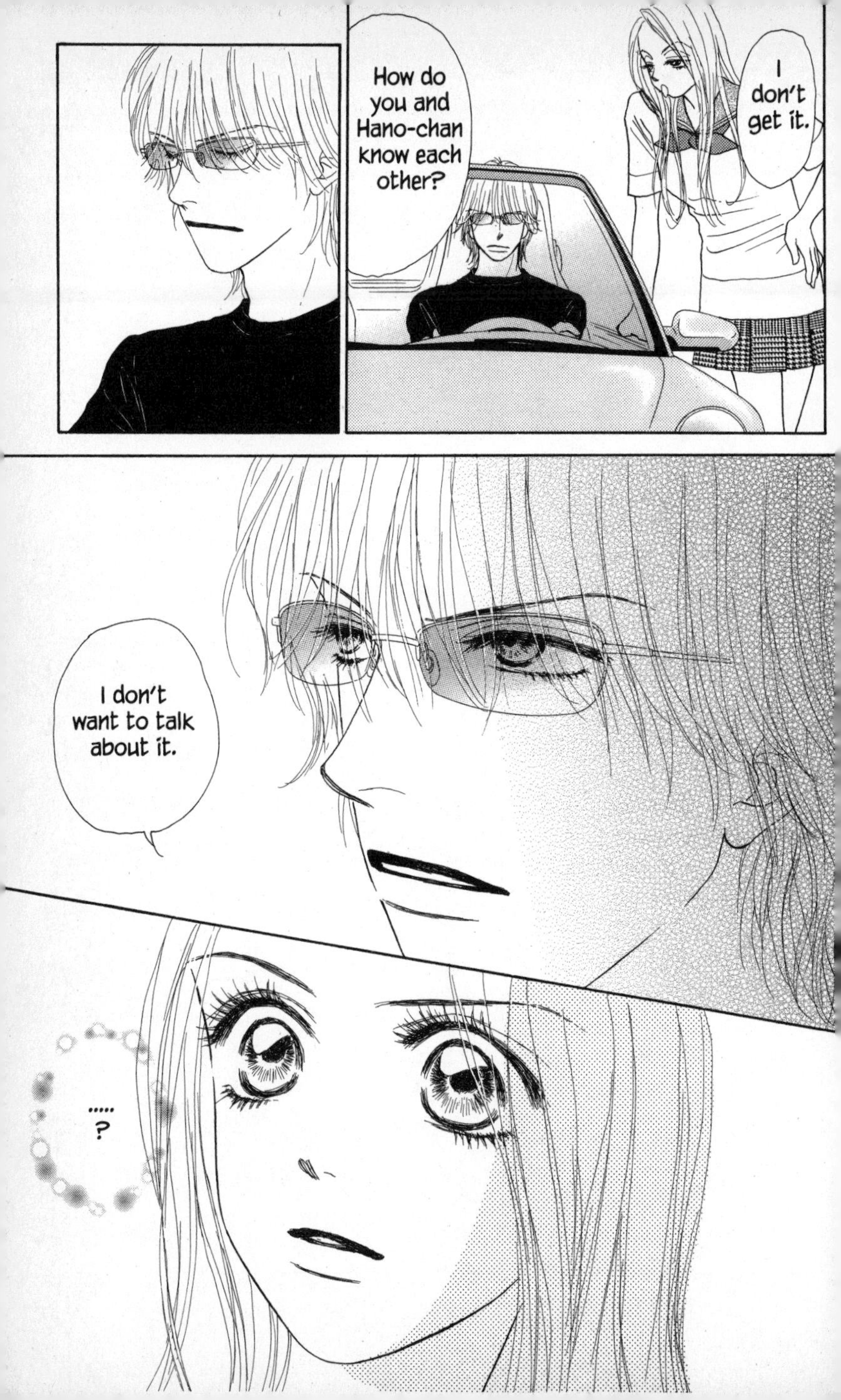
I don't get it.
How do you and Hano-chan know each other?
I don't want to talk about it.
.....?

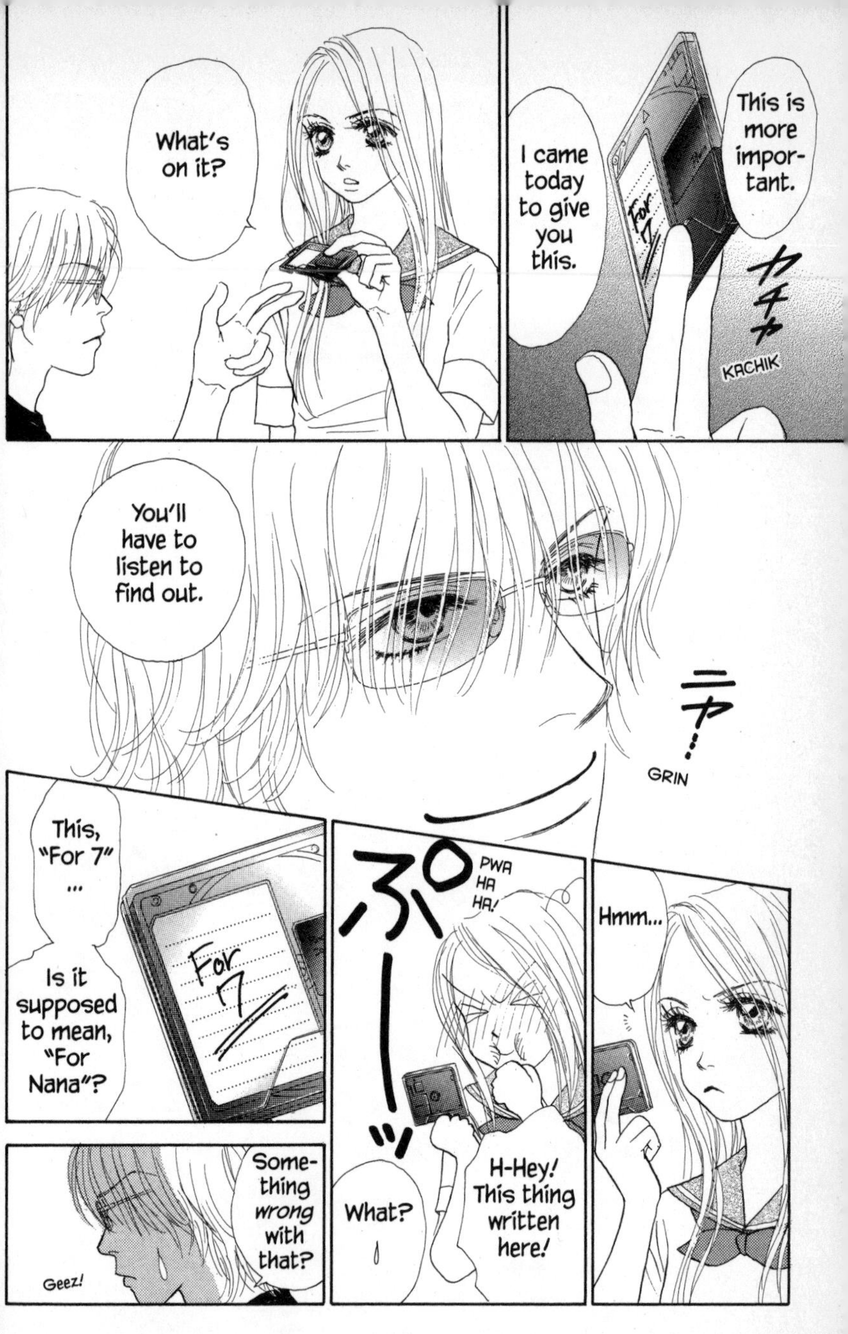
This is more impor-tant.
I came today to give you this.
For 7
KACHIK
What's on it?
You'll have to listen to find out.
GRIN
Hmm...
PWA HA HA!
H-Hey! This thing written here!
What?
This, "For 7" ...
For 7
Is it supposed to mean, "For Nana"?
Some-thing *wrong* with that?
Geez!

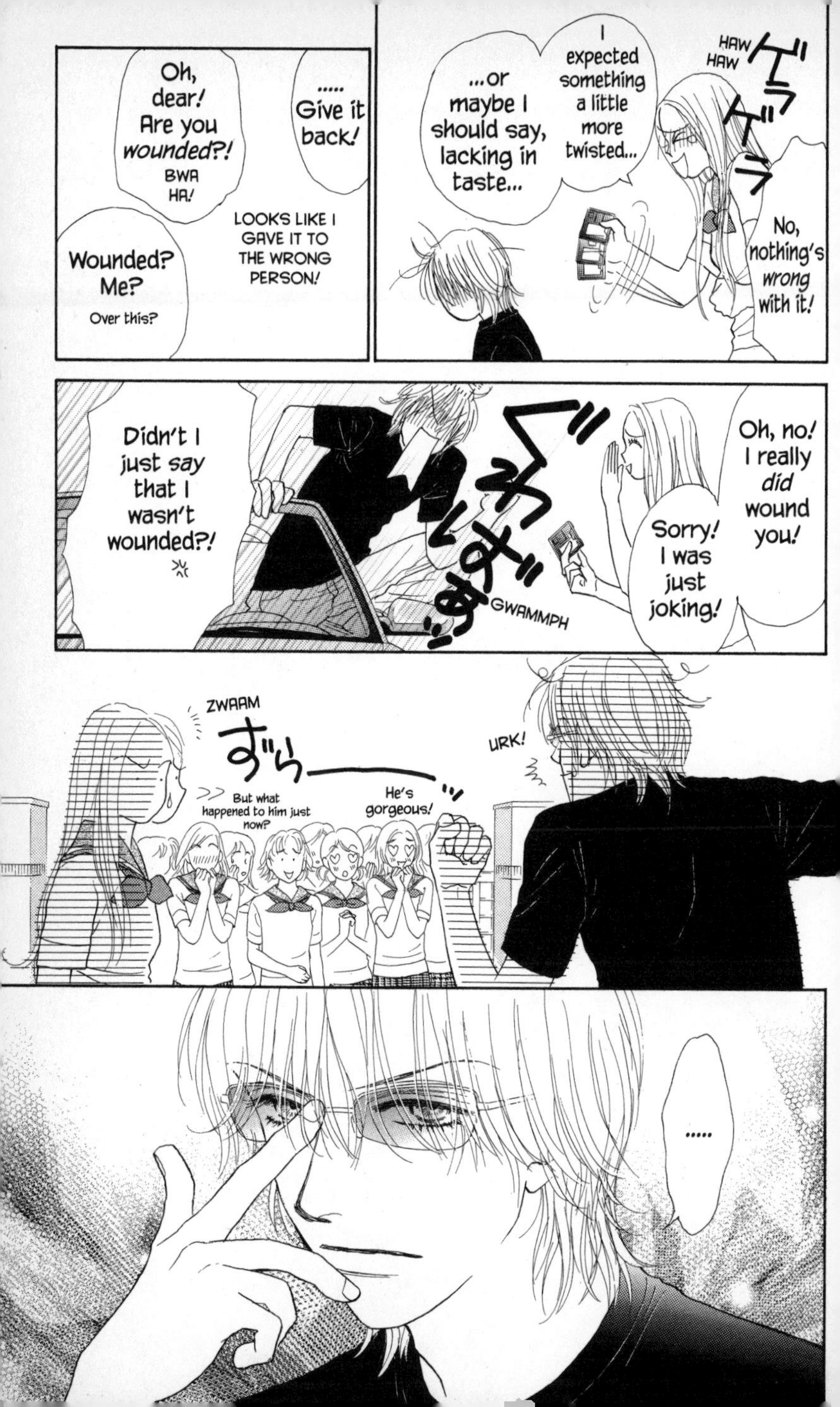
HAW HAW
ゲラゲラ
No, nothing's *wrong* with it!
I expected something a little more twisted...
...or maybe I should say, lacking in taste...
..... Give it back!
Oh, dear! Are you *wounded?!*
BWA HA!
LOOKS LIKE I GAVE IT TO THE WRONG PERSON!
Wounded? Me?
Over this?
Oh, no! I really *did* wound you!
Sorry! I was just joking!
ぐわしゃあ
GWAMMPH
Didn't I just *say* that I wasn't wounded?!
URK!
ZWAAM
ずら
He's gorgeous!
But what happened to him just now?
.....

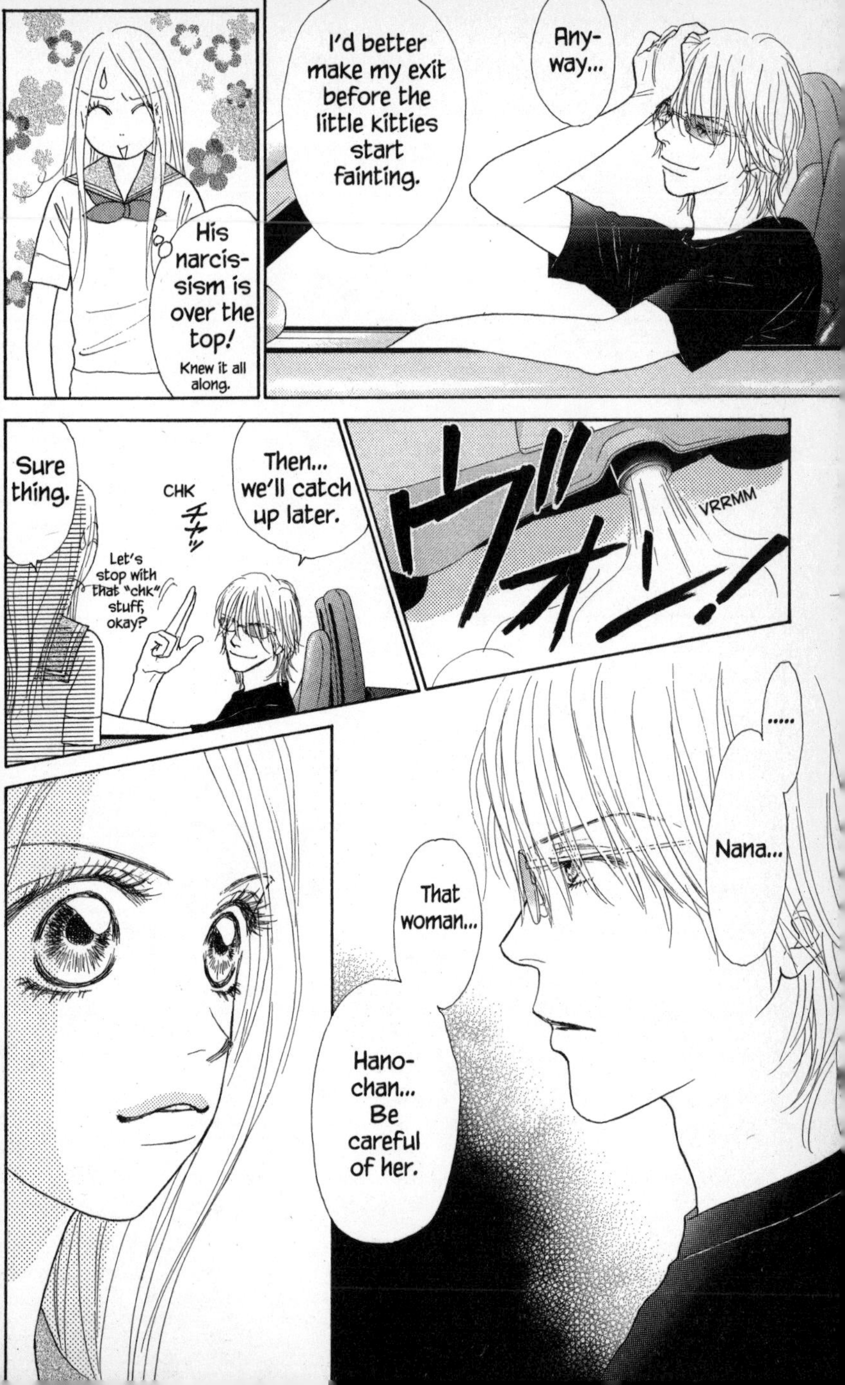
Any-way...
I'd better make my exit before the little kitties start fainting.
His narcis-sism is over the top!
Knew it all along.
VRRMM
Then... we'll catch up later.
CHK
Sure thing.
Let's stop with that "chk" stuff, okay?
.....
Nana...
That woman...
Hano-chan... Be careful of her.

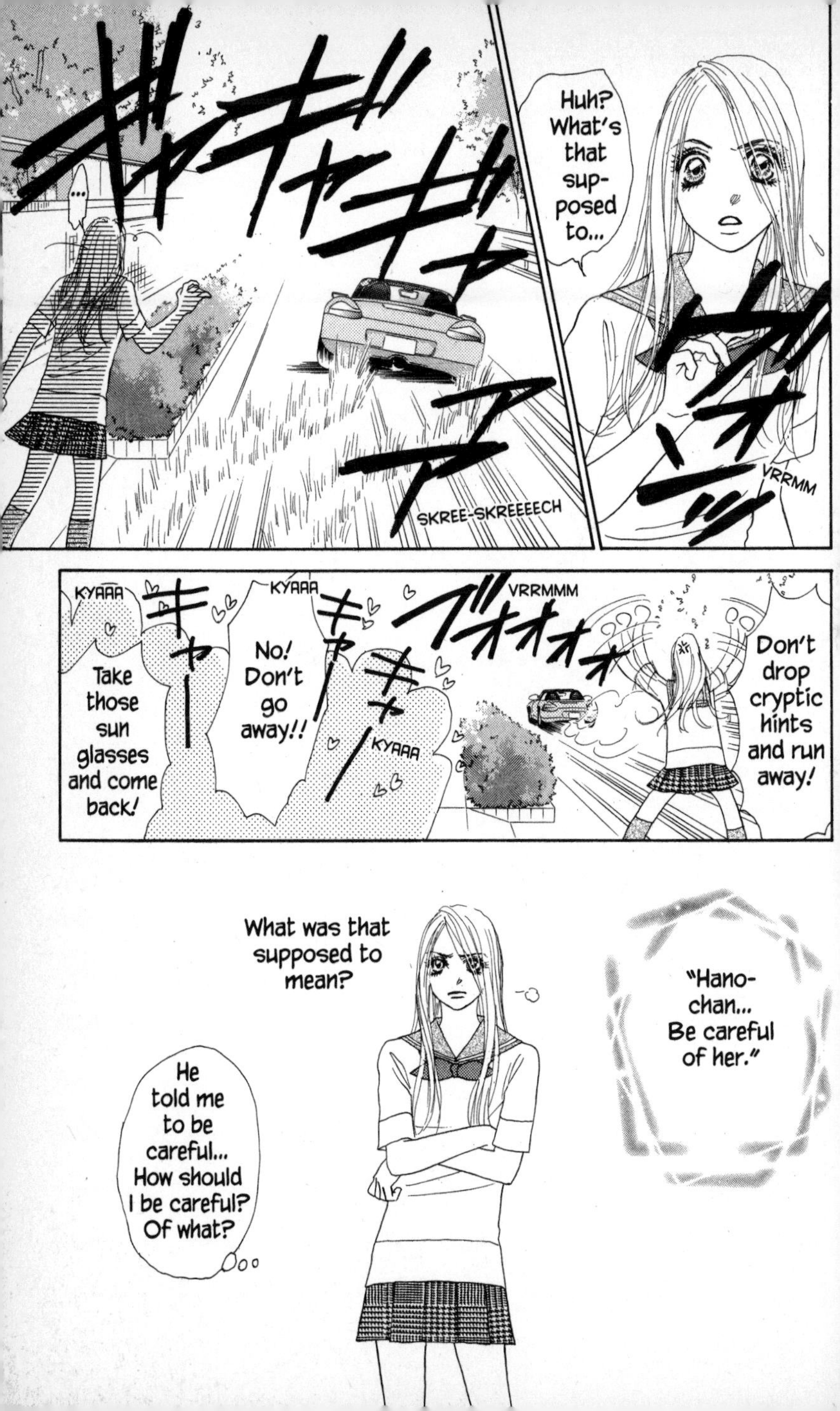

Huh? What's that sup-posed to...
VRRMM
SKREE-SKREEEECH
Don't drop cryptic hints and run away!
VRRMMM
KYAAA
No! Don't go away!!
KYAAA
Take those sun glasses and come back!
KYAAA
"Hano-chan... Be careful of her."
What was that supposed to mean?
He told me to be careful... How should I be careful? Of what?

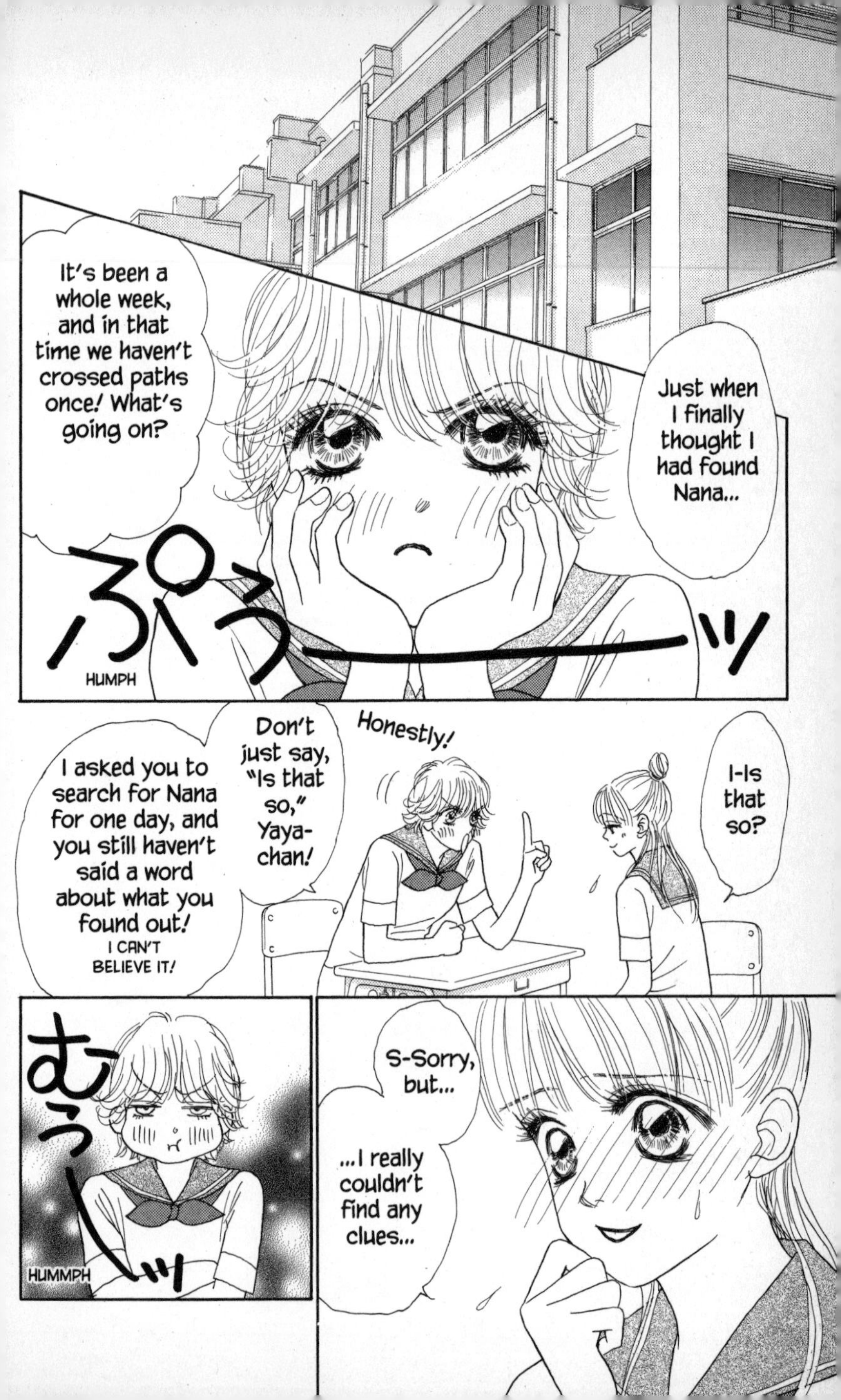
Just when I finally thought I had found Nana...
It's been a whole week, and in that time we haven't crossed paths once! What's going on?
ぷう―――ッ
HUMPH
I-Is that so?
Honestly!
Don't just say, "Is that so," Yaya-chan!
I asked you to search for Nana for one day, and you still haven't said a word about what you found out!
I CAN'T BELIEVE IT!
S-Sorry, but...
...I really couldn't find any clues...
むう―ッ
HUMMPH

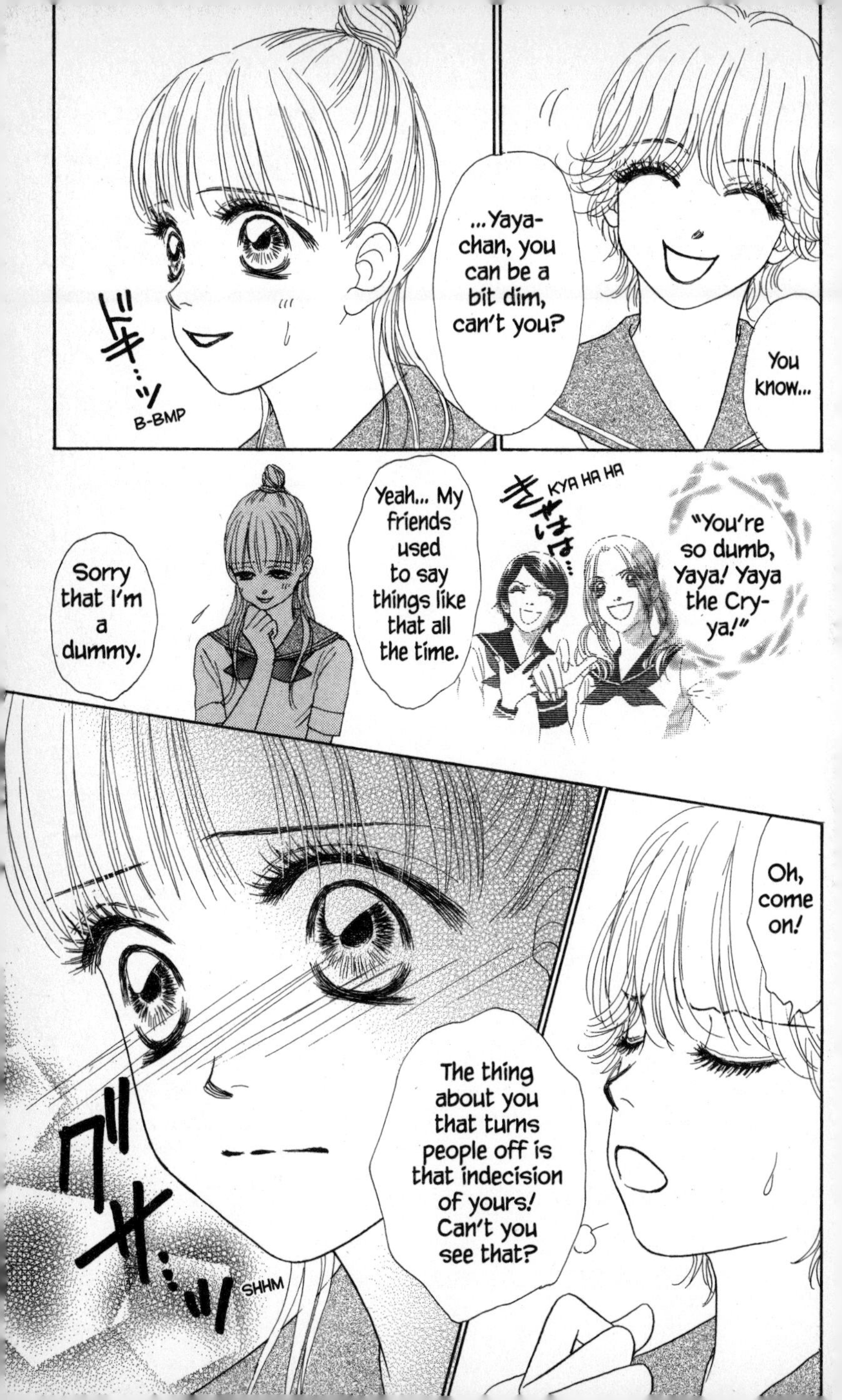
You know...
...Yaya-chan, you can be a bit dim, can't you?
ドキッ
B-BMP
"You're so dumb, Yaya! Yaya the Cry-ya!"
きゃはは
KYA HA HA
Yeah... My friends used to say things like that all the time.
Sorry that I'm a dummy.
Oh, come on!
The thing about you that turns people off is that indecision of yours! Can't you see that?
グサッ
SHHM

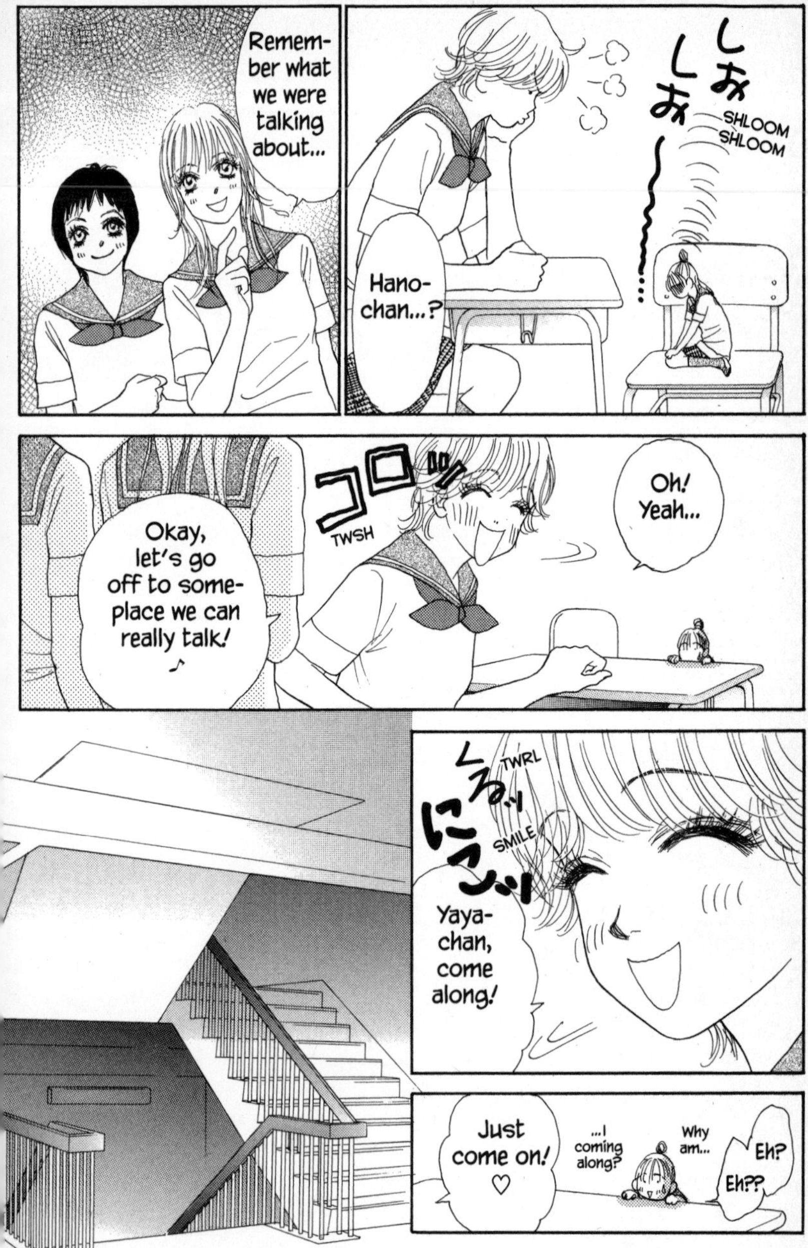
しおしお~~~……
SHLOOM SHLOOM
Hano-chan...?
Remember what we were talking about...
Oh! Yeah...
コロッ
TWSH
Okay, let's go off to someplace we can really talk! ♪
くるっ
TWRL
にこっ
SMILE
Yaya-chan, come along!
Eh?
Eh??
Why am...
...I coming along?
Just come on! ♡

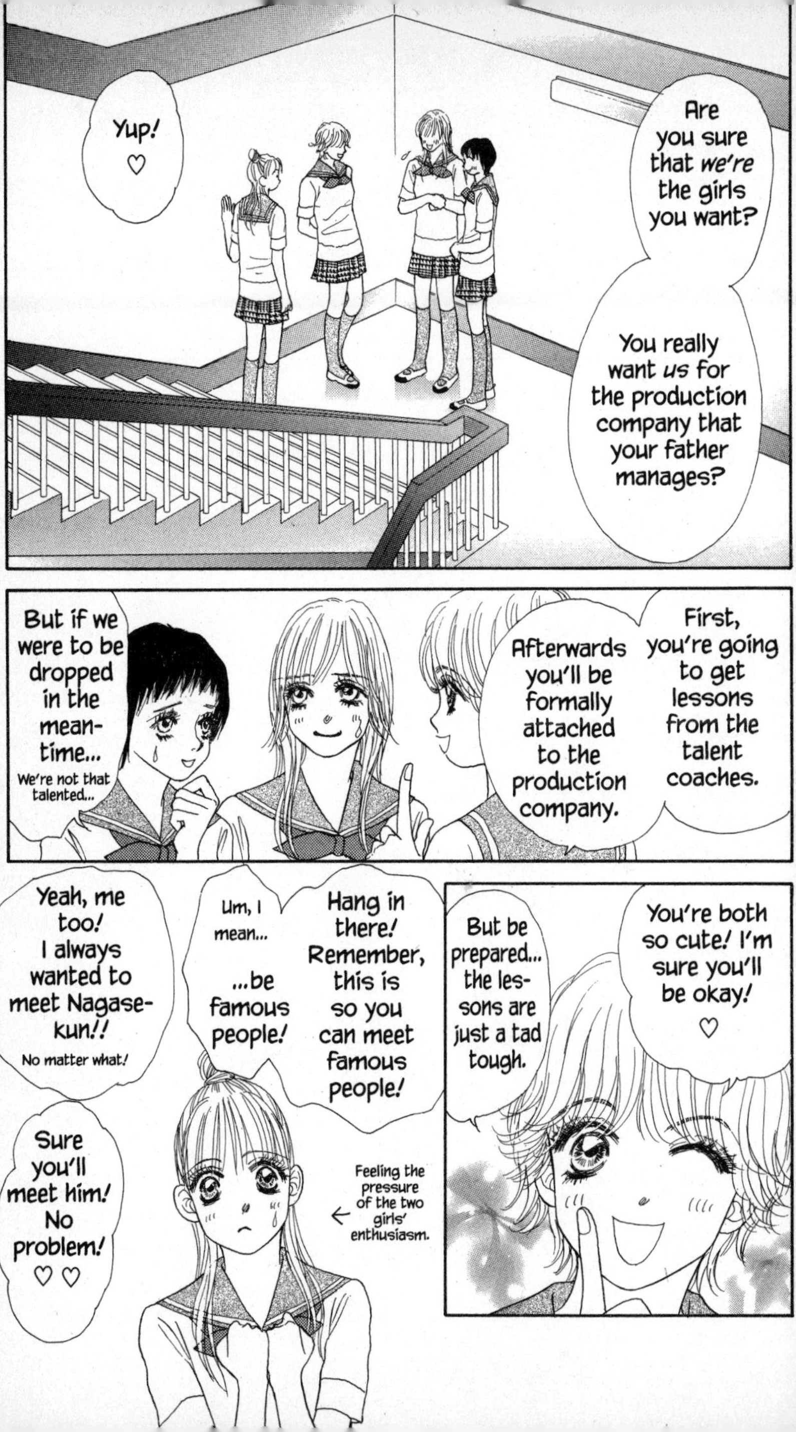

Are you sure that *we're* the girls you want?
You really want *us* for the production company that your father manages?
Yup! ♡
First, you're going to get lessons from the talent coaches.
Afterwards you'll be formally attached to the production company.
But if we were to be dropped in the mean-time...
We're not that talented...
You're both so cute! I'm sure you'll be okay! ♡
But be prepared... the les-sons are just a tad tough.
Hang in there! Remember, this is so you can meet famous people!
Um, I mean...
...be famous people!
Yeah, me too! I always wanted to meet Nagase-kun!!
No matter what!
Sure you'll meet him! No problem! ♡ ♡
Feeling the pressure of the two girls' enthusiasm.

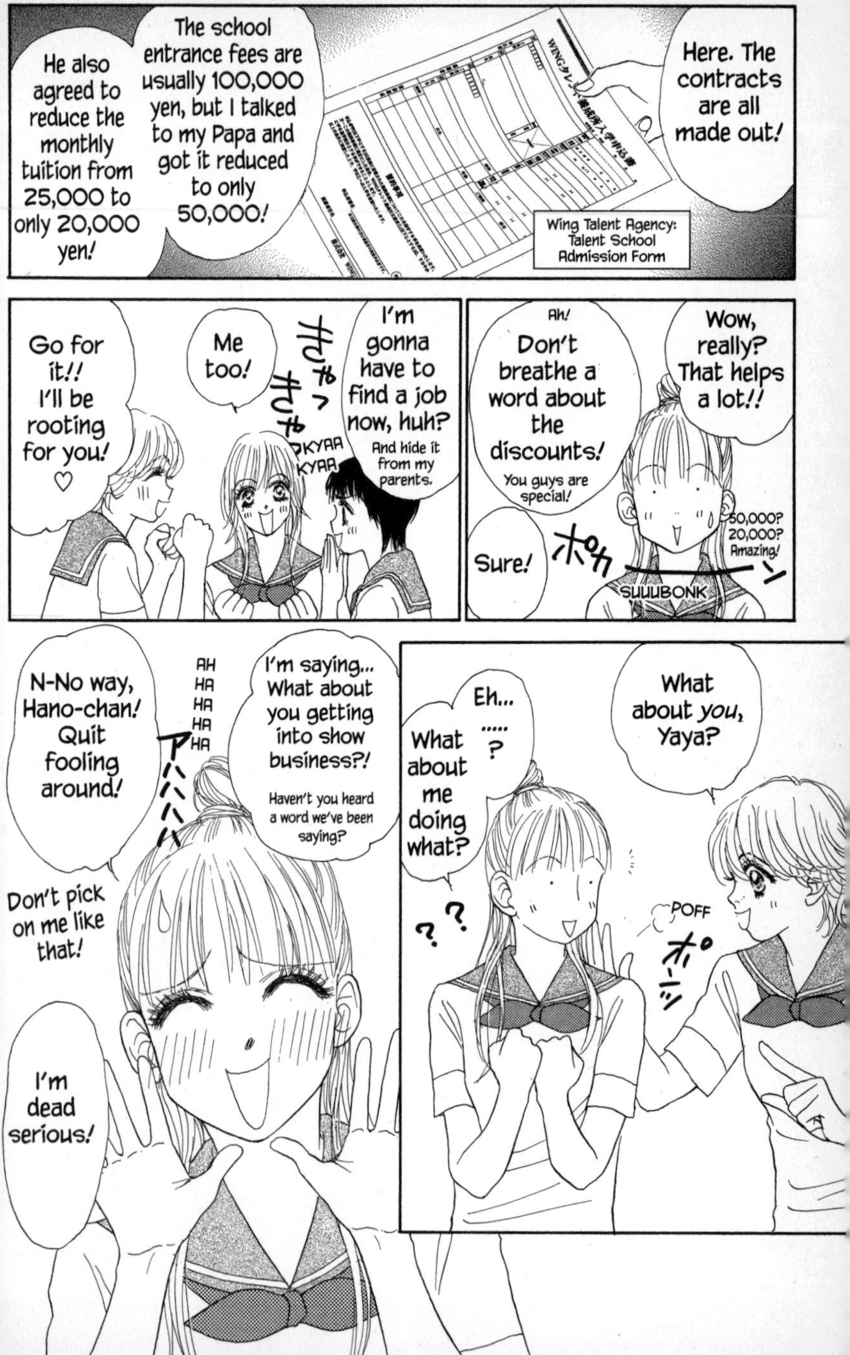
Here. The contracts are all made out!
Wing Talent Agency: Talent School Admission Form
The school entrance fees are usually 100,000 yen, but I talked to my Papa and got it reduced to only 50,000!
He also agreed to reduce the monthly tuition from 25,000 to only 20,000 yen!
Wow, really? That helps a lot!!
50,000? 20,000? Amazing!
Ah! Don't breathe a word about the discounts! You guys are special!
Sure!
SUUUBONK
I'm gonna have to find a job now, huh? And hide it from my parents.
KYAA KYAA
Me too!
Go for it!! I'll be rooting for you! ♡
What about *you*, Yaya?
POFF
Eh... ..... ?
What about me doing what?
I'm saying... What about you getting into show business?! Haven't you heard a word we've been saying?
AH HA HA HA HA
N-No way, Hano-chan! Quit fooling around!
Don't pick on me like that!
I'm dead serious!

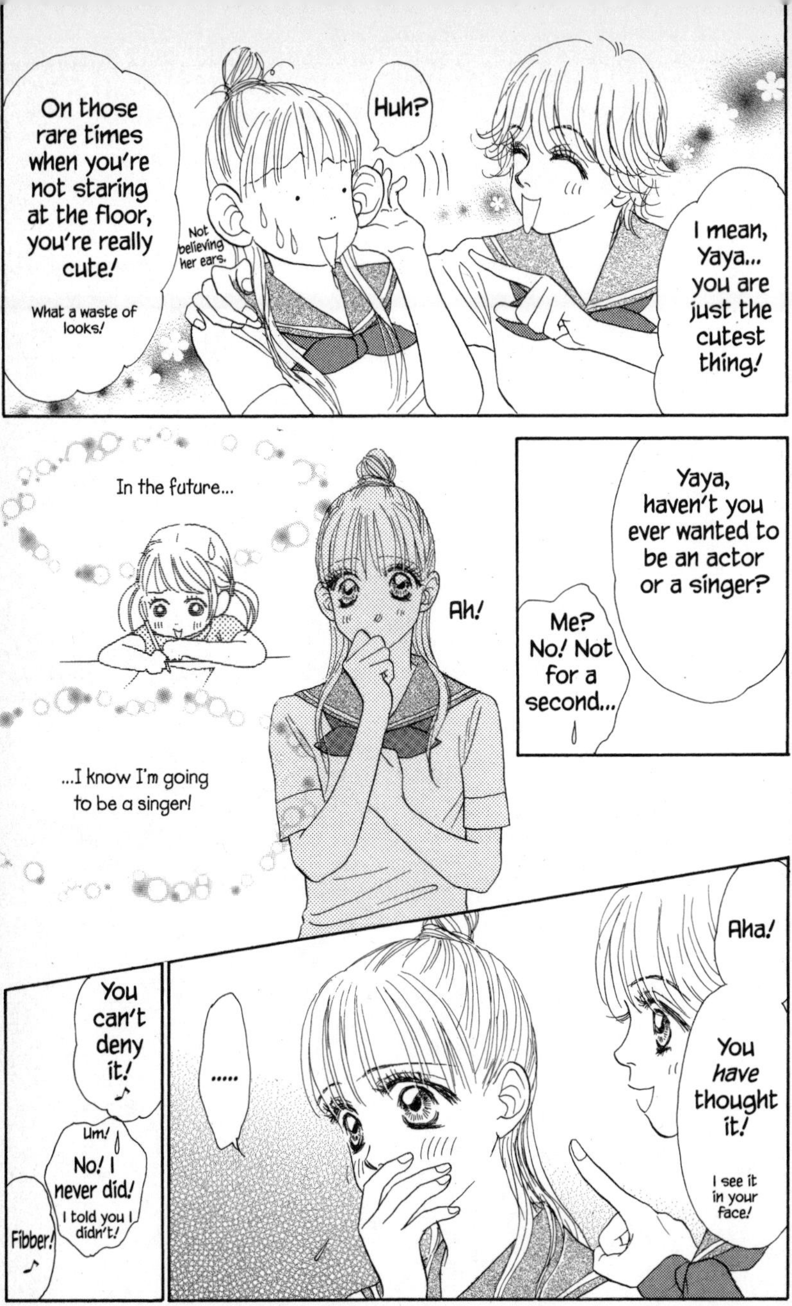
I mean, Yaya... you are just the cutest thing!
Huh?
Not believing her ears.
On those rare times when you're not staring at the floor, you're really cute!
What a waste of looks!
Yaya, haven't you ever wanted to be an actor or a singer?
Me? No! Not for a second...
Ah!
In the future...
...I know I'm going to be a singer!
Aha!
You *have* thought it!
I see it in your face!
.....
You can't deny it! ♪
Um! No! I never did!
I told you I didn't!
Fibber! ♪

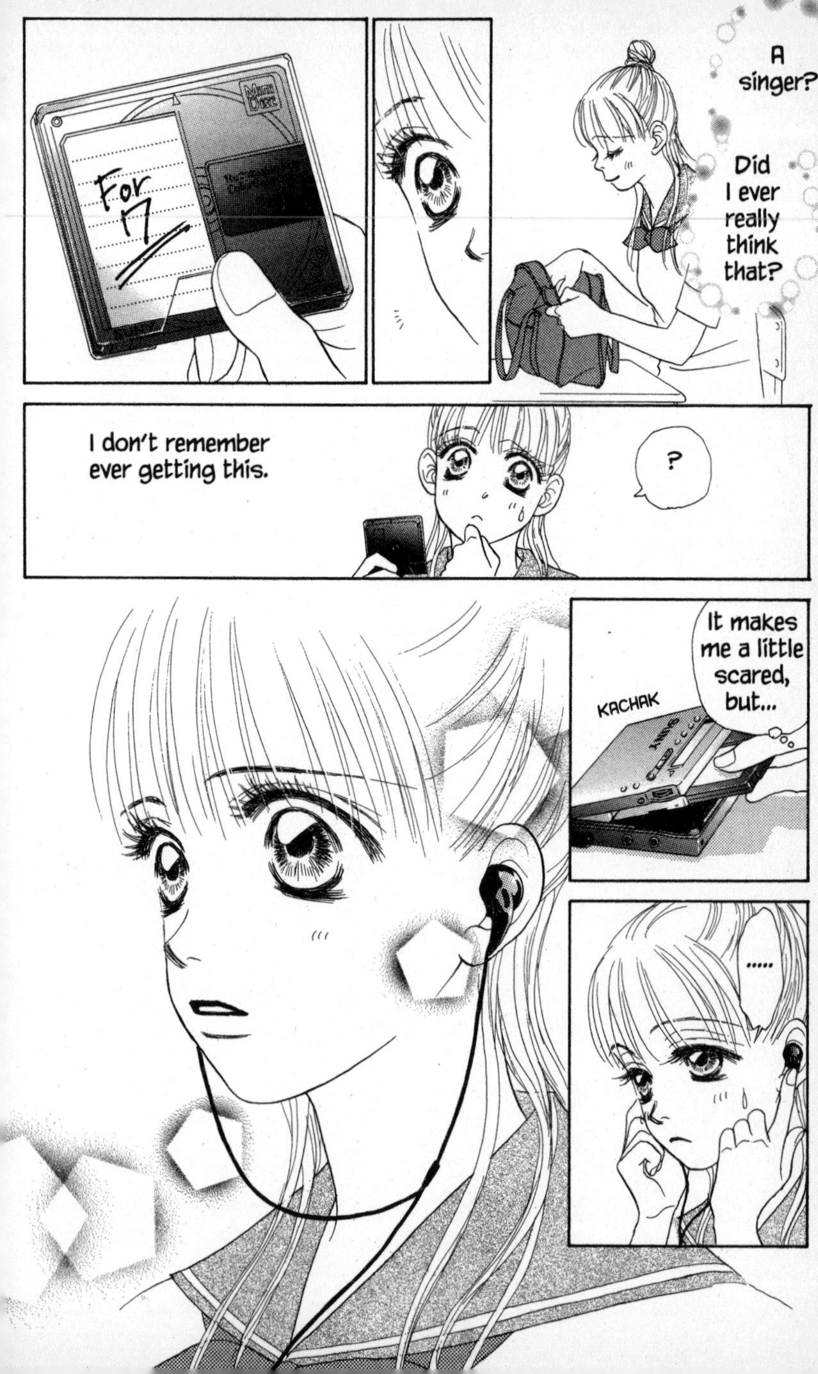
A singer?
Did I ever really think that?
For 17
I don't remember ever getting this.
?
It makes me a little scared, but...
KACHAK
.....

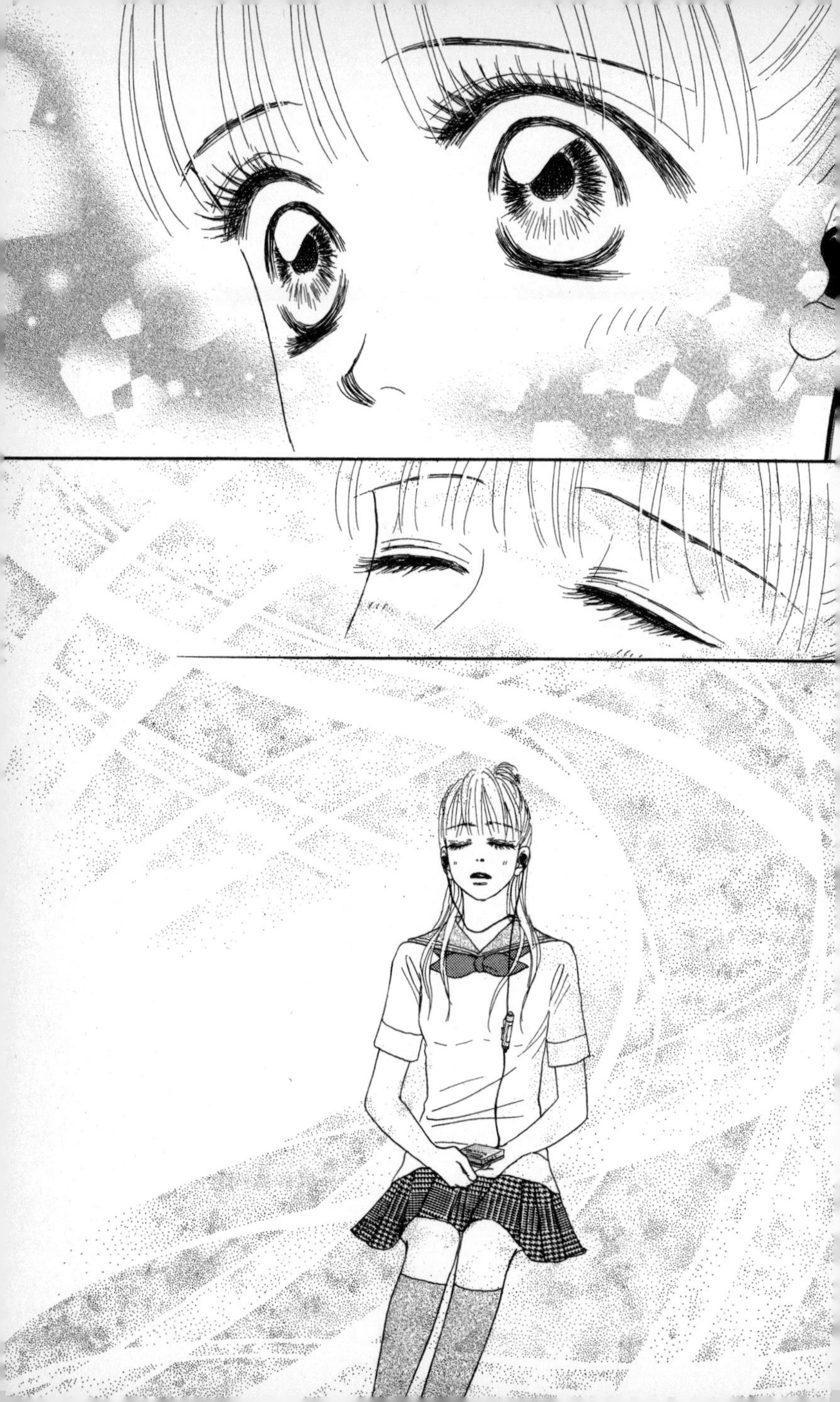

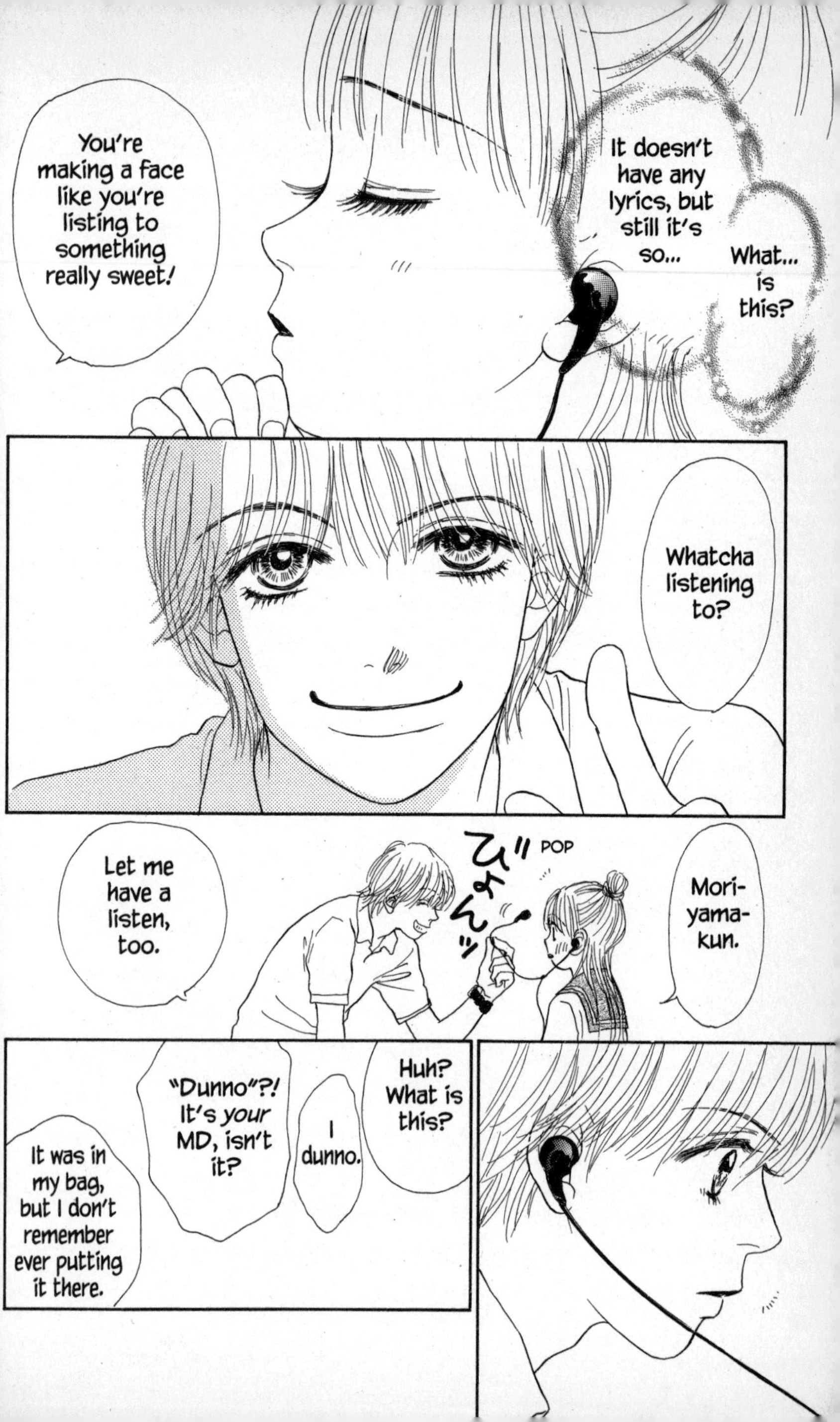
It doesn't have any lyrics, but still it's so...
What... is this?
You're making a face like you're listing to something really sweet!
Whatcha listening to?
Mori-yama-kun.
POP
Let me have a listen, too.
Huh? What is this?
I dunno.
"Dunno"?! It's *your* MD, isn't it?
It was in my bag, but I don't remember ever putting it there.

A long time ago, I wanted to grow up to be a singer.

Sure.

Um... Moriyama-kun?

Can I say something a little embarrassing to you?

But listening to this music, it really made me want to sing.

Of course, I gave up on it.

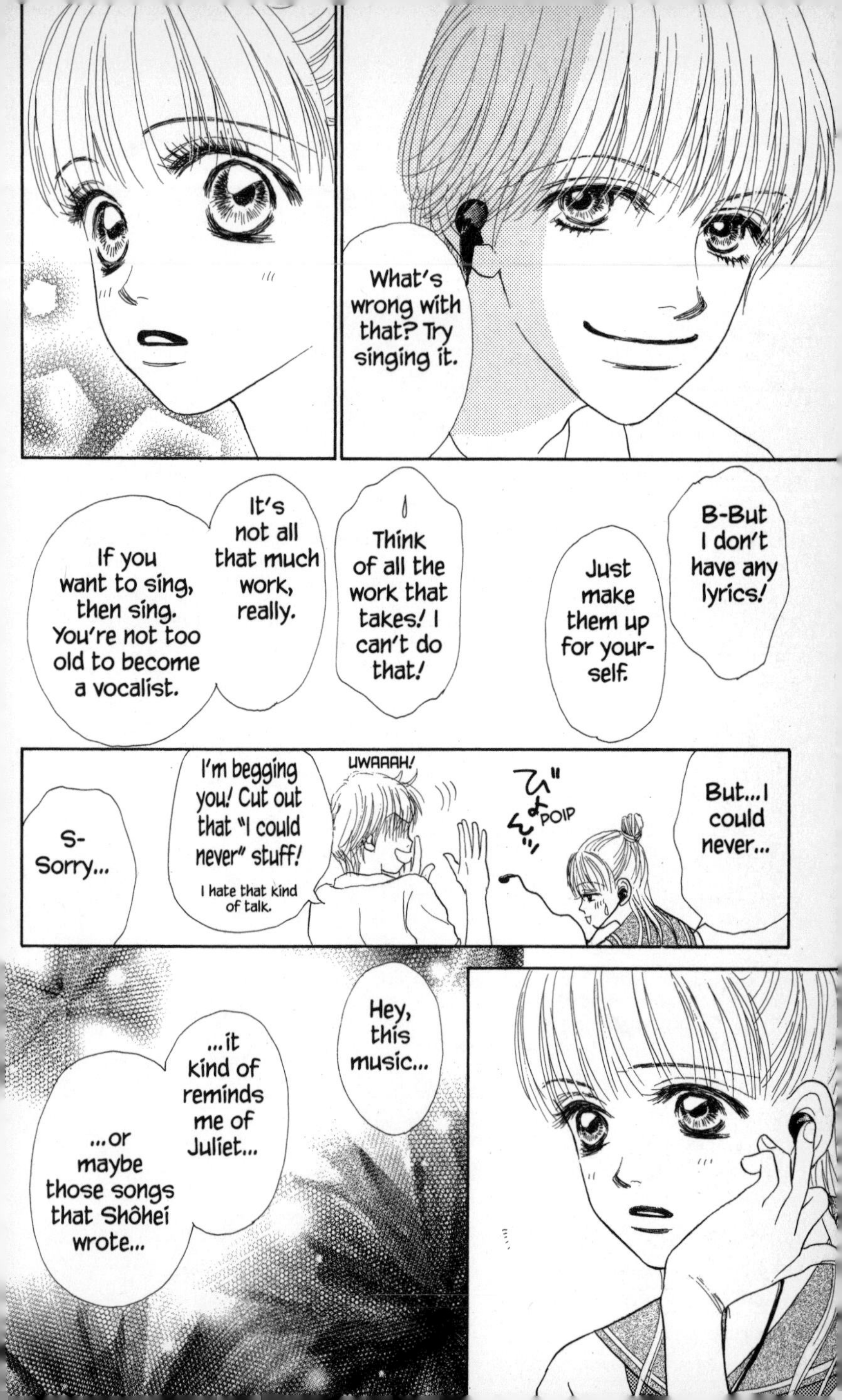

What's wrong with that? Try singing it.
B-But I don't have any lyrics!
Just make them up for your-self.
Think of all the work that takes! I can't do that!
It's not all that much work, really.
If you want to sing, then sing. You're not too old to become a vocalist.
But...I could never...
POIP
UWAAAH!
I'm begging you! Cut out that "I could never" stuff!
I hate that kind of talk.
S- Sorry...
Hey, this music...
...it kind of reminds me of Juliet...
...or maybe those songs that Shôhei wrote...

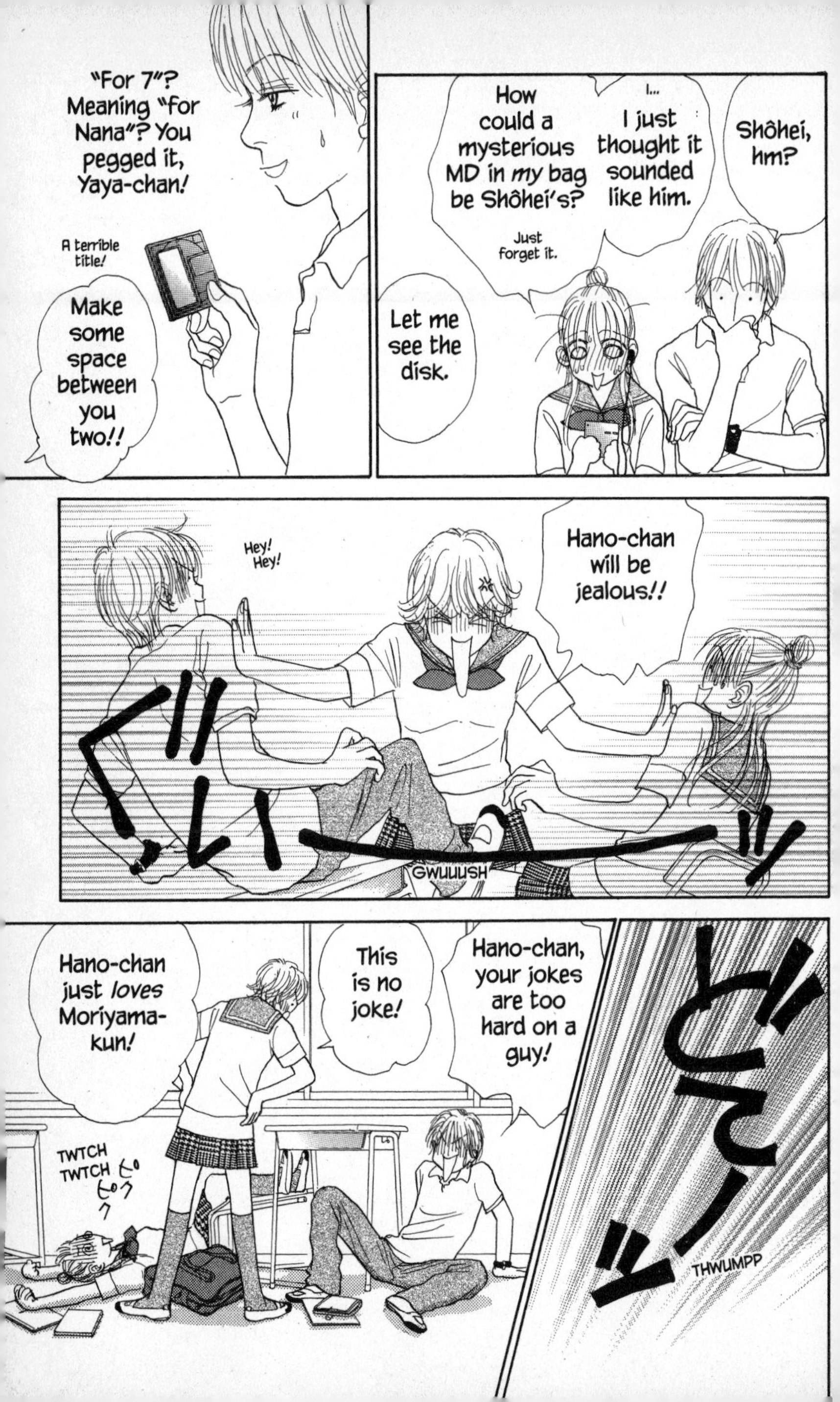

Shôhei, hm?
I... I just thought it sounded like him.
How could a mysterious MD in *my* bag be Shôhei's?
Just forget it.
Let me see the disk.
"For 7"? Meaning "for Nana"? You pegged it, Yaya-chan!
A terrible title!
Make some space between you two!!
Hano-chan will be jealous!!
Hey! Hey!
GWUUUSH
THWUMPP
Hano-chan, your jokes are too hard on a guy!
This is no joke!
Hano-chan just *loves* Moriyama-kun!
TWTCH TWTCH

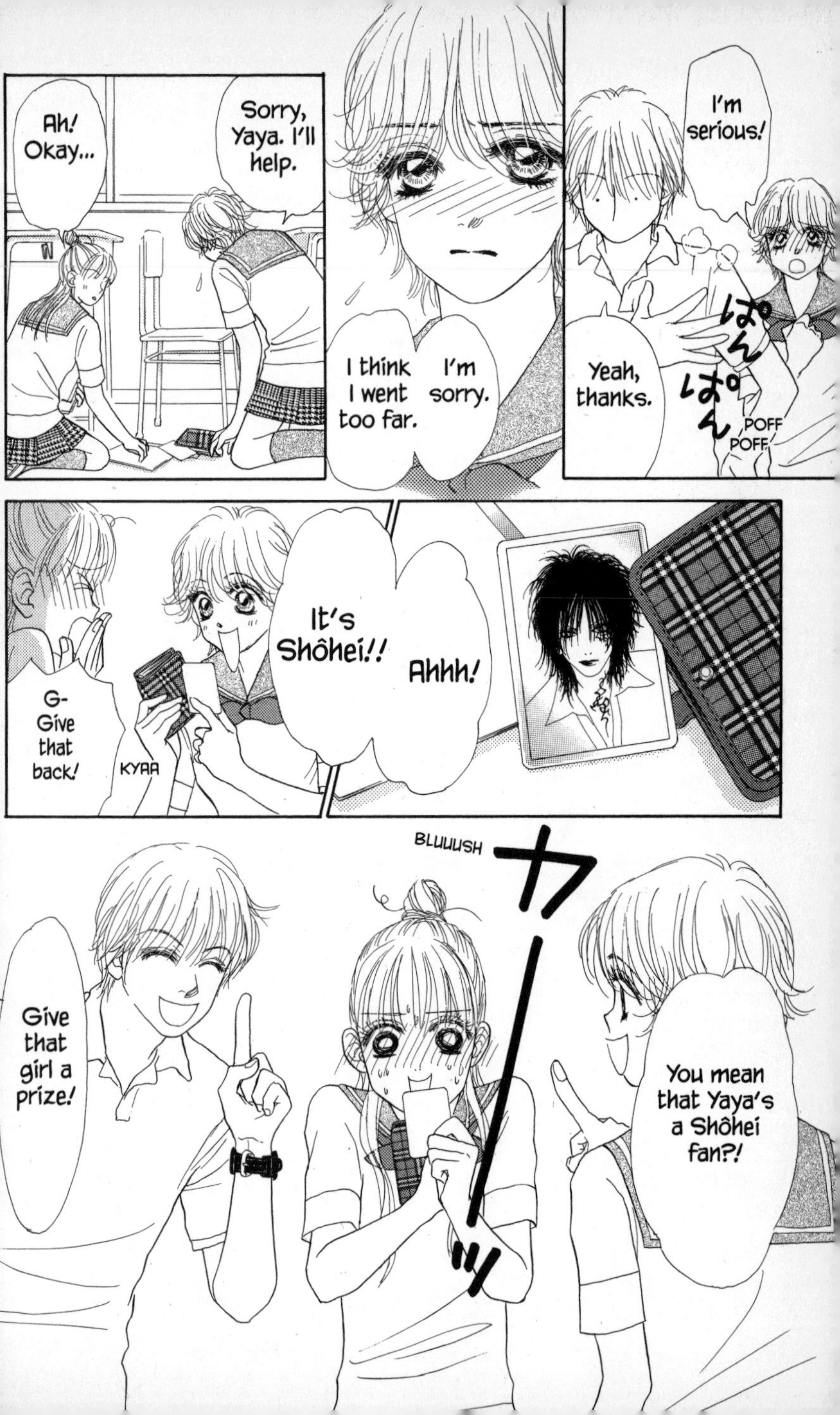
I'm serious!
Yeah, thanks.
ぱんぱん
POFF POFF
I'm sorry.
I think I went too far.
Sorry, Yaya. I'll help.
Ah! Okay...
Ahhh!
It's Shôhei!!
KYAA
G-Give that back!
BLUUUSH
You mean that Yaya's a Shôhei fan?!
Give that girl a prize!

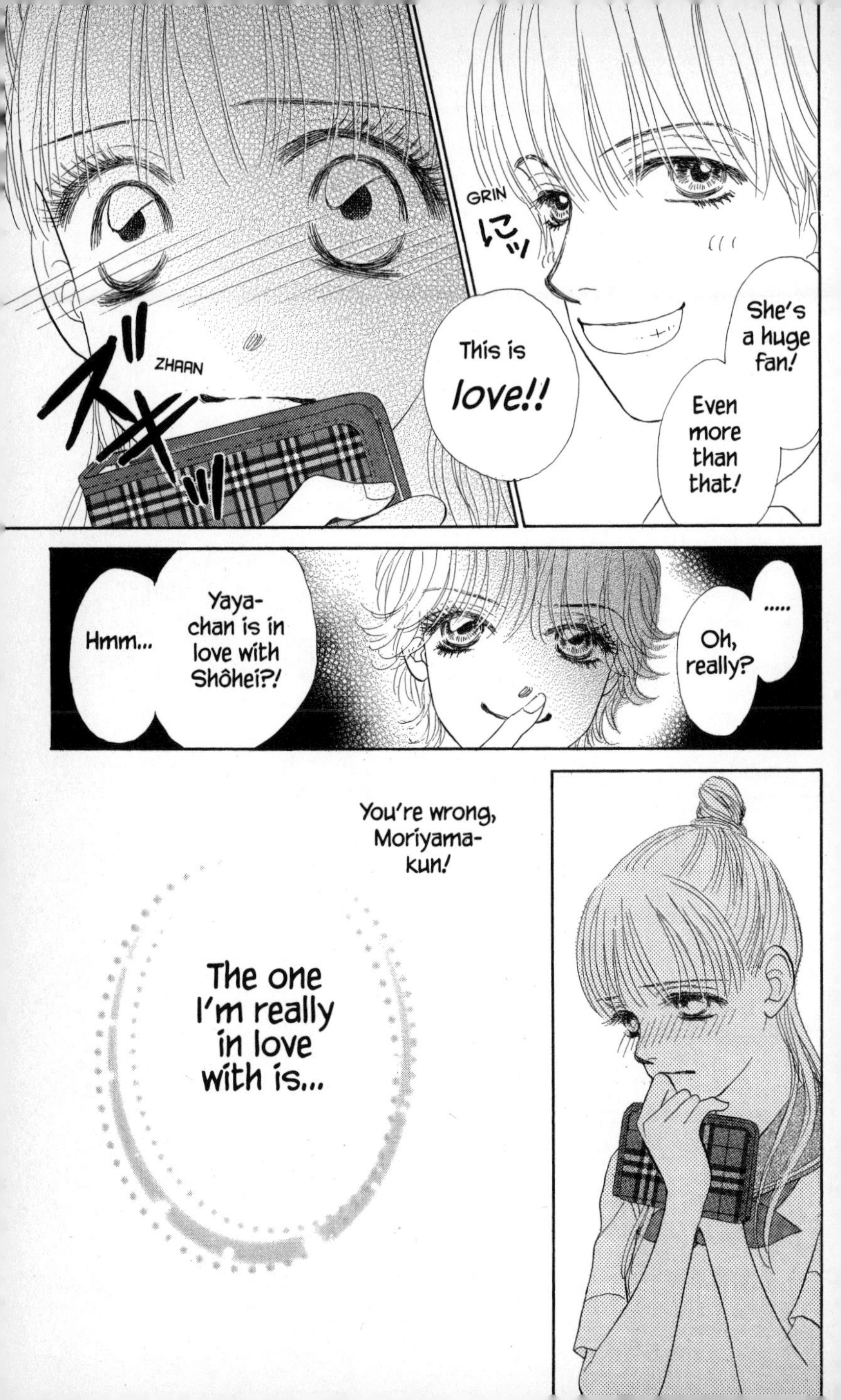
GRIN
にッ
She's a huge fan!
Even more than that!
This is love!!
ZHAAN
.....
Oh, really?
Yaya-chan is in love with Shôhei?!
Hmm...
You're wrong, Moriyama-kun!
The one I'm really in love with is...

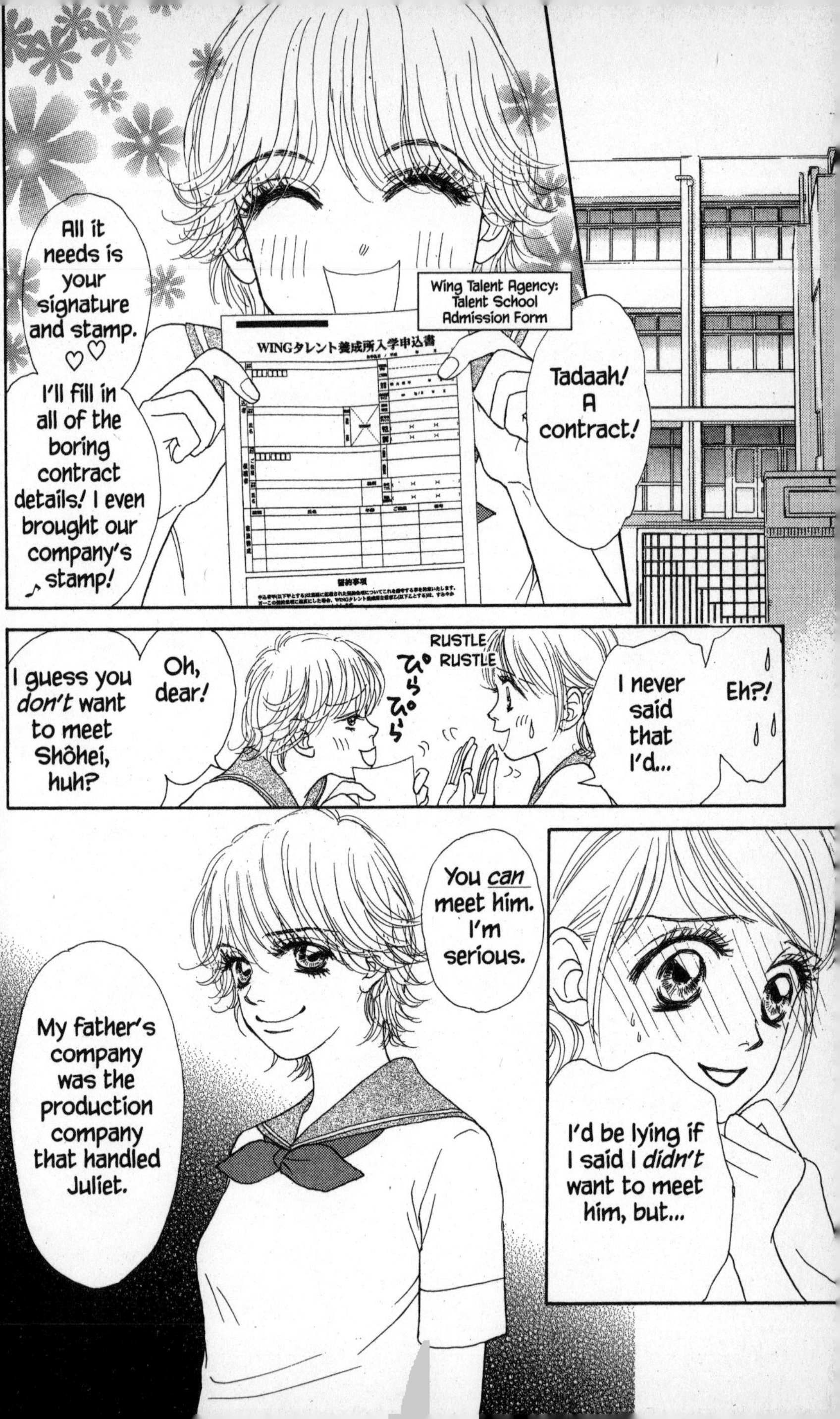

Tadaah! A contract!
Wing Talent Agency: Talent School Admission Form
WINGタレント養成所入学申込書
All it needs is your signature and stamp. ♡♡
I'll fill in all of the boring contract details! I even brought our company's stamp! ♪
Eh?!
I never said that I'd...
RUSTLE RUSTLE
ぴらぴら
Oh, dear!
I guess you *don't* want to meet Shôhei, huh?
I'd be lying if I said I *didn't* want to meet him, but...
You *can* meet him. I'm serious.
My father's company was the production company that handled Juliet.

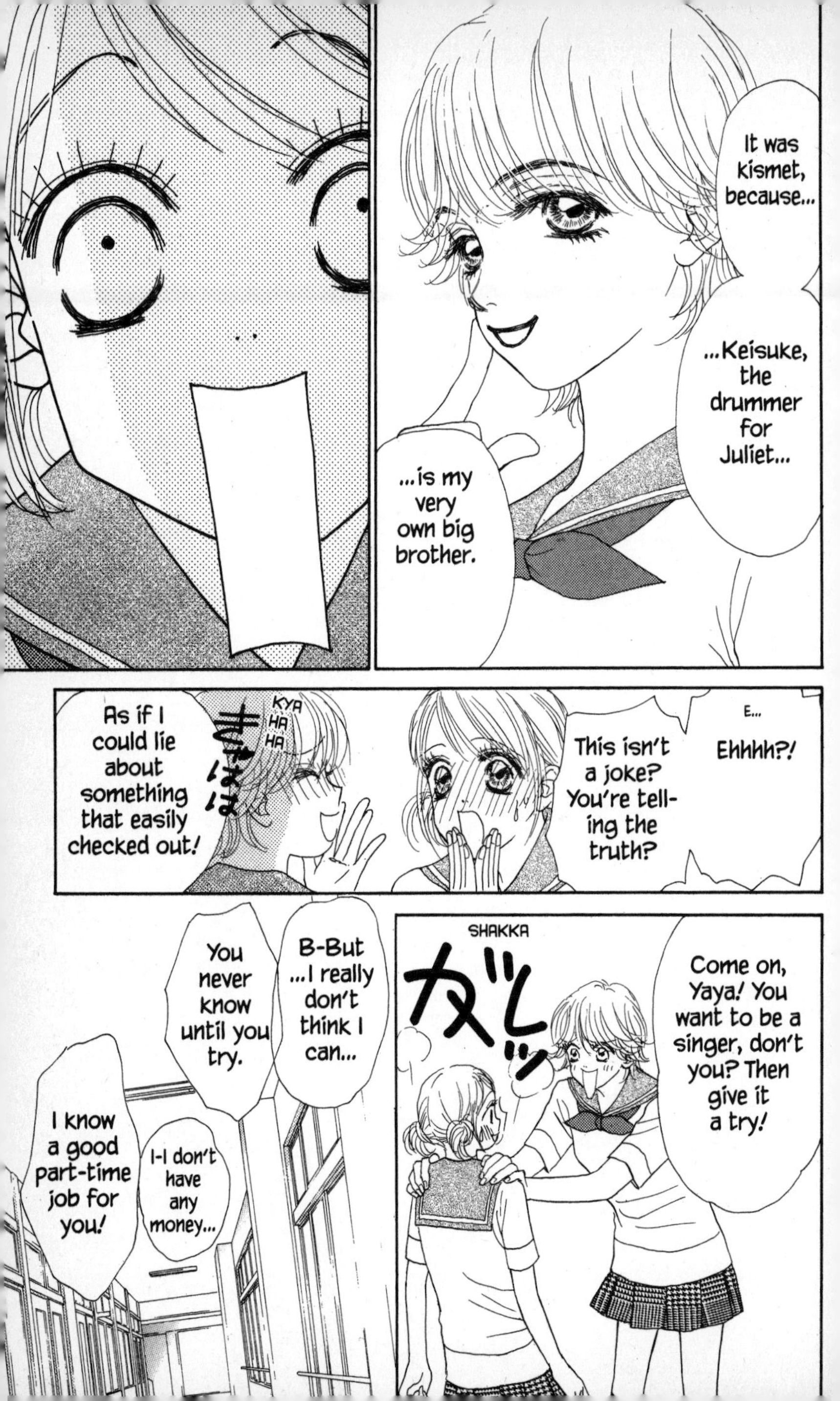
It was kismet, because...
...Keisuke, the drummer for Juliet...
...is my very own big brother.
E...
Ehhhh?!
This isn't a joke? You're telling the truth?
KYA HA HA
きゃはは
As if I could lie about something that easily checked out!
Come on, Yaya! You want to be a singer, don't you? Then give it a try!
SHAKKA
B-But ...I really don't think I can...
You never know until you try.
I-I don't have any money...
I know a good part-time job for you!

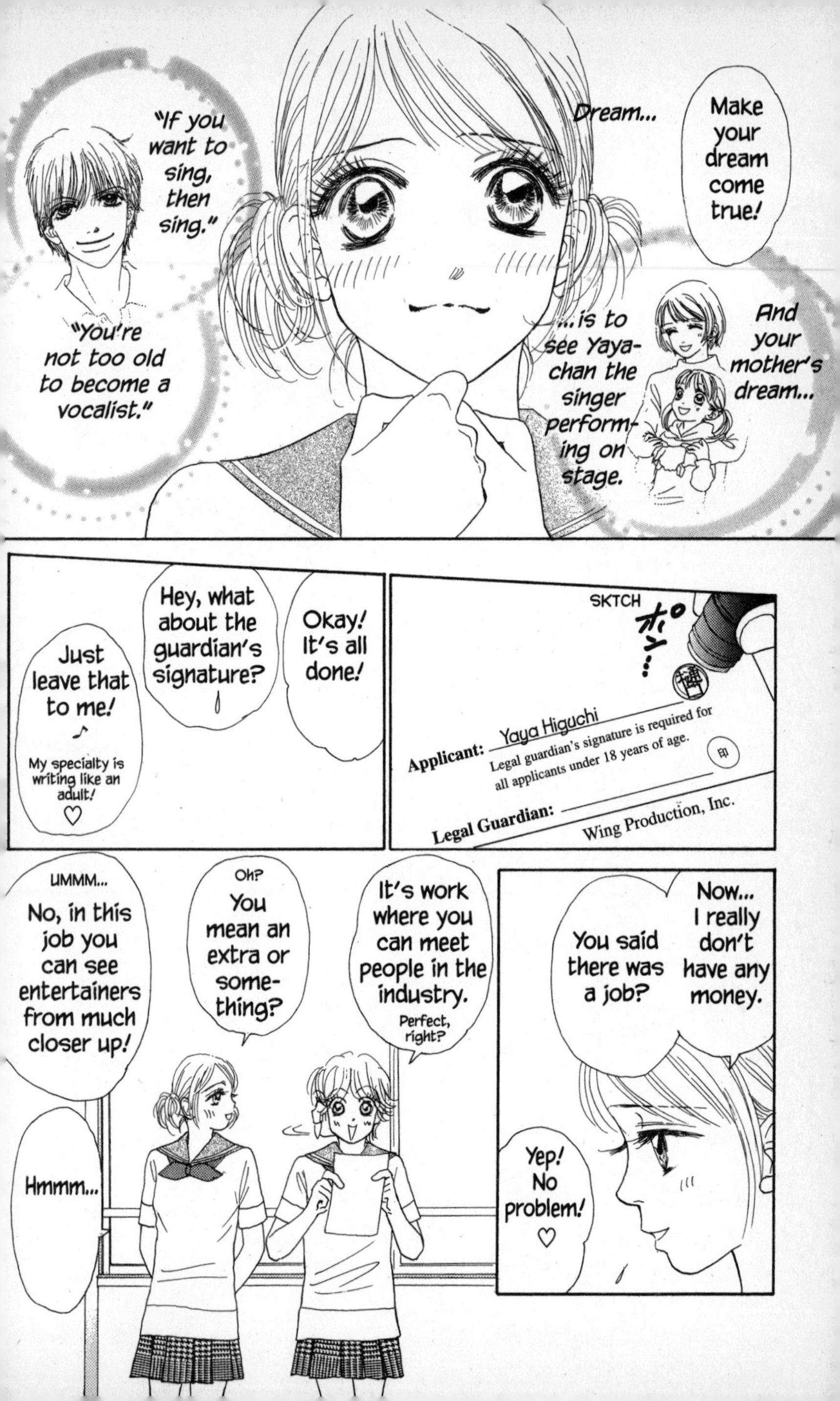
Make your dream come true!
Dream...
And your mother's dream...
...is to see Yaya-chan the singer performing on stage.
"If you want to sing, then sing."
"You're not too old to become a vocalist."
SKTCH
ポン…
Applicant: Yaya Higuchi
Legal guardian's signature is required for all applicants under 18 years of age.
印
Legal Guardian:
Wing Production, Inc.
Okay! It's all done!
Hey, what about the guardian's signature?
Just leave that to me! ♪
My specialty is writing like an adult! ♡
Now... I really don't have any money.
You said there was a job?
Yep! No problem! ♡
It's work where you can meet people in the industry.
Perfect, right?
Oh? You mean an extra or something?
UMMM... No, in this job you can see entertainers from much closer up!
Hmmm...

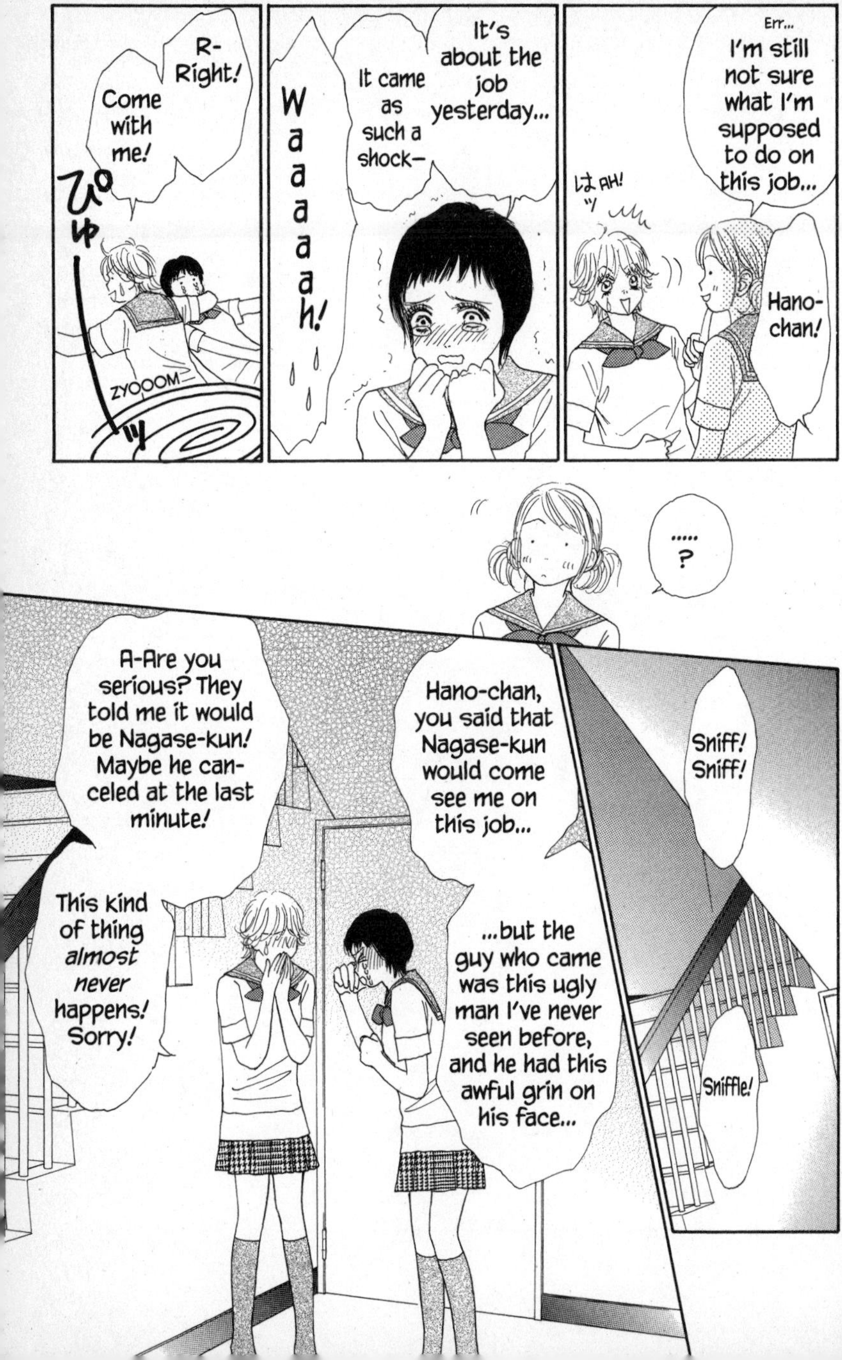

Err...
I'm still not sure what I'm supposed to do on this job...
はッ AH!
Hano-chan!
It's about the job yesterday...
It came as such a shock—
Waaaaah!
R-Right!
Come with me!
ぴゅ
ZYOOOM
ッ
.....
?
Sniff! Sniff!
Sniffle!
Hano-chan, you said that Nagase-kun would come see me on this job...
...but the guy who came was this ugly man I've never seen before, and he had this awful grin on his face...
A-Are you serious? They told me it would be Nagase-kun! Maybe he canceled at the last minute!
This kind of thing *almost never* happens! Sorry!

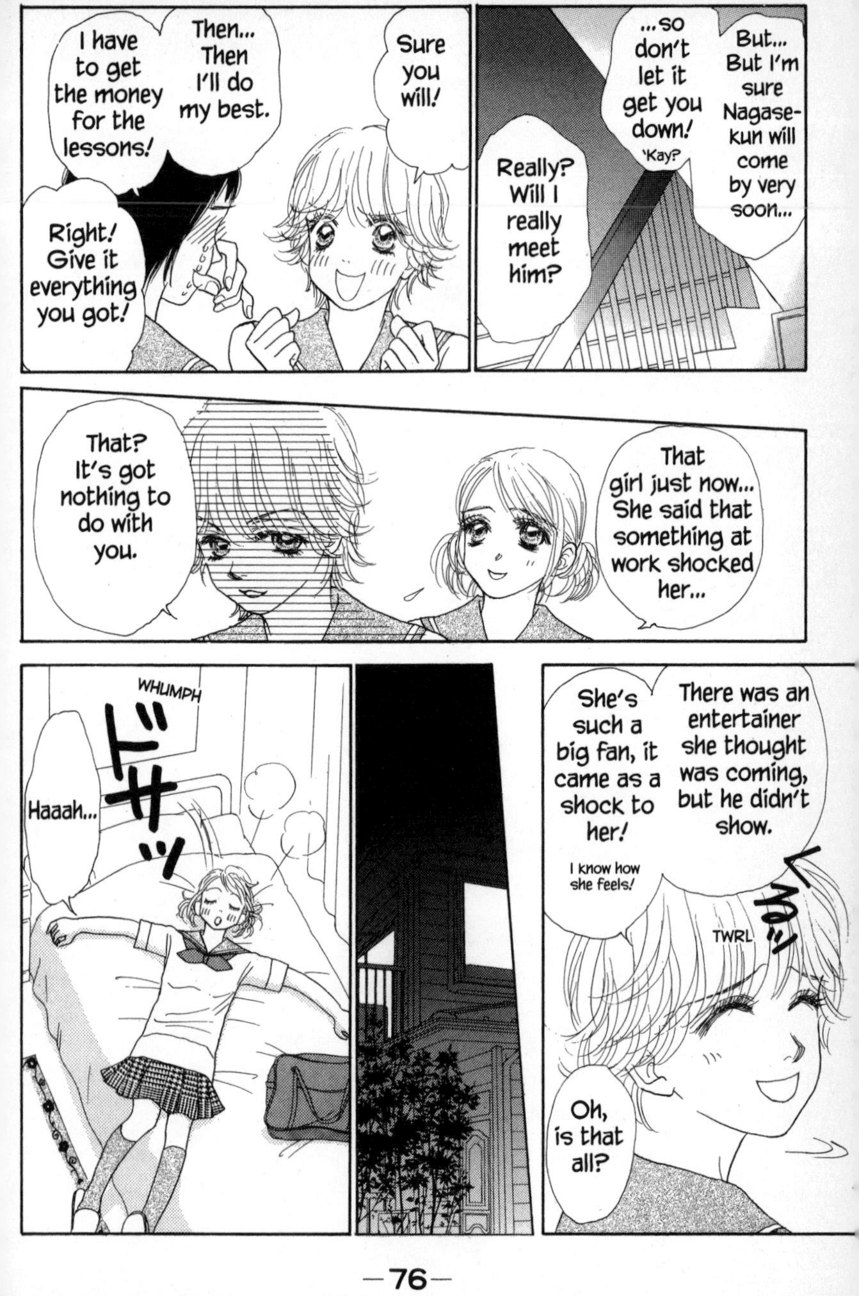
But... But I'm sure Nagase-kun will come by very soon...
...so don't let it get you down!
'Kay?
Really? Will I really meet him?
Sure you will!
Then... Then I'll do my best.
I have to get the money for the lessons!
Right! Give it everything you got!
That girl just now... She said that something at work shocked her...
That? It's got nothing to do with you.
There was an entertainer she thought was coming, but he didn't show.
She's such a big fan, it came as a shock to her!
I know how she feels!
くるっ
TWRL
Oh, is that all?
ドサッ
WHUMPH
Haaah...

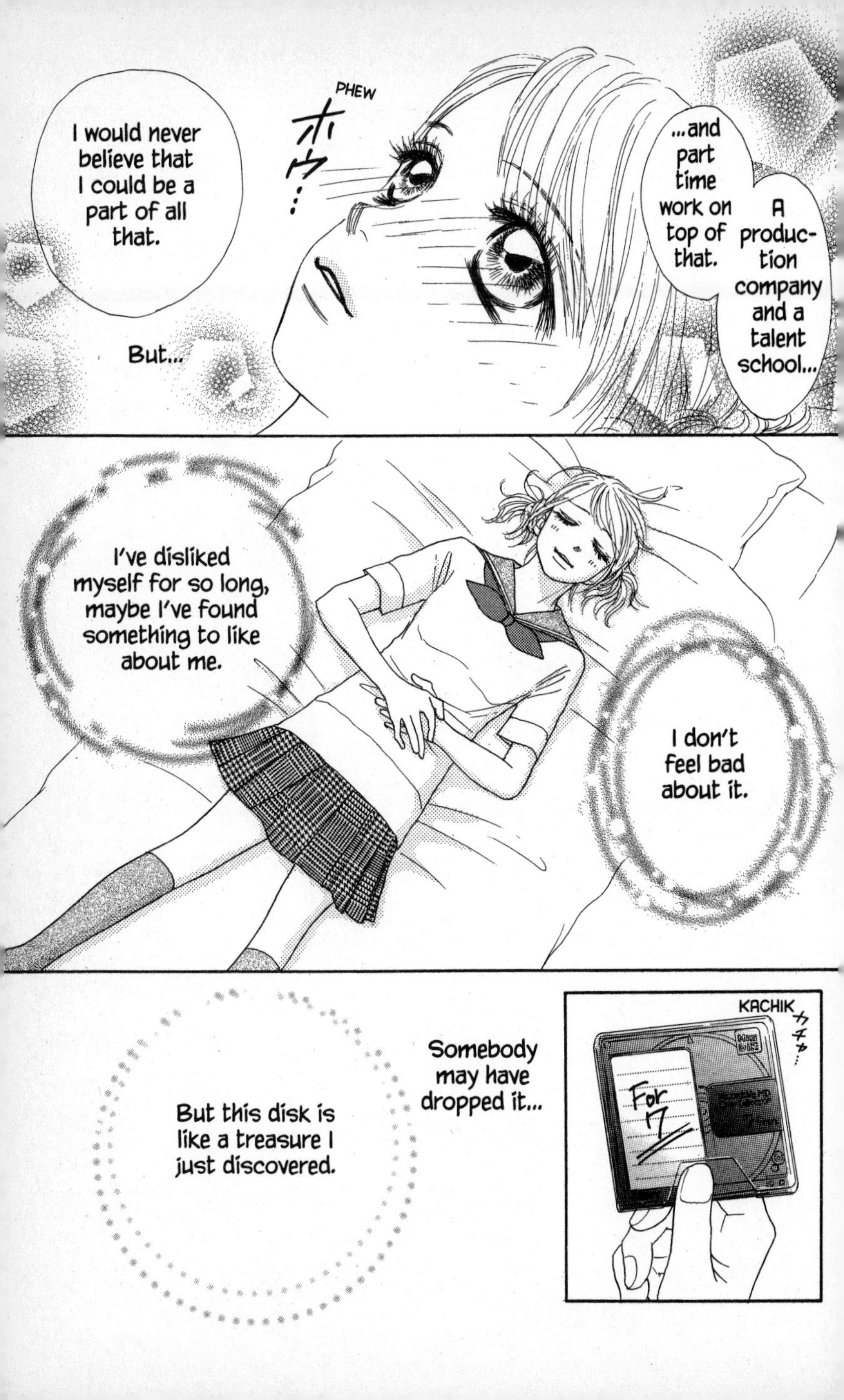
A production company and a talent school...
...and part time work on top of that.
PHEW
I would never believe that I could be a part of all that.
But...
I've disliked myself for so long, maybe I've found something to like about me.
I don't feel bad about it.
KACHIK
For 7
Somebody may have dropped it...
But this disk is like a treasure I just discovered.

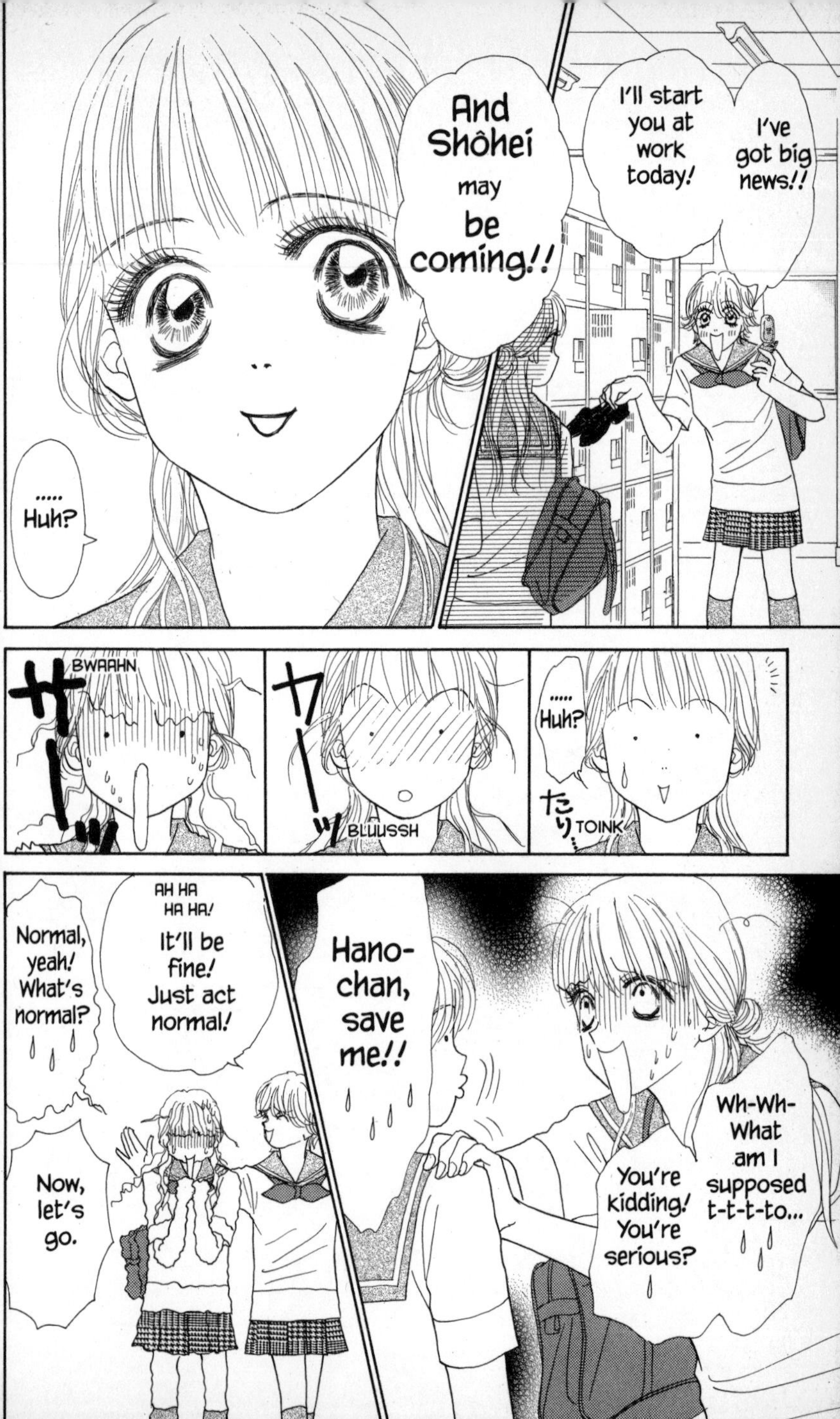

I've got big news!!
I'll start you at work today!
And Shôhei may be coming!!
..... Huh?
..... Huh?
たり TOINK
ヤーッ BLUUSSH
サーッ BWAAHN
Wh-Wh-What am I supposed t-t-t-to...
You're kidding! You're serious?
Hano-chan, save me!!
AH HA HA HA! It'll be fine! Just act normal!
Normal, yeah! What's normal?
Now, let's go.

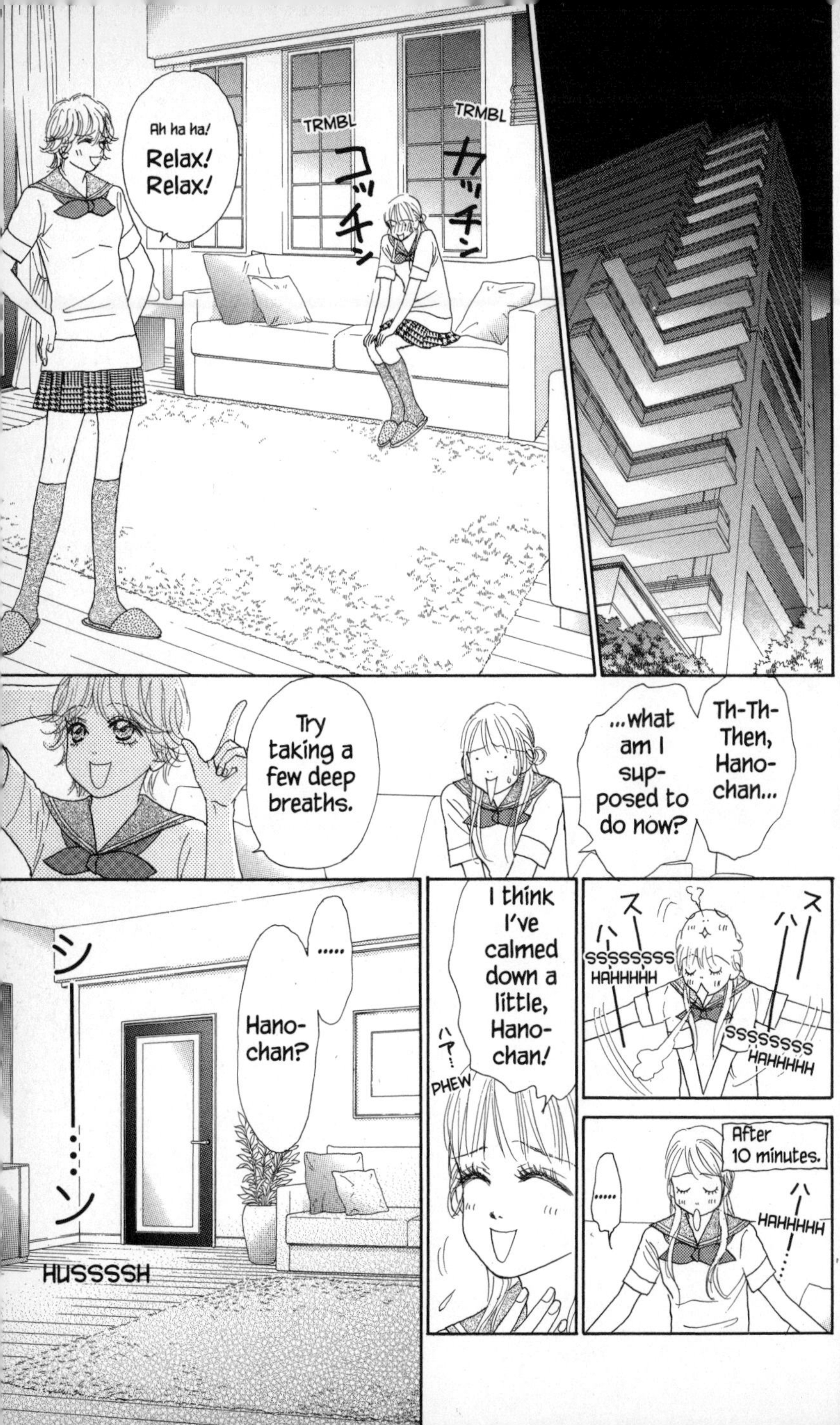

TRMBL
カッチン
TRMBL
コッチン
Ah ha ha!
Relax! Relax!
Th-Th-Then, Hano-chan...
...what am I sup-posed to do now?
Try taking a few deep breaths.
スーハー
SSSSSSSS HAHHHHH
スーハー
SSSSSSSS HAHHHHH
I think I've calmed down a little, Hano-chan!
ハア...
PHEW
After 10 minutes.
ハー
HAHHHHHH
.....
.....
Hano-chan?
シーン
HUSSSSH

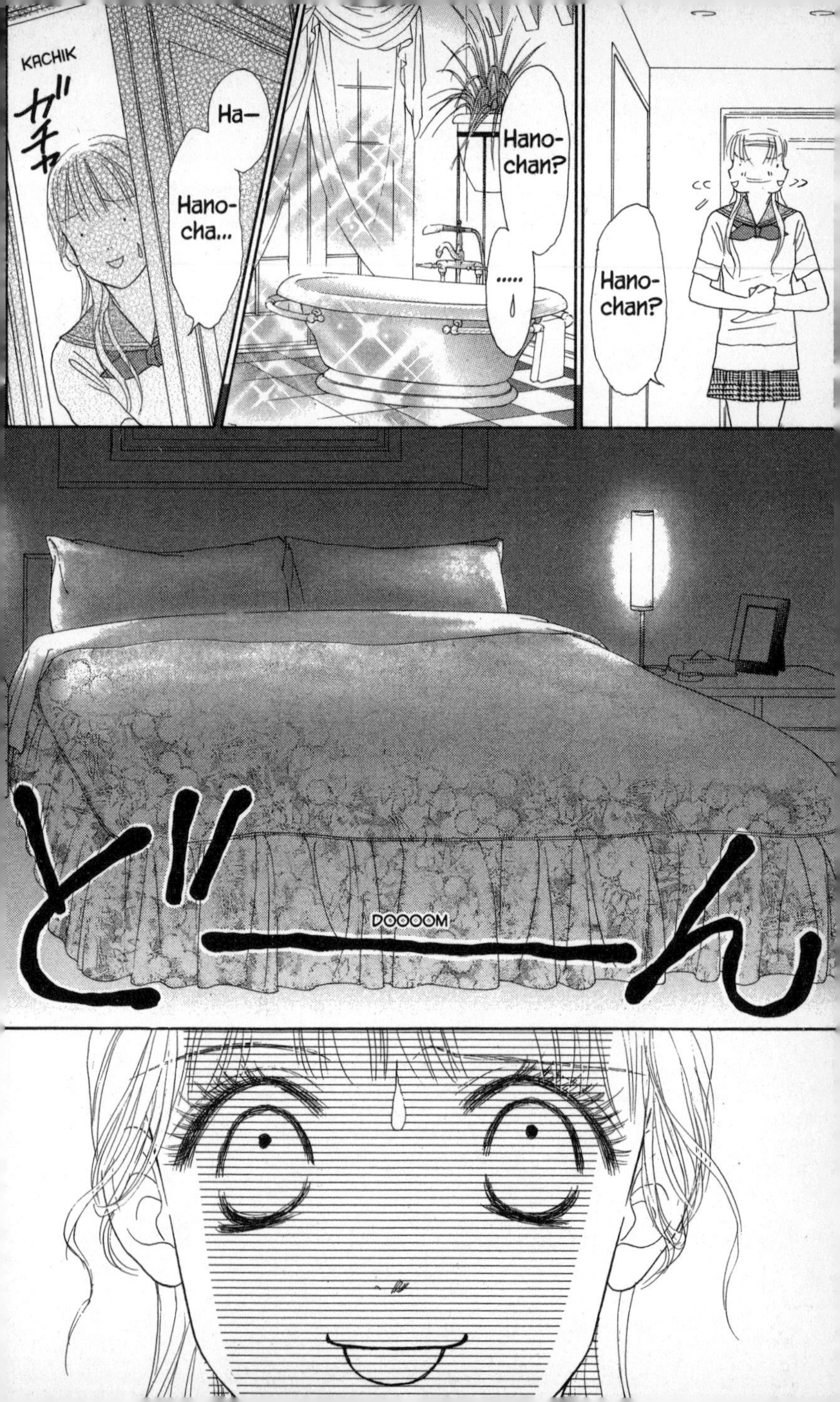

Hano-chan?
Hano-chan?
.....
KACHIK
ガチャ
Ha–
Hano-cha...
どーーん
DOOOOM

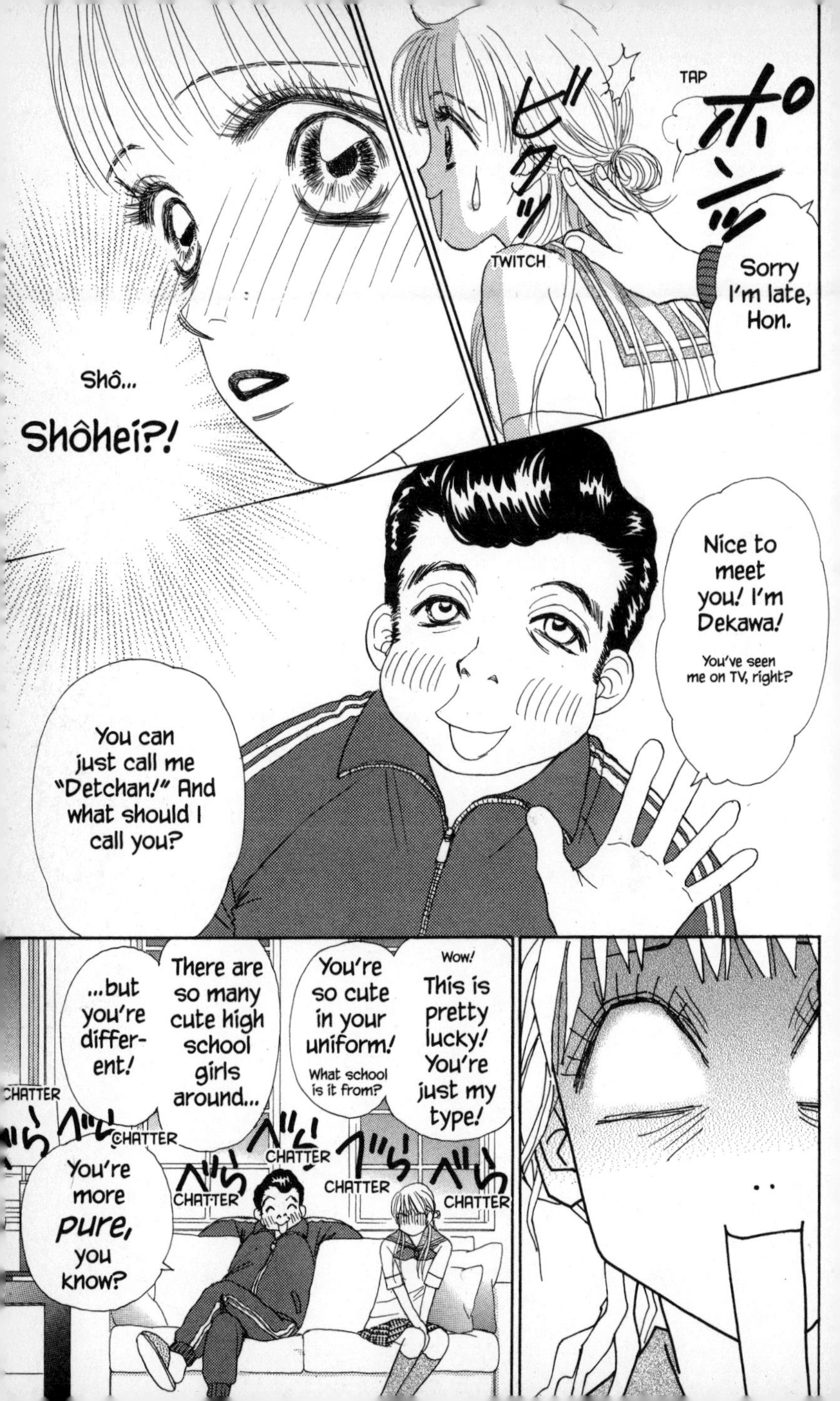
TAP
ポンッ
Sorry I'm late, Hon.
ビクッ
TWITCH
Shô...
Shôhei?!
Nice to meet you! I'm Dekawa!
You've seen me on TV, right?
You can just call me "Detchan!" And what should I call you?
..
Wow!
This is pretty lucky! You're just my type!
You're so cute in your uniform!
What school is it from?
There are so many cute high school girls around...
...but you're different!
You're more *pure*, you know?
CHATTER
CHATTER
CHATTER
CHATTER
CHATTER
CHATTER

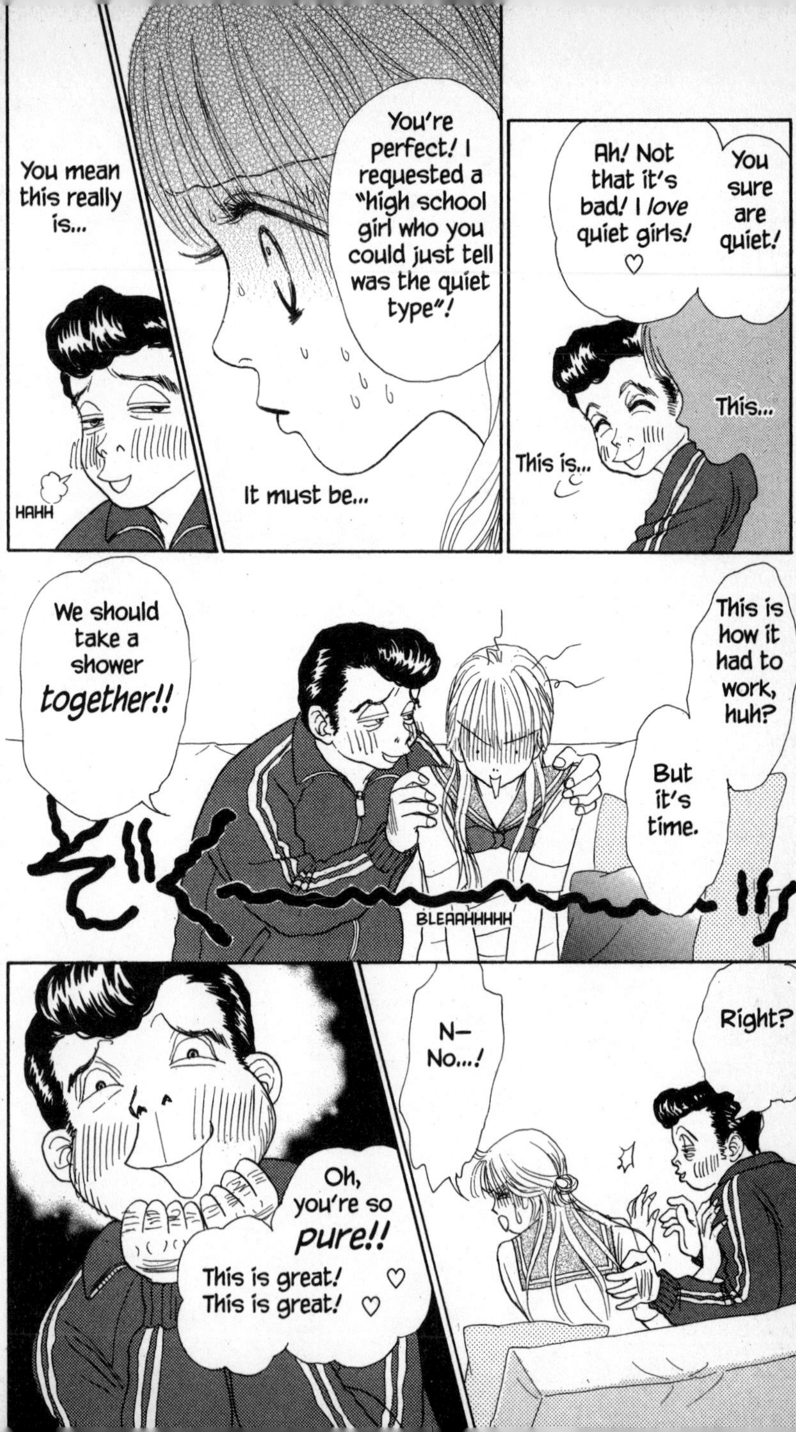

You sure are quiet!
Ah! Not that it's bad! I *love* quiet girls! ♡
This...
This is...
You're perfect! I requested a "high school girl who you could just tell was the quiet type"!
It must be...
You mean this really is...
HAHH
This is how it had to work, huh?
But it's time.
We should take a shower *together!!*
BLEAAHHHHH
Right?
N– No...!
Oh, you're so *pure!!*
This is great! ♡ This is great! ♡

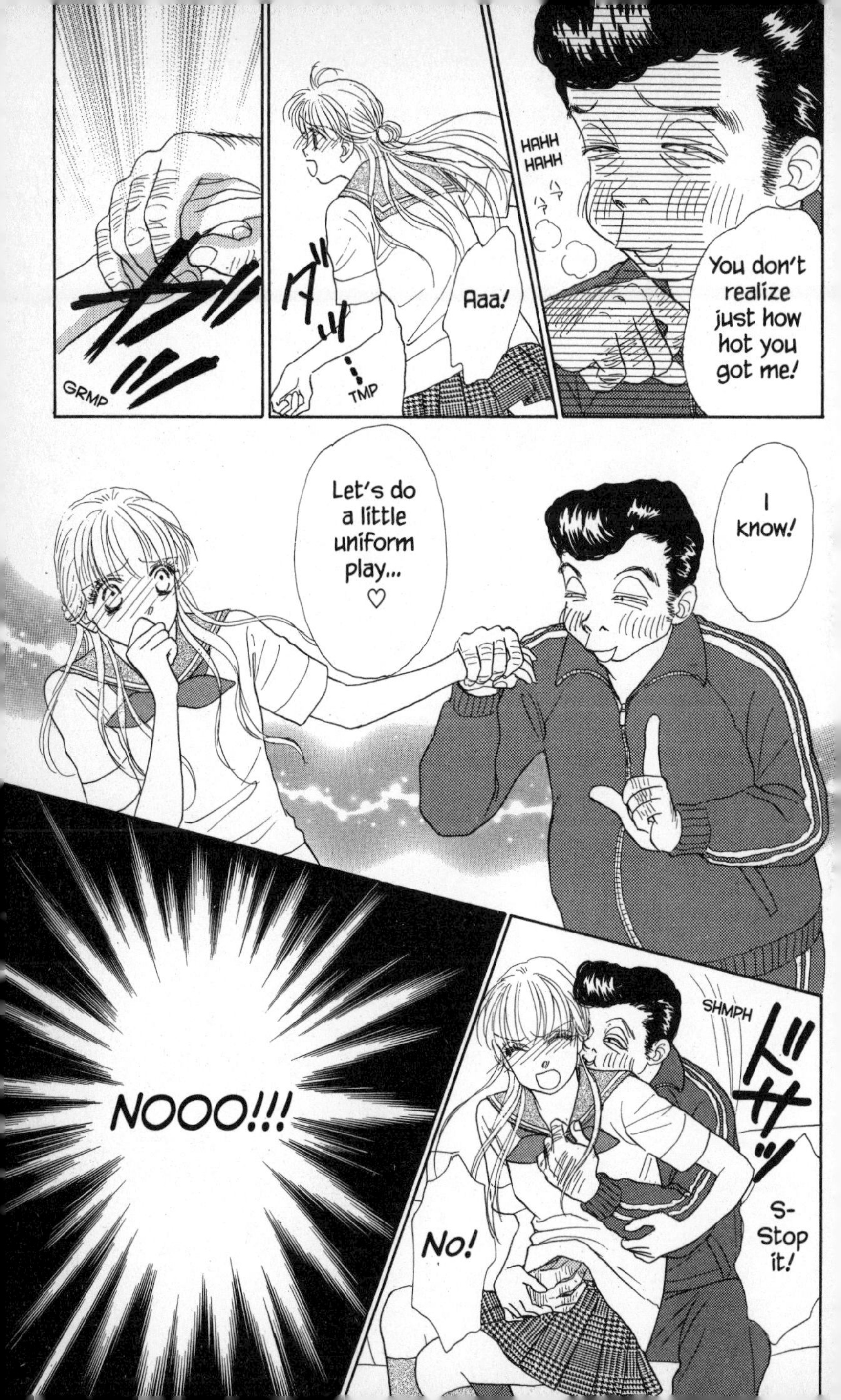
HAHH HAHH
You don't realize just how hot you got me!
Aaa!
TMP
GRMP
I know!
Let's do a little uniform play... ♡
SHMPH
S- Stop it!
No!
NOOO!!!

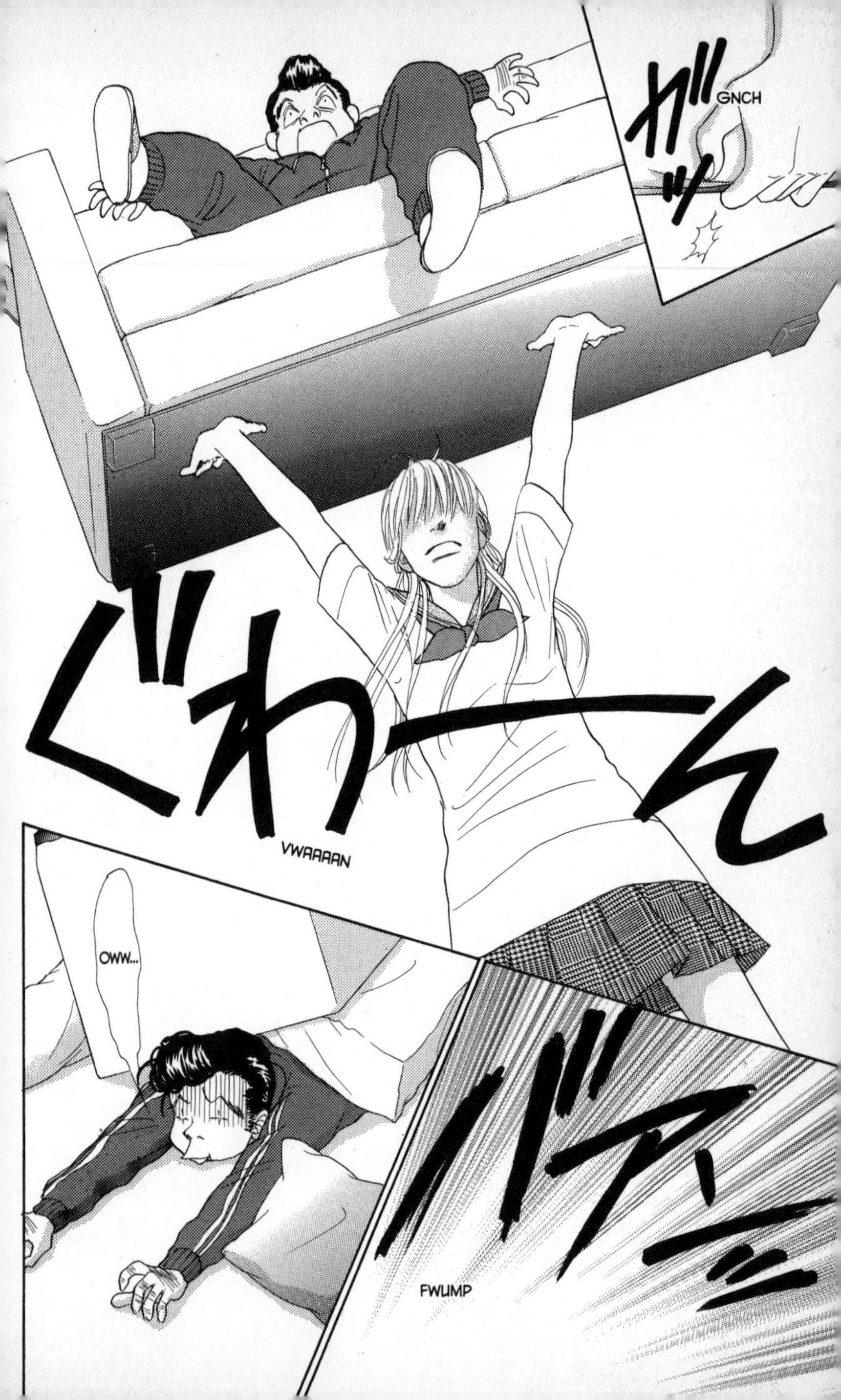

ガッ
GNCH
ぐわーん
VWAAAAN
OWW...
バン
FWUMP

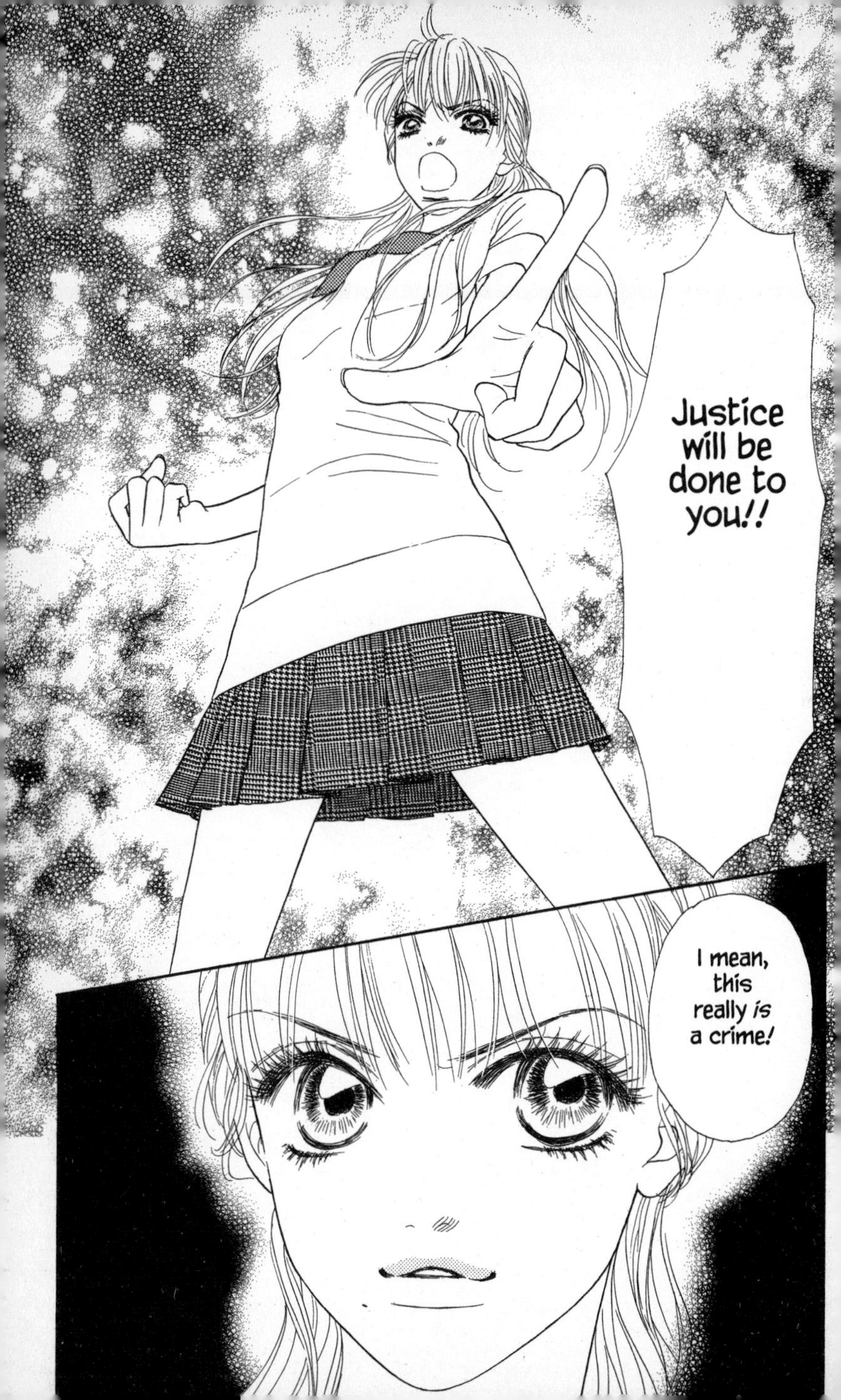
Justice will be done to you!!
I mean, this really *is* a crime!

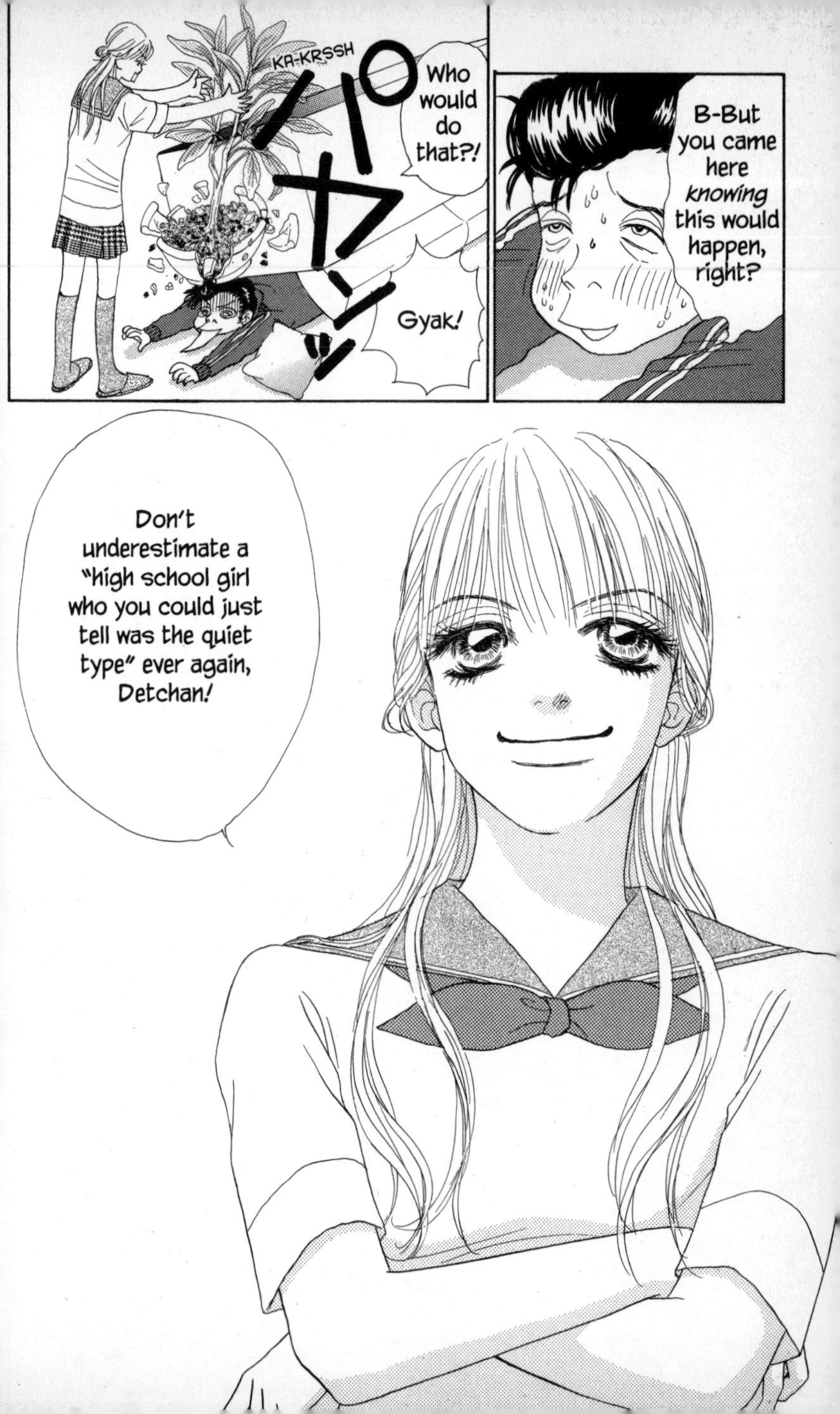
B-But you came here *knowing* this would happen, right?
Who would do that?!
KA-KRSSH
パヤン
Gyak!
Don't underestimate a "high school girl who you could just tell was the quiet type" ever again, Detchan!

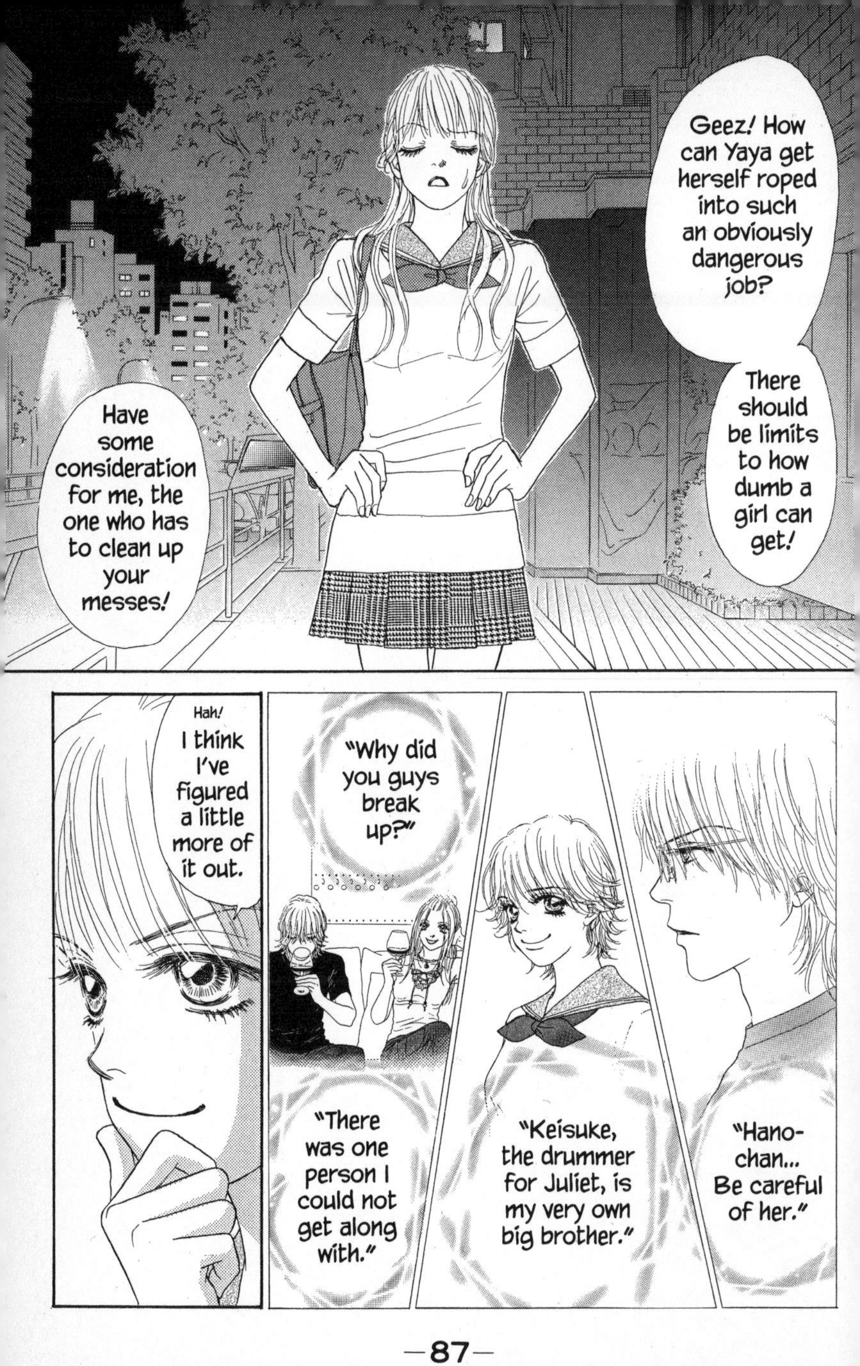
Geez! How can Yaya get herself roped into such an obviously dangerous job?
There should be limits to how dumb a girl can get!
Have some consideration for me, the one who has to clean up your messes!
"Hano-chan... Be careful of her."
"Keisuke, the drummer for Juliet, is my very own big brother."
"Why did you guys break up?"
"There was one person I could not get along with."
Hah!
I think I've figured a little more of it out.

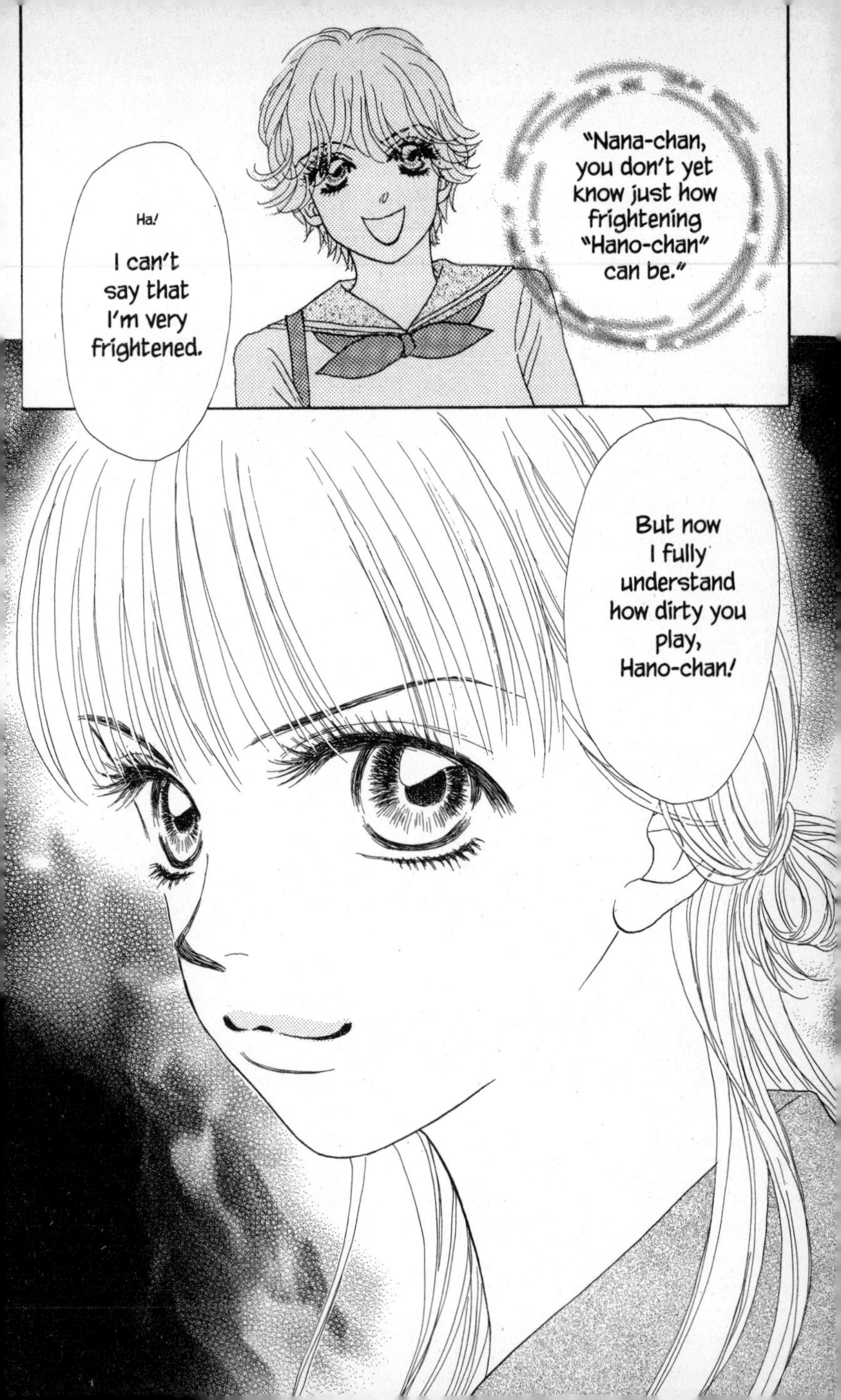
"Nana-chan, you don't yet know just how frightening "Hano-chan" can be."
Ha! I can't say that I'm very frightened.
But now I fully understand how dirty you play, Hano-chan!

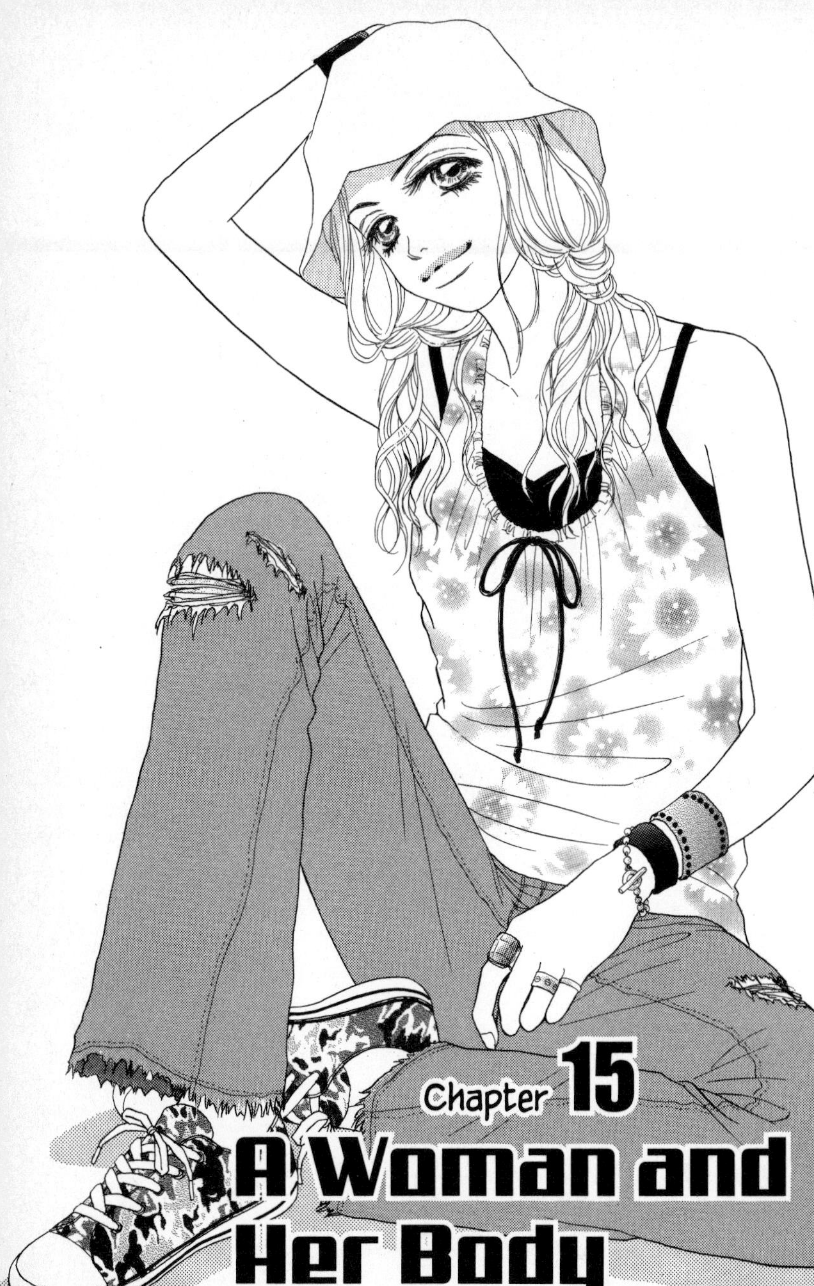

Chapter 15

A Woman and Her Body

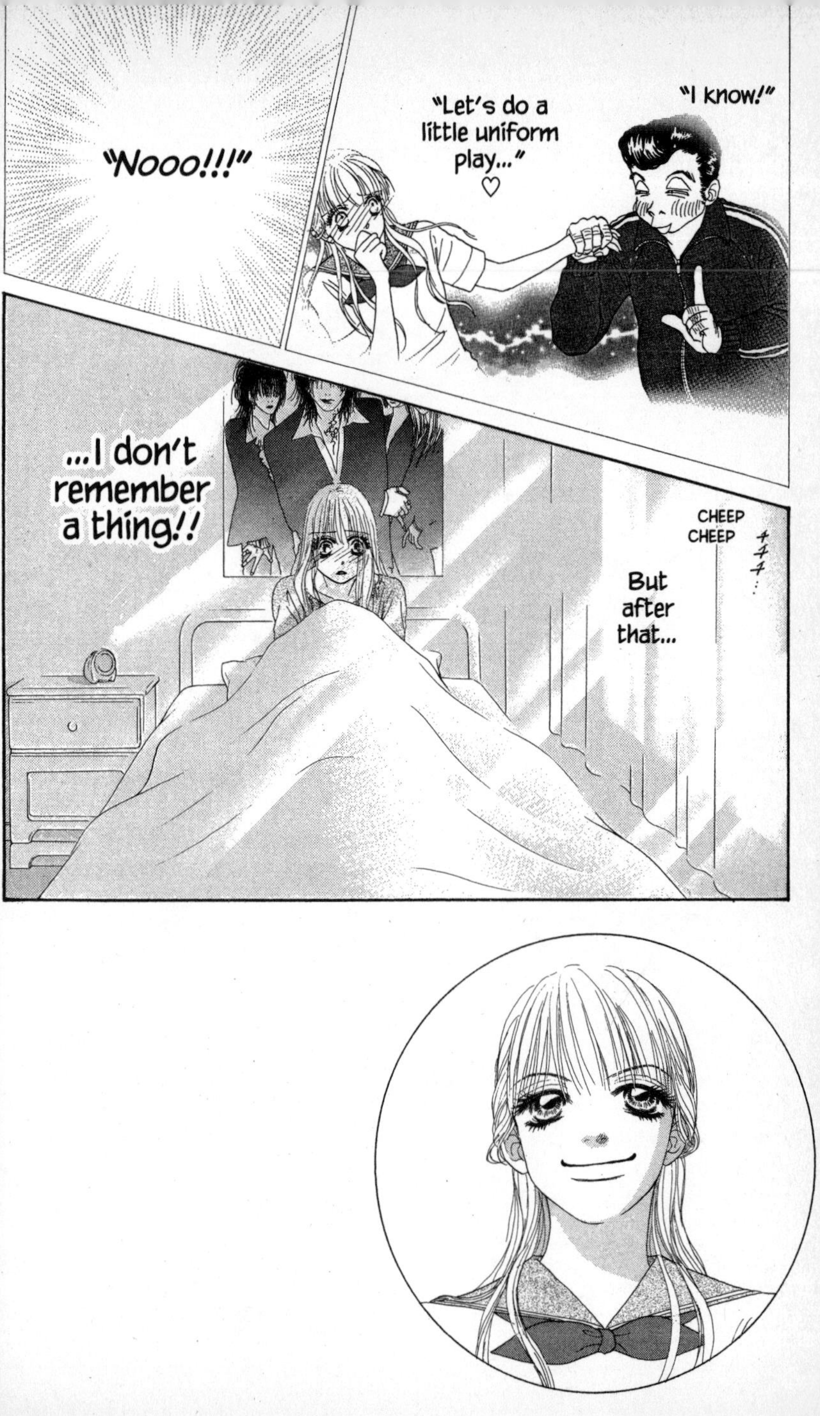
"I know!"
"Let's do a little uniform play..." ♡
"Nooo!!!"
CHEEP CHEEP
But after that...
...I don't remember a thing!!

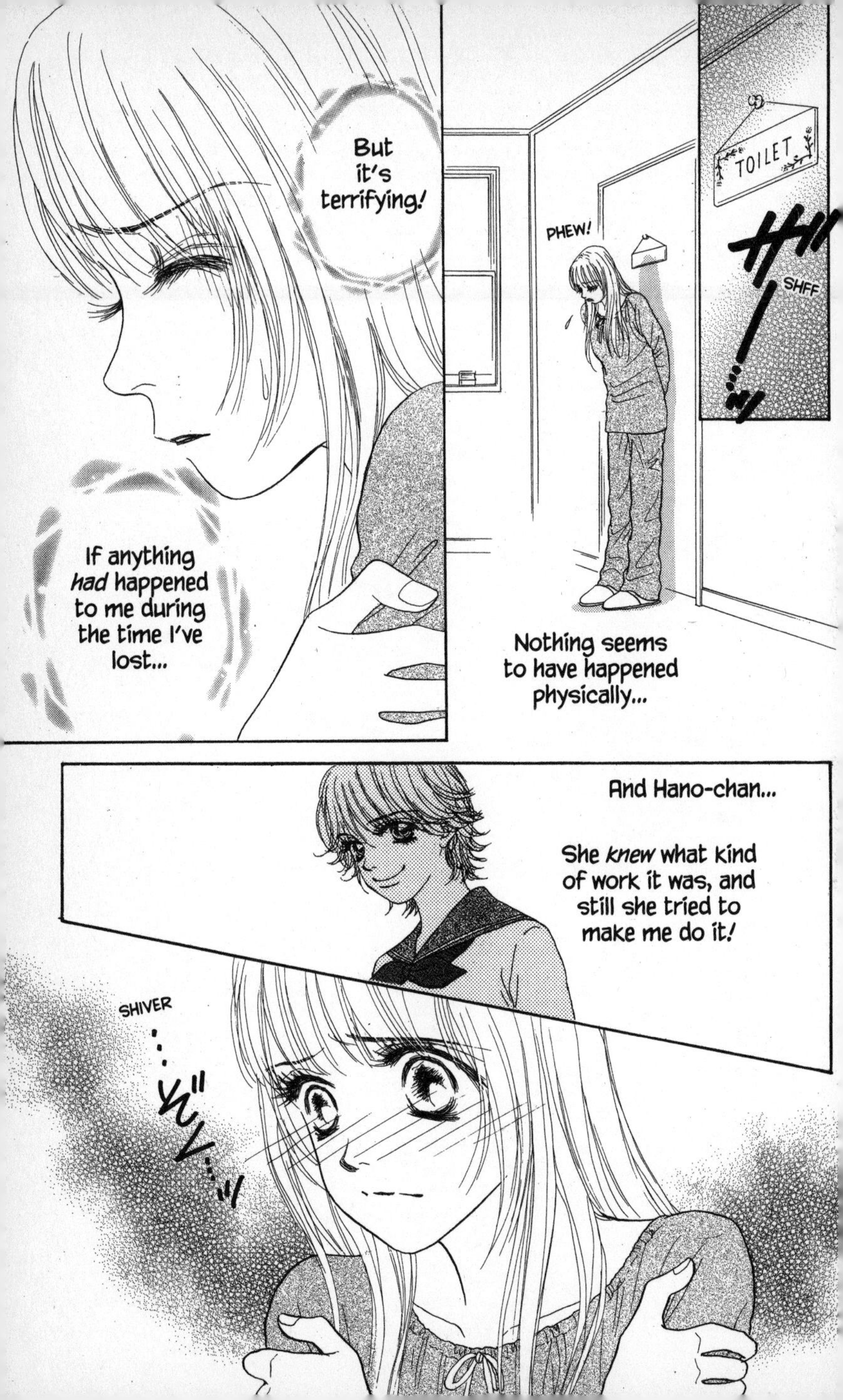
But it's terrifying!
If anything *had* happened to me during the time I've lost...
PHEW!
TOILET
SHFF
Nothing seems to have happened physically...
And Hano-chan...
She *knew* what kind of work it was, and still she tried to make me do it!
SHIVER

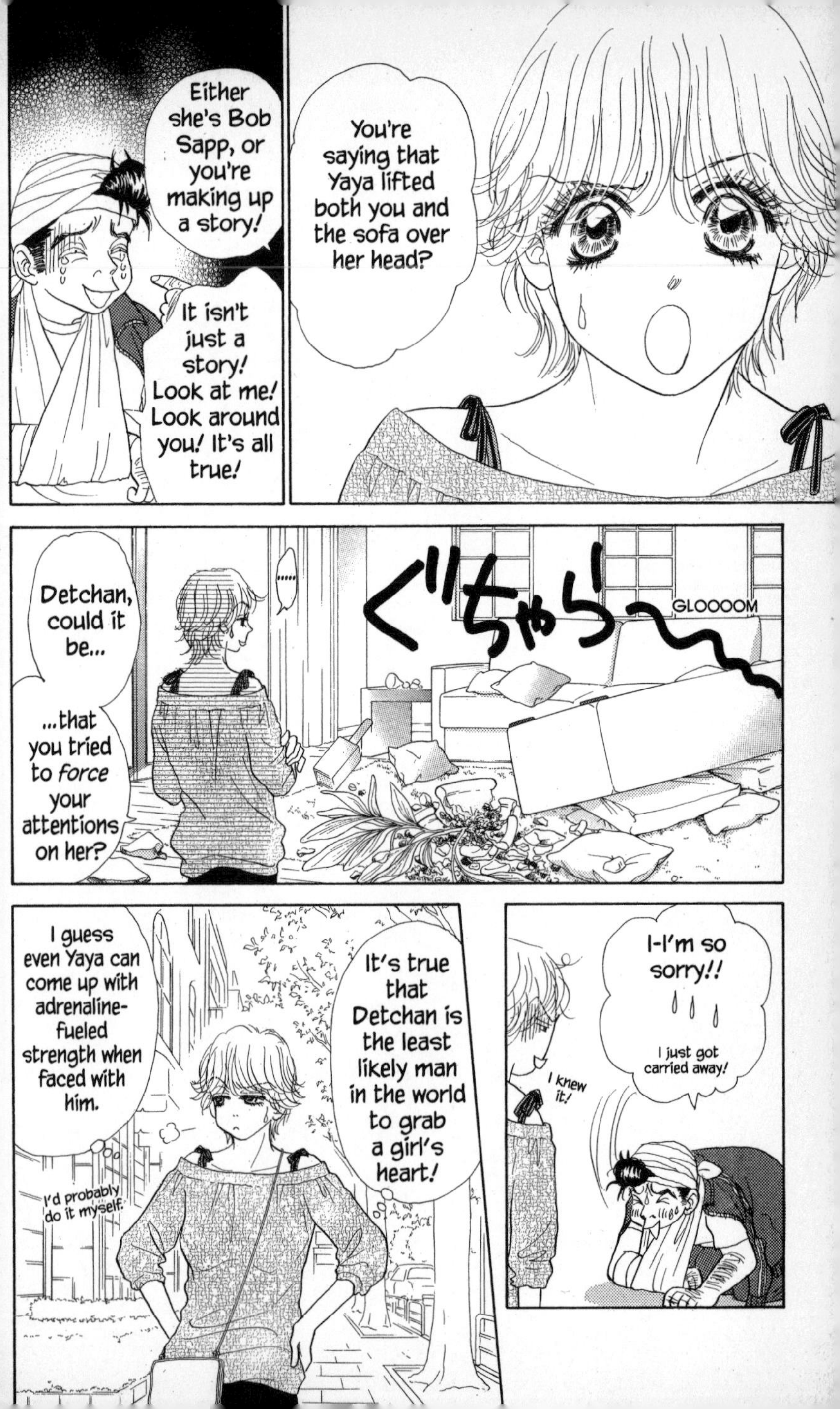

You're saying that Yaya lifted both you and the sofa over her head?
Either she's Bob Sapp, or you're making up a story!
It isn't just a story! Look at me! Look around you! It's all true!
......
GLOOOOM
Detchan, could it be...
...that you tried to *force* your attentions on her?
I-I'm so sorry!!
I just got carried away!
I knew it!
It's true that Detchan is the least likely man in the world to grab a girl's heart!
I guess even Yaya can come up with adrenaline-fueled strength when faced with him.
I'd probably do it myself.

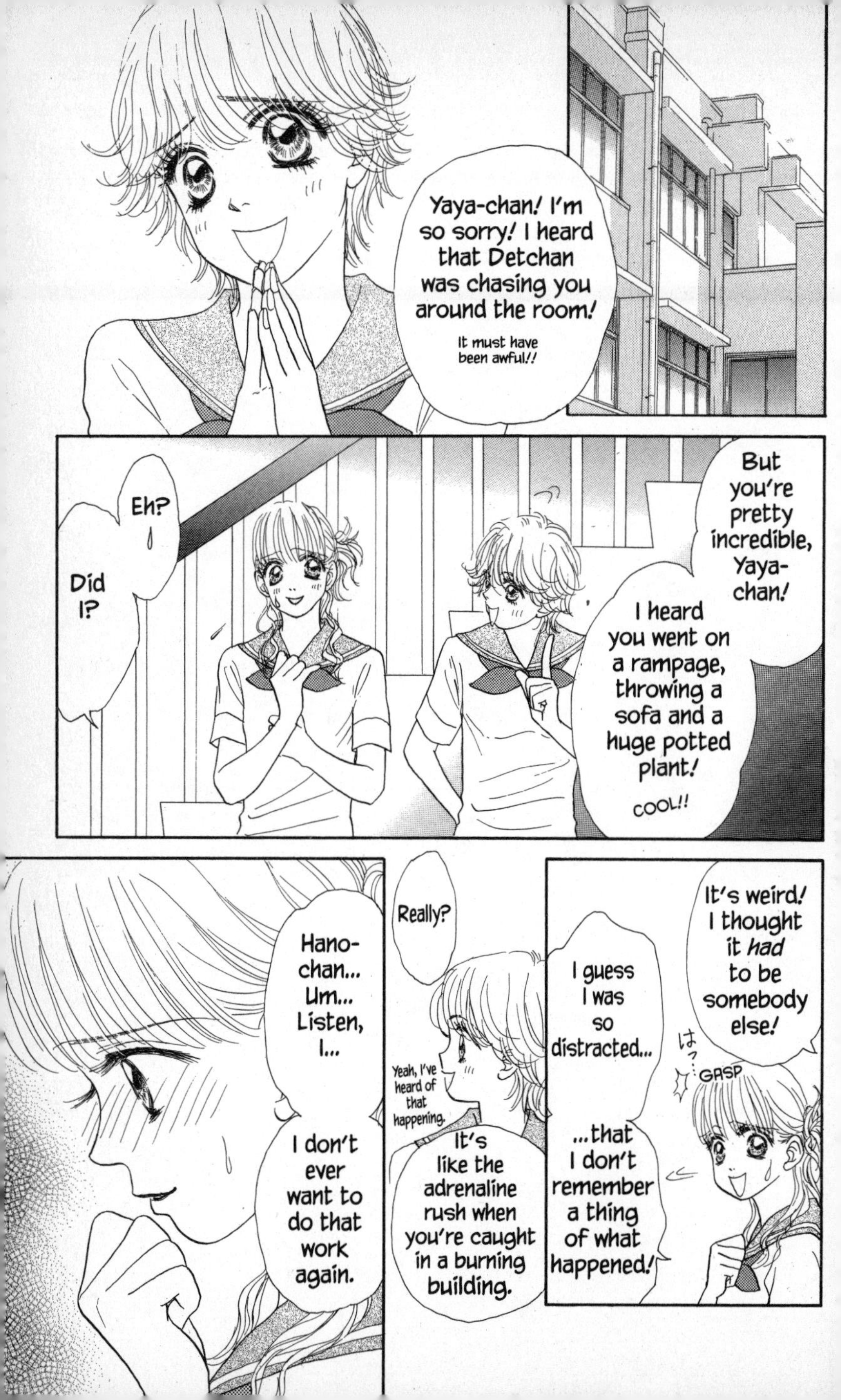
Yaya-chan! I'm so sorry! I heard that Detchan was chasing you around the room!
It must have been awful!!
But you're pretty incredible, Yaya-chan!
I heard you went on a rampage, throwing a sofa and a huge potted plant!
COOL!!
Eh?
Did I?
It's weird! I thought it *had* to be somebody else!
はっ
GASP
I guess I was so distracted...
...that I don't remember a thing of what happened!
Really?
Yeah, I've heard of that happening.
It's like the adrenaline rush when you're caught in a burning building.
Hano-chan... Um... Listen, I...
I don't ever want to do that work again.

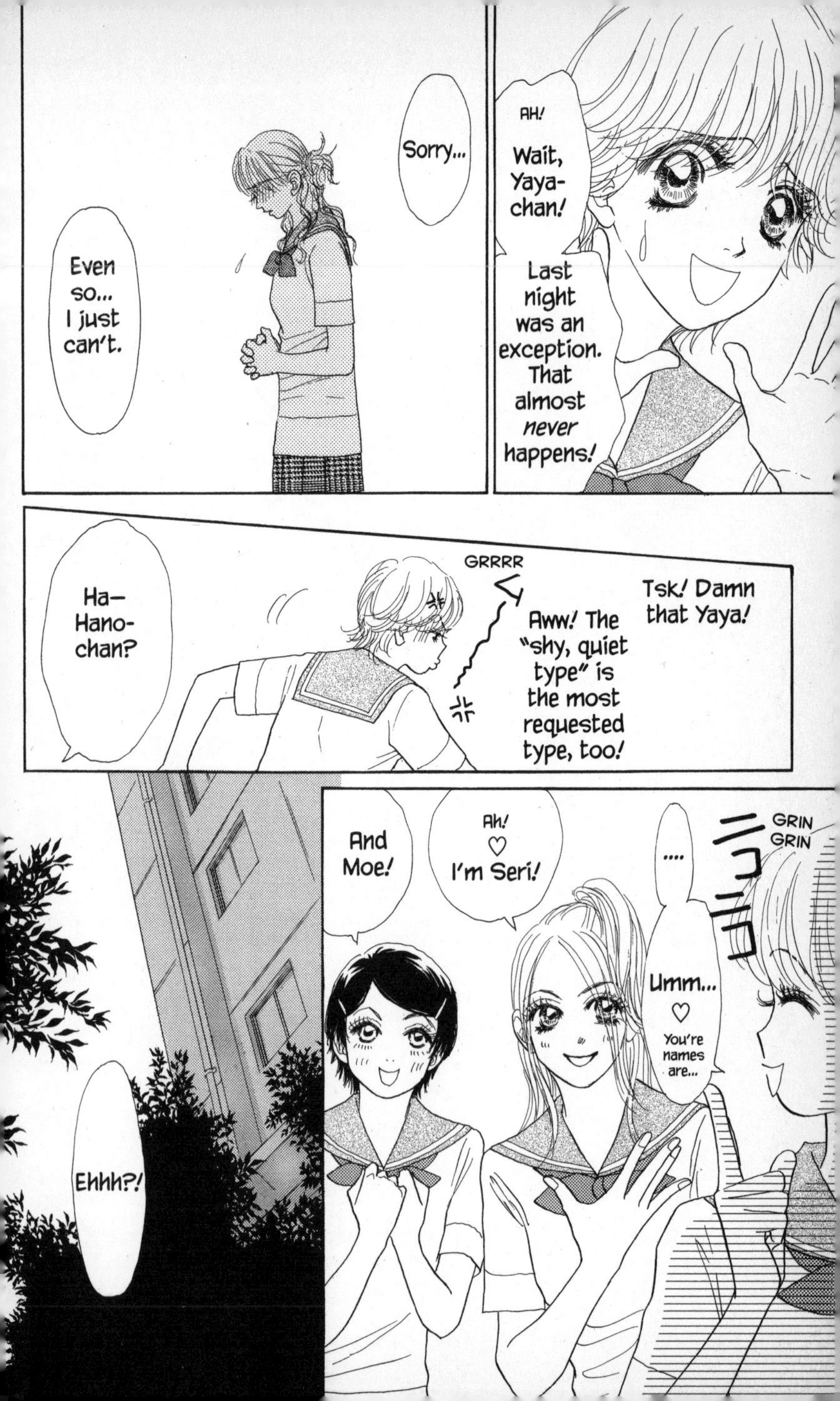

AH! Wait, Yaya-chan!
Last night was an exception. That almost *never* happens!
Sorry...
Even so... I just can't.
Tsk! Damn that Yaya!
Aww! The "shy, quiet type" is the most requested type, too!
GRRRR
Ha— Hano-chan?
GRIN GRIN
....
Umm... ♡ You're names are...
Ah! ♡ I'm Seri!
And Moe!
Ehhh?!

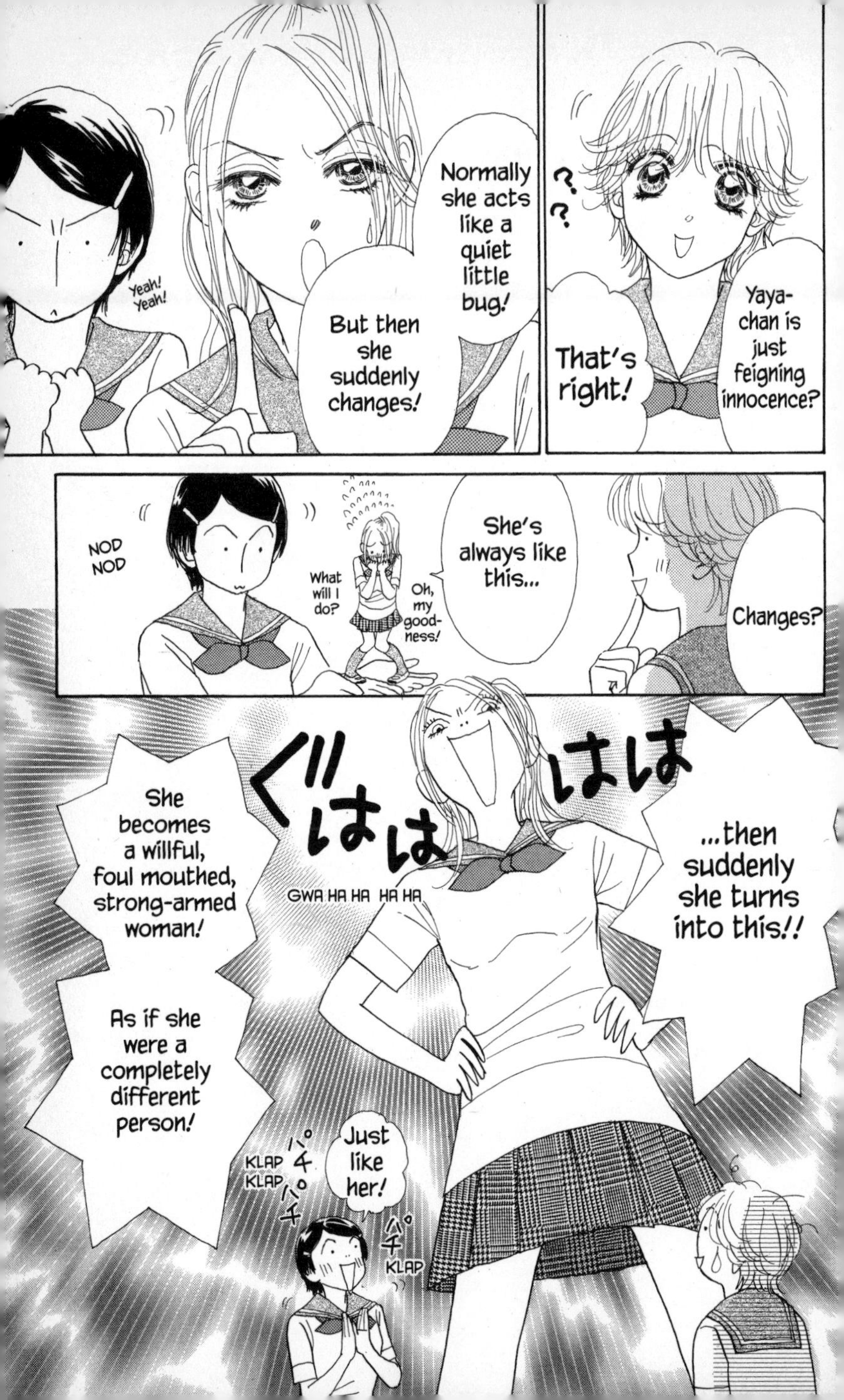

Yaya-chan is just feigning innocence?
That's right!
Normally she acts like a quiet little bug!
But then she suddenly changes!
Yeah! Yeah!
Changes?
She's always like this...
Oh, my goodness!
What will I do?
NOD NOD
...then suddenly she turns into this!!
ぐはは はは
GWA HA HA HA HA
She becomes a willful, foul mouthed, strong-armed woman!
As if she were a completely different person!
Just like her!
パチ
KLAP
パチパチ
KLAP KLAP

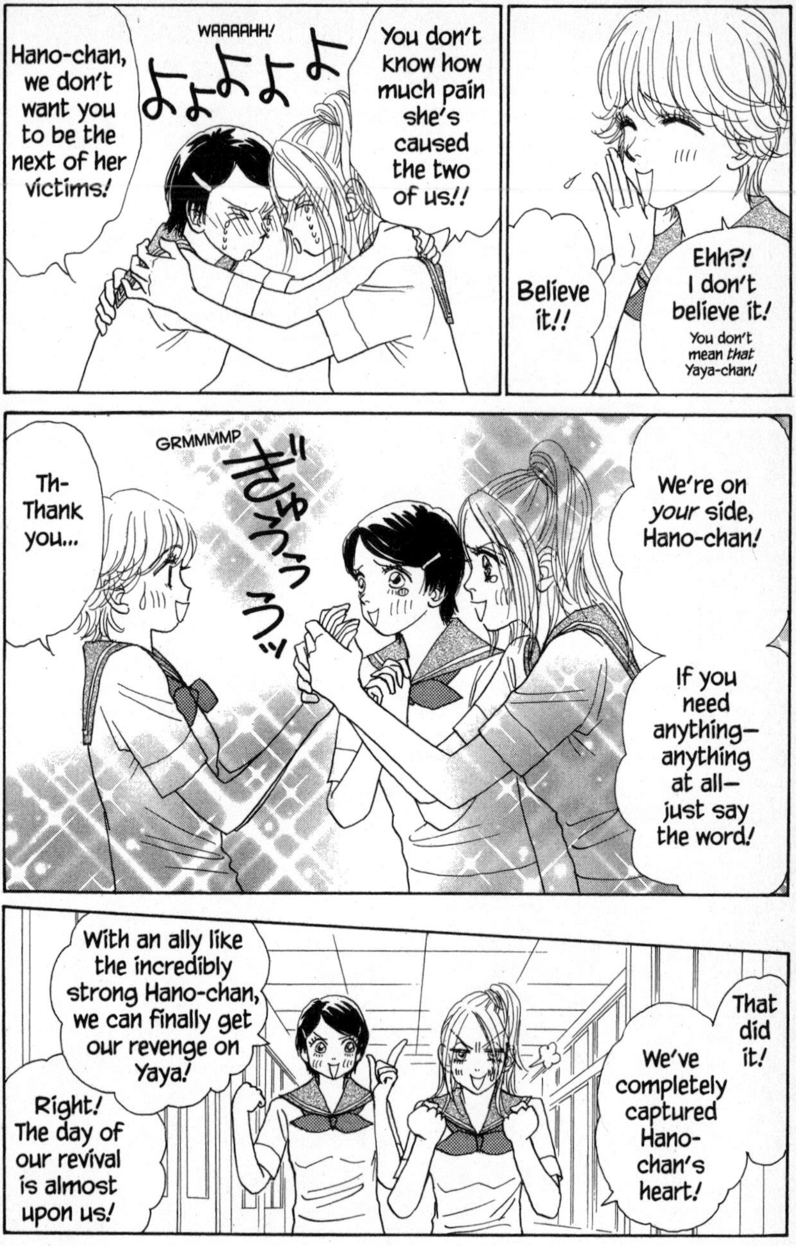

You don't know how much pain she's caused the two of us!!
WAAAAHH!
よよよよ
Hano-chan, we don't want you to be the next of her victims!
Ehh?! I don't believe it!
You don't mean *that* Yaya-chan!
Believe it!!
We're on *your* side, Hano-chan!
If you need anything—anything at all—just say the word!
GRMMMMP
ぎゅううう
Th-Thank you...
That did it!
We've completely captured Hano-chan's heart!
With an ally like the incredibly strong Hano-chan, we can finally get our revenge on Yaya!
Right! The day of our revival is almost upon us!

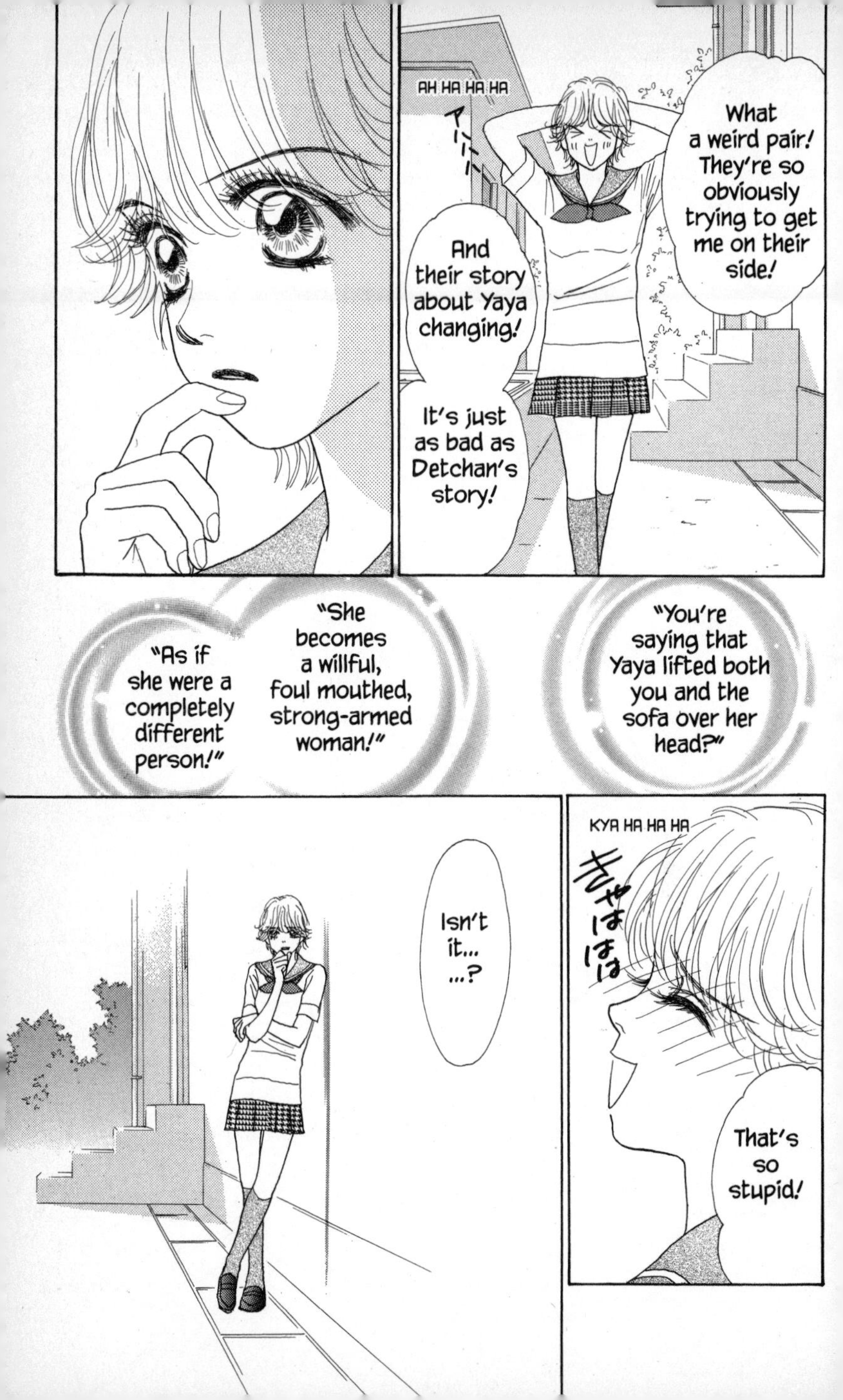
AH HA HA HA
What a weird pair! They're so obviously trying to get me on their side!
And their story about Yaya changing!
It's just as bad as Detchan's story!
"You're saying that Yaya lifted both you and the sofa over her head?"
"She becomes a willful, foul mouthed, strong-armed woman!"
"As if she were a completely different person!"
KYA HA HA HA
きゃははは
That's so stupid!
Isn't it... ...?

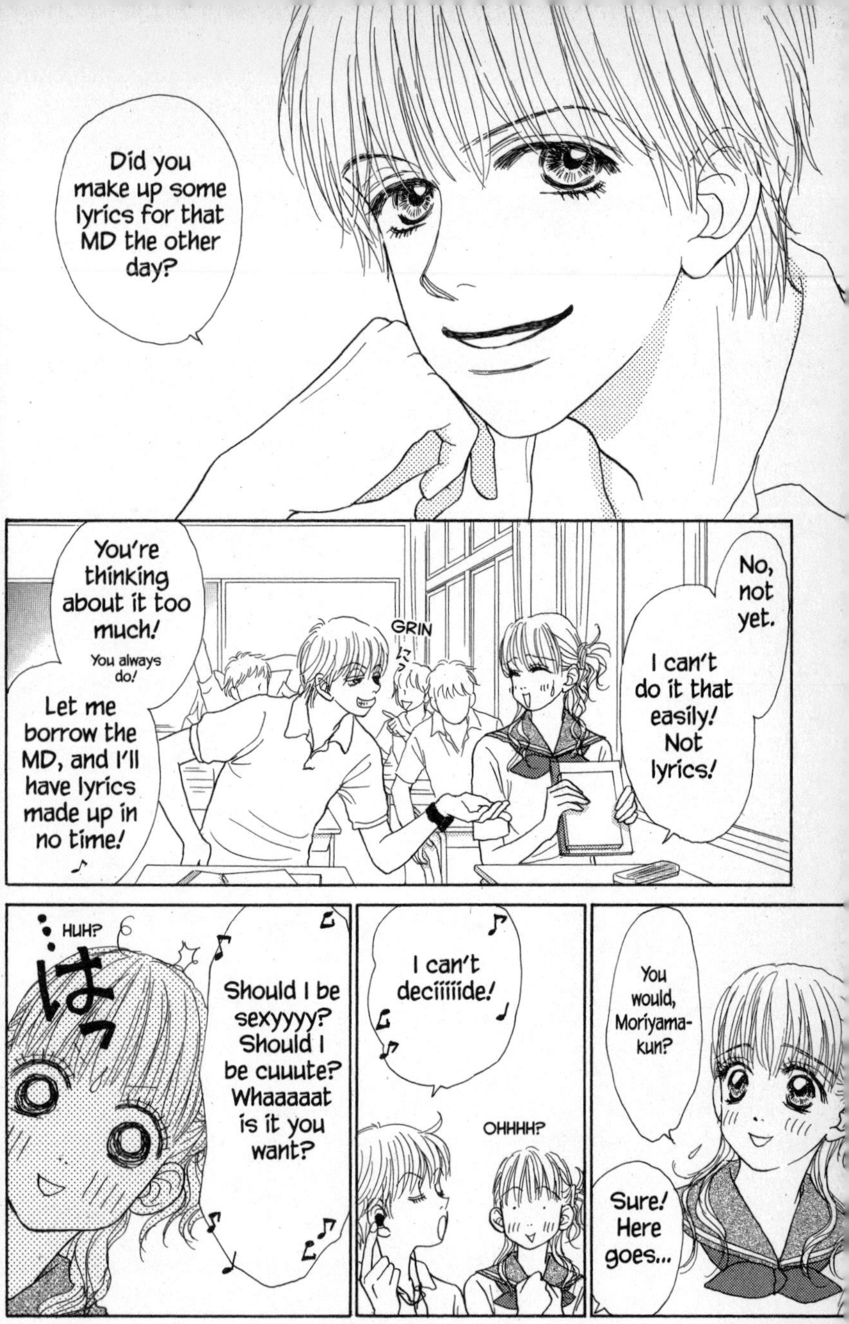
Did you make up some lyrics for that MD the other day?
No, not yet.
I can't do it that easily! Not lyrics!
GRIN
You're thinking about it too much!
You always do!
Let me borrow the MD, and I'll have lyrics made up in no time!
You would, Moriyama-kun?
Sure! Here goes...
I can't deciiiiide!
OHHHH?
Should I be sexyyyy? Should I be cuuute? Whaaaaat is it you want?
HUH?
はっ

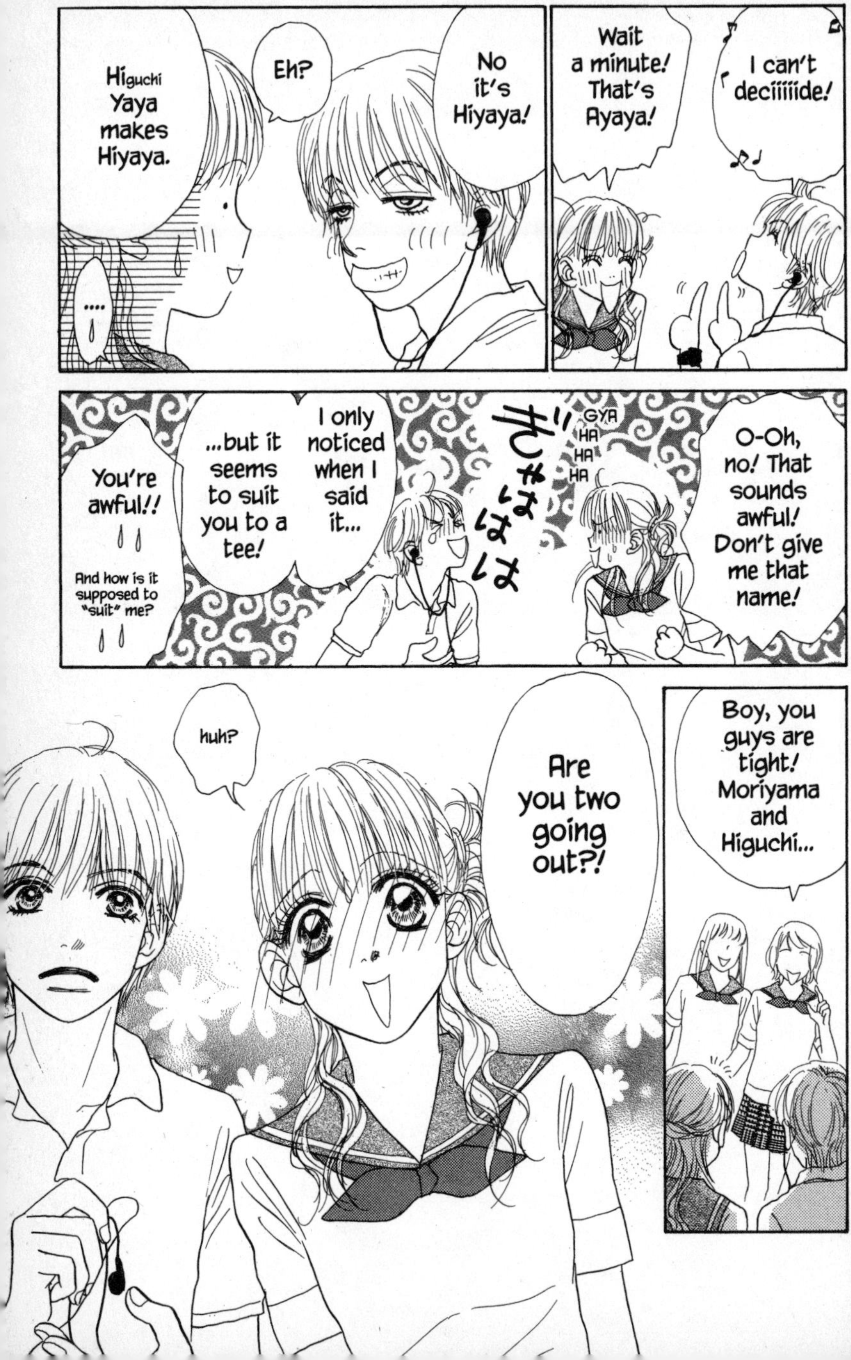

I can't deciiiide!
Wait a minute! That's Ayaya!
No it's Hiyaya!
Eh?
Higuchi Yaya makes Hiyaya.
....
O-Oh, no! That sounds awful! Don't give me that name!
ぎゃははは
GYA HA HA HA
I only noticed when I said it...
...but it seems to suit you to a tee!
You're awful!!
And how is it supposed to "suit" me?
Boy, you guys are tight! Moriyama and Higuchi...
Are you two going out?!
huh?

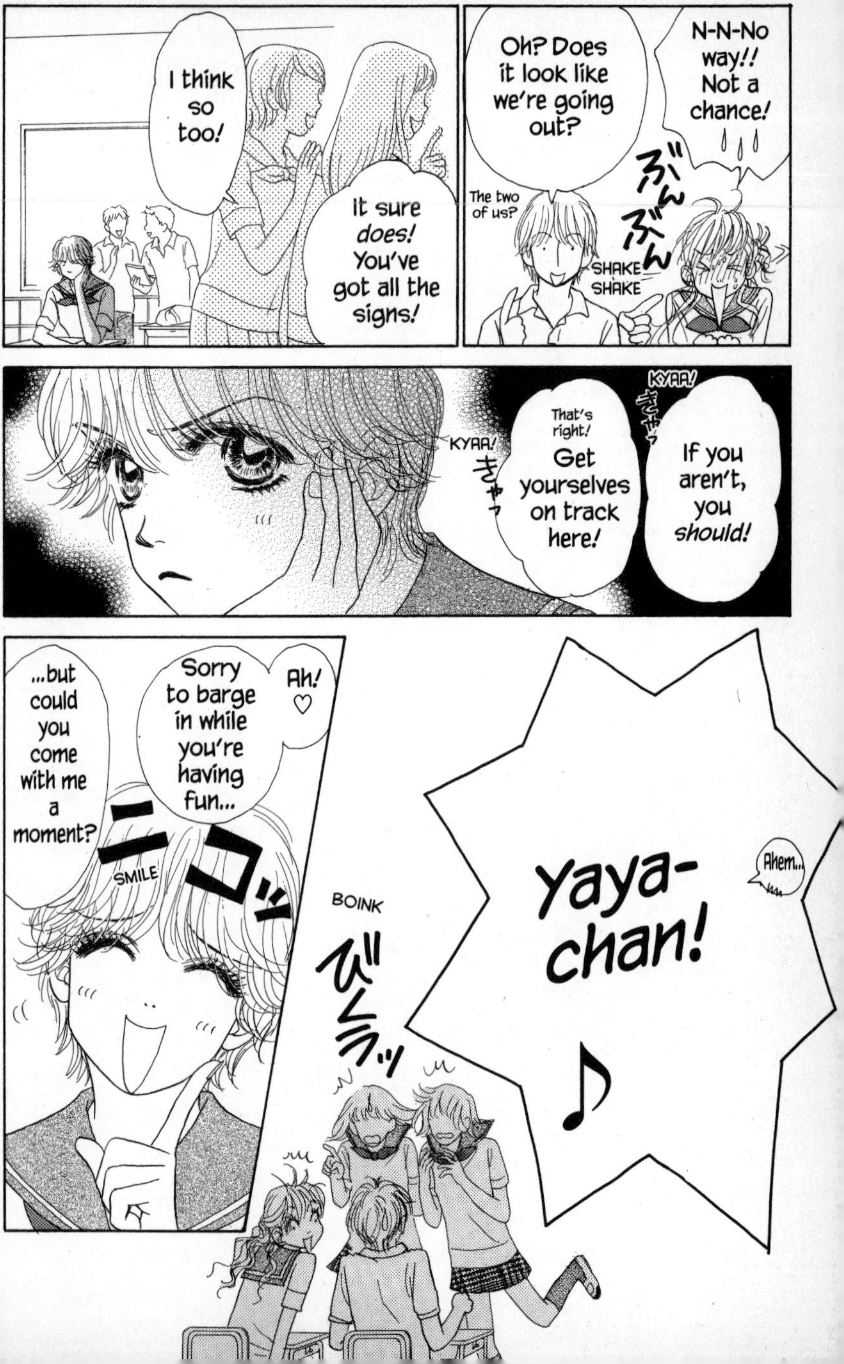
N-N-No way!! Not a chance!
Oh? Does it look like we're going out?
The two of us?
ぶんぶん
SHAKE SHAKE
It sure does! You've got all the signs!
I think so too!
KYAA!
きゃっ
If you aren't, you should!
KYAA!
きゃっ
That's right! Get yourselves on track here!
Ahem...
Yaya-chan! ♪
BOINK
Ah! ♡
Sorry to barge in while you're having fun...
...but could you come with me a moment?
ニコッ
SMILE

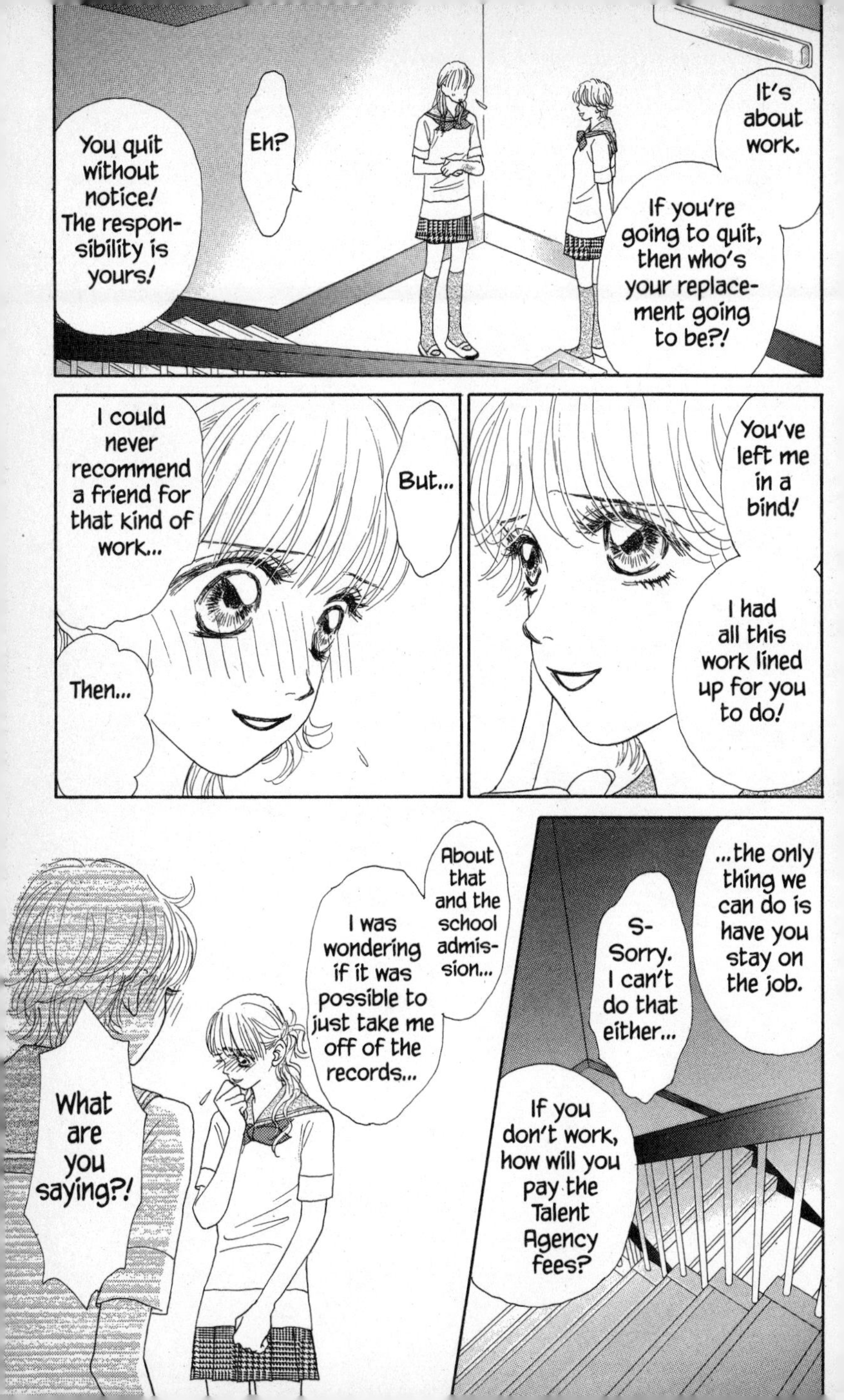
It's about work.
If you're going to quit, then who's your replacement going to be?!
Eh?
You quit without notice! The responsibility is yours!
You've left me in a bind!
I had all this work lined up for you to do!
But...
I could never recommend a friend for that kind of work...
Then...
...the only thing we can do is have you stay on the job.
S-Sorry. I can't do that either...
If you don't work, how will you pay the Talent Agency fees?
About that and the school admission...
I was wondering if it was possible to just take me off of the records...
What are you saying?!

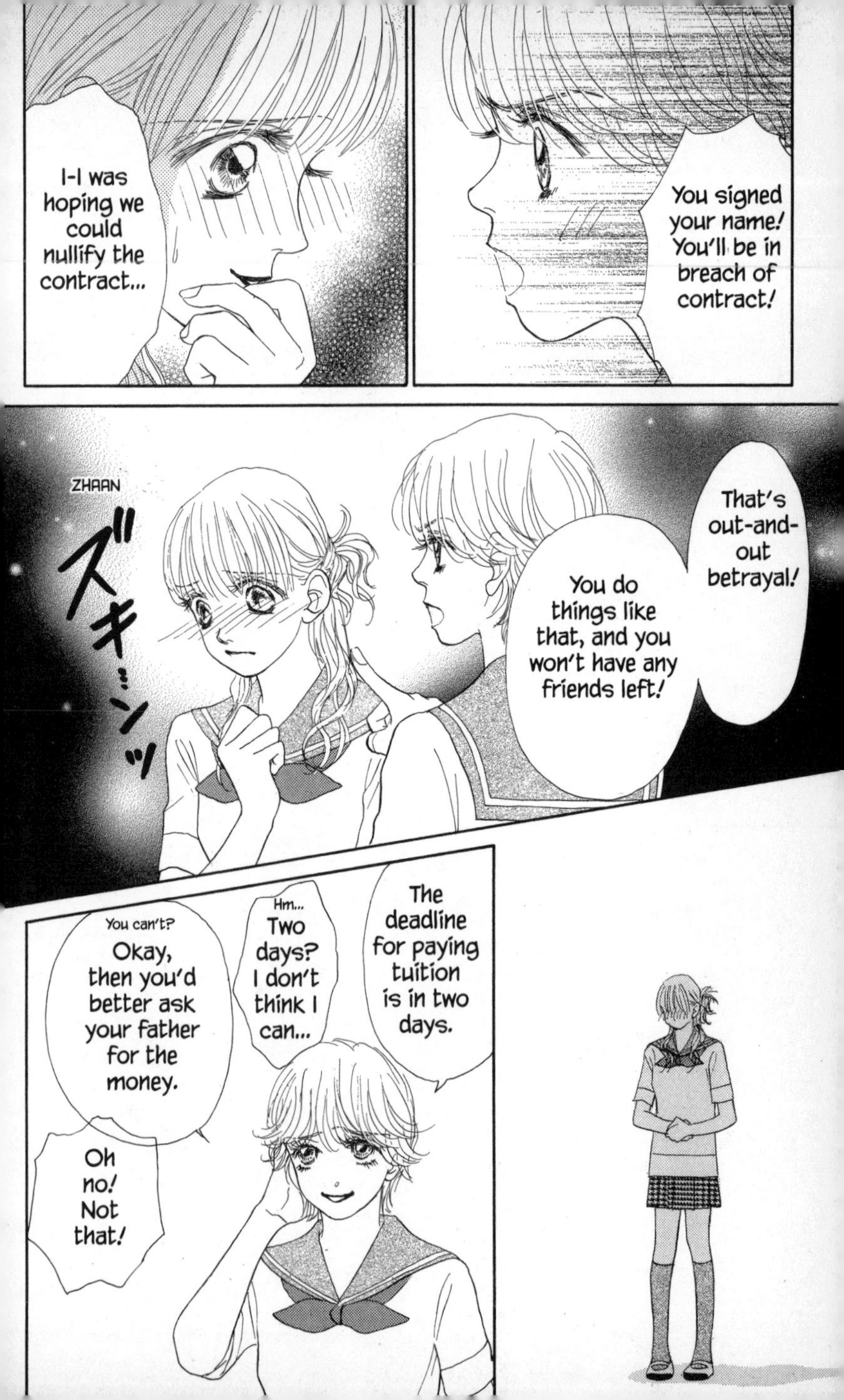

You signed your name! You'll be in breach of contract!
I-I was hoping we could nullify the contract...
That's out-and-out betrayal!
You do things like that, and you won't have any friends left!
ZHAAN
The deadline for paying tuition is in two days.
Hm... Two days? I don't think I can...
You can't? Okay, then you'd better ask your father for the money.
Oh no! Not that!

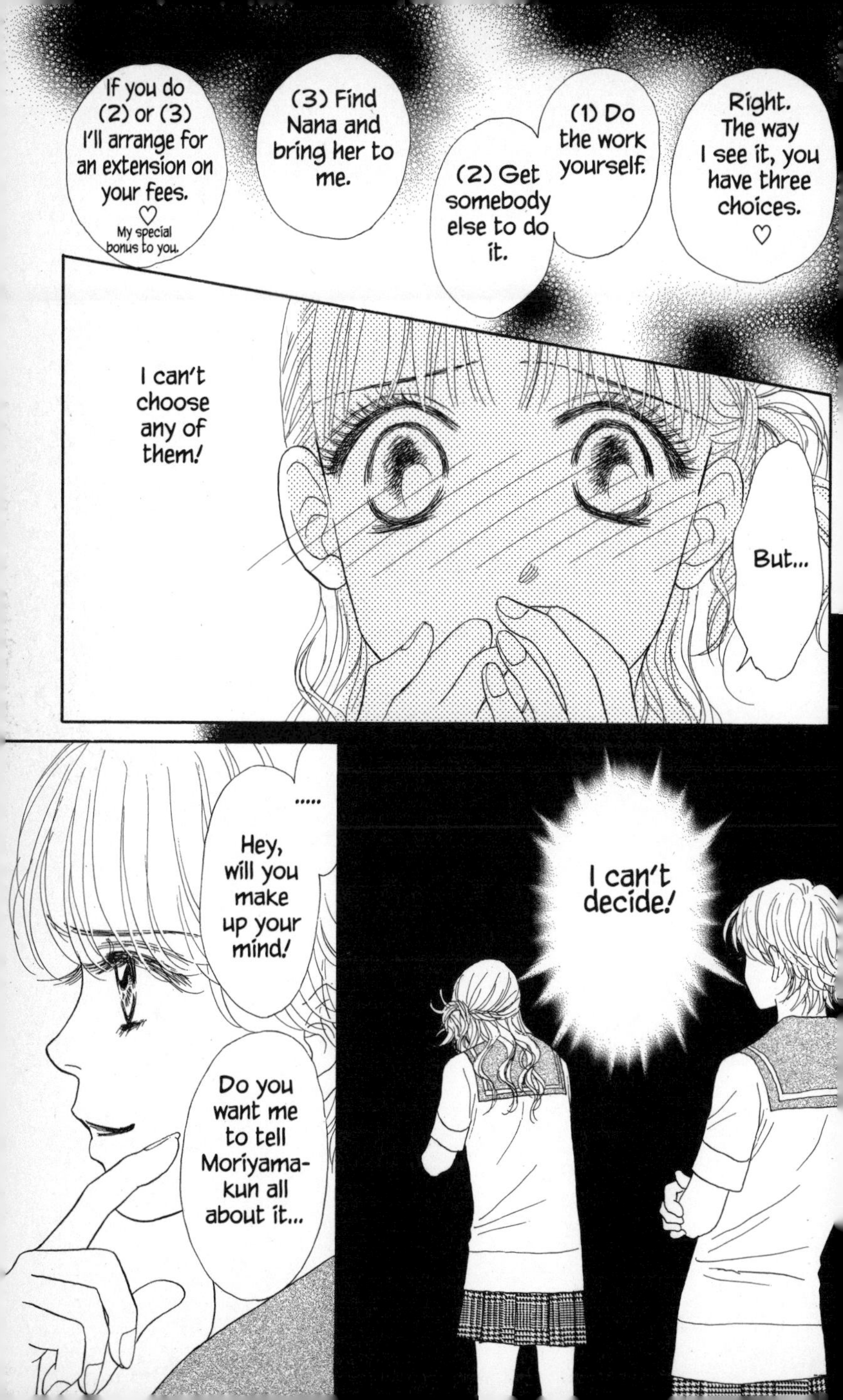

Right. The way I see it, you have three choices. ♡
(1) Do the work yourself.
(2) Get somebody else to do it.
(3) Find Nana and bring her to me.
If you do (2) or (3) I'll arrange for an extension on your fees. ♡
My special bonus to you.
But...
I can't choose any of them!
I can't decide!
.....
Hey, will you make up your mind!
Do you want me to tell Moriyama-kun all about it...

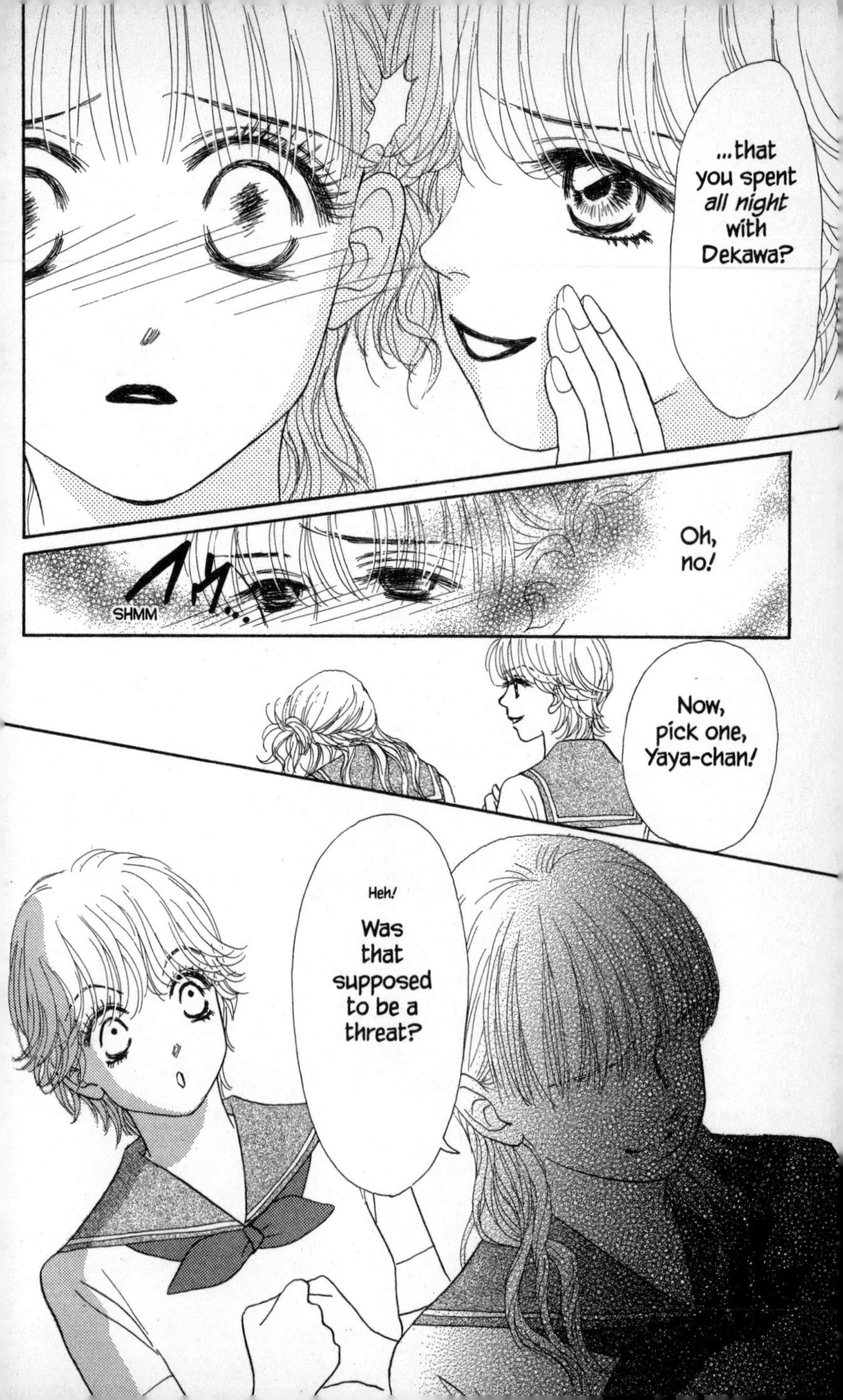
...that you spent *all night* with Dekawa?
Oh, no!
SHMM
Now, pick one, Yaya-chan!
Heh!
Was that supposed to be a threat?

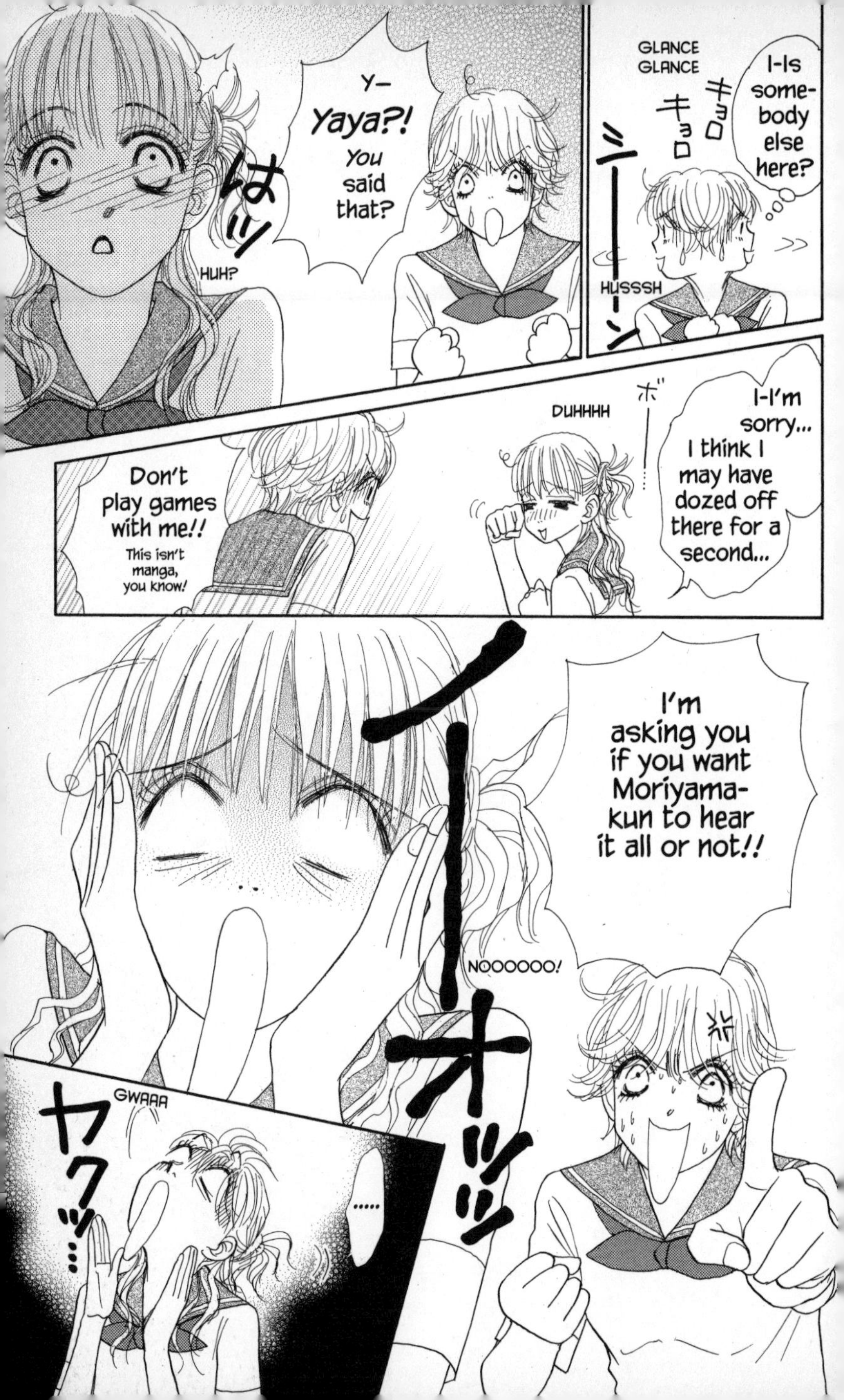

GLANCE GLANCE
キョロキョロ
シーーン
HUSSSH
I-Is somebody else here?
Y– Yaya?! You said that?
はッ
HUH?
I-I'm sorry... I think I may have dozed off there for a second...
ボー
DUHHHH
Don't play games with me!!
This isn't manga, you know!
I'm asking you if you want Moriyama-kun to hear it all or not!!
NOOOOOO!
.....
GWAAA
ヤクッ

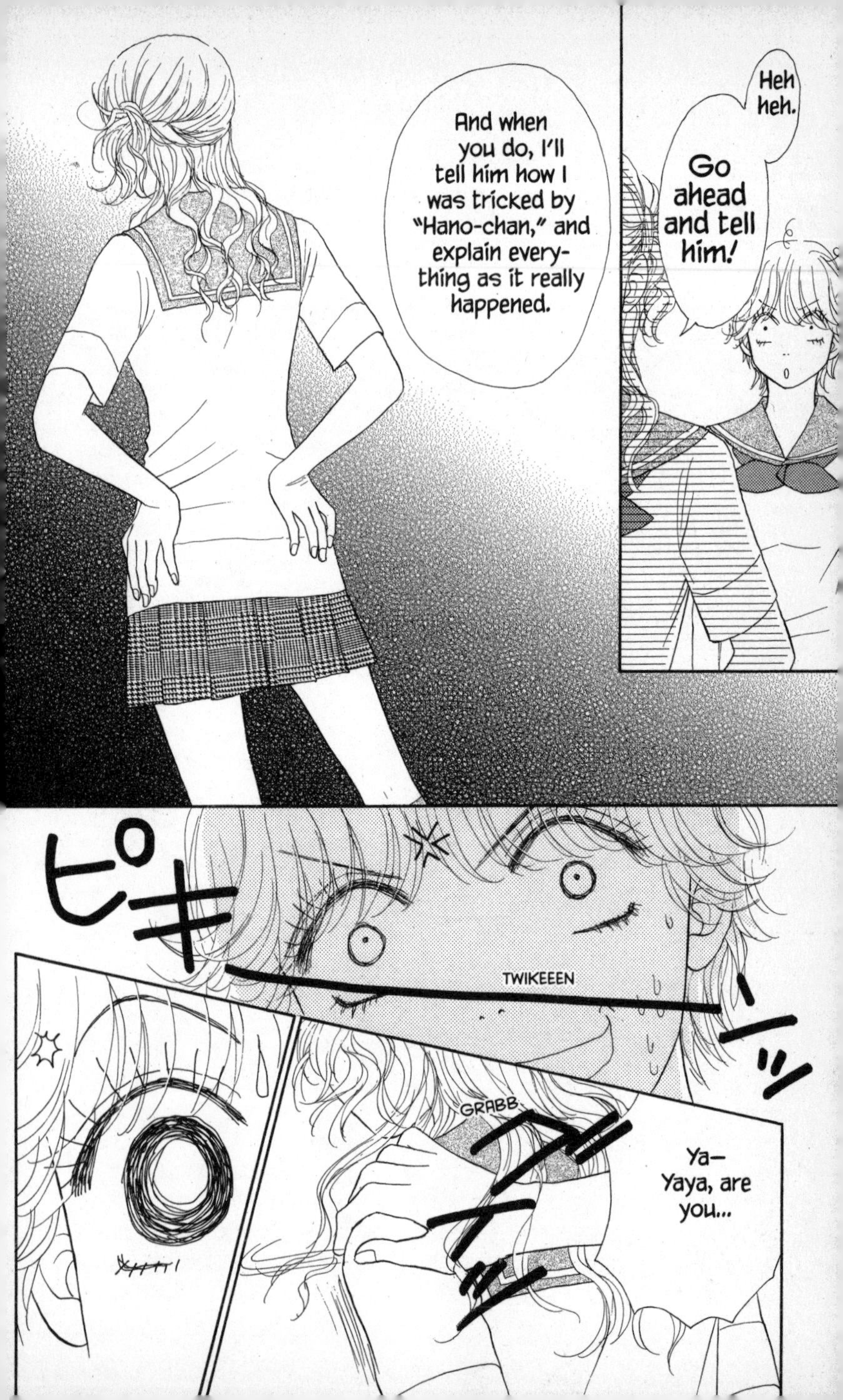
Heh heh.
Go ahead and tell him!
And when you do, I'll tell him how I was tricked by "Hano-chan," and explain every-thing as it really happened.
ピキーンッ
TWIKEEEN
ガシッ
GRABB
Ya— Yaya, are you...

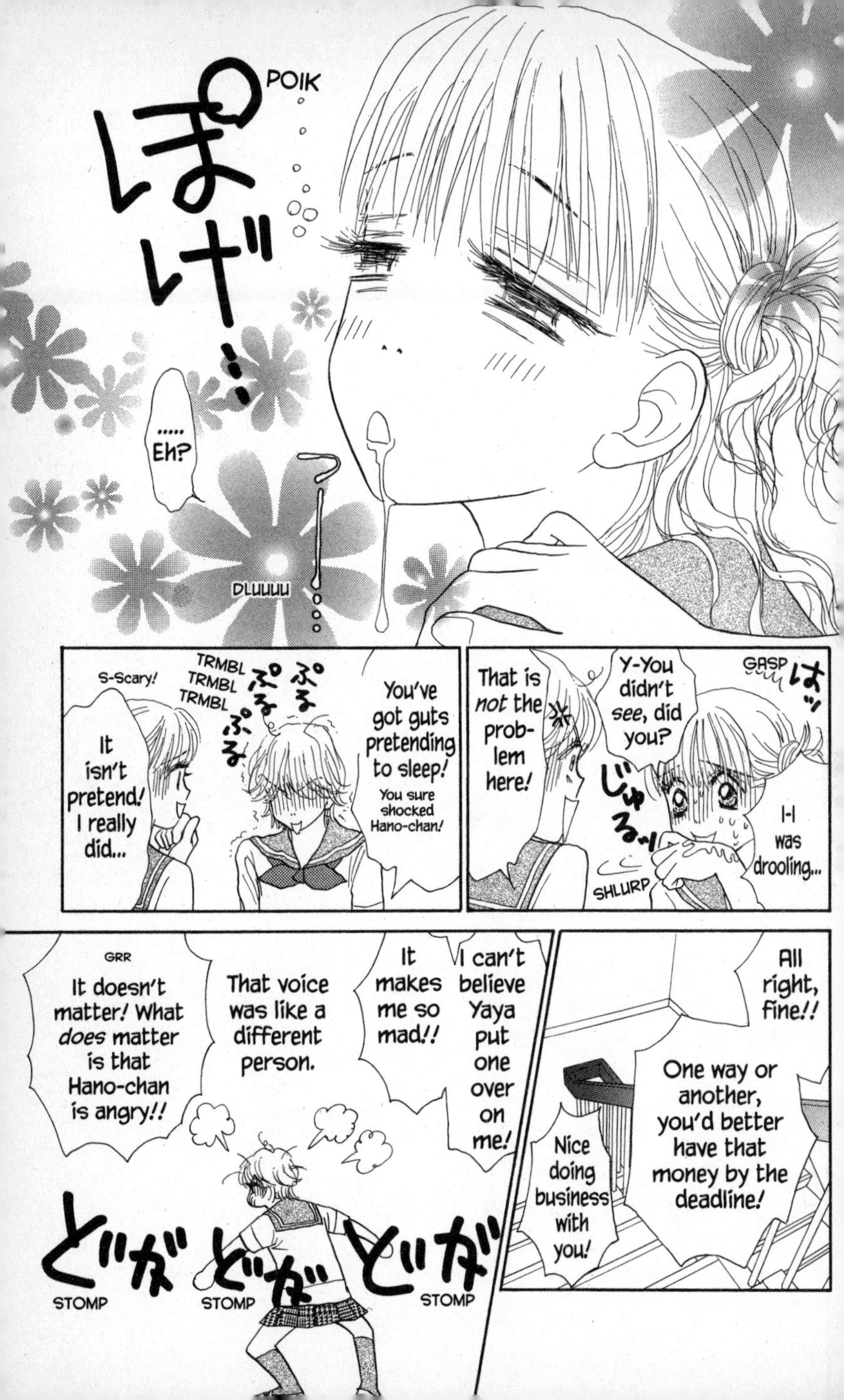

ぽげ…
POIK
.....
Eh?
つー
DLUUUU
はっ
GASP
Y-You didn't see, did you?
That is *not* the prob-lem here!
じゅるっ
SHLURP
I-I was drooling...
You've got guts pretending to sleep!
You sure shocked Hano-chan!
ぷるぷるぷる
TRMBL TRMBL TRMBL
S-Scary!
It isn't pretend! I really did...
All right, fine!!
One way or another, you'd better have that money by the deadline!
Nice doing business with you!
I can't believe Yaya put one over on me!
It makes me so mad!!
That voice was like a different person.
GRR
It doesn't matter! What *does* matter is that Hano-chan is angry!!
どがどがどが
STOMP STOMP STOMP

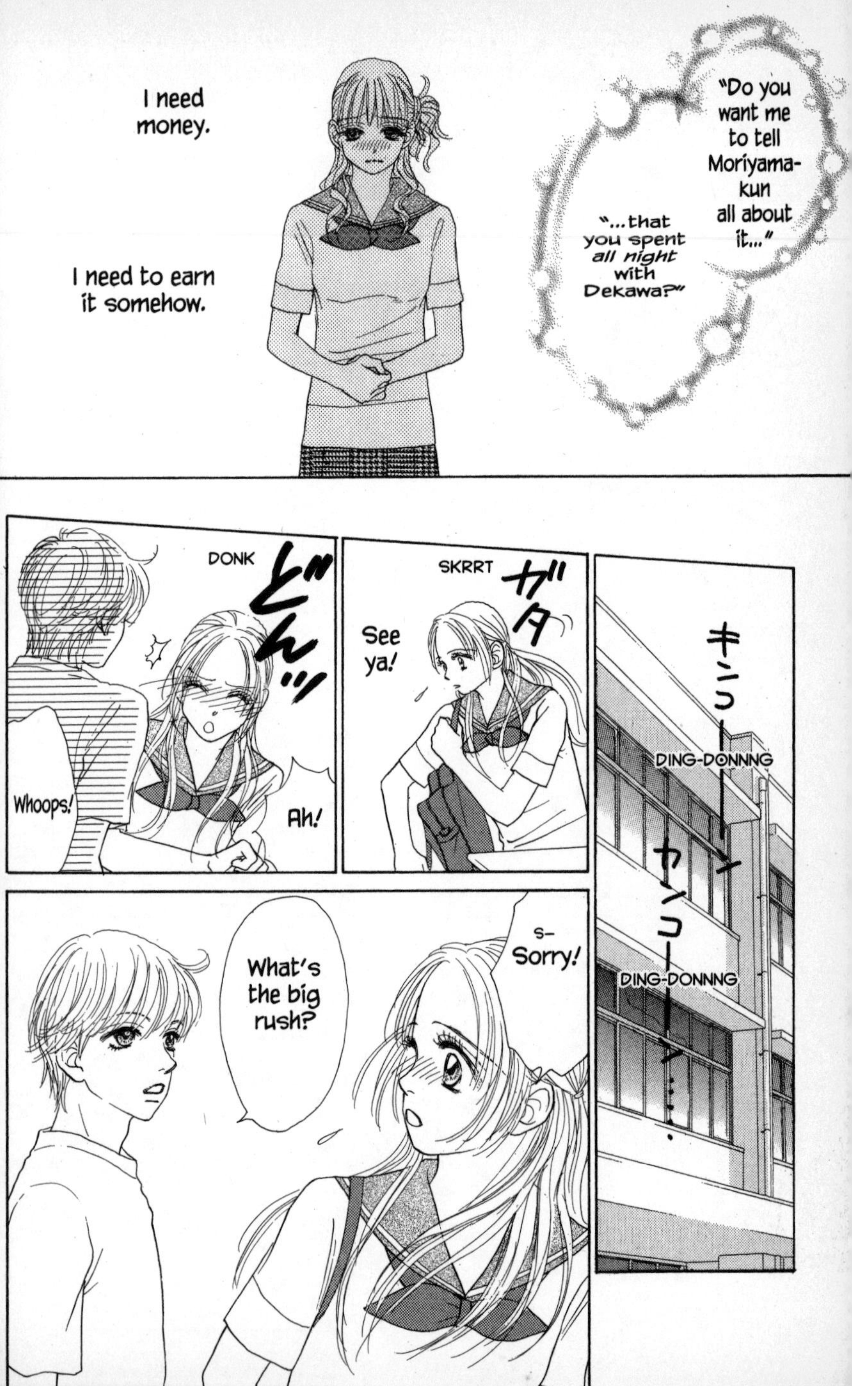
"Do you want me to tell Moriyama-kun all about it..."
"...that you spent all night with Dekawa?"
I need money.
I need to earn it somehow.
キンコーン
DING-DONNNG
カンコーン……
DING-DONNNG
SKRRT
ガタ
See ya!
DONK
どんッ
Whoops!
Ah!
S-Sorry!
What's the big rush?

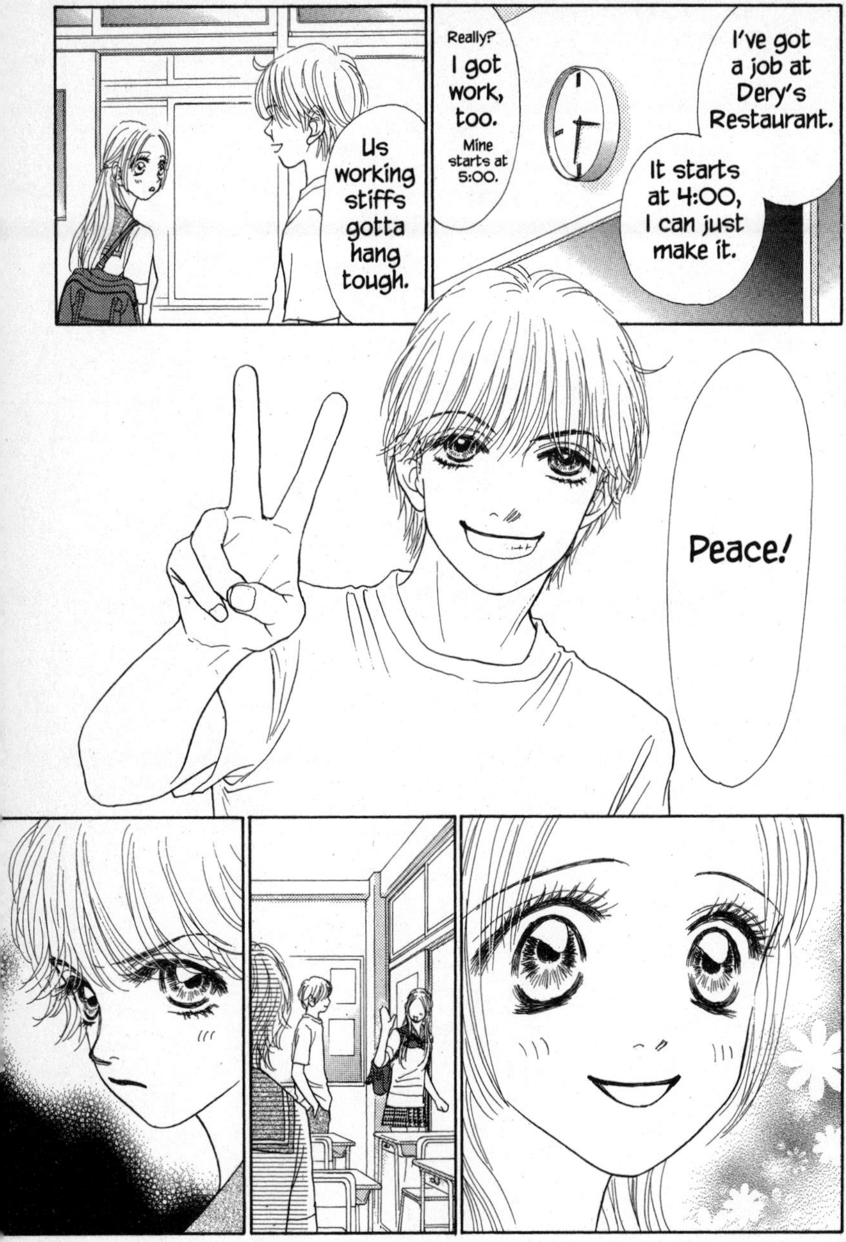
I've got a job at Dery's Restaurant.
It starts at 4:00, I can just make it.
Really? I got work, too.
Mine starts at 5:00.
Us working stiffs gotta hang tough.
Peace!

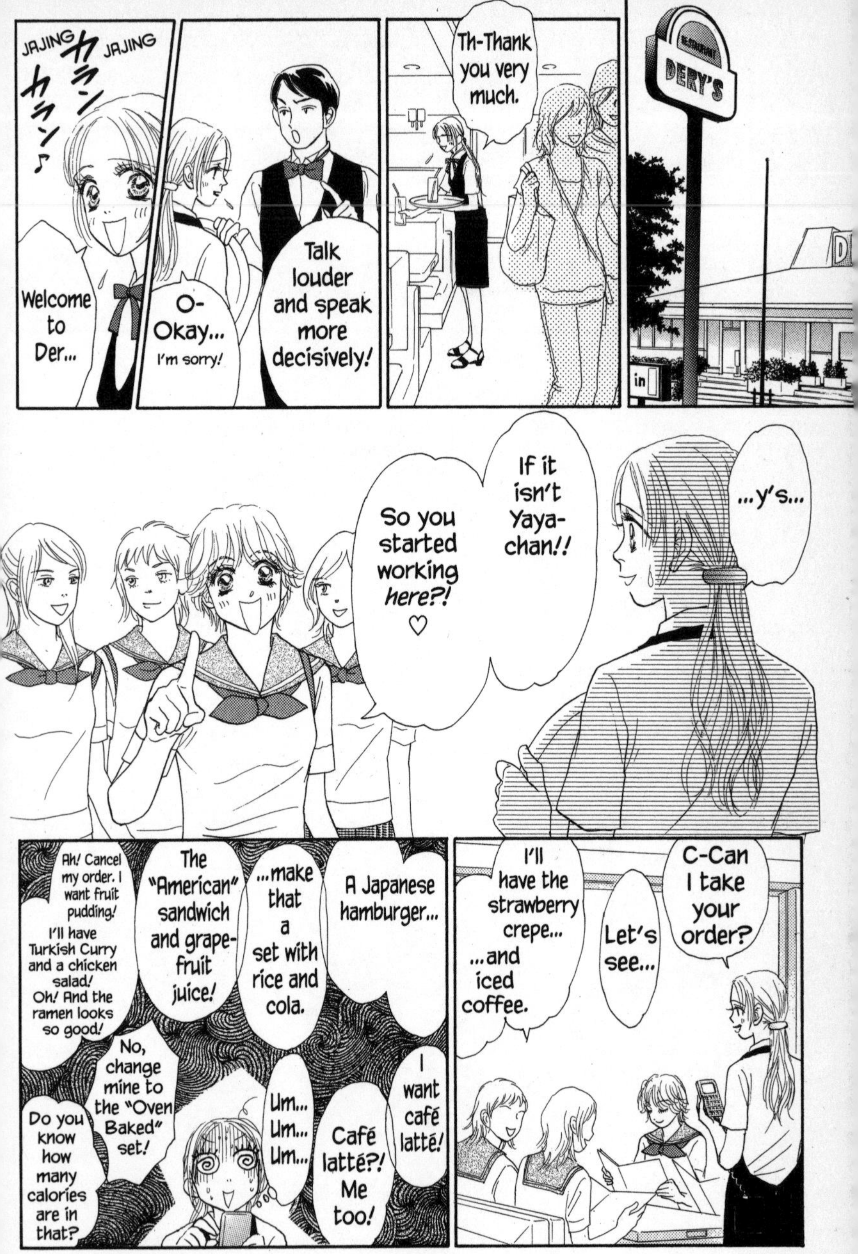
DERY'S
in
Th-Thank you very much.
Talk louder and speak more decisively!
O-Okay... I'm sorry!
JAJING カラン JAJING カラン♪
Welcome to Der...
...y's...
If it isn't Yaya-chan!!
So you started working *here*?! ♡
C-Can I take your order?
Let's see...
I'll have the strawberry crepe... ...and iced coffee.
A Japanese hamburger...
...make that a set with rice and cola.
The "American" sandwich and grape-fruit juice!
Ah! Cancel my order. I want fruit pudding!
I'll have Turkish Curry and a chicken salad! Oh! And the ramen looks so good!
I want café latté!
Café latté?! Me too!
Um... Um... Um...
No, change mine to the "Oven Baked" set!
Do you know how many calories are in that?

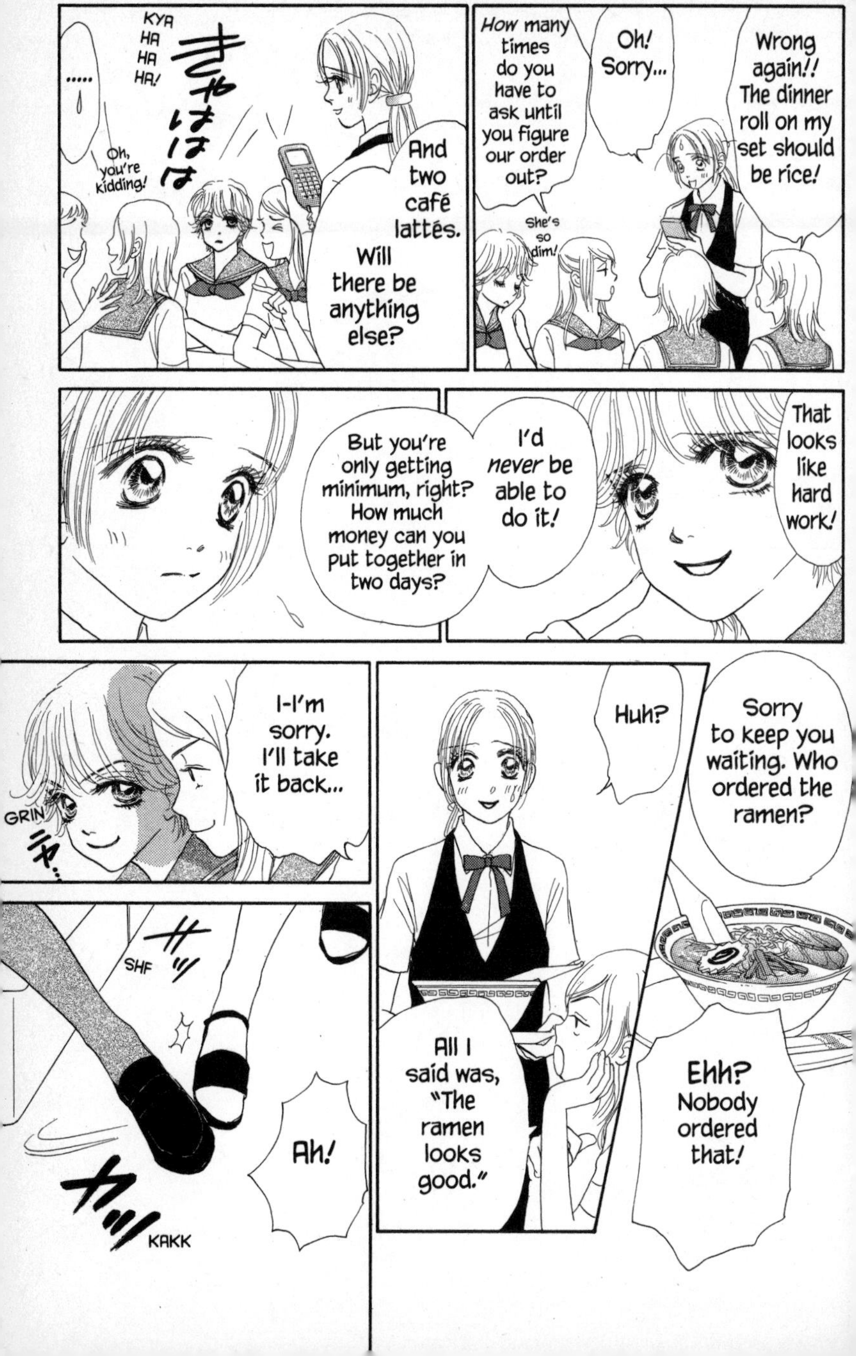

Wrong again!! The dinner roll on my set should be rice!
Oh! Sorry...
How many times do you have to ask until you figure our order out?
She's so dim!
And two café lattés.
Will there be anything else?
KYA HA HA HA!
きゃははは
Oh, you're kidding!
.....
That looks like hard work!
I'd *never* be able to do it!
But you're only getting minimum, right? How much money can you put together in two days?
Sorry to keep you waiting. Who ordered the ramen?
Huh?
Ehh? Nobody ordered that!
All I said was, "The ramen looks good."
I-I'm sorry. I'll take it back...
GRIN
ニヤ...
SHF
Ah!
KAKK

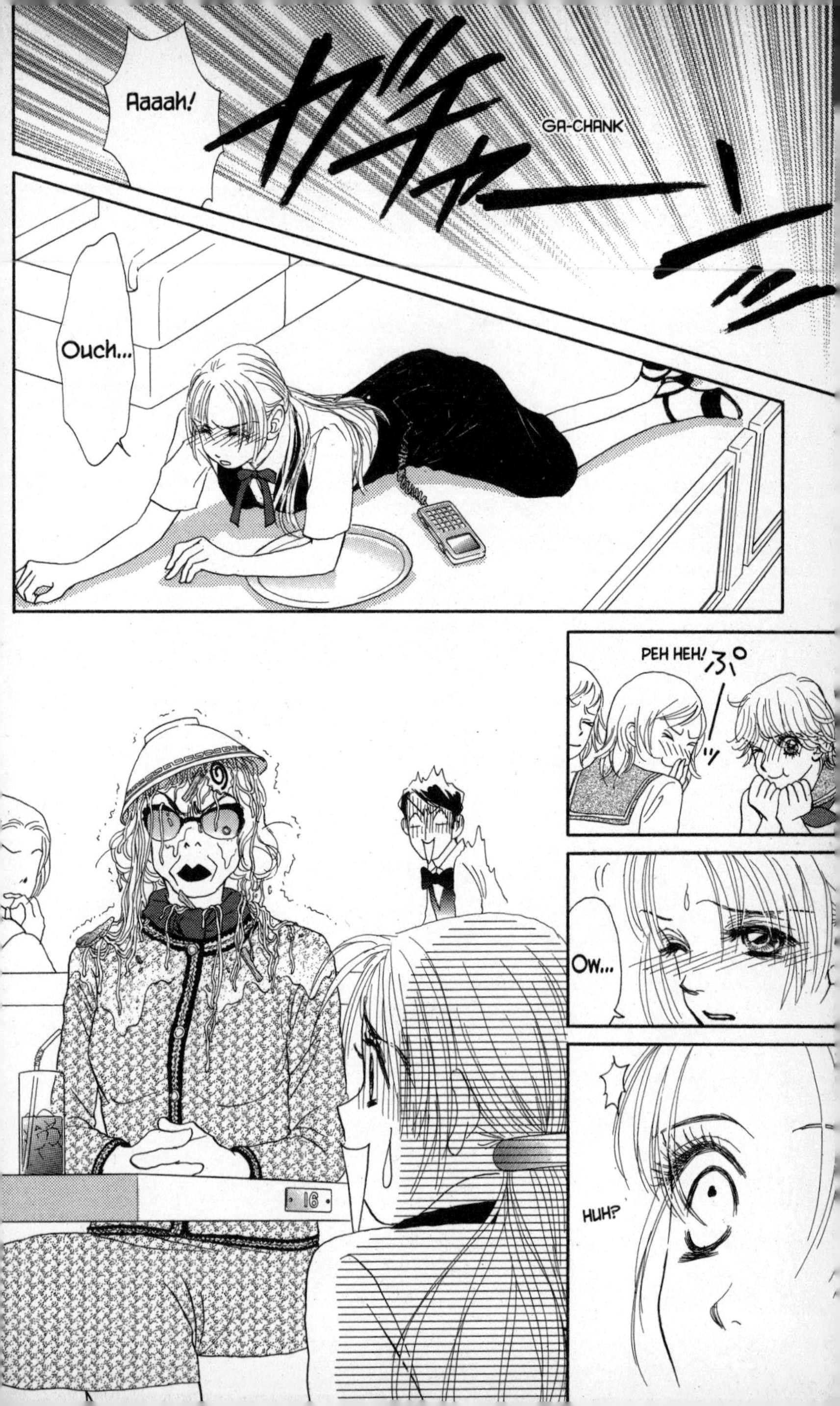

Aaaah!
GA-CHANK
Ouch...
PEH HEH!
ぷ
Ow...
HUH?
16

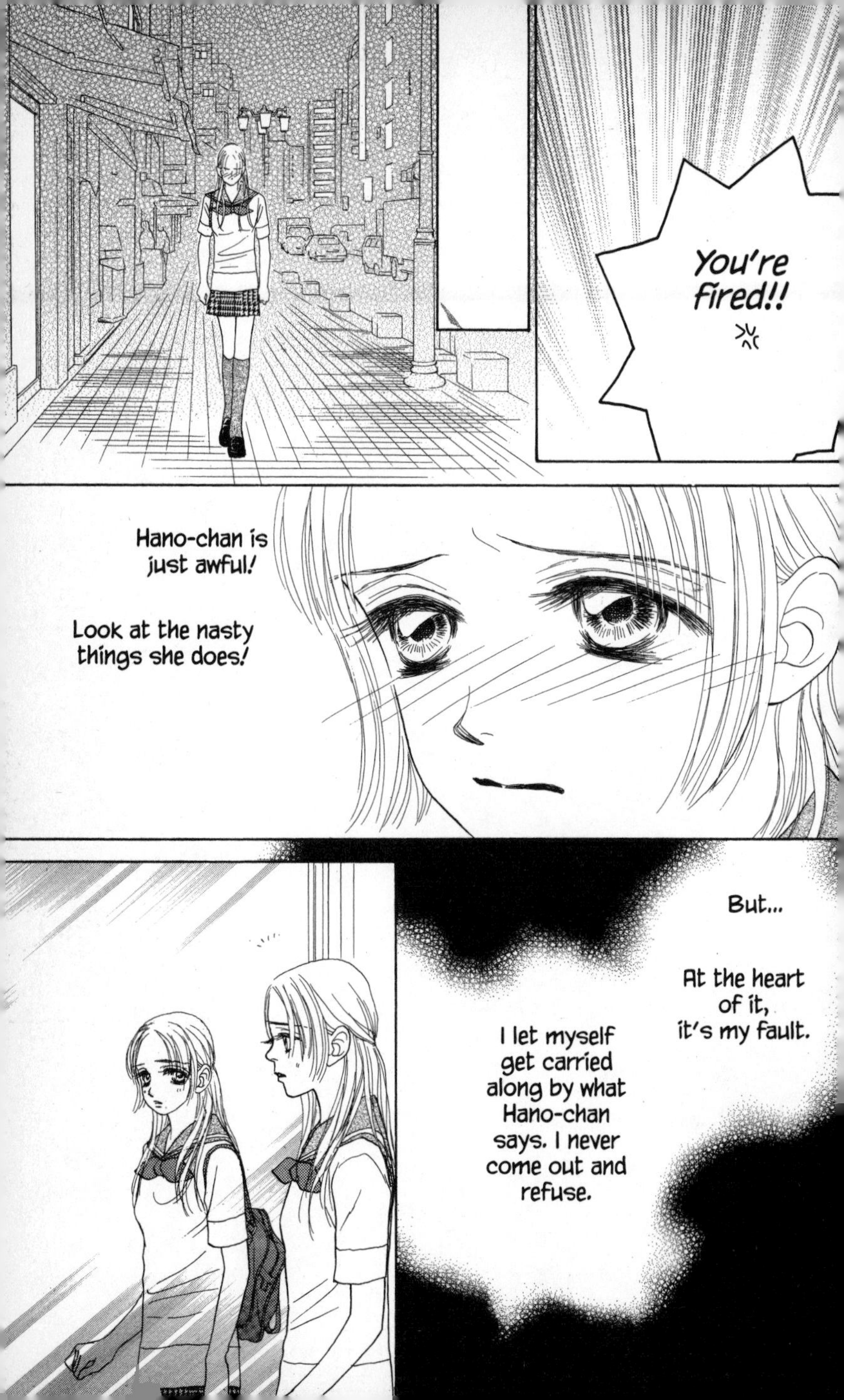
You're fired!!
Hano-chan is just awful!
Look at the nasty things she does!
But...
At the heart of it, it's my fault.
I let myself get carried along by what Hano-chan says. I never come out and refuse.

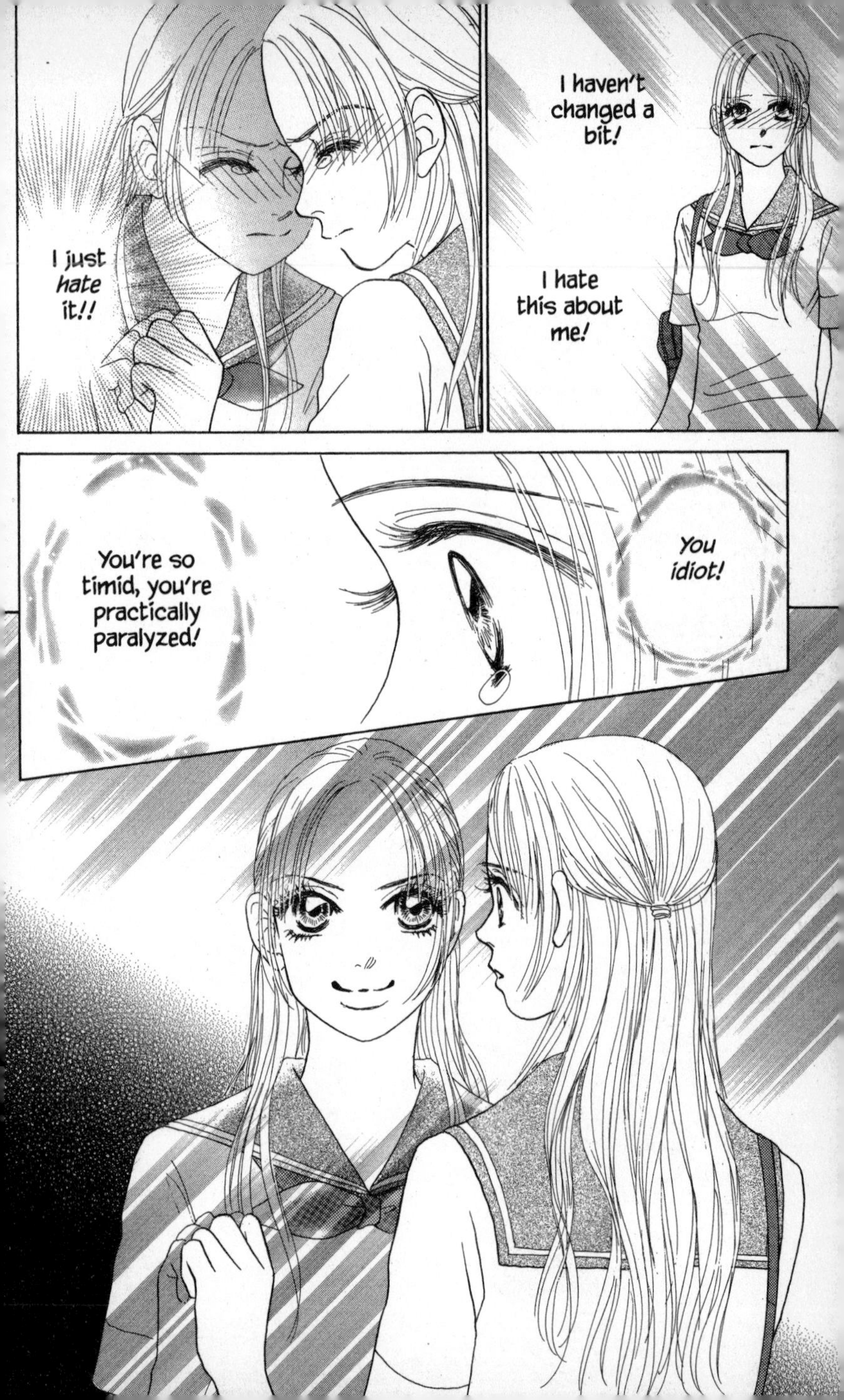
I haven't changed a bit!
I hate this about me!
I just *hate* it!!
You idiot!
You're so timid, you're practically paralyzed!

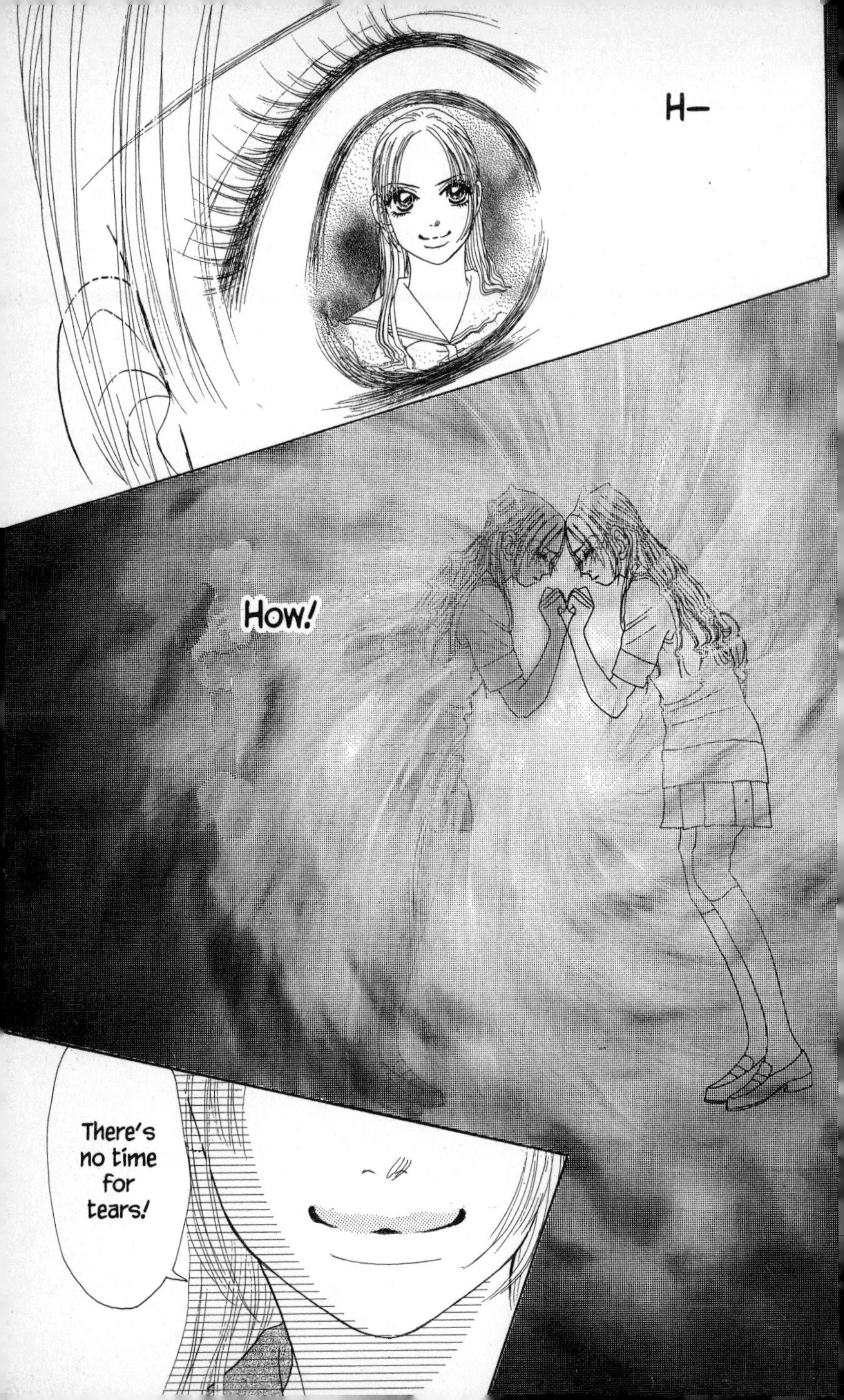
H—
How!
There's no time for tears!

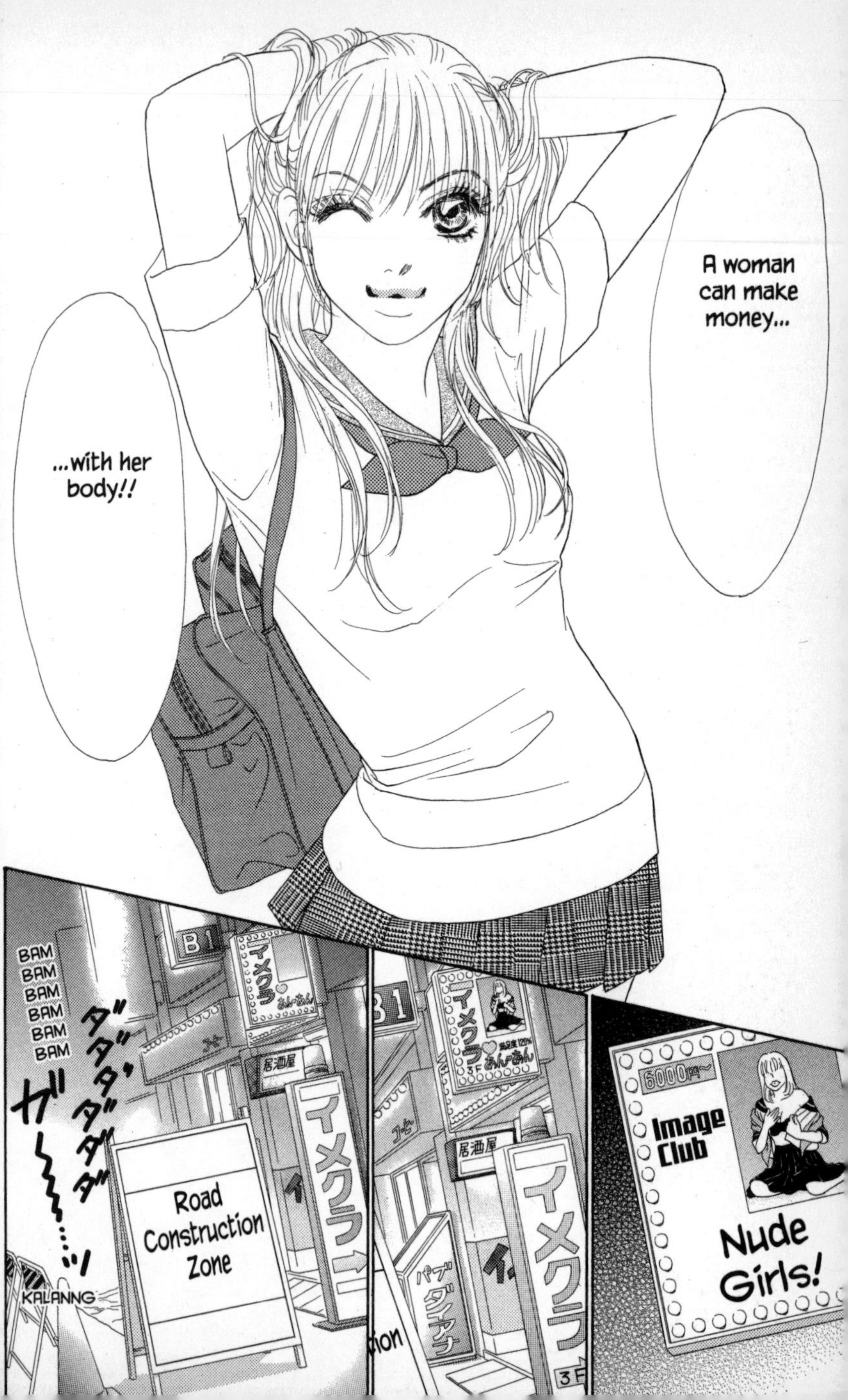
A woman can make money...
...with her body!!
6000円~
Image Club
Nude Girls!
イメクラ
3F
居酒屋
イメクラ
パブ ダイアナ
3F
B1
イメクラ
居酒屋
イメクラ
Road Construction Zone
BAM BAM BAM BAM BAM BAM
ダダダダダ
ガ〜〜…ッ
KALANNG

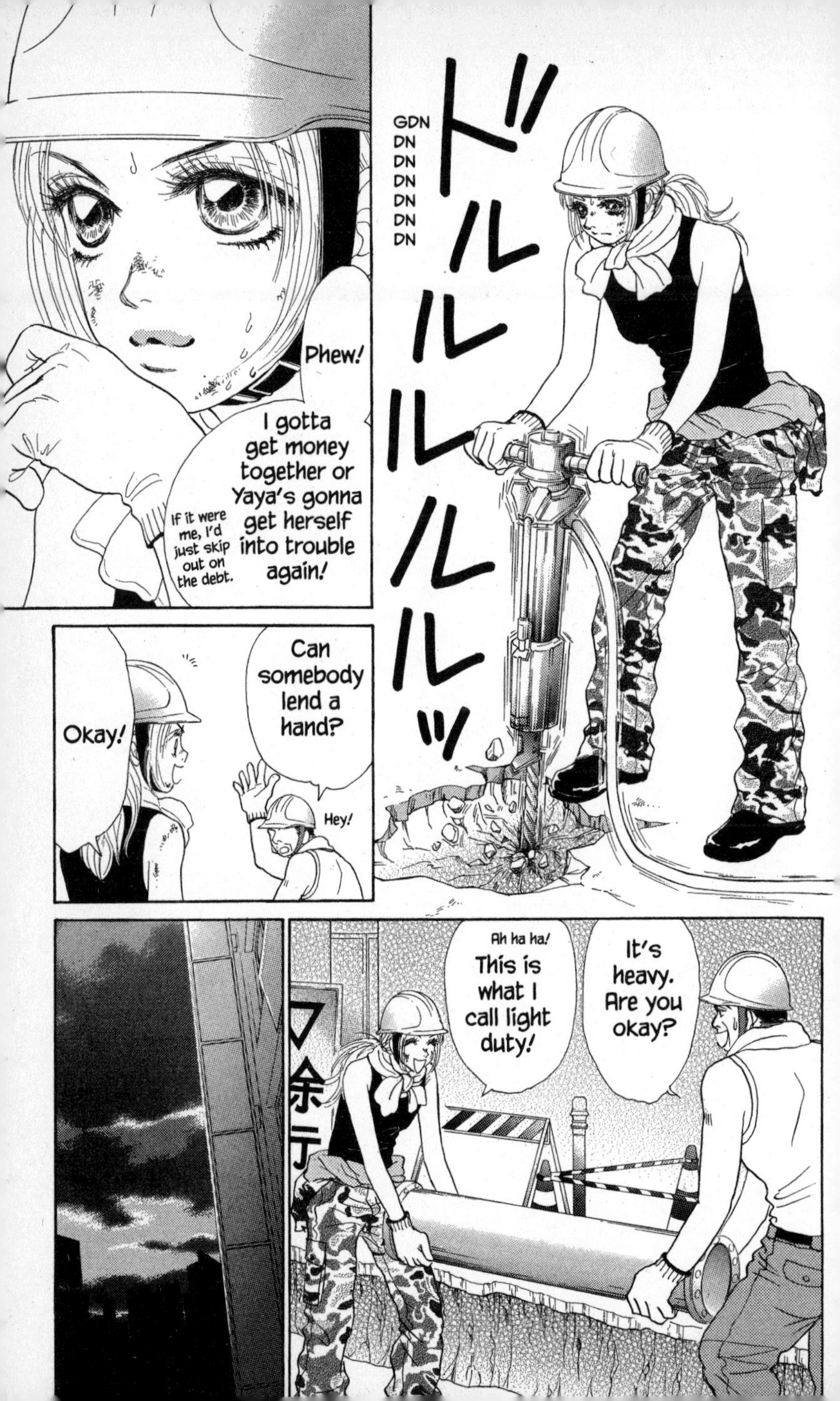
ドルルルルルッ
GDN DN DN DN DN DN DN
Phew!
I gotta get money together or Yaya's gonna get herself into trouble again!
If it were me, I'd just skip out on the debt.
Can somebody lend a hand?
Hey!
Okay!
It's heavy. Are you okay?
Ah ha ha!
This is what I call light duty!

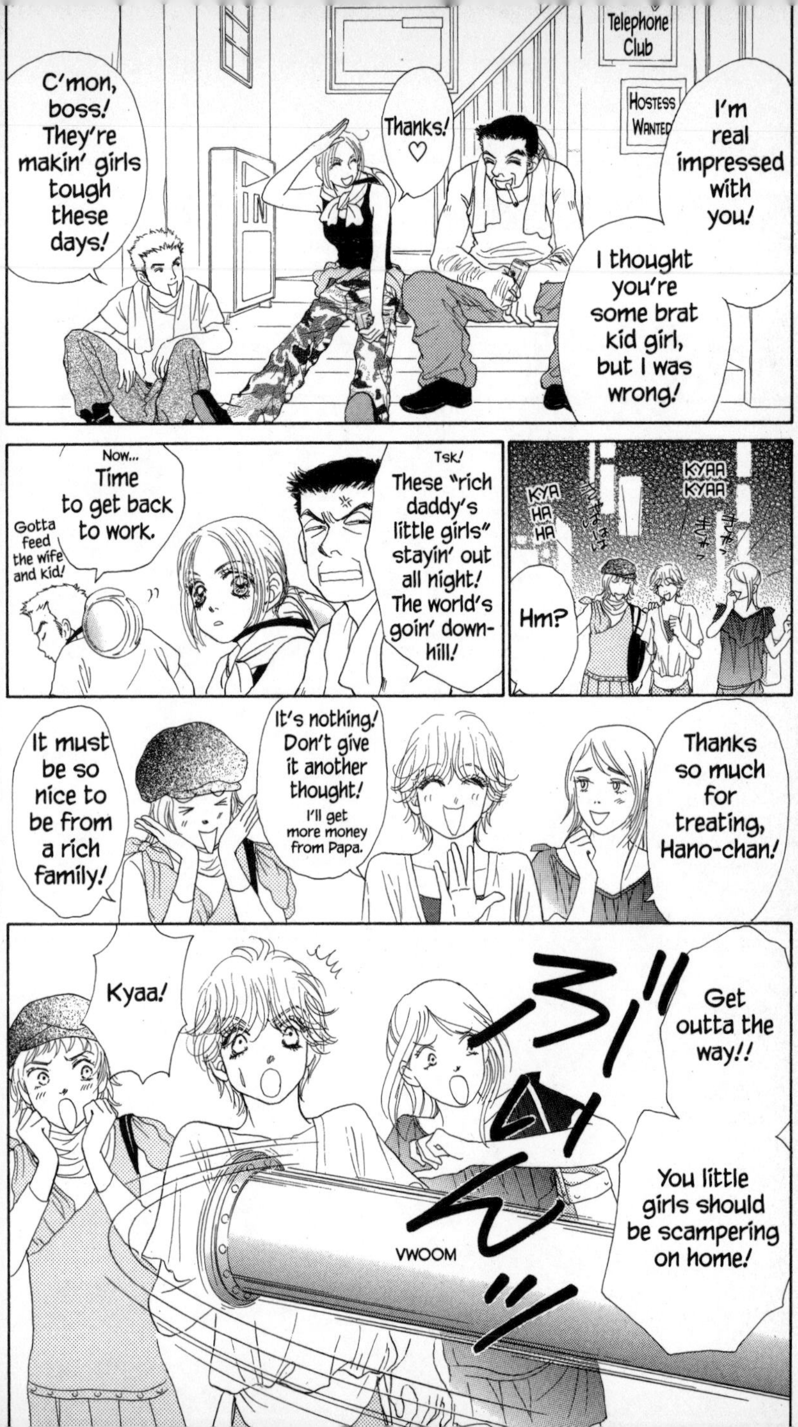

Telephone Club
Hostess Wanted
I'm real impressed with you!
I thought you're some brat kid girl, but I was wrong!
Thanks! ♡
C'mon, boss! They're makin' girls tough these days!
KYAA KYAA
KYA HA HA
Hm?
Tsk! These "rich daddy's little girls" stayin' out all night! The world's goin' downhill!
Now... Time to get back to work.
Gotta feed the wife and kid!
Thanks so much for treating, Hano-chan!
It's nothing! Don't give it another thought! I'll get more money from Papa.
It must be so nice to be from a rich family!
Get outta the way!!
You little girls should be scampering on home!
VWOOM
Kyaa!

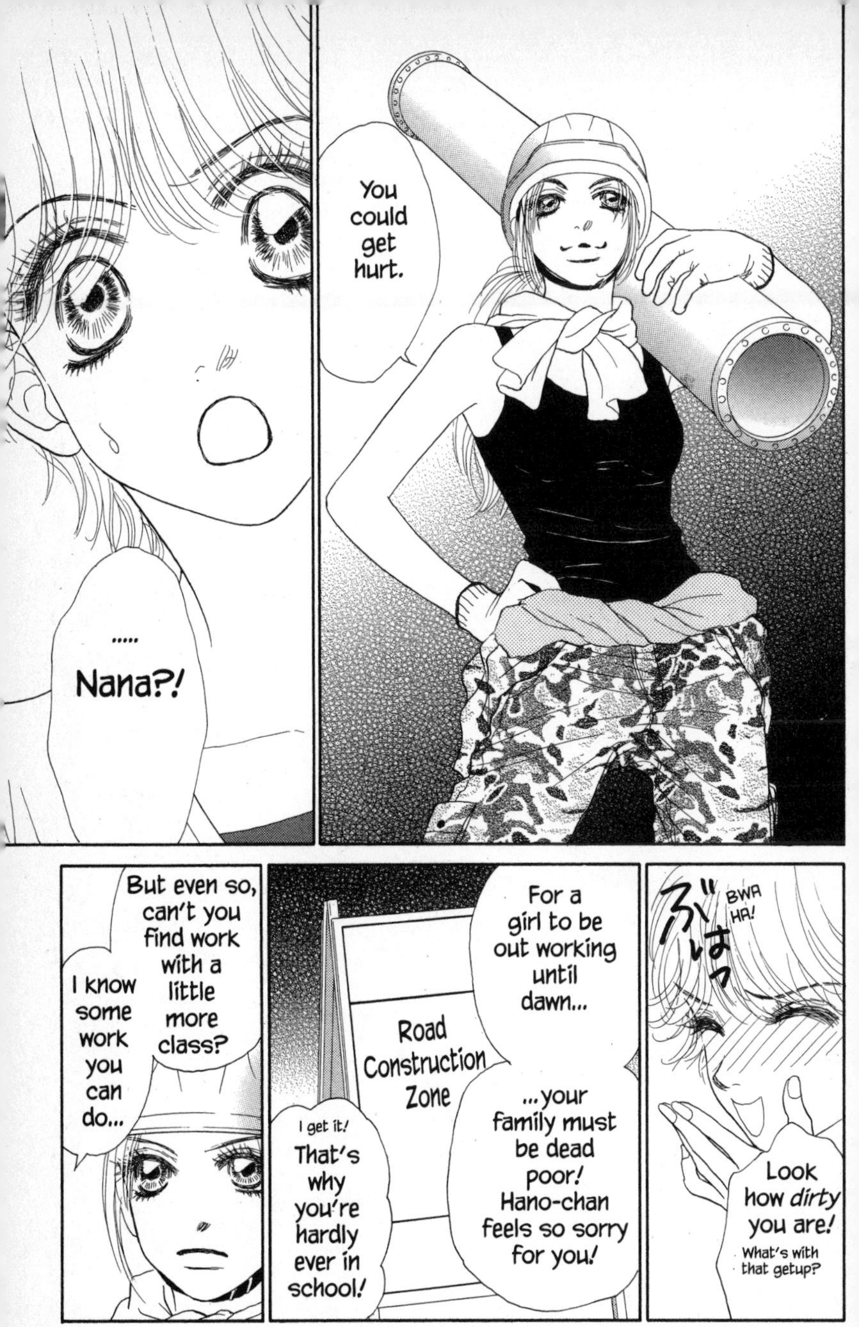
You could get hurt.
..... Nana?!
ぶはっ
BWA HA!
Look how *dirty* you are!
What's with that getup?
For a girl to be out working until dawn...
...your family must be dead poor! Hano-chan feels so sorry for you!
I get it!
That's why you're hardly ever in school!
Road Construction Zone
But even so, can't you find work with a little more class?
I know some work you can do...

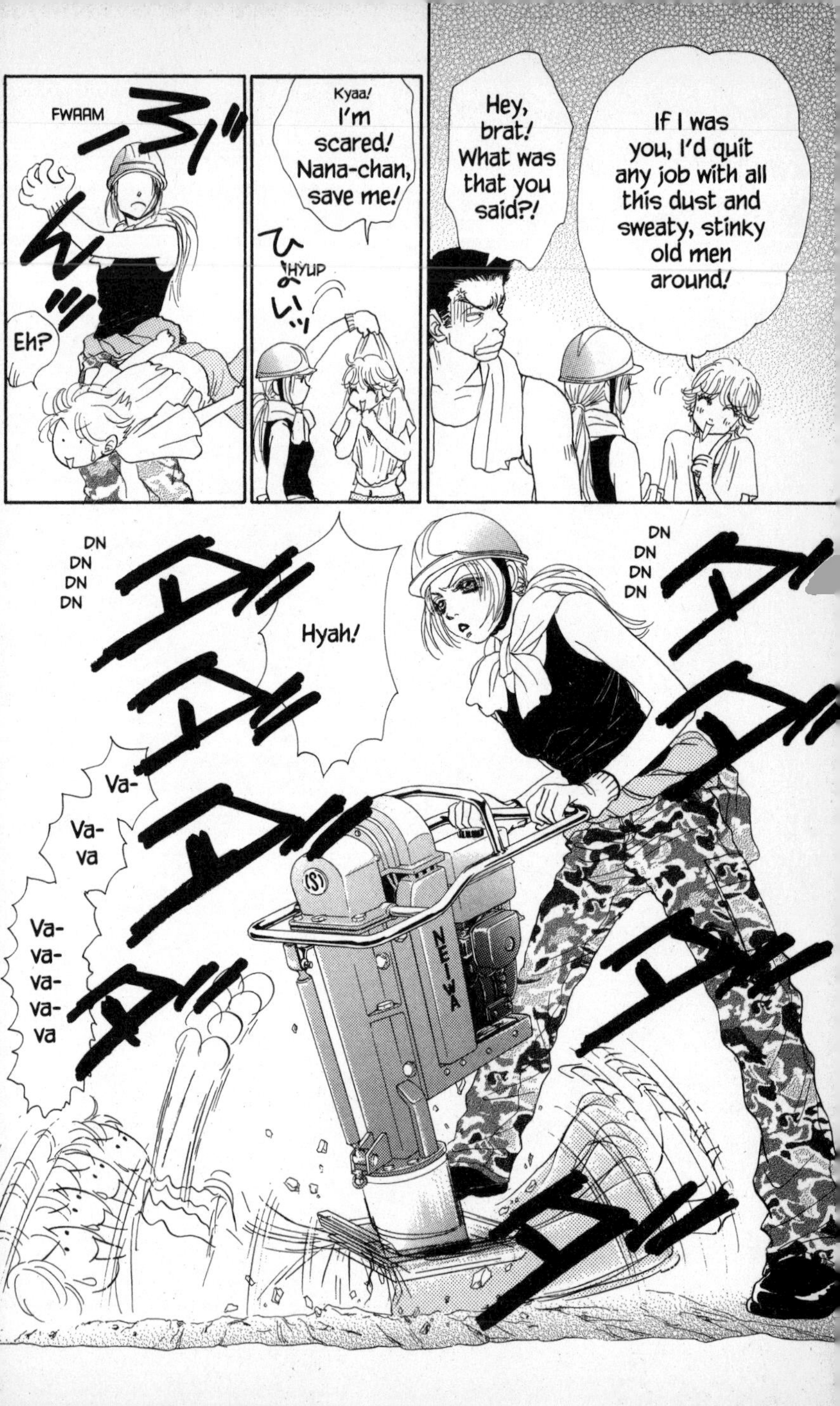
If I was you, I'd quit any job with all this dust and sweaty, stinky old men around!
Hey, brat! What was that you said?!
Kyaa! I'm scared! Nana-chan, save me!
HYUP
FWAAM
Eh?
DN DN DN DN
Hyah!
DN DN DN DN
Va- Va-va Va-va-va-va-va

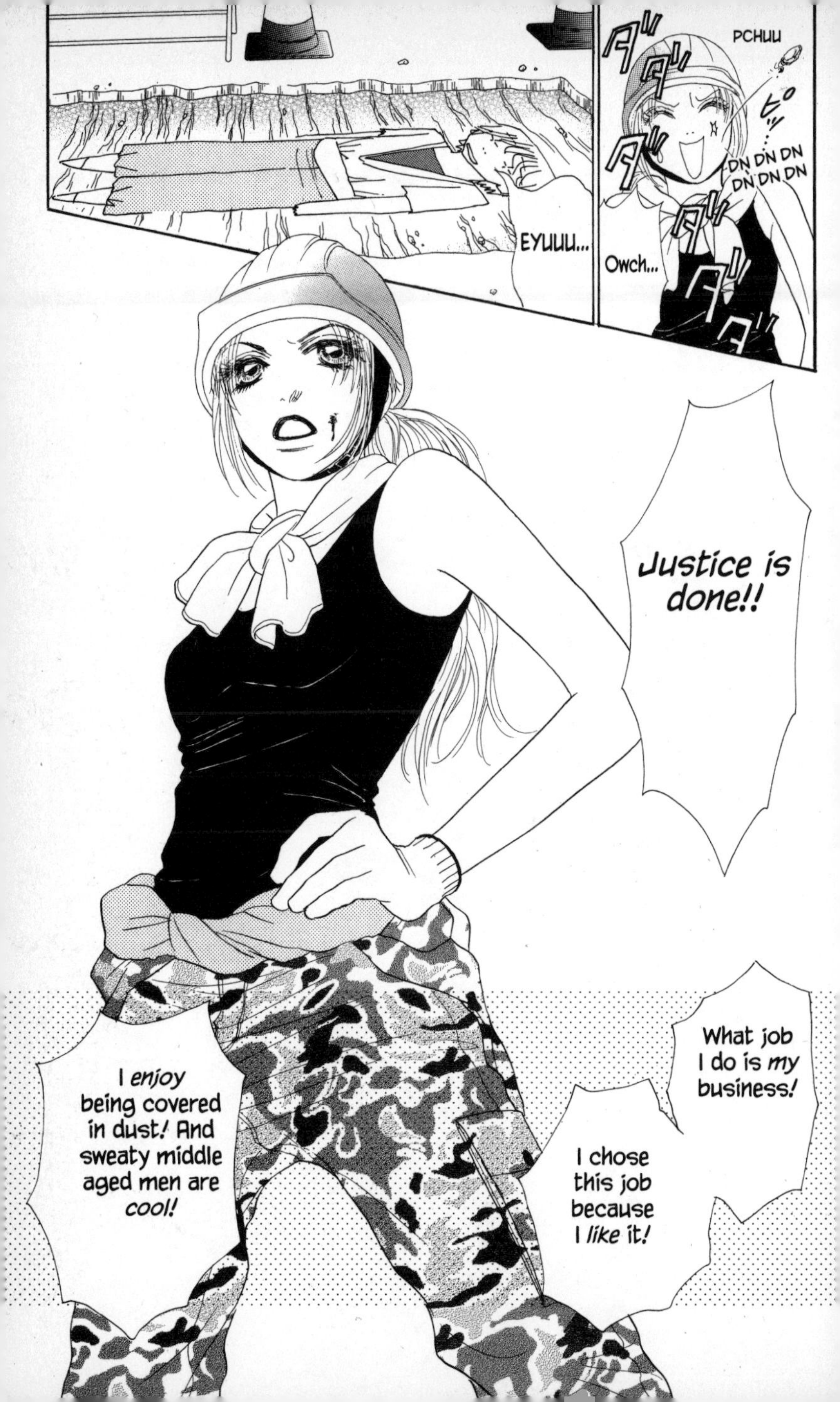
PCHUU
DN DN DN DN DN DN
Owch...
EYUUU...
Justice is done!!
What job I do is *my* business!
I chose this job because I *like* it!
I *enjoy* being covered in dust! And sweaty middle aged men are *cool*!

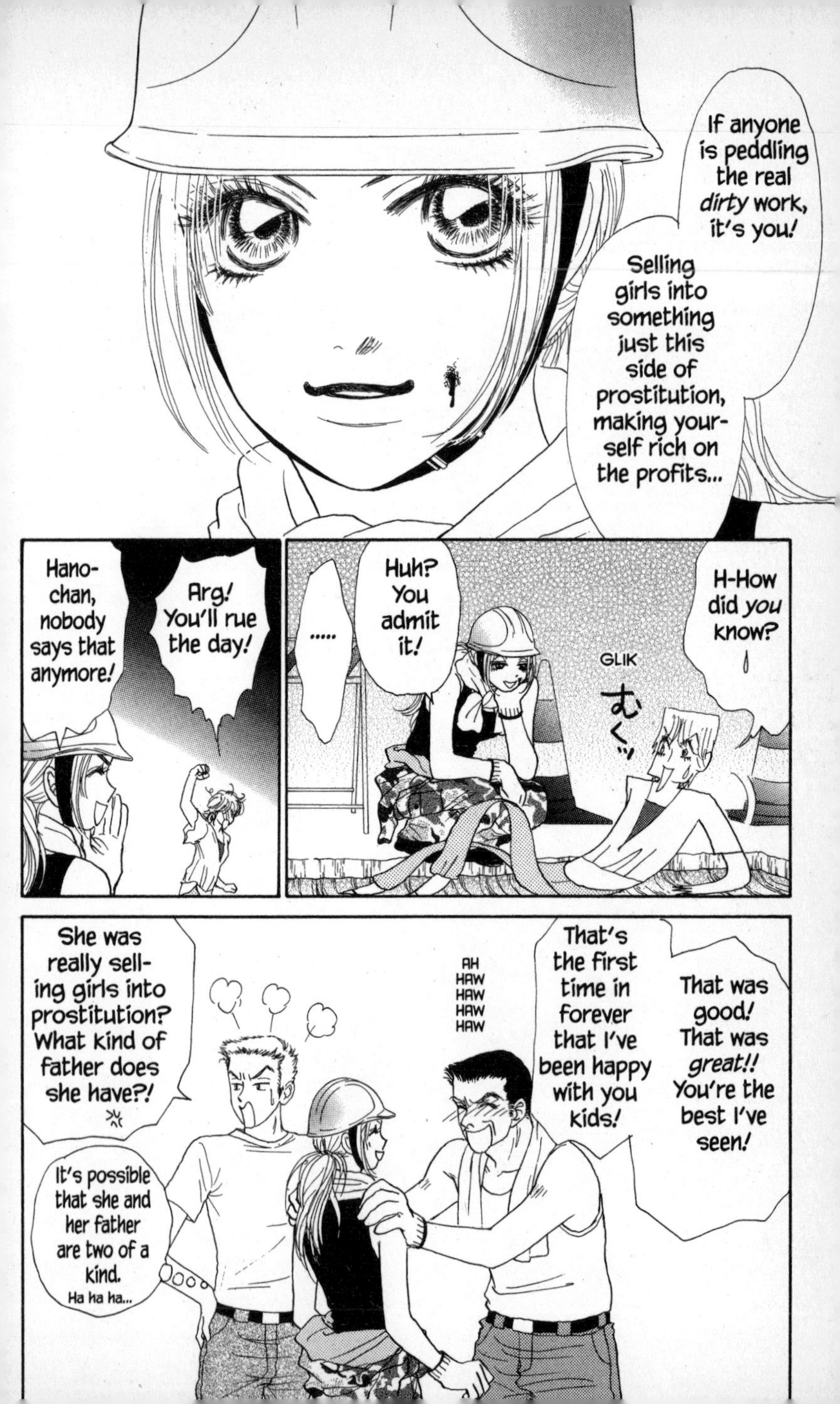
If anyone is peddling the real *dirty* work, it's you!
Selling girls into something just this side of prostitution, making your-self rich on the profits...
H-How did *you* know?
GLIK
むくッ
Huh? You admit it!
.....
Arg! You'll rue the day!
Hano-chan, nobody says that anymore!
That was good! That was *great!!* You're the best I've seen!
That's the first time in forever that I've been happy with you kids!
AH HAW HAW HAW HAW
She was really sell-ing girls into prostitution? What kind of father does she have?!
It's possible that she and her father are two of a kind.
Ha ha ha...

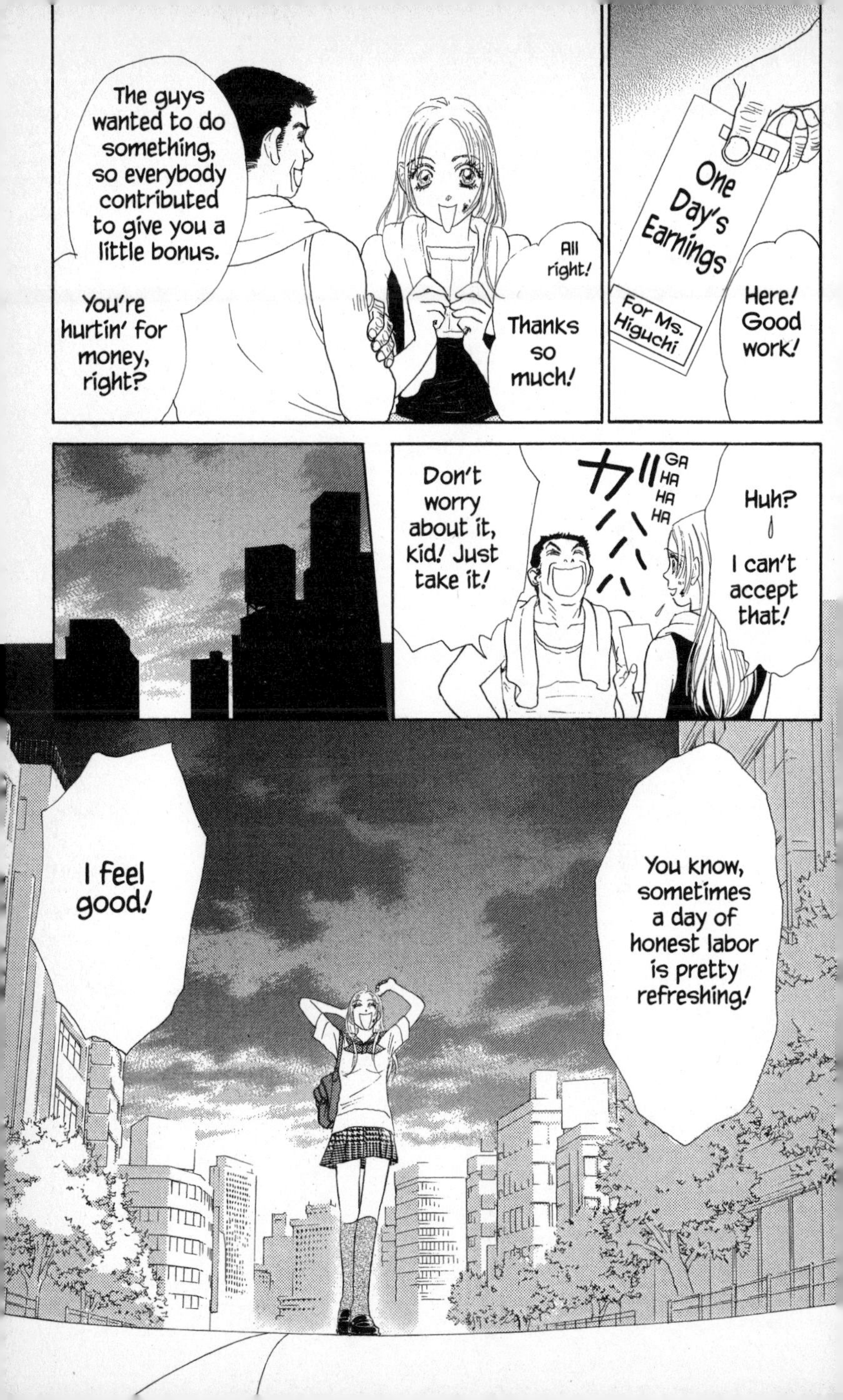
One Day's Earnings
For Ms. Higuchi
Here! Good work!
All right!
Thanks so much!
The guys wanted to do something, so everybody contributed to give you a little bonus.
You're hurtin' for money, right?
Huh?
I can't accept that!
GA HA HA HA
Don't worry about it, kid! Just take it!
You know, sometimes a day of honest labor is pretty refreshing!
I feel good!

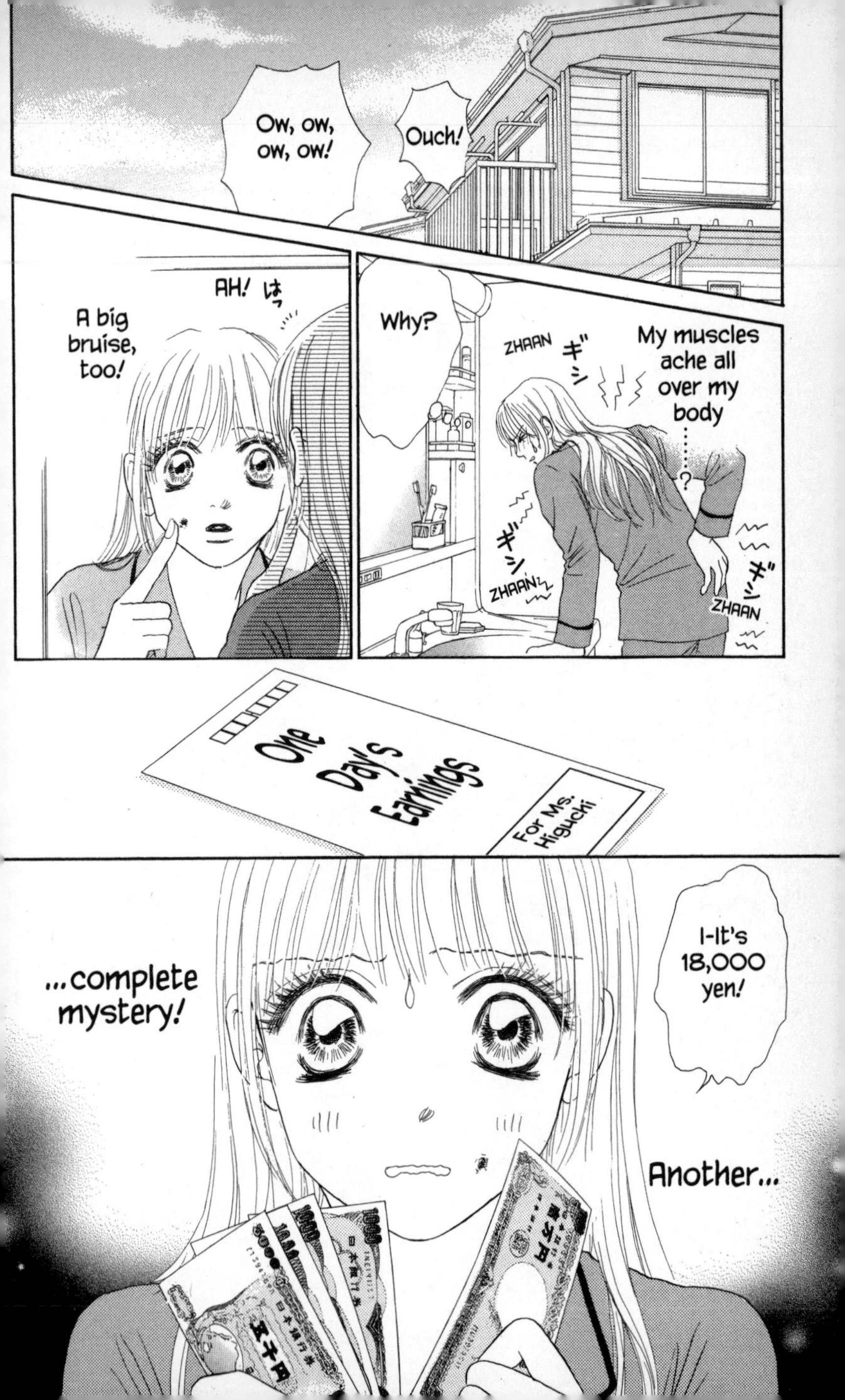
Ow, ow, ow, ow!
Ouch!
Why?
My muscles ache all over my body......?
ZHAAN
ギシ
ZHAAN
ギシ
ZHAAN
ギシ
AH! はっ
A big bruise, too!
One Day's Earnings
For Ms. Higuchi
I-It's 18,000 yen!
Another...
...complete mystery!

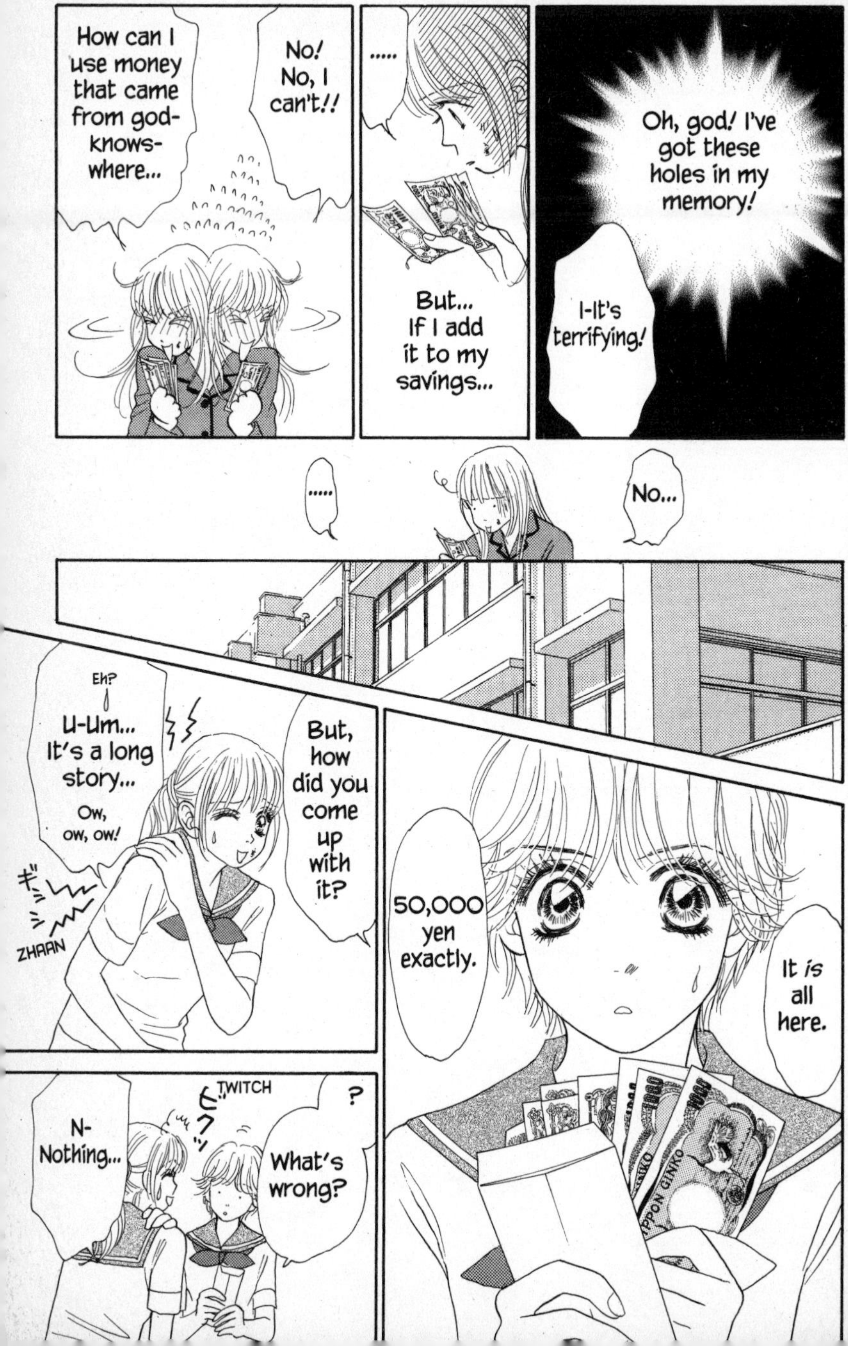

How can I use money that came from god-knows-where...
No! No, I can't!!
.....
But... If I add it to my savings...
Oh, god! I've got these holes in my memory!
I-It's terrifying!
.....
No...
50,000 yen exactly.
It *is* all here.
But, how did you come up with it?
U-Um... It's a long story...
Eh?
Ow, ow, ow!
ZHAAN
?
What's wrong?
TWITCH
N-Nothing...

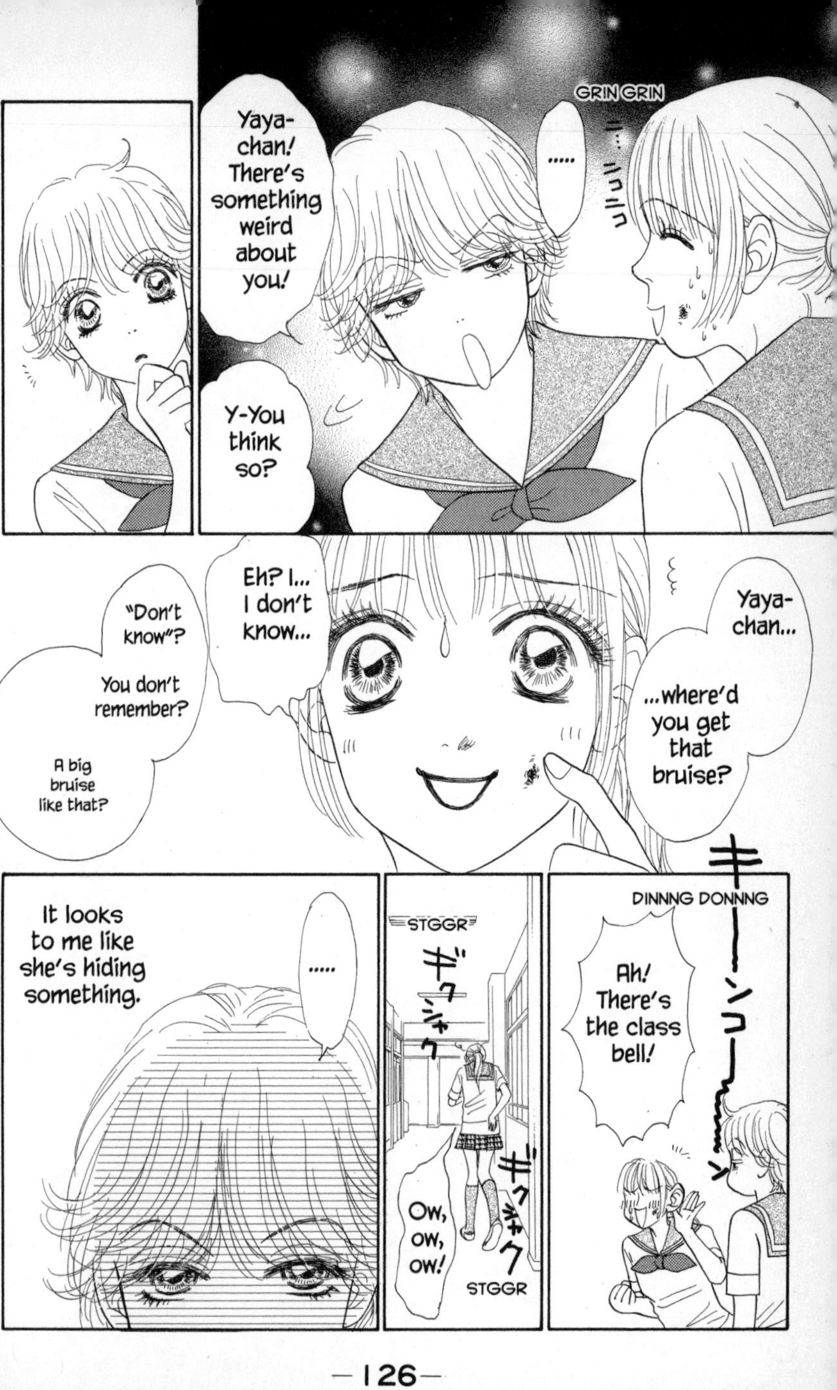
GRIN GRIN
.....
Yaya-chan! There's something weird about you!
Y-You think so?
Yaya-chan...
...where'd you get that bruise?
Eh? I... I don't know...
"Don't know"?
You don't remember?
A big bruise like that?
DINNNG DONNNG
Ah! There's the class bell!
STGGR
ギクシャク
Ow, ow, ow!
STGGR
.....
It looks to me like she's hiding something.

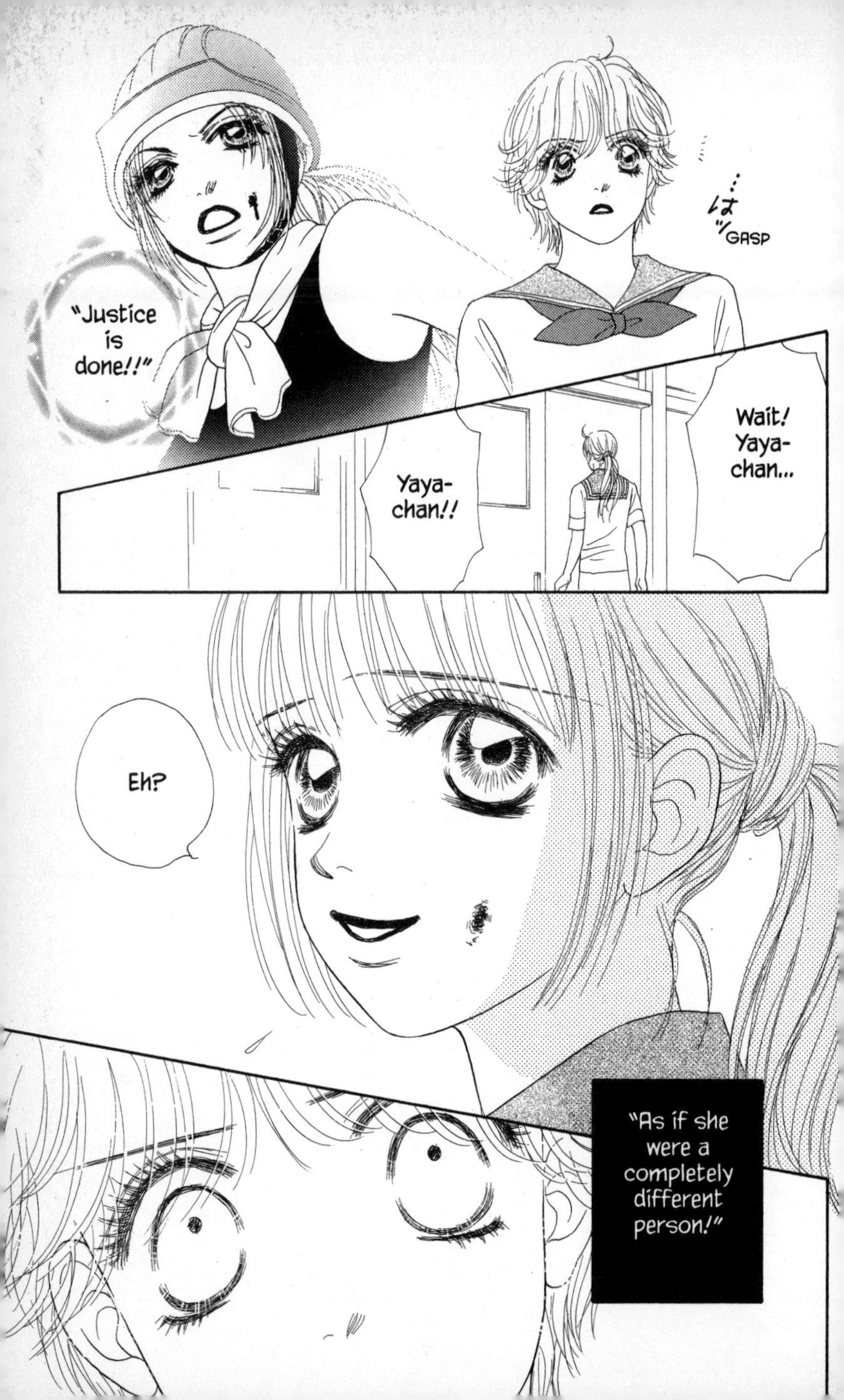

…はッ
GASP
"Justice is done!!"
Wait! Yaya-chan...
Yaya-chan!!
Eh?
"As if she were a completely different person!"

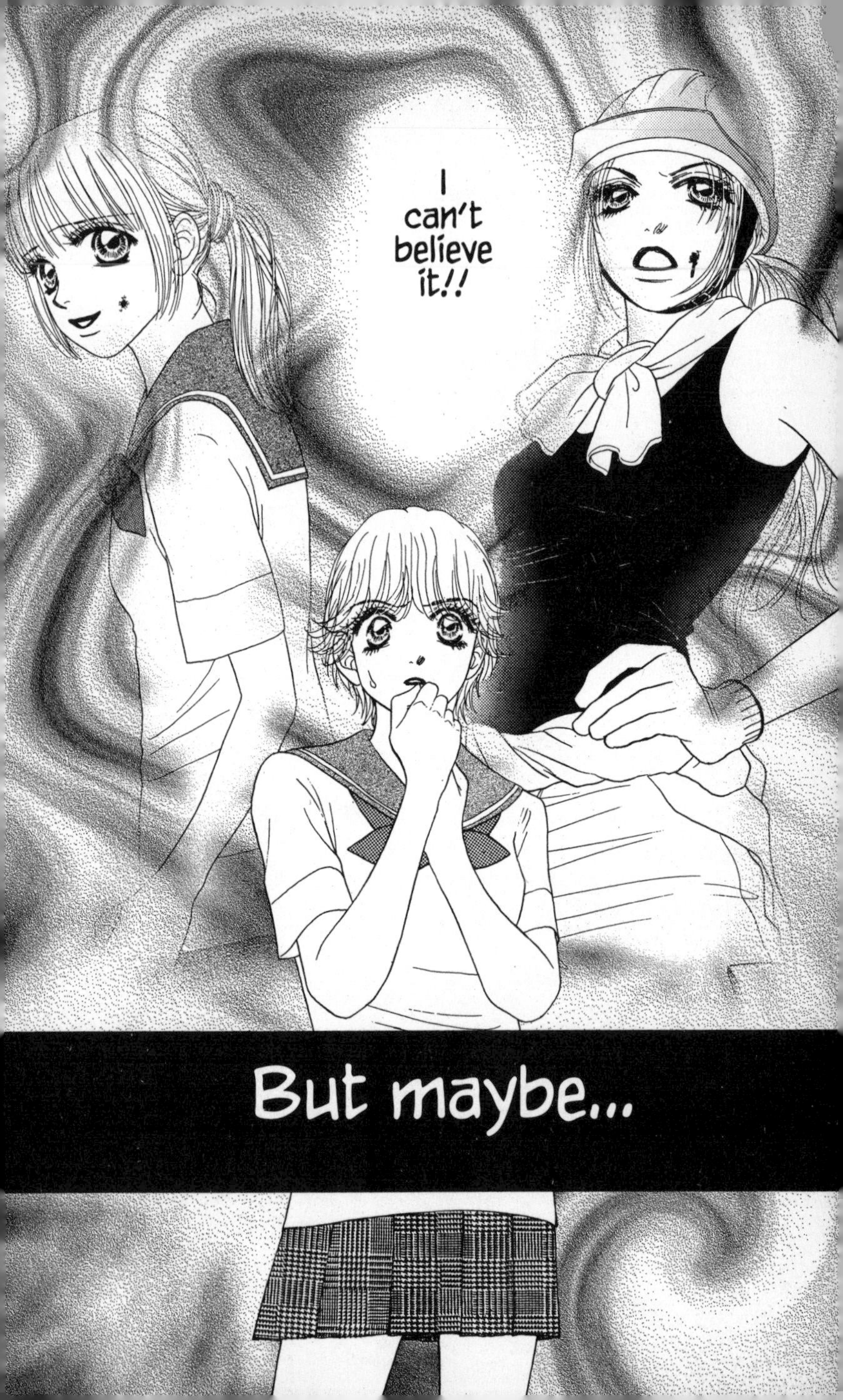
I can't believe it!!
But maybe...

Chapter 16
The Confrontation

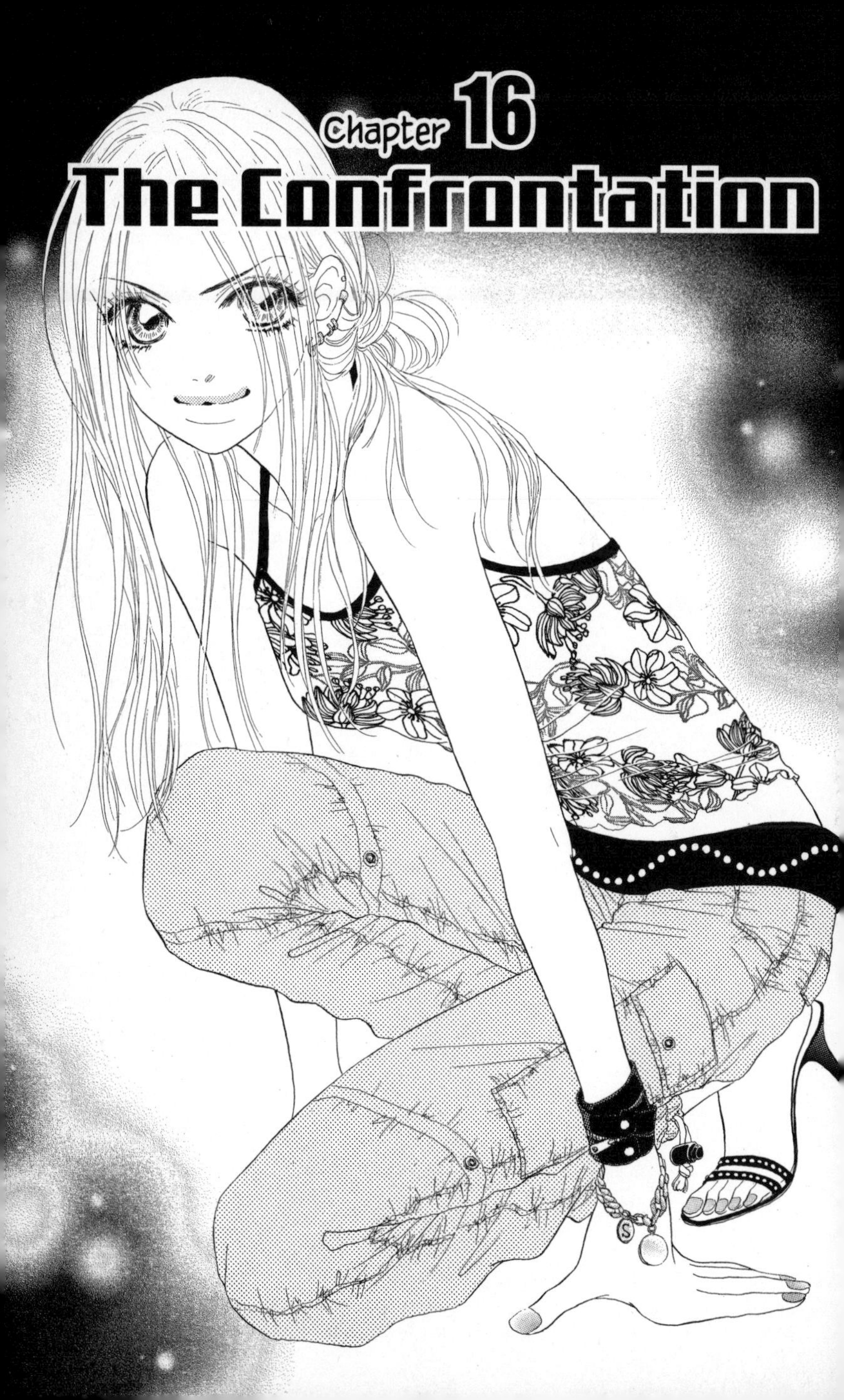

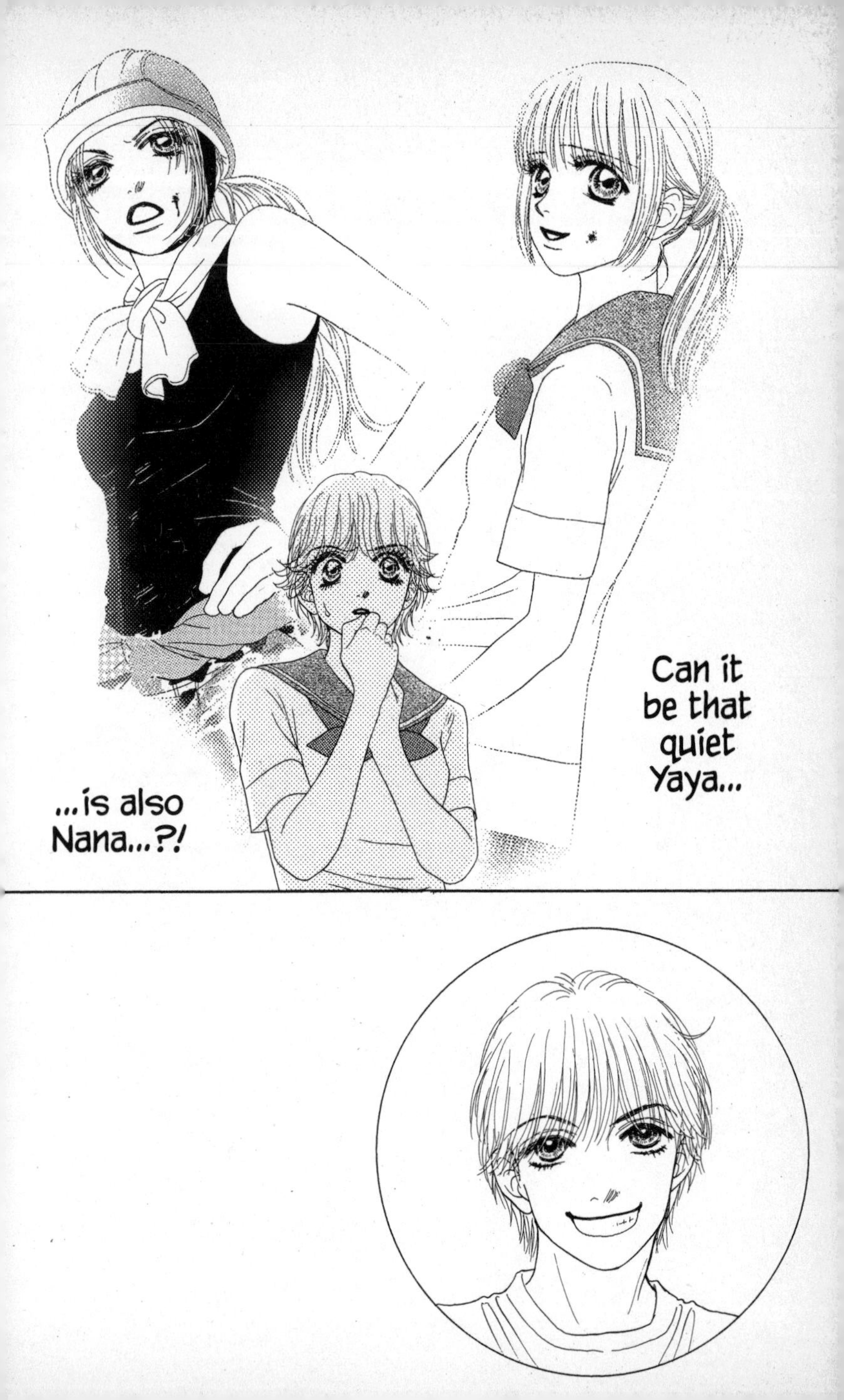
Can it be that quiet Yaya...
...is also Nana...?!

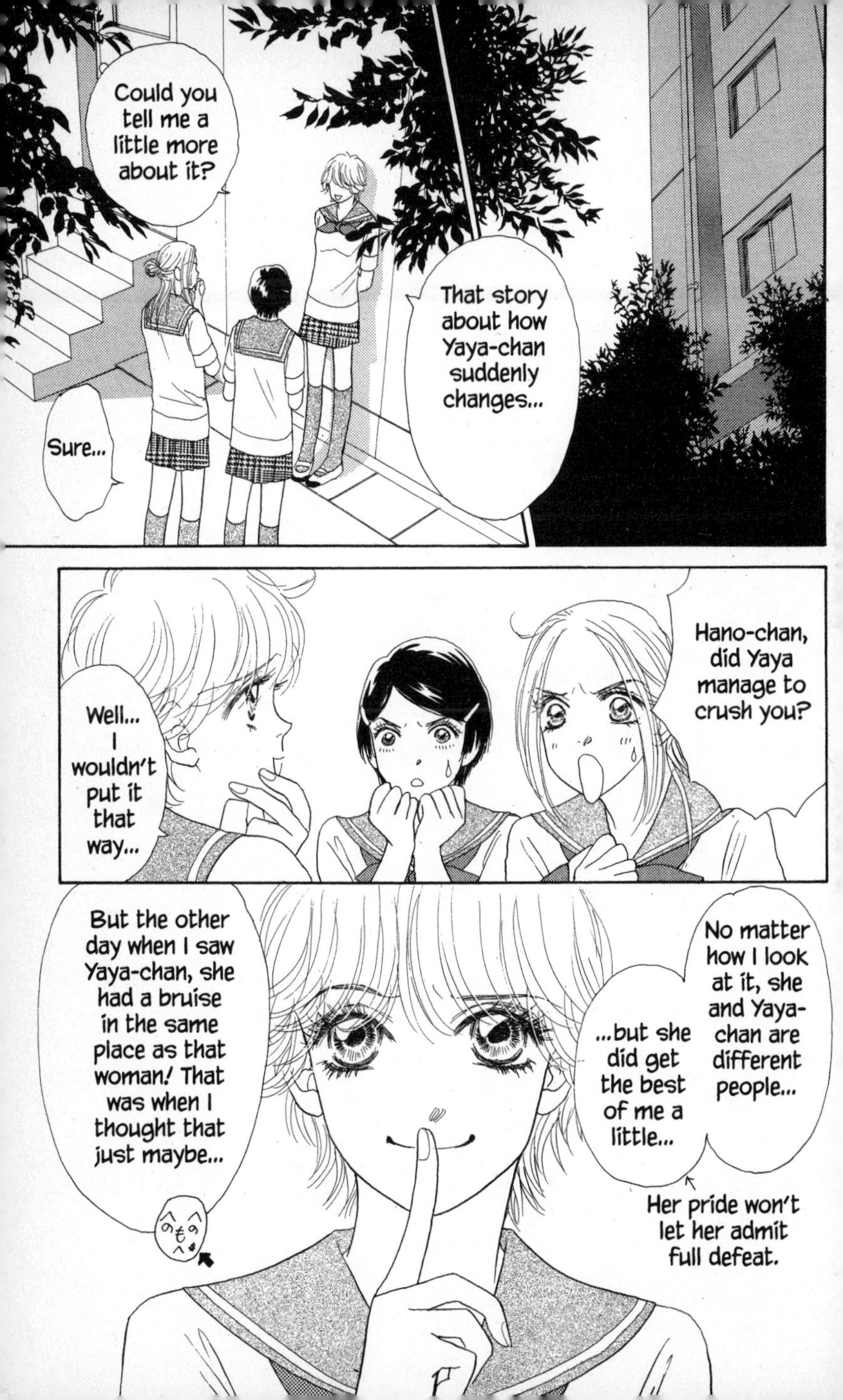
Could you tell me a little more about it?
That story about how Yaya-chan suddenly changes...
Sure...
Hano-chan, did Yaya manage to crush you?
Well... I wouldn't put it that way...
No matter how I look at it, she and Yaya-chan are different people...
...but she did get the best of me a little...
Her pride won't let her admit full defeat.
But the other day when I saw Yaya-chan, she had a bruise in the same place as that woman! That was when I thought that just maybe...

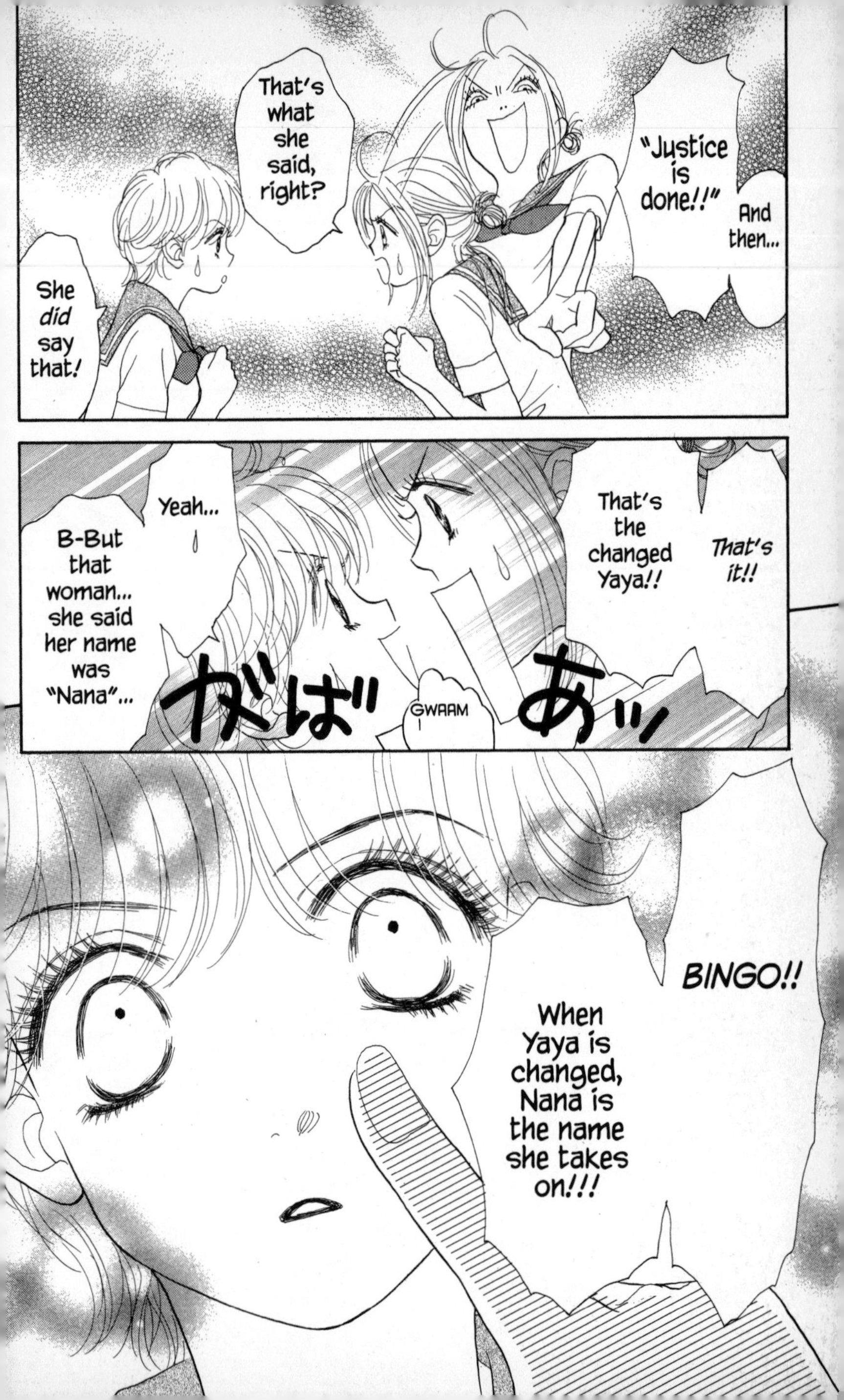
"Justice is done!!"
And then...
That's what she said, right?
She *did* say that!
That's it!!
That's the changed Yaya!!
Yeah...
B-But that woman... she said her name was "Nana"...
GWAAM
BINGO!!
When Yaya is changed, Nana is the name she takes on!!!

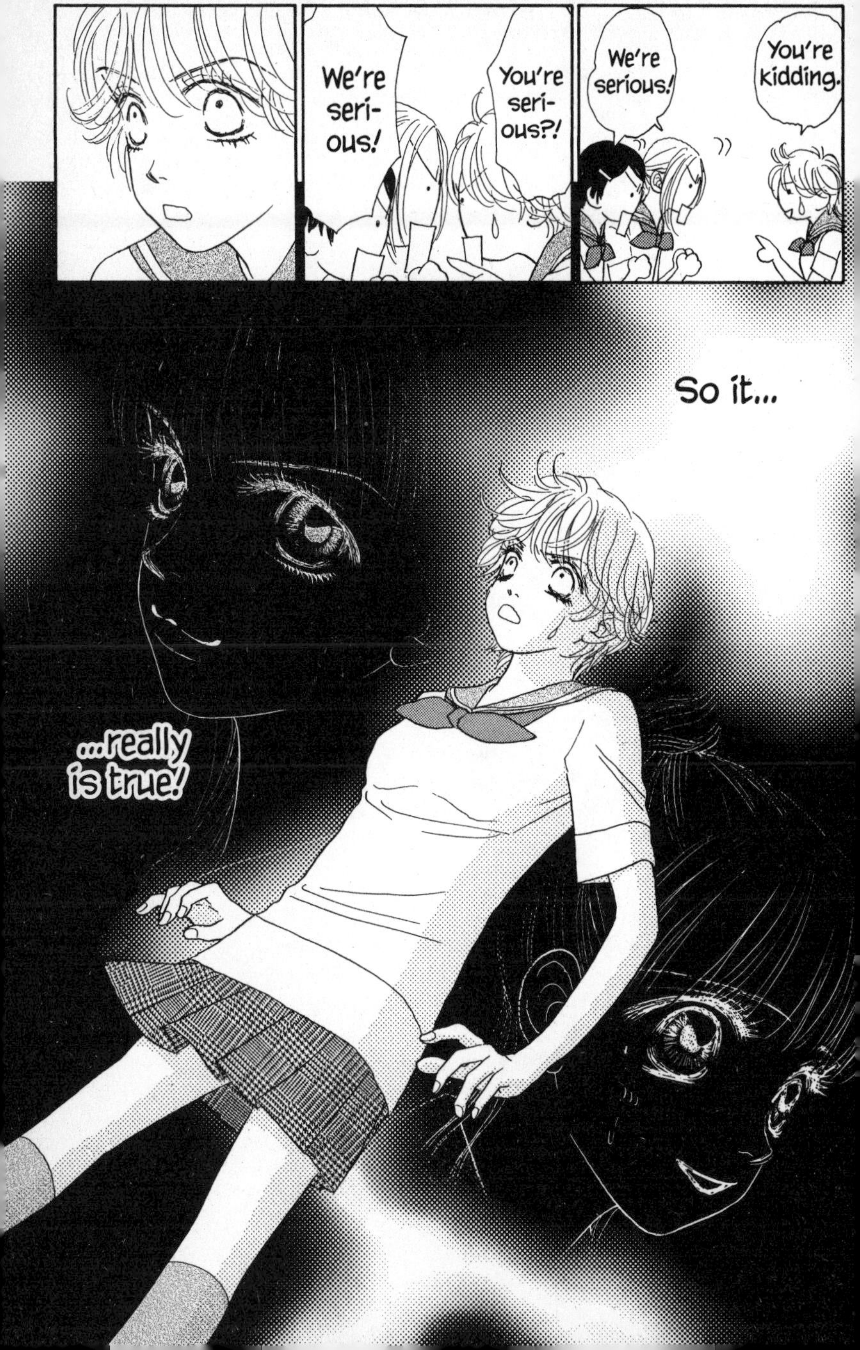
You're kidding.
We're serious!
You're seri-ous?!
We're seri-ous!
So it...
...really is true!

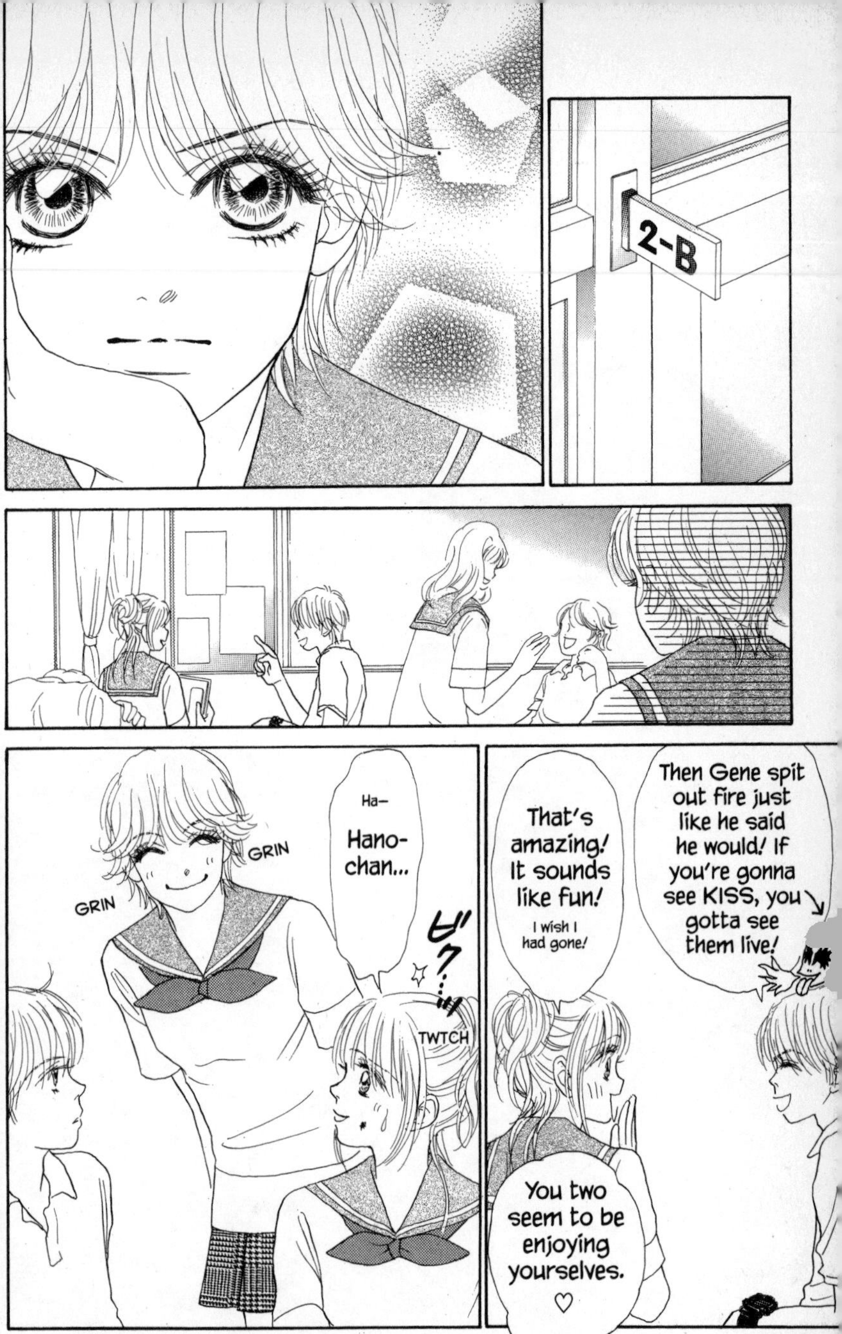
2-B
Then Gene spit out fire just like he said he would! If you're gonna see KISS, you gotta see them live!
That's amazing! It sounds like fun!
I wish I had gone!
You two seem to be enjoying yourselves. ♡
GRIN
GRIN
Ha– Hano-chan...
ビク
TWTCH

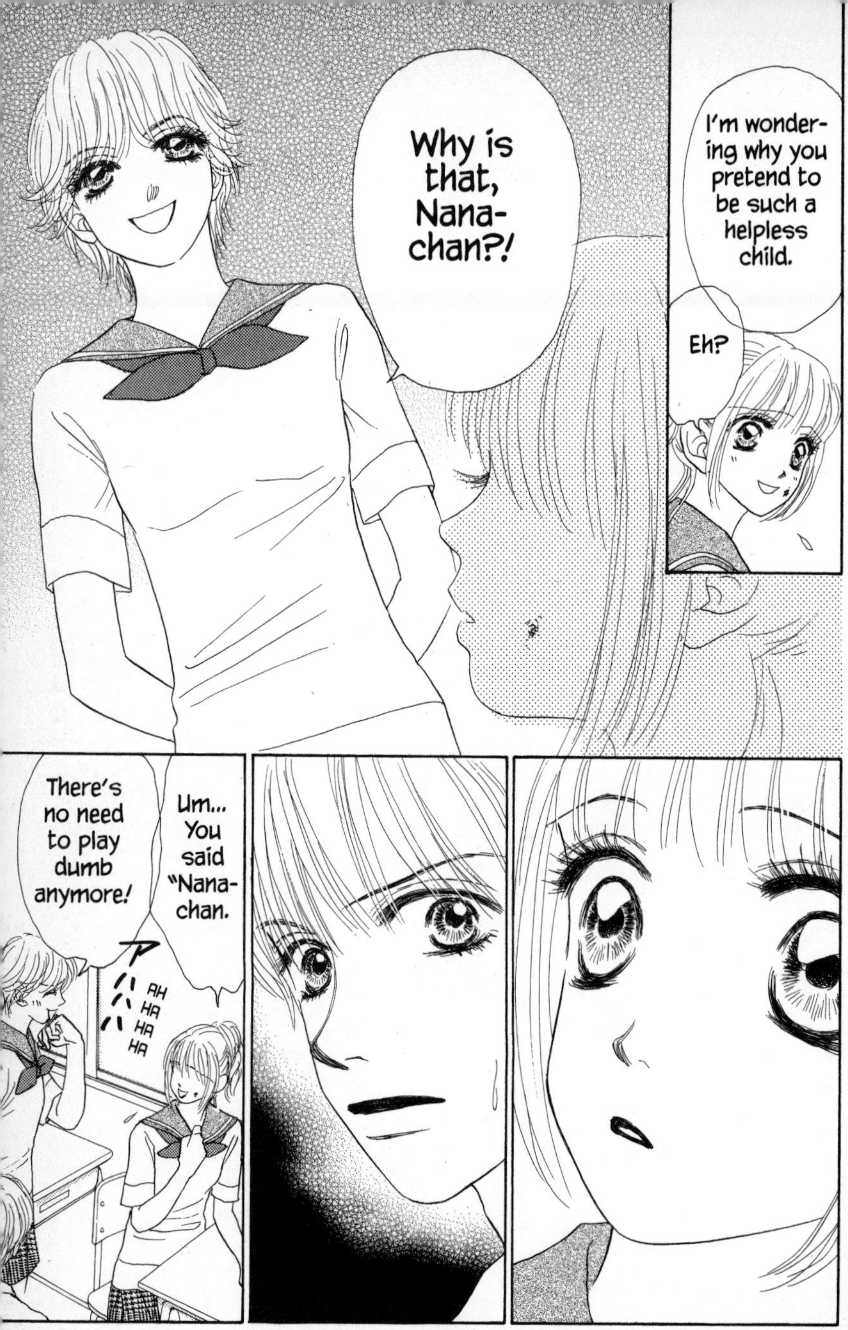

I'm wondering why you pretend to be such a helpless child.
Eh?
Why is that, Nana-chan?!
Um... You said "Nana-chan.
There's no need to play dumb anymore!
AH HA HA HA

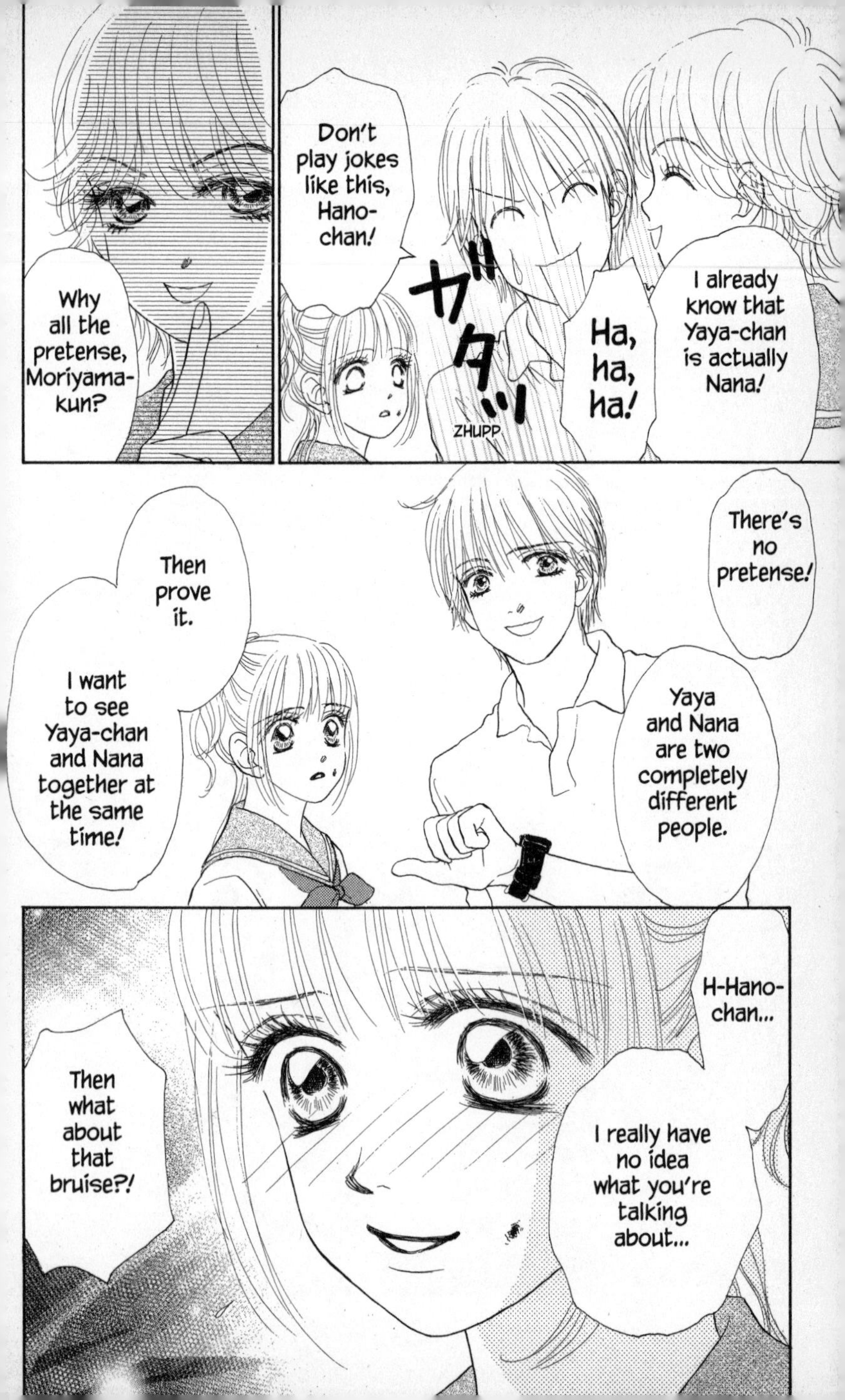
I already know that Yaya-chan is actually Nana!
Ha, ha, ha!
ZHUPP
Don't play jokes like this, Hano-chan!
Why all the pretense, Moriyama-kun?
There's no pretense!
Yaya and Nana are two completely different people.
Then prove it.
I want to see Yaya-chan and Nana together at the same time!
H-Hano-chan...
I really have no idea what you're talking about...
Then what about that bruise?!

Are you *still* trying to play dumb?!

Construction... site?

That's the exact same bruise that Nana got when we faced off at the construction site!

Let's go.

She doesn't know what she's talking about.

Don't let it bother you.

Wait there one minute!

Wait!!

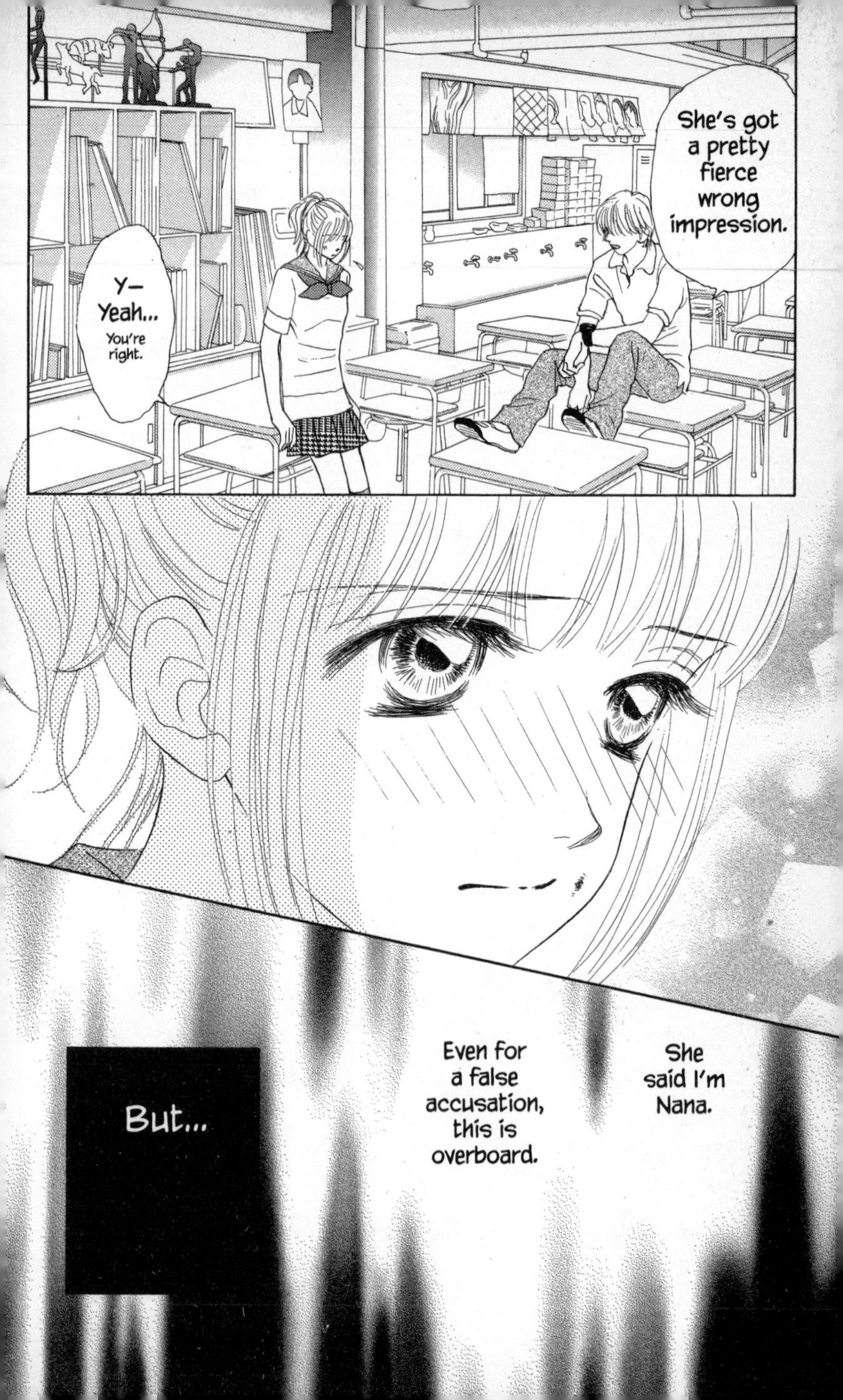
She's got a pretty fierce wrong impression.
Y— Yeah... You're right.
She said I'm Nana.
Even for a false accusation, this is overboard.
But...

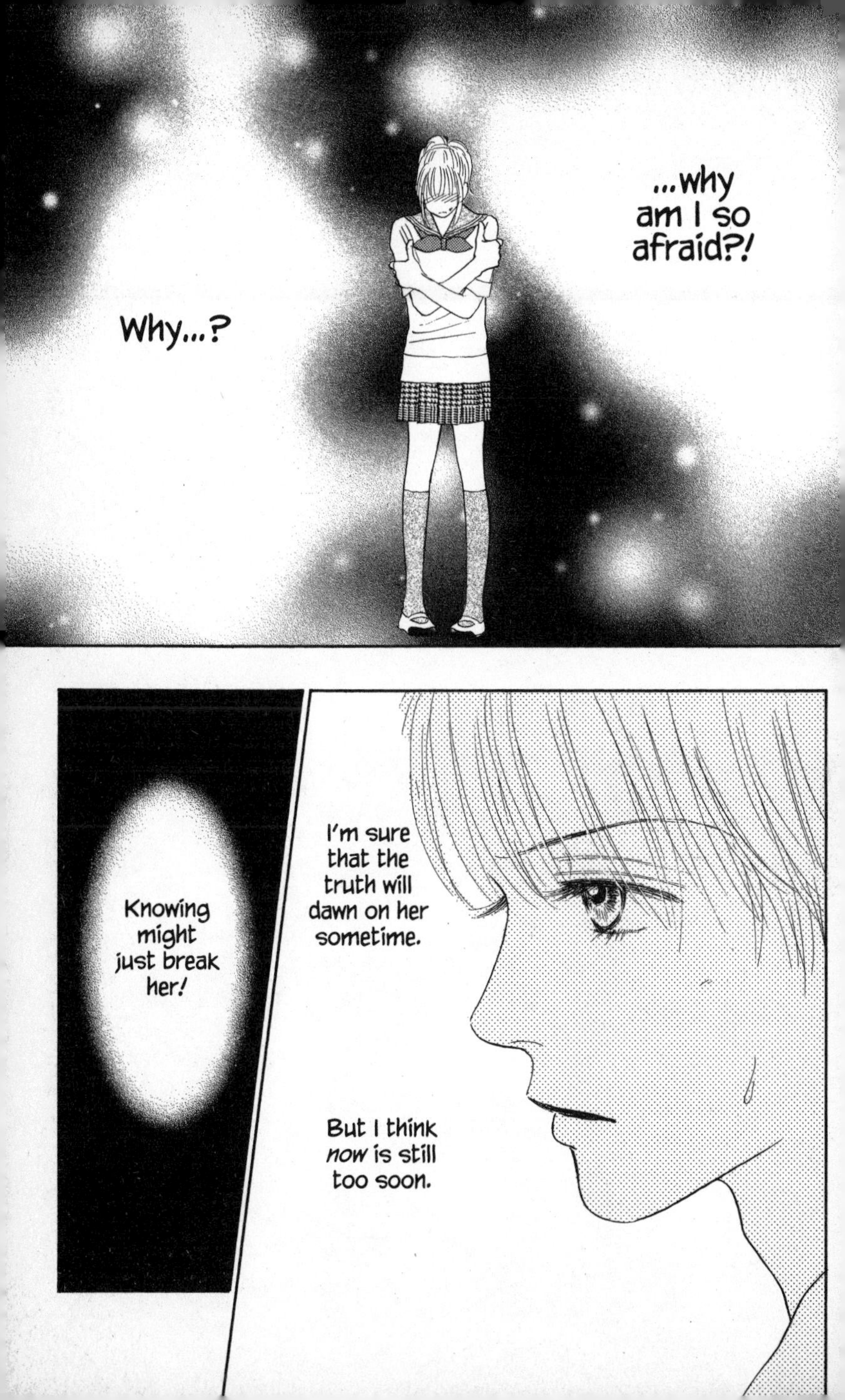
Why...?
...why am I so afraid?!
I'm sure that the truth will dawn on her sometime.
But I think *now* is still too soon.
Knowing might just break her!

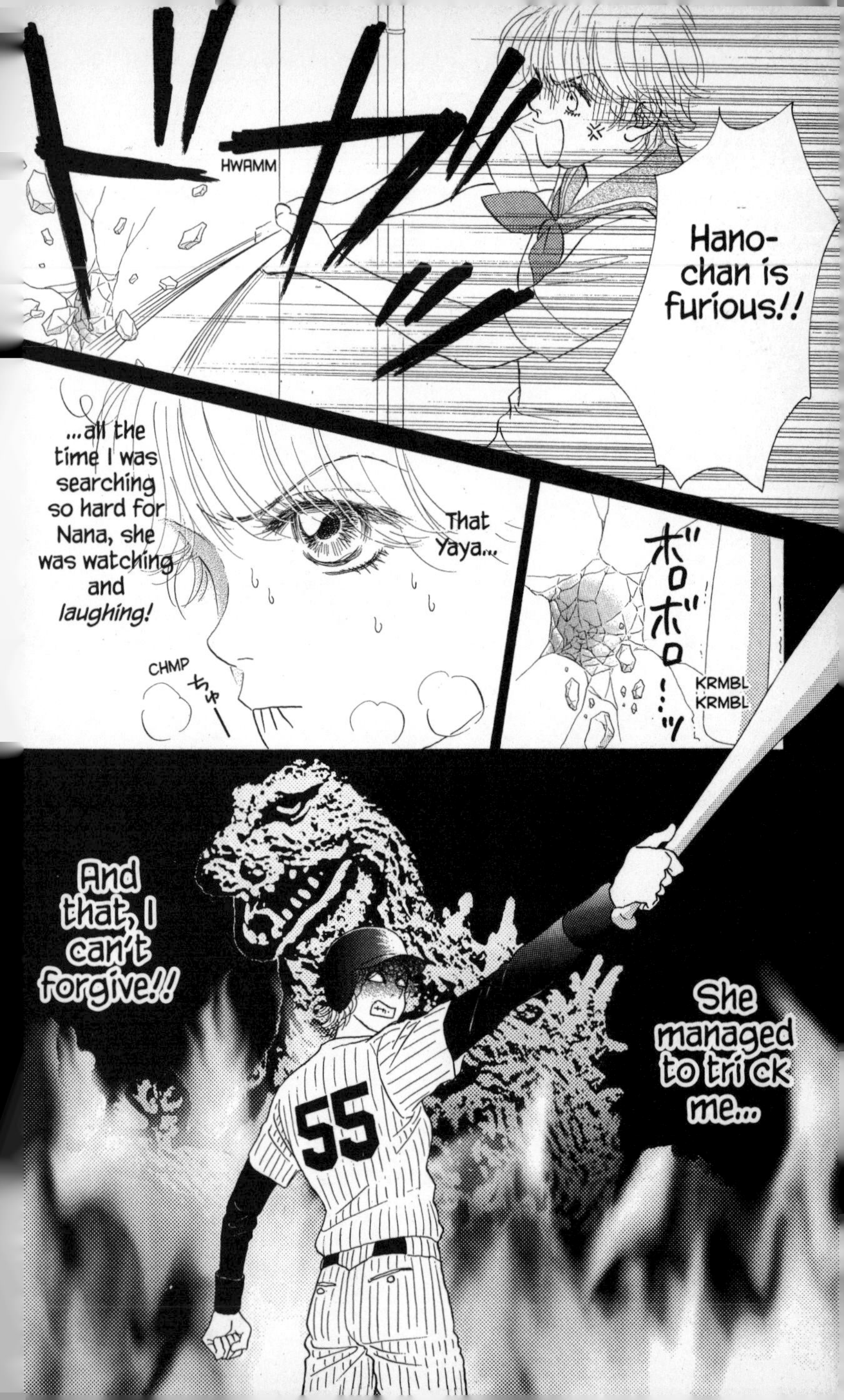
HWAMM
Hano-chan is furious!!
ボロボロ…ッ
KRMBL KRMBL
That Yaya...
...all the time I was searching so hard for Nana, she was watching and *laughing!*
CHMP
ちゅー
She managed to tri ck me...
And that, I can't forgive!!

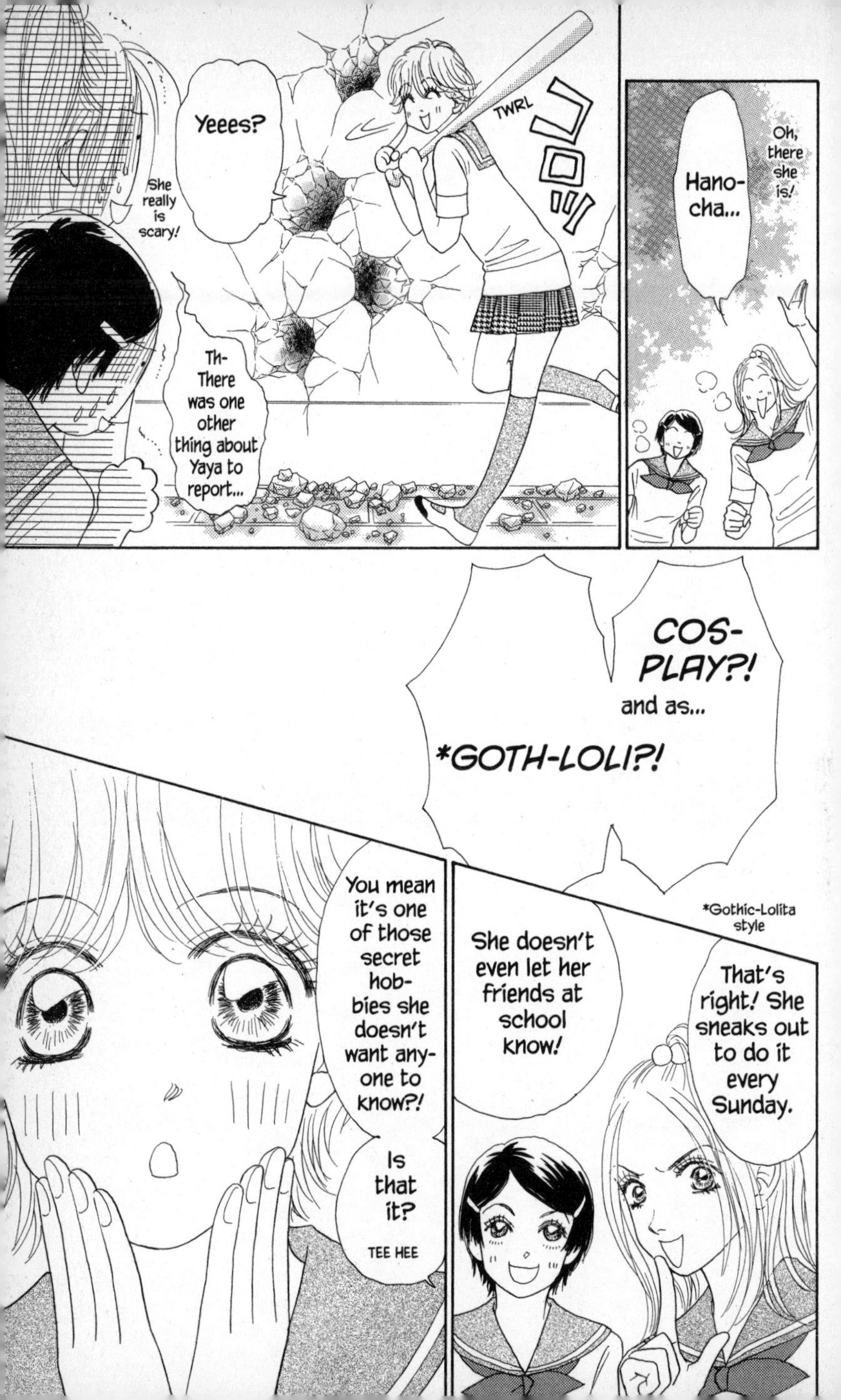

Oh, there she is!
Hano-cha...
TWRL
Yeees?
She really is scary!
Th- There was one other thing about Yaya to report...
COS-PLAY?!
and as...
*GOTH-LOLI?!
*Gothic-Lolita style
That's right! She sneaks out to do it every Sunday.
She doesn't even let her friends at school know!
You mean it's one of those secret hob-bies she doesn't want any-one to know?!
Is that it?
TEE HEE

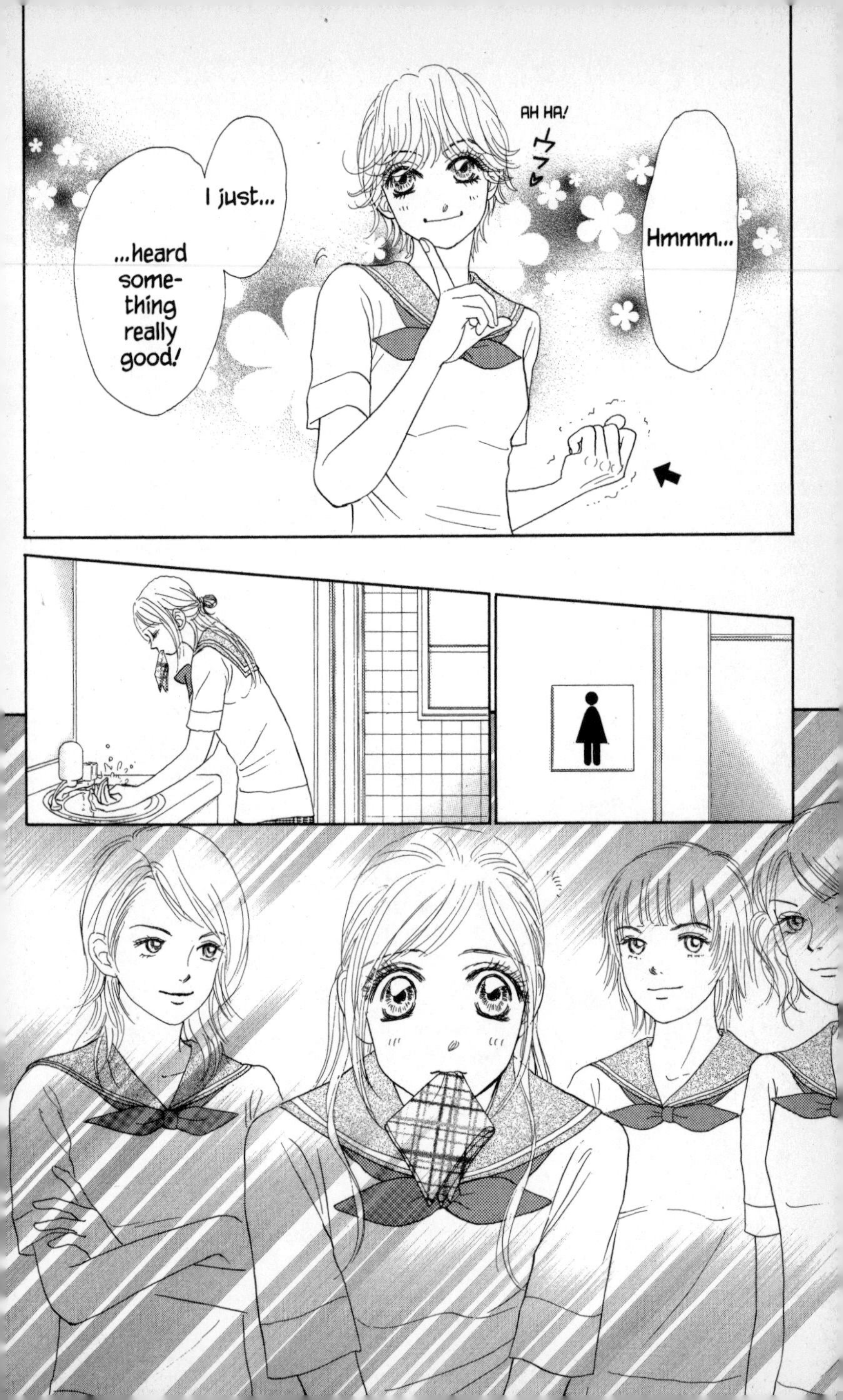

Hmmm...
AH HA!
ウフ♡
I just...
...heard something really good!

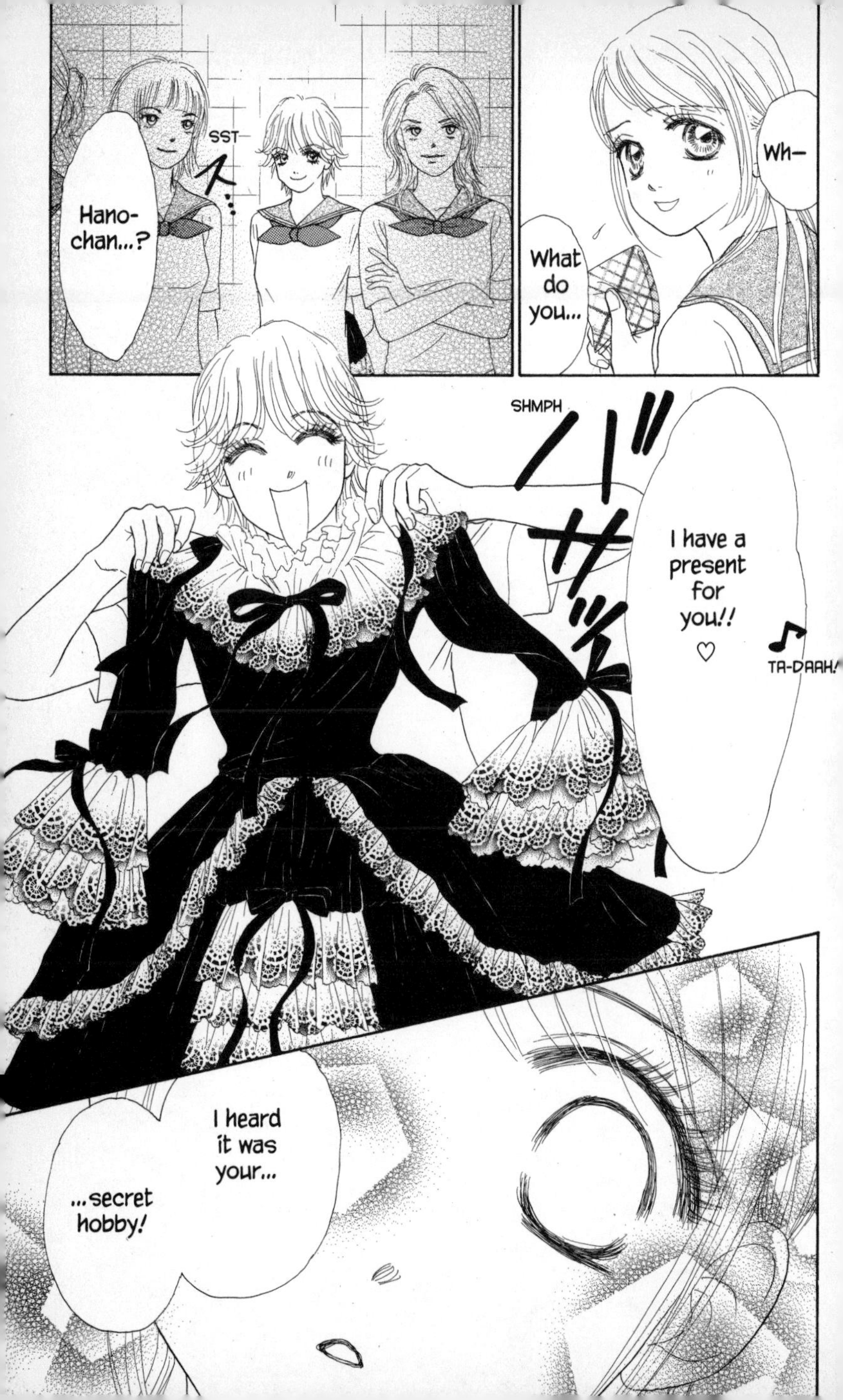
Wh—
What do you...
SST
Hano-chan...?
SHMPH
I have a present for you!! ♡
TA-DAAH!
I heard it was your...
...secret hobby!

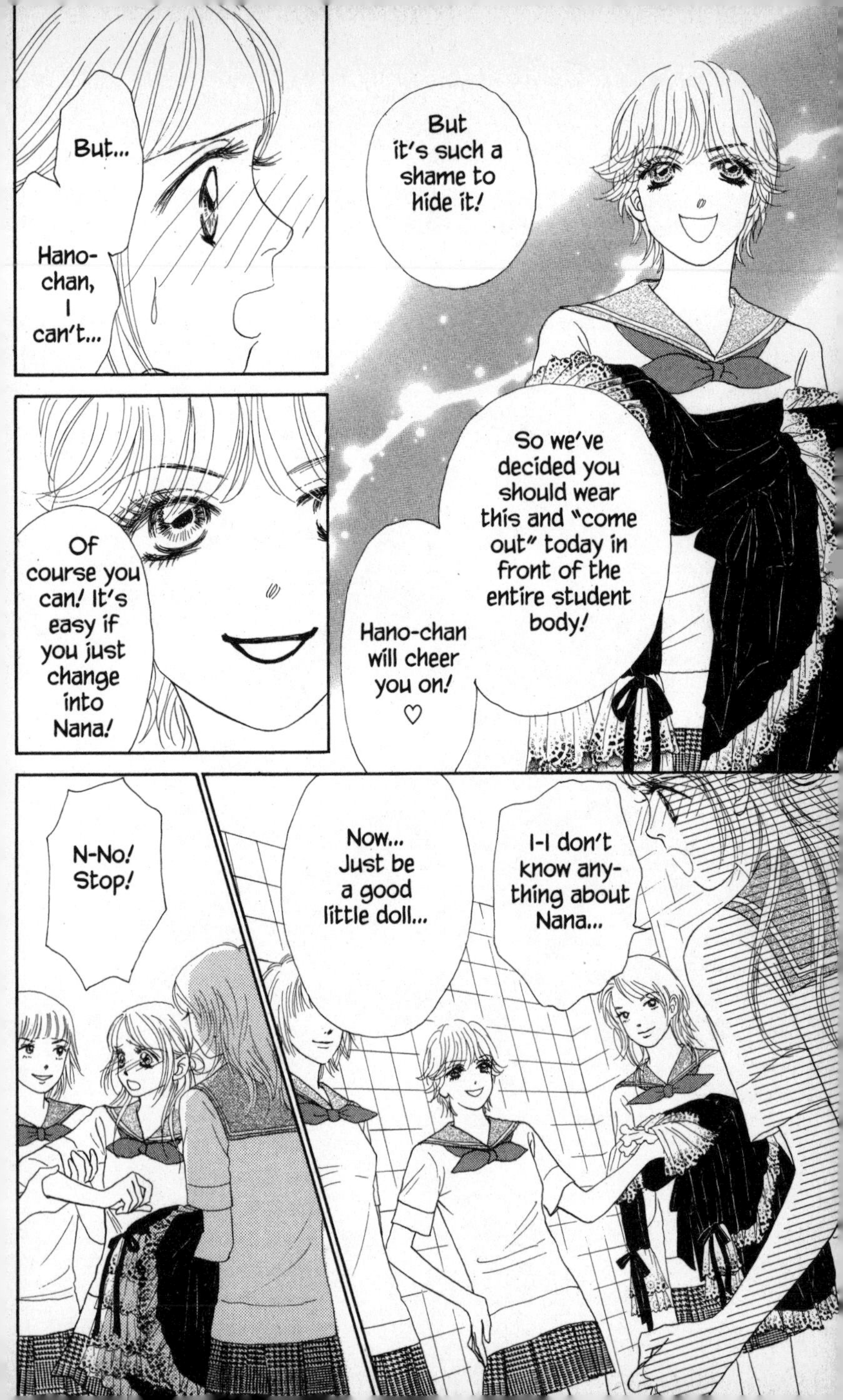
But it's such a shame to hide it!
So we've decided you should wear this and "come out" today in front of the entire student body!
Hano-chan will cheer you on! ♡
But...
Hano-chan, I can't...
Of course you can! It's easy if you just change into Nana!
I-I don't know anything about Nana...
Now... Just be a good little doll...
N-No! Stop!

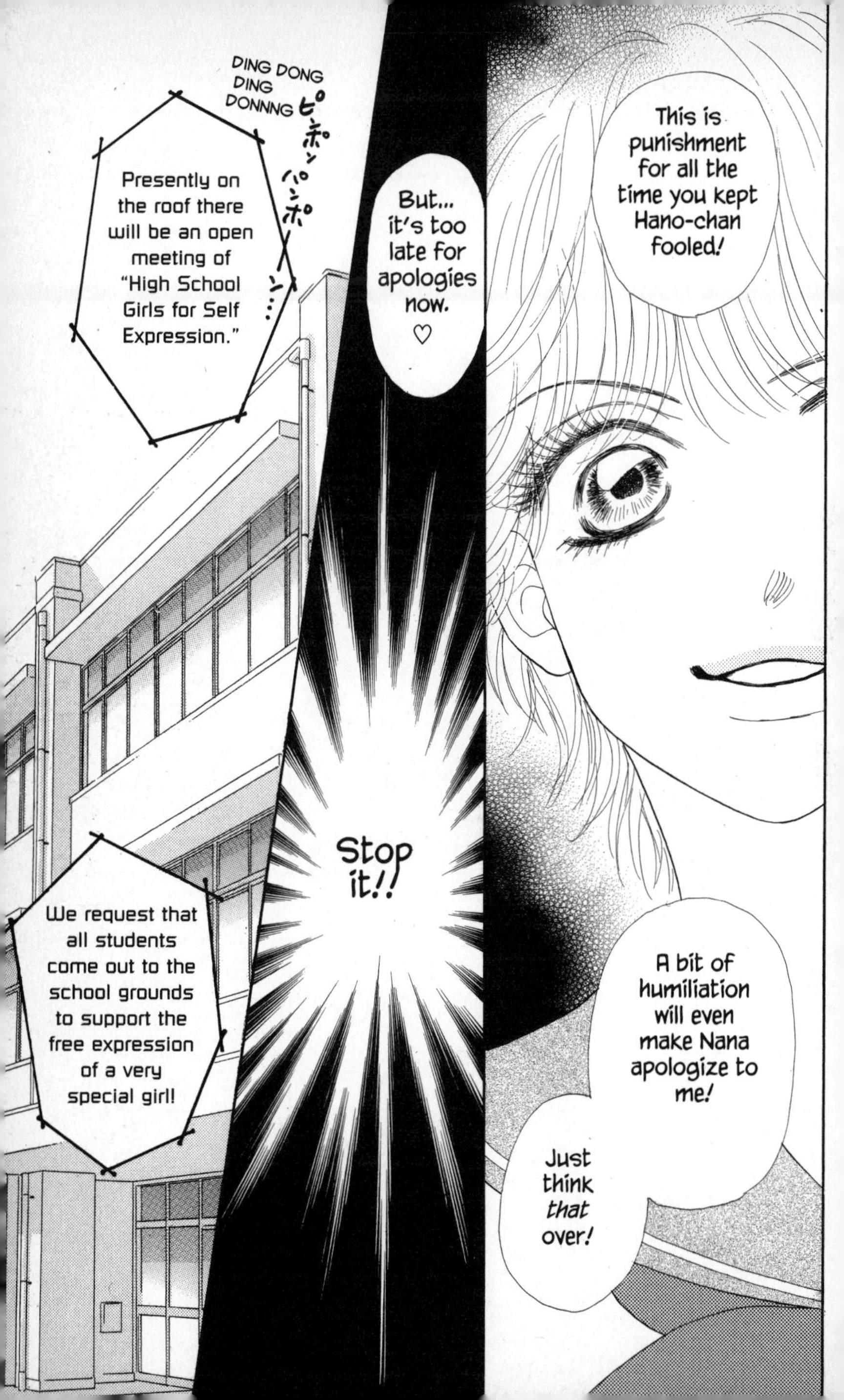
This is punishment for all the time you kept Hano-chan fooled!
A bit of humiliation will even make Nana apologize to me!
Just think *that* over!
But... it's too late for apologies now. ♡
Stop it!!
DING DONG DING DONNNG
Presently on the roof there will be an open meeting of "High School Girls for Self Expression."
We request that all students come out to the school grounds to support the free expression of a very special girl!

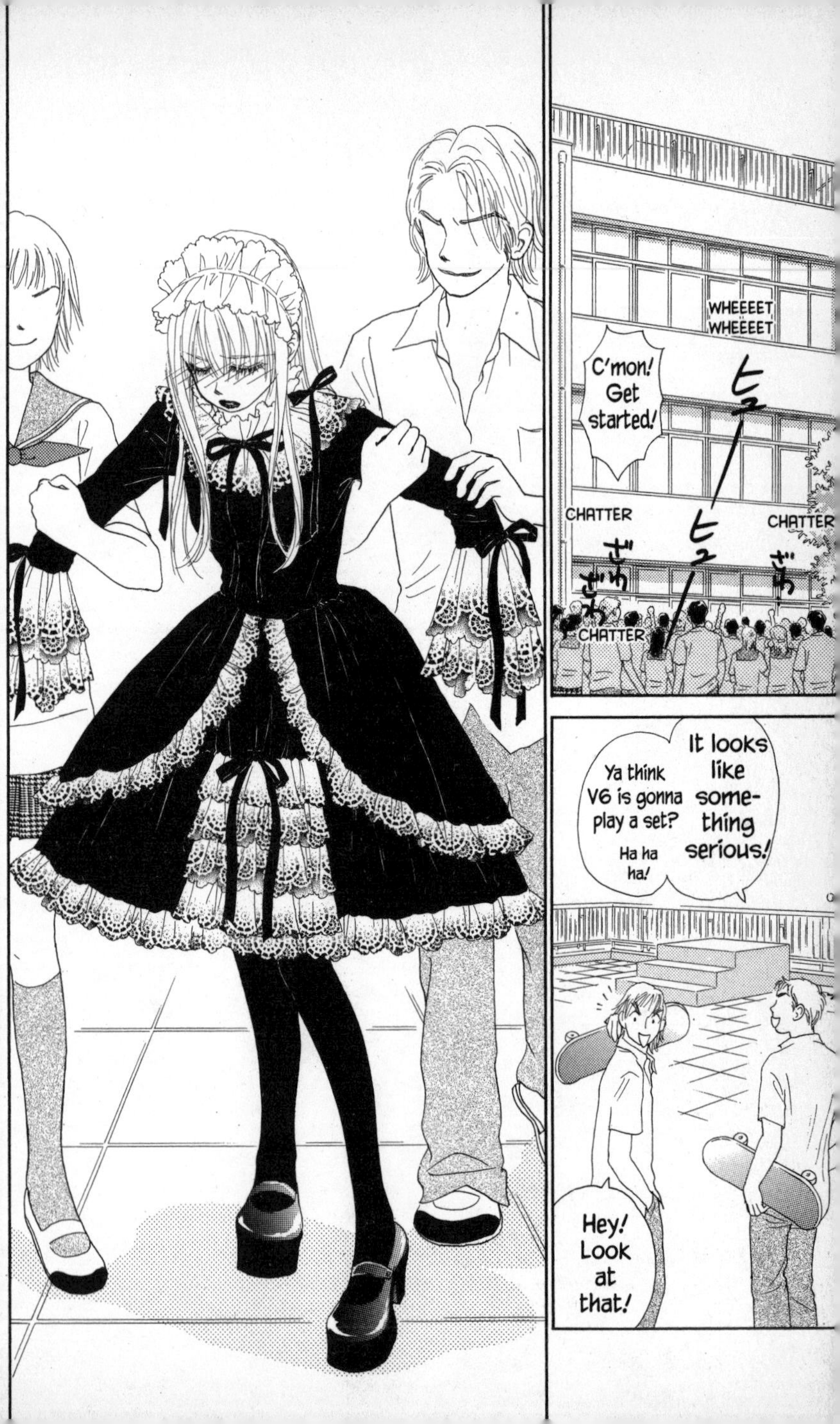
WHEEEET
WHEEEET
C'mon! Get started!
ヒュ
ヒュ
CHATTER
ざわ
CHATTER
ざわ
ざわ
CHATTER
It looks like some-thing serious!
Ya think V6 is gonna play a set?
Ha ha ha!
Hey! Look at that!

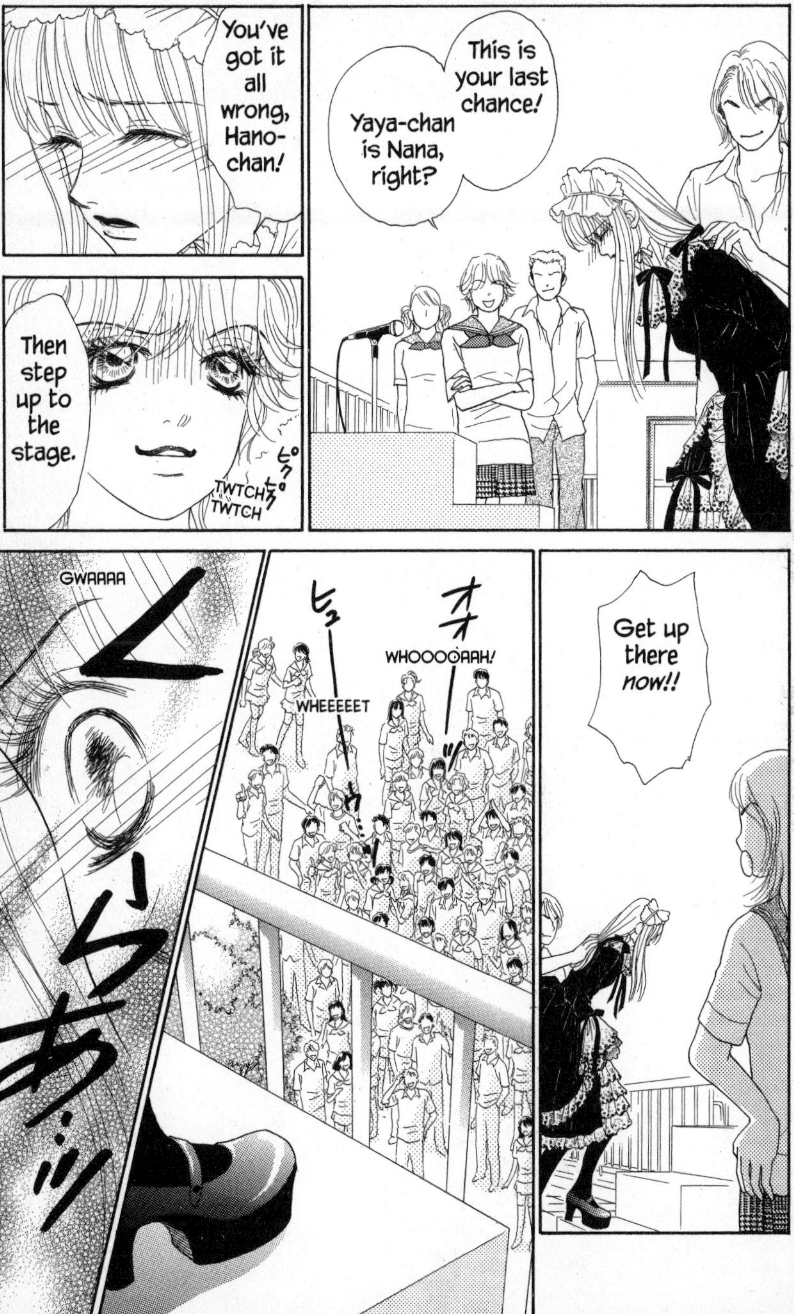
This is your last chance!
Yaya-chan is Nana, right?
You've got it all wrong, Hano-chan!
Then step up to the stage.
TWTCH TWTCH
Get up there now!!
WHOOOOAAH!
WHEEEEET
GWAAAA

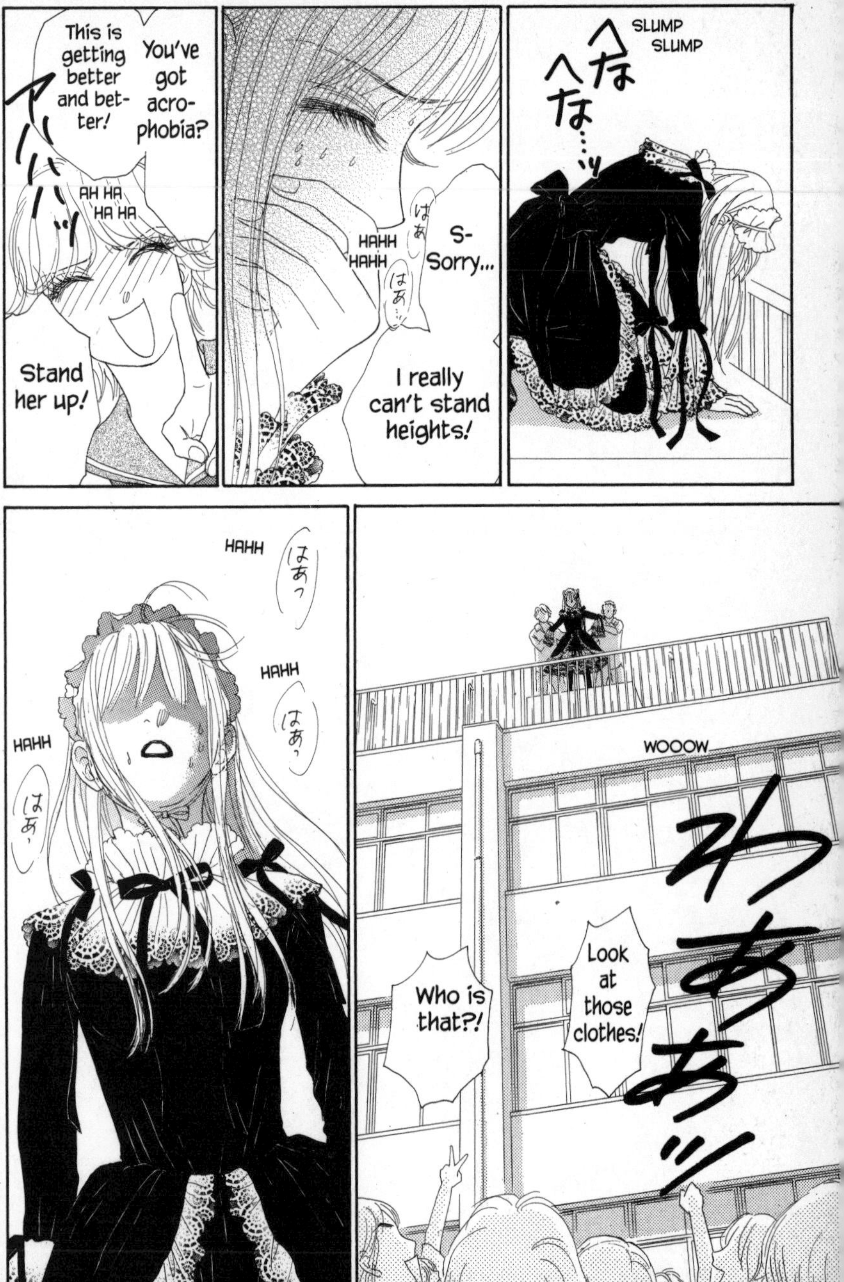
へなへな…ッ
SLUMP SLUMP
S-Sorry...
はあ はあ…
HAHH HAHH
I really can't stand heights!
You've got acrophobia?
This is getting better and better!
アハハハッ
AH HA HA HA
Stand her up!
わあああッ
WOOOW
Look at those clothes!
Who is that?!
はあっ
HAHH
はあっ
HAHH
はあ
HAHH

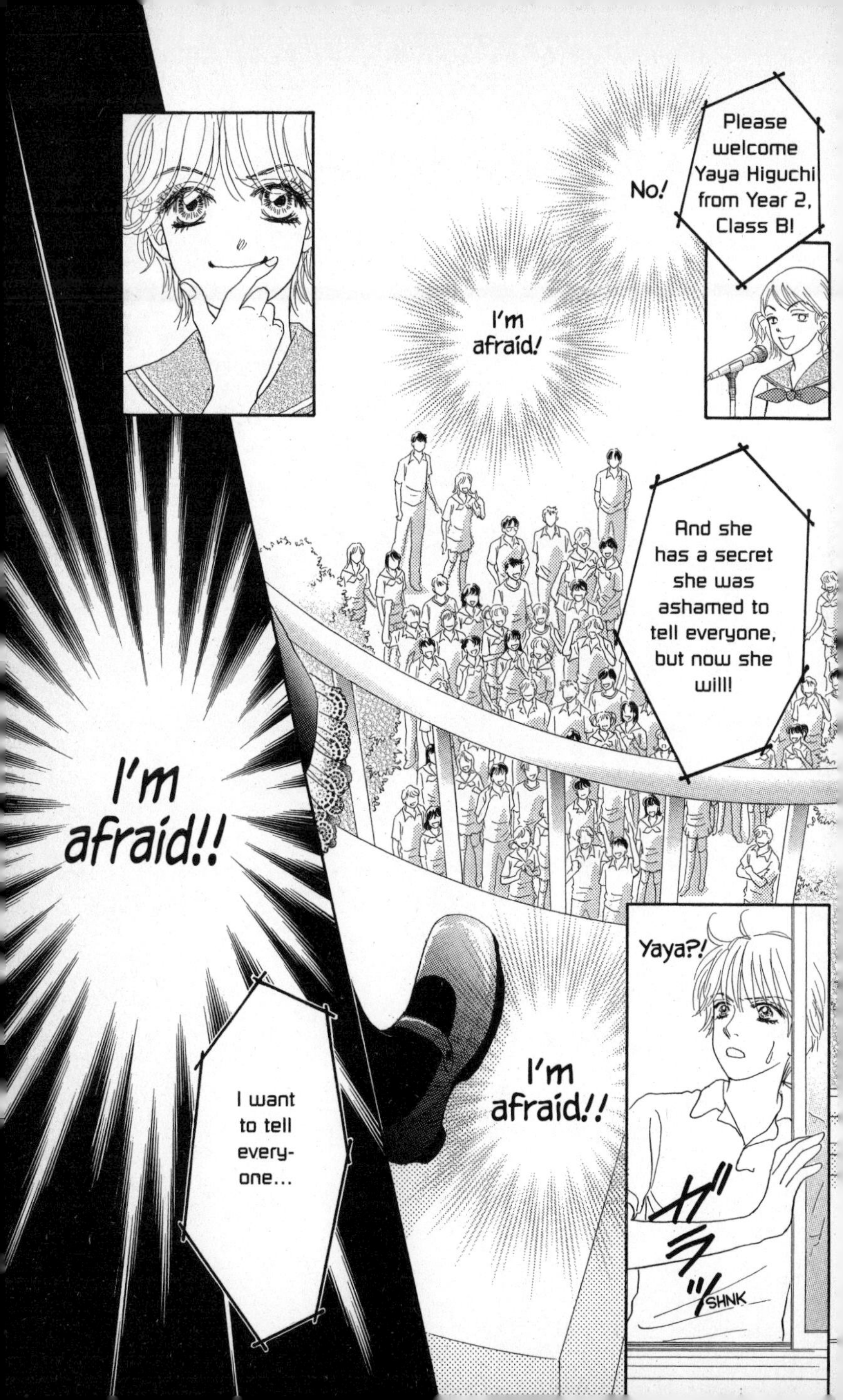
Please welcome Yaya Higuchi from Year 2, Class B!
No!
I'm afraid!
And she has a secret she was ashamed to tell everyone, but now she will!
I'm afraid!!
Yaya?!
I'm afraid!!
I want to tell every-one...
SHNK

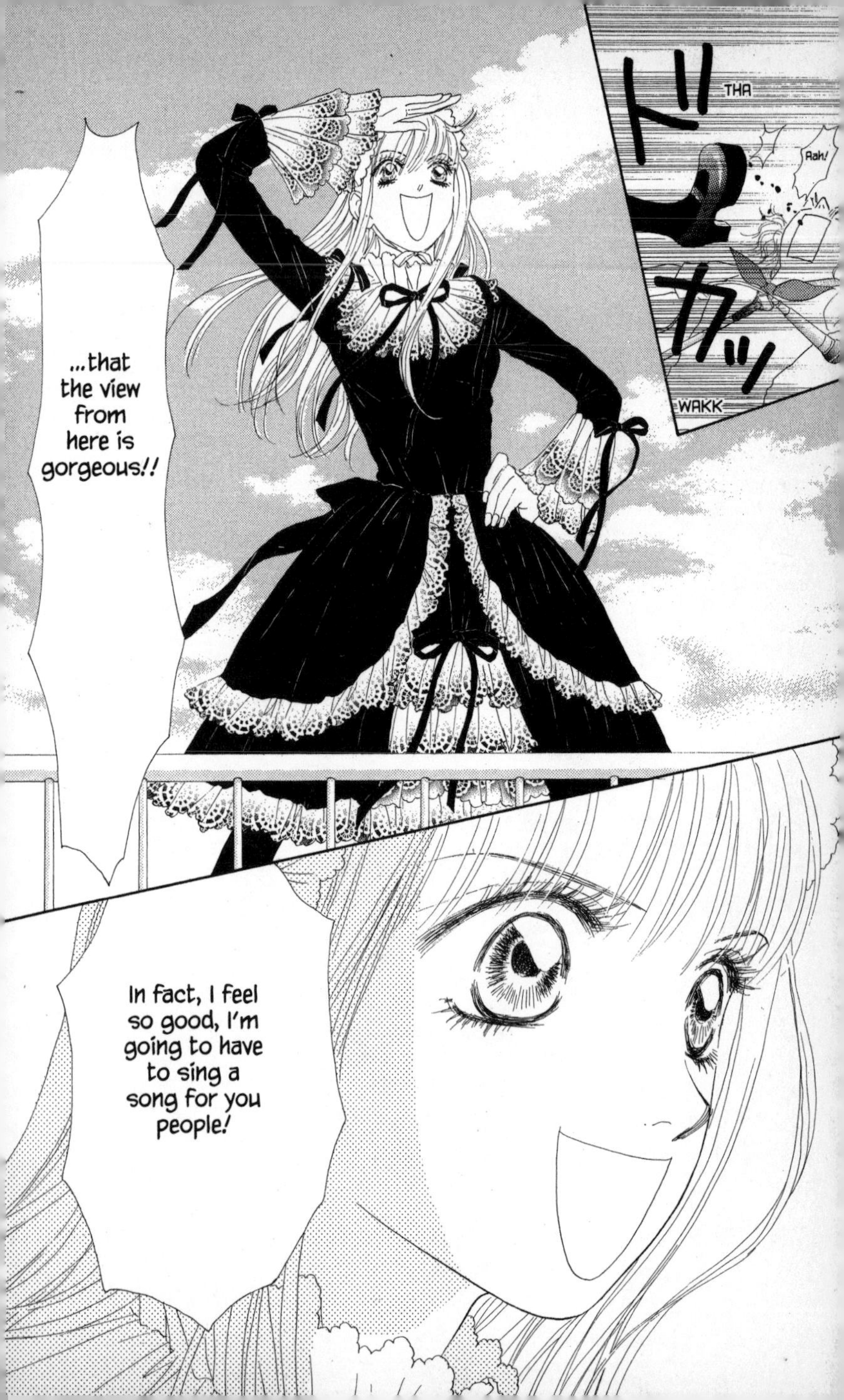

ドッ
THA
Aah!
カッ
WAKK
...that the view from here is gorgeous!!
In fact, I feel so good, I'm going to have to sing a song for you people!

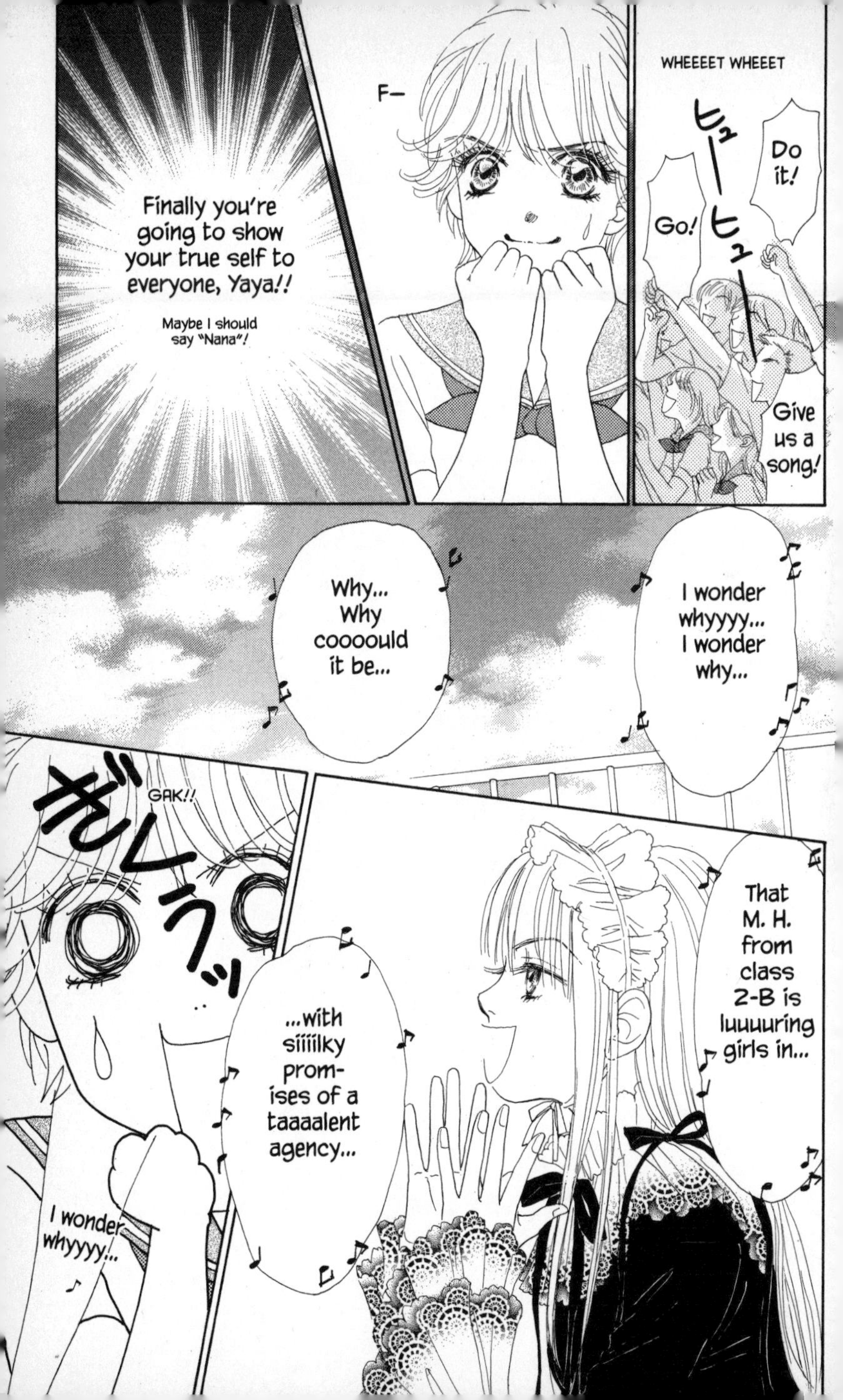
WHEEEET WHEEET
ヒューヒュー
Do it!
Go!
Give us a song!
F—
Finally you're going to show your true self to everyone, Yaya!!
Maybe I should say "Nana"!
I wonder whyyyy... I wonder why...
Why... Why coooould it be...
That M. H. from class 2-B is luuuuring girls in...
...with siiiilky prom-ises of a taaaalent agency...
ぎくうッ
GAK!!
I wonder whyyyy...

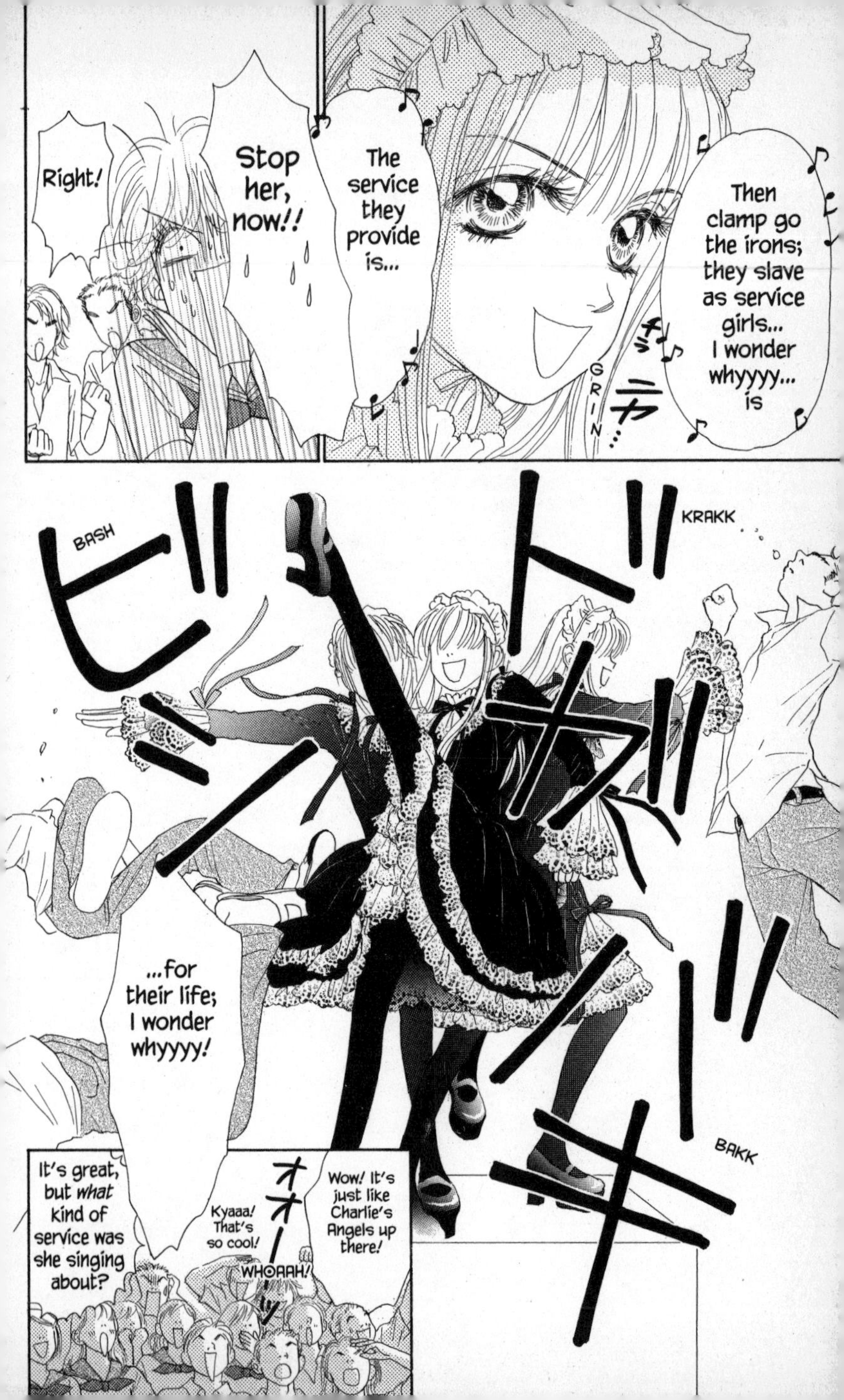
Then clamp go the irons; they slave as service girls... I wonder whyyyy... is
GRIN...
The service they provide is...
Stop her, now!!
Right!
KRAKK
BASH
...for their life; I wonder whyyyy!
BAKK
Wow! It's just like Charlie's Angels up there!
WHOAAH!
Kyaaa! That's so cool!
It's great, but *what* kind of service was she singing about?

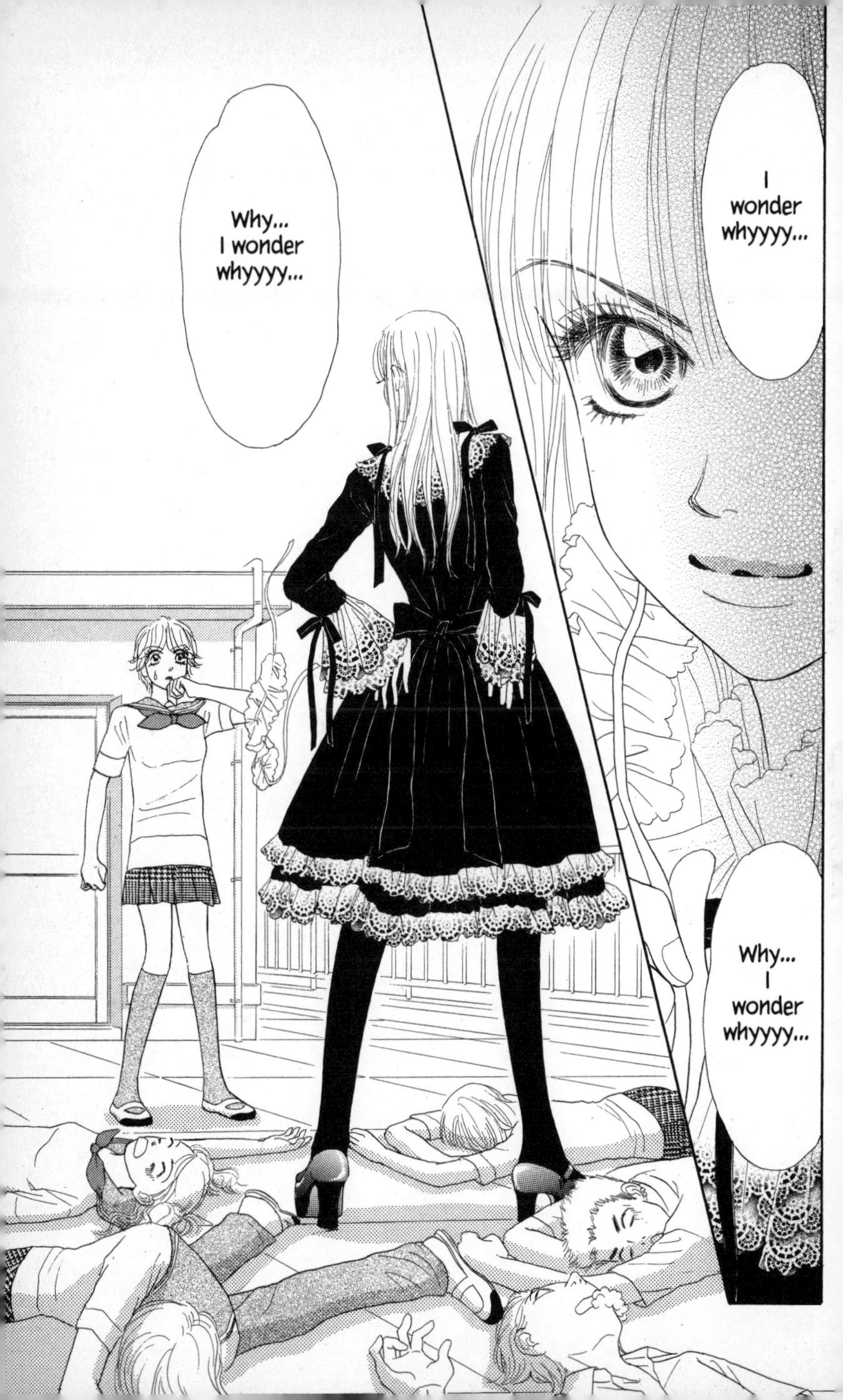
I wonder whyyyy...
Why... I wonder whyyyy...
Why... I wonder whyyyy...

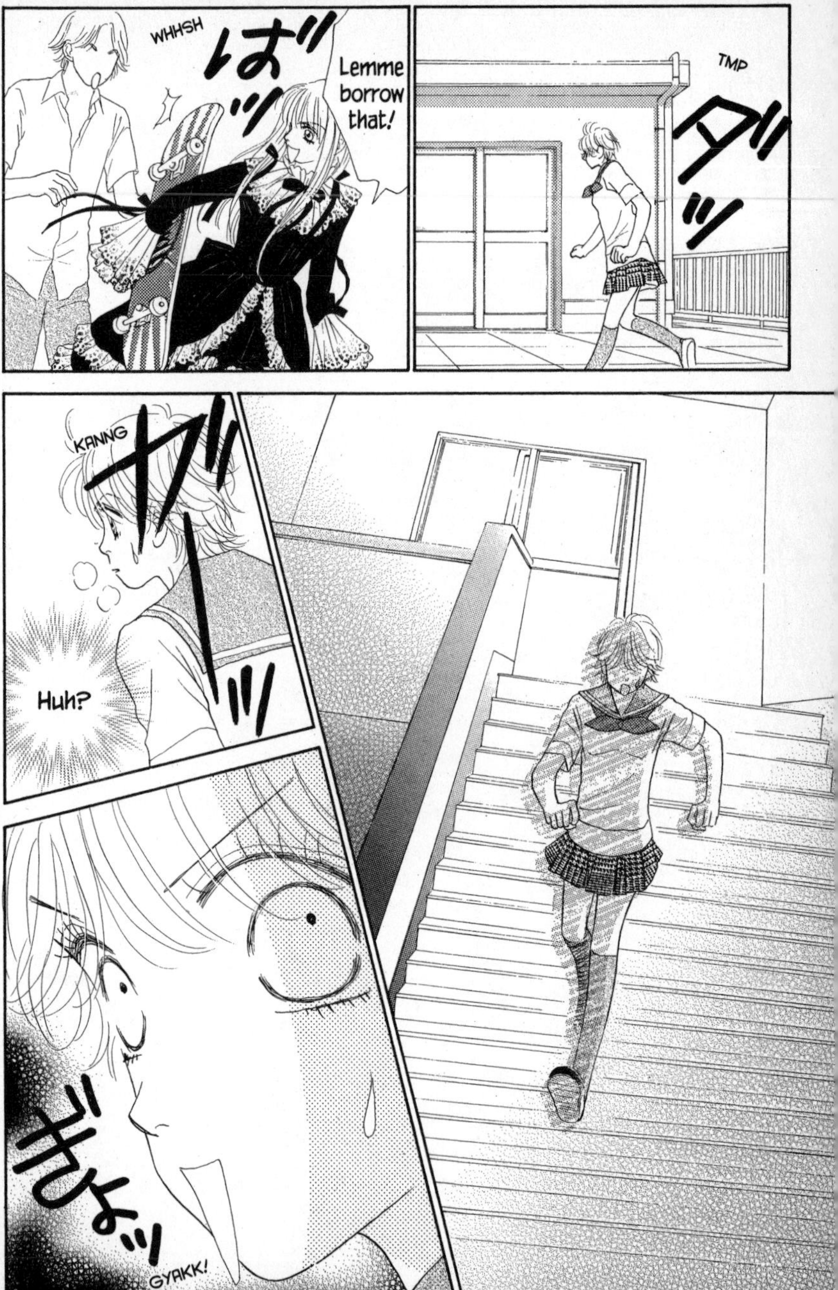
ダッ
TMP
ばッ
WHHSH
Lemme borrow that!
ガッ
KANNG
Huh?
ぎょッ
GYAKK!

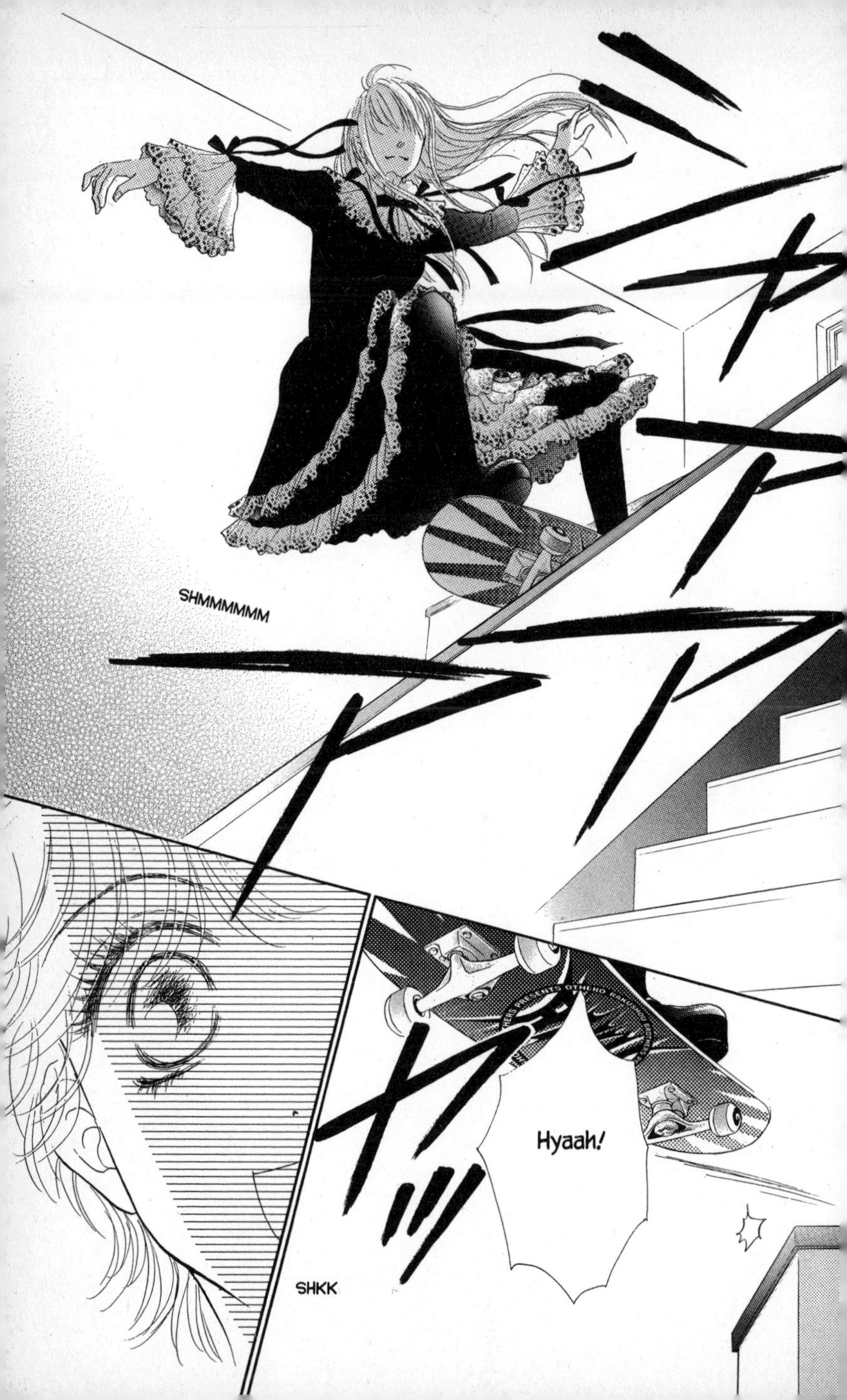
SHMMMMMM
Hyaah!
SHKK

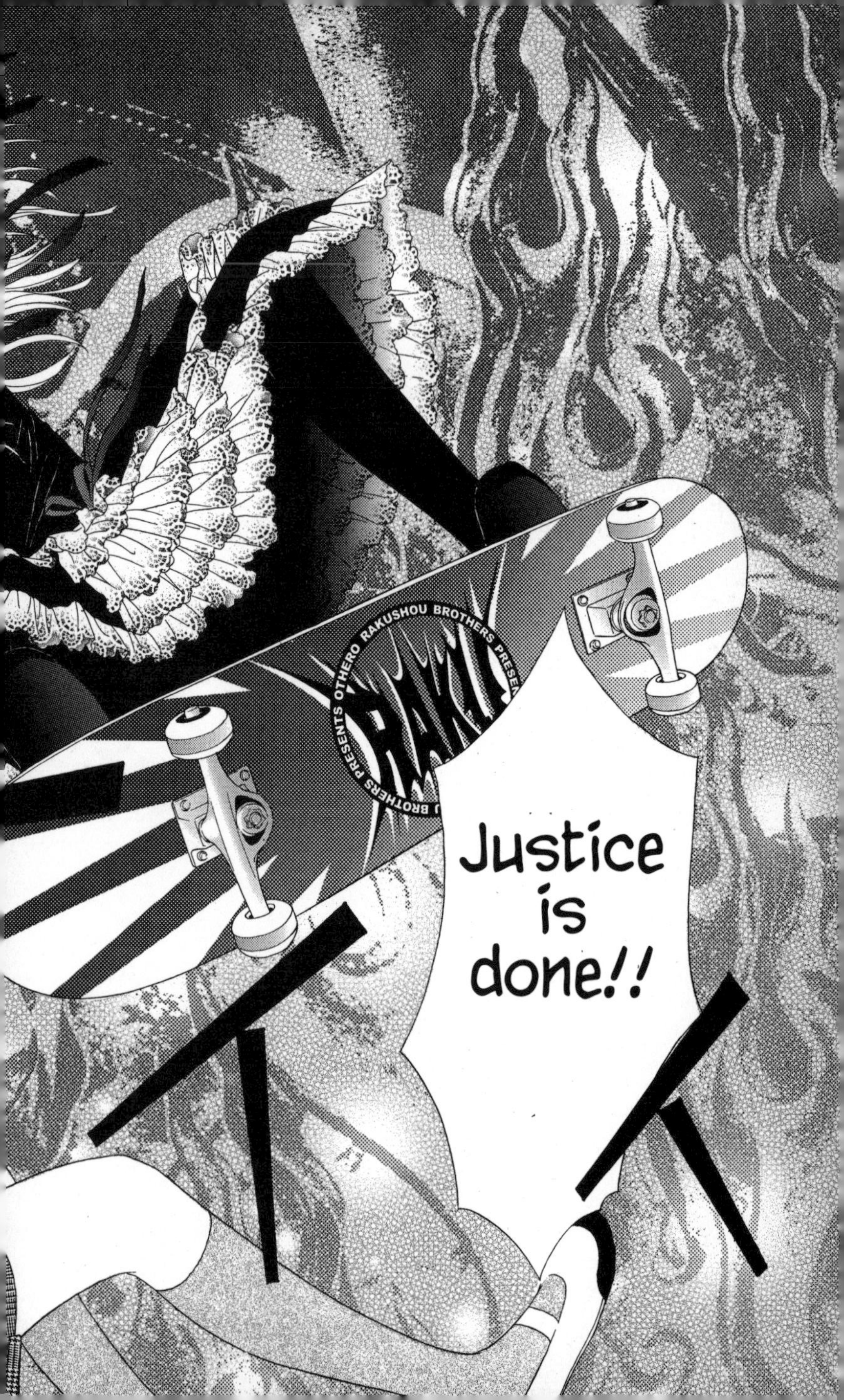
Justice is done!!

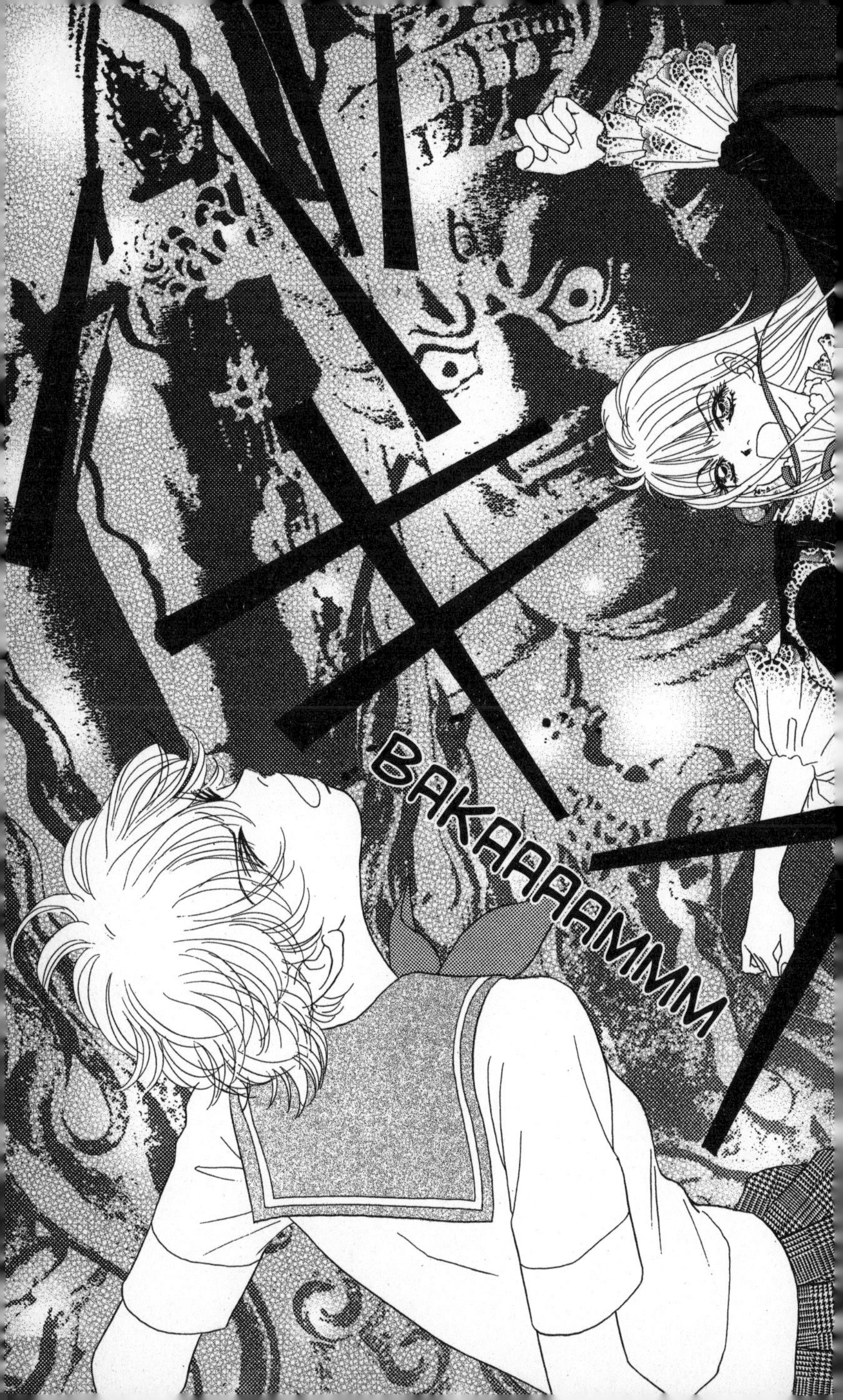
BAKAAAAAMMM

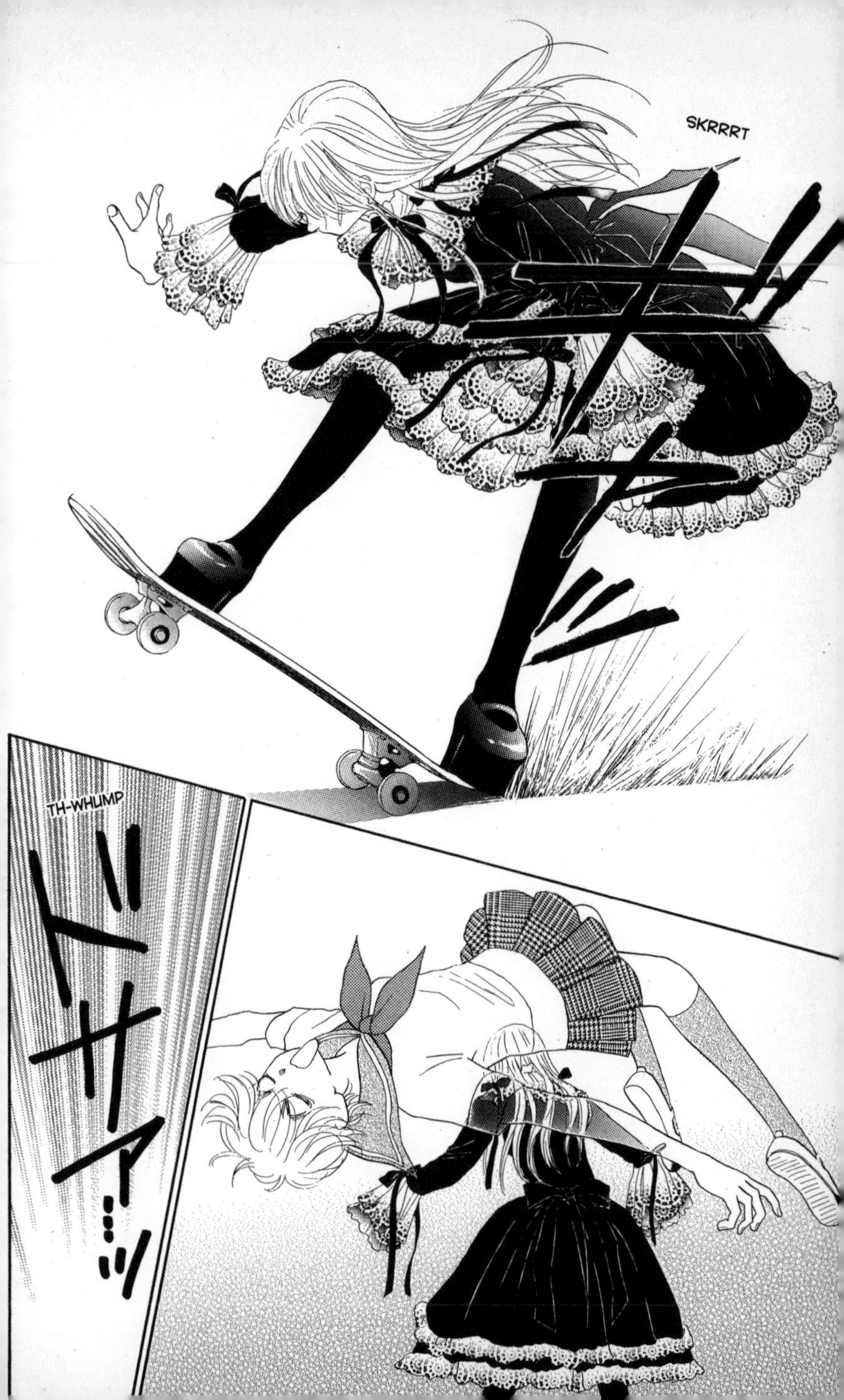
SKRRRT
TH-WHUMP
ドサァ…ッ

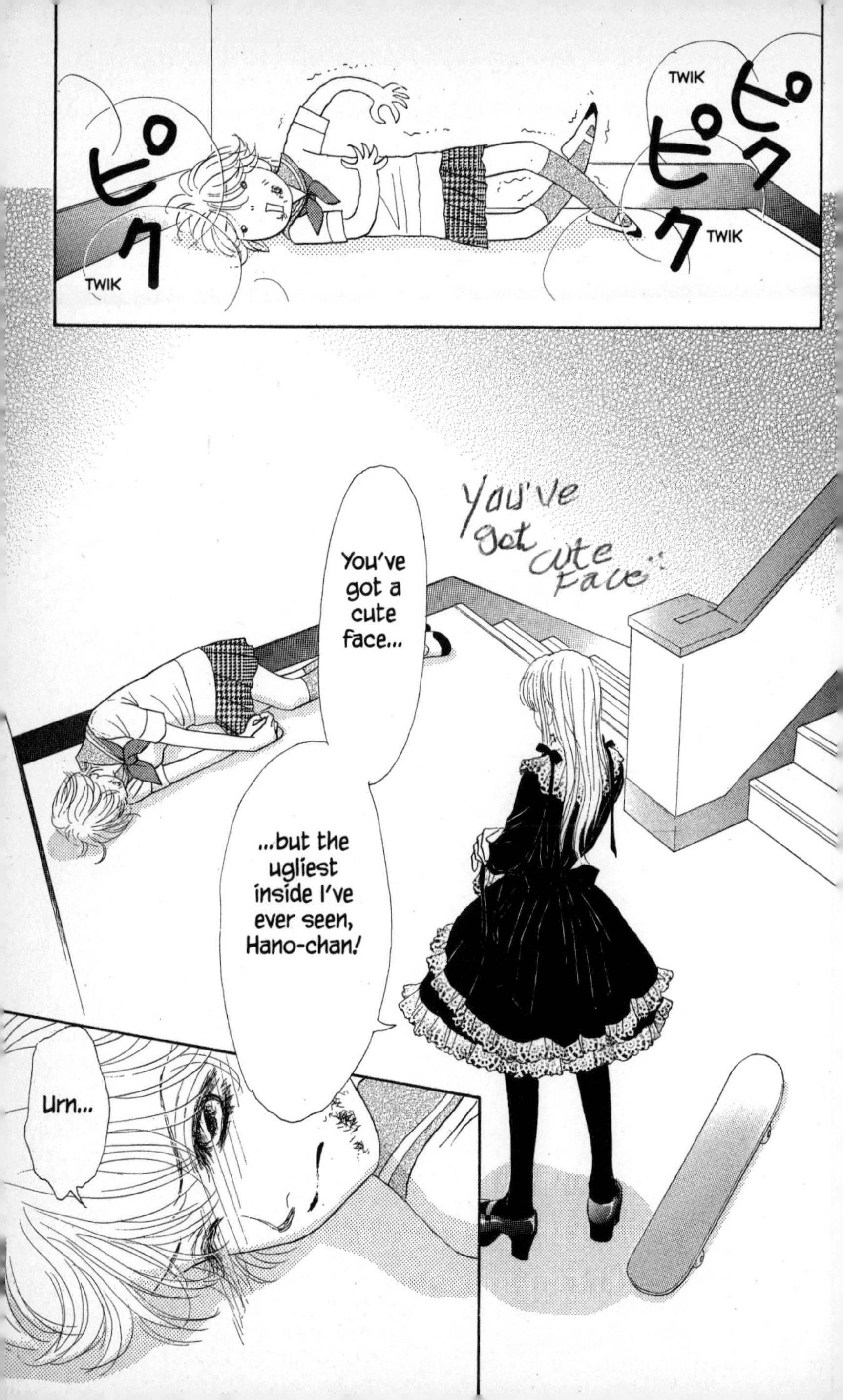

TWIK
ピクピク
TWIK
ピク
TWIK
You've got cute face
You've got a cute face...
...but the ugliest inside I've ever seen, Hano-chan!
Urn...

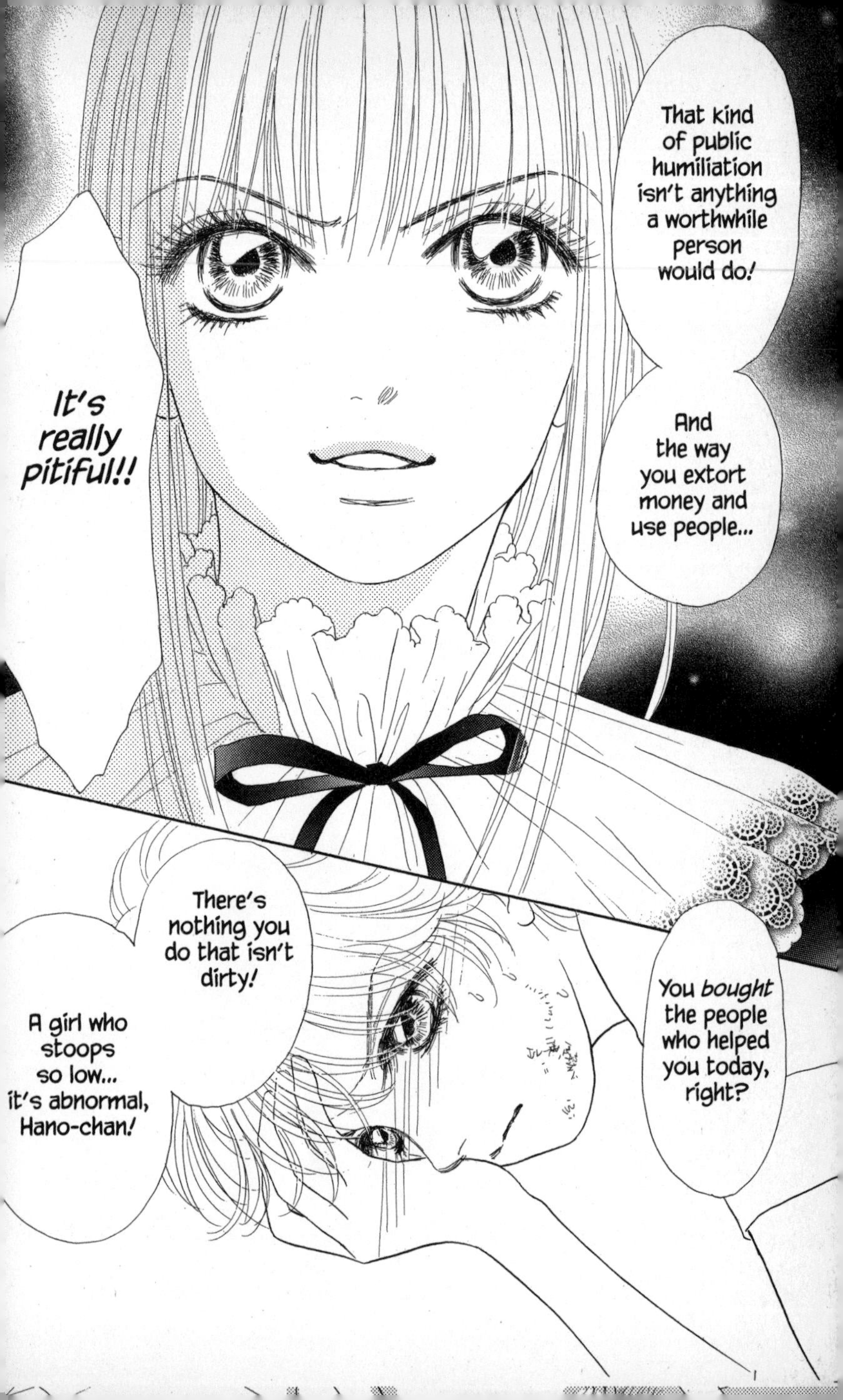

That kind of public humiliation isn't anything a worthwhile person would do!
And the way you extort money and use people...
It's really pitiful!!
You *bought* the people who helped you today, right?
There's nothing you do that isn't dirty!
A girl who stoops so low... it's abnormal, Hano-chan!

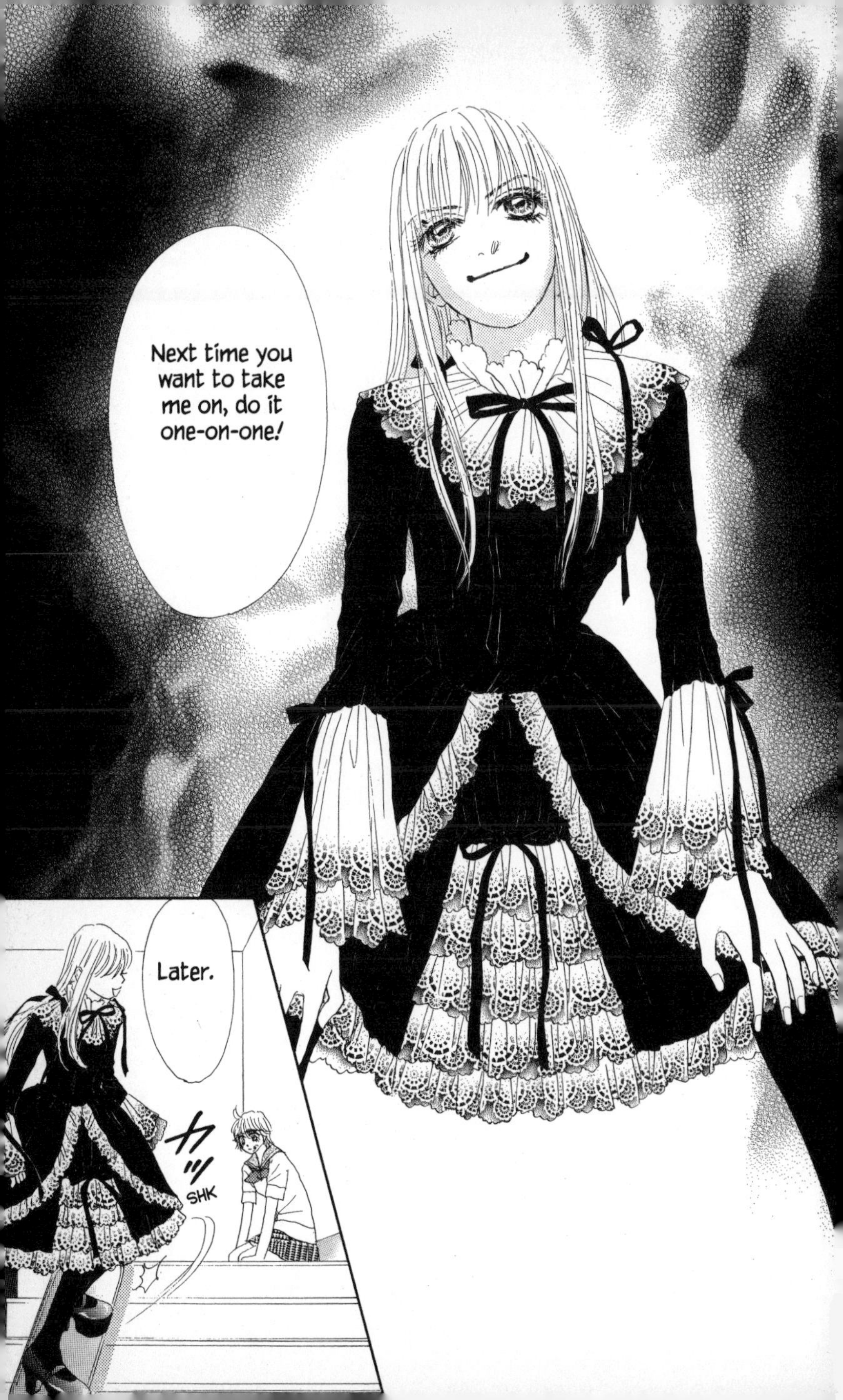
Next time you want to take me on, do it one-on-one!
Later.
SHK

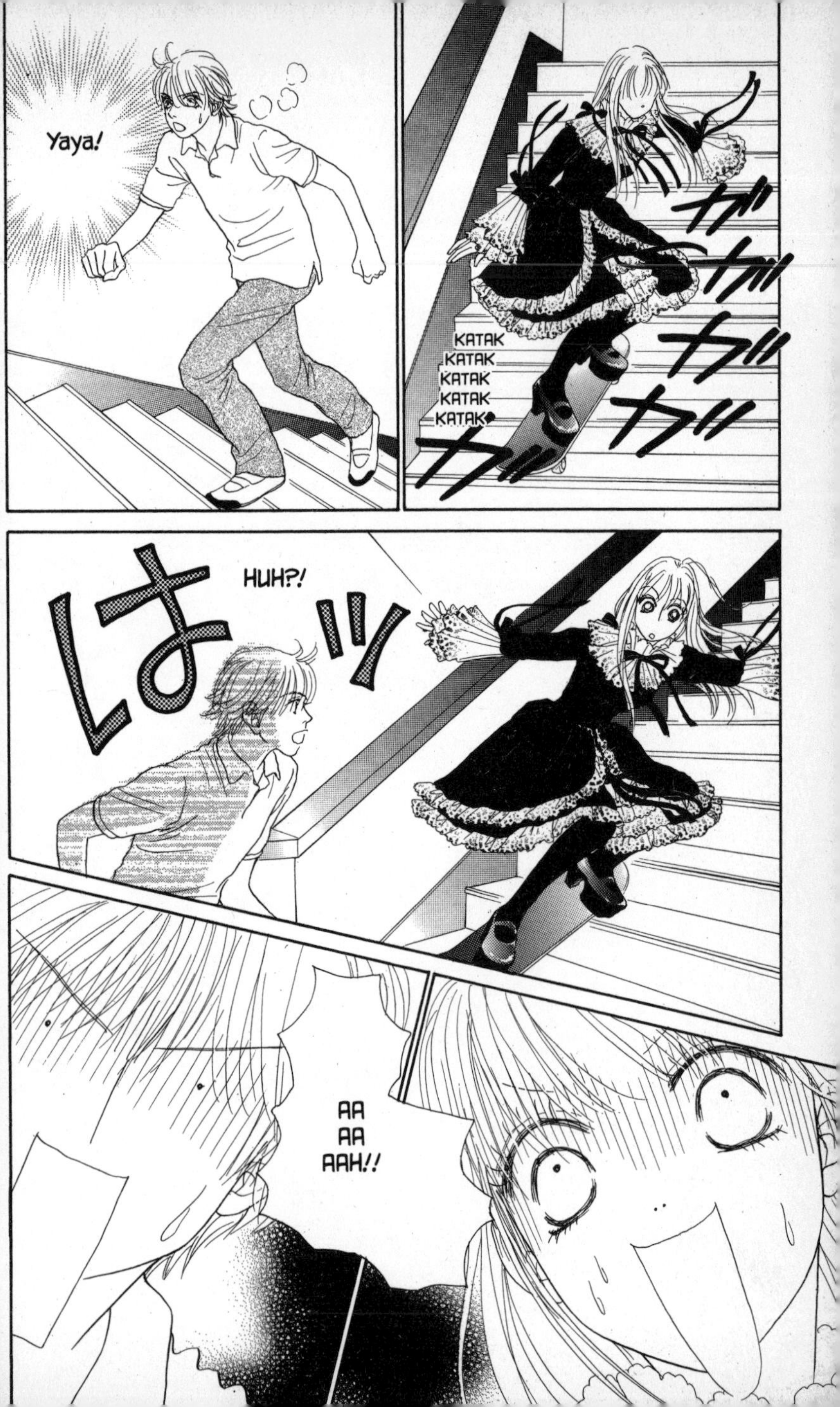
ガガガガガ
KATAK
KATAK
KATAK
KATAK
KATAK
Yaya!
HUH?!
はッ
AA
AA
AAH!!

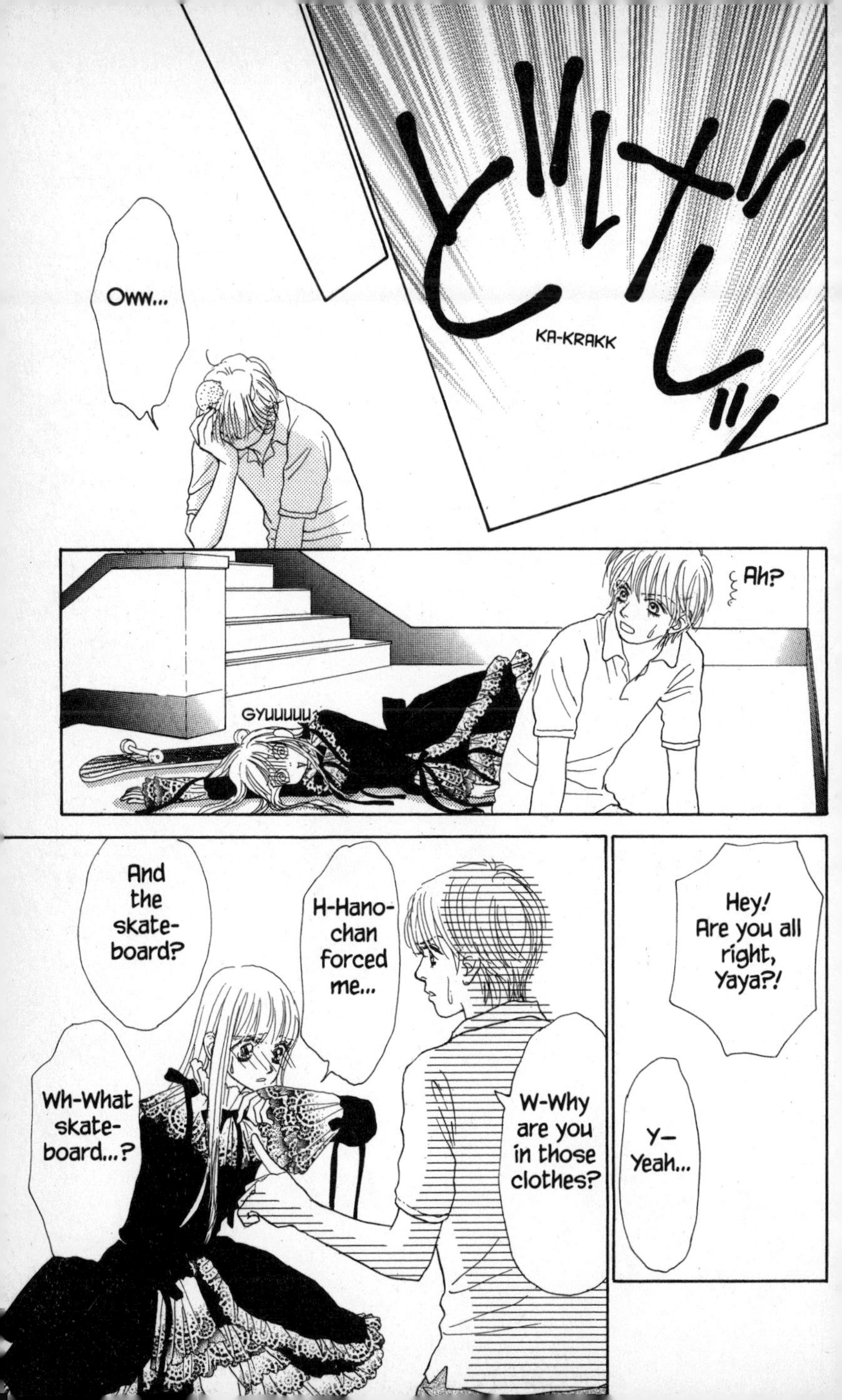
KA-KRAKK
Oww...
Ah?
GYUUUUU
Hey! Are you all right, Yaya?!
Y— Yeah...
W-Why are you in those clothes?
H-Hano-chan forced me...
And the skate-board?
Wh-What skate-board...?

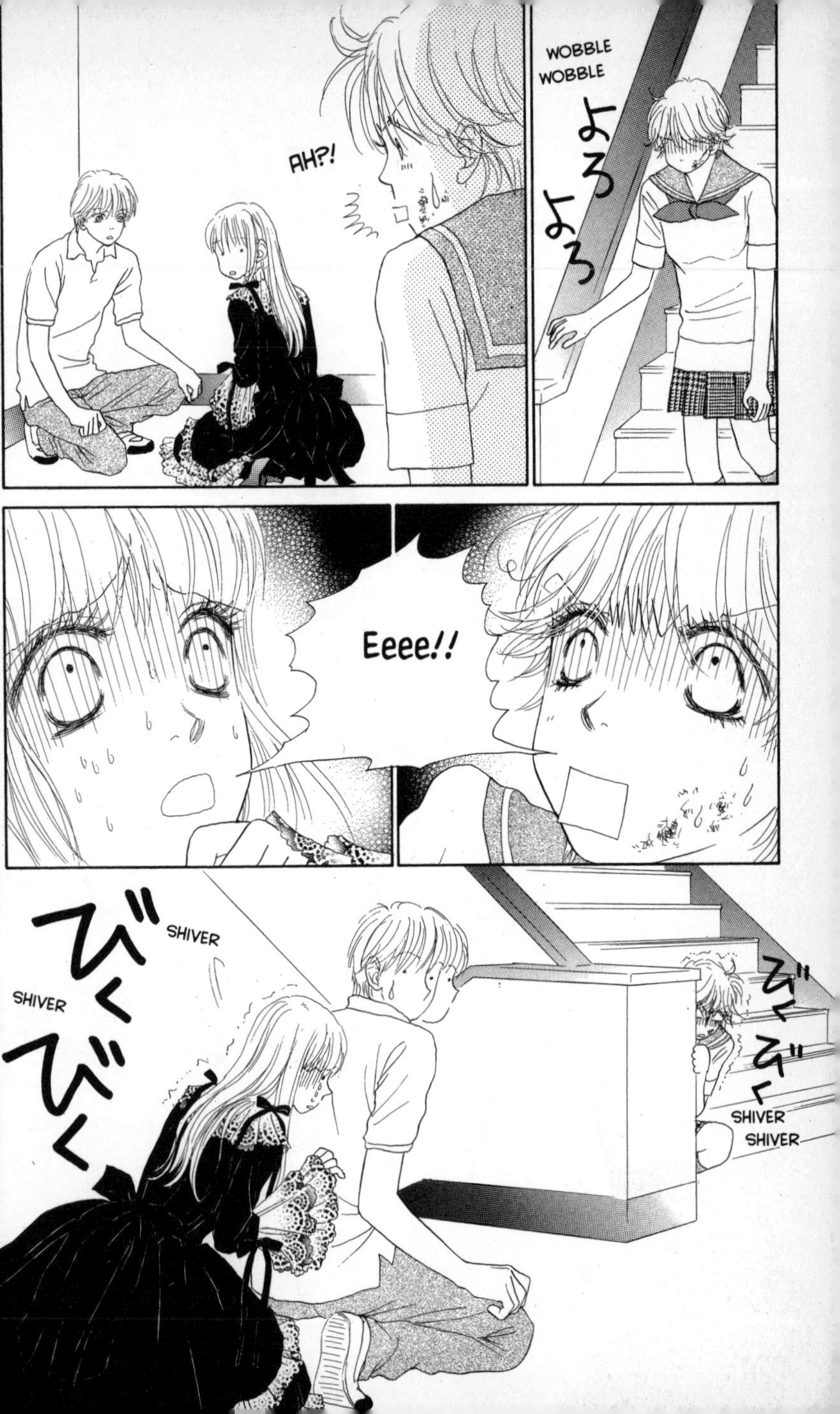
WOBBLE WOBBLE
よろよろ
AH?!
Eeee!!
びくびく
SHIVER SHIVER
びくびく
SHIVER
SHIVER

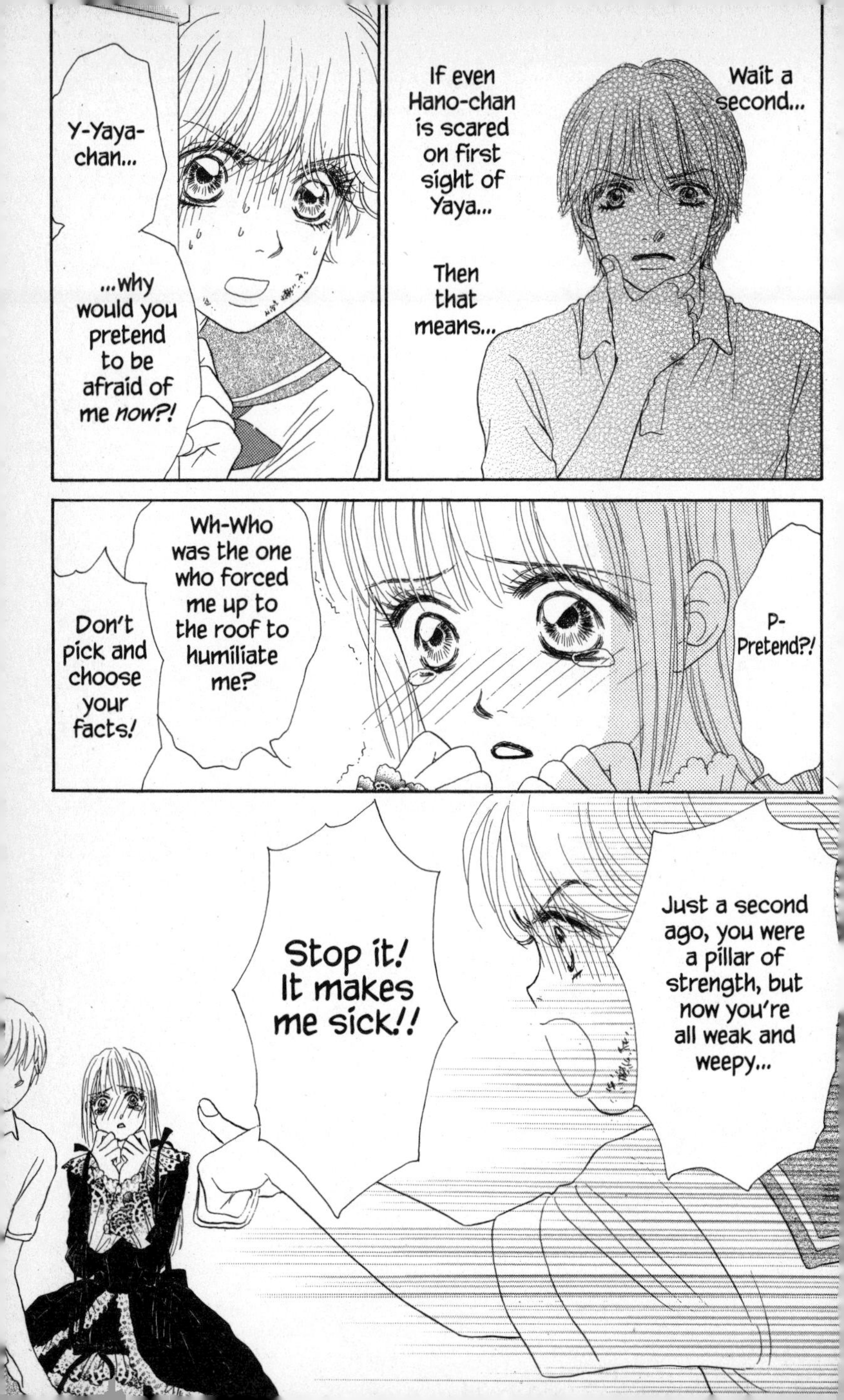
Wait a second...
If even Hano-chan is scared on first sight of Yaya...
Then that means...
Y-Yaya-chan...
...why would you pretend to be afraid of me *now*?!
P-Pretend?!
Wh-Who was the one who forced me up to the roof to humiliate me?
Don't pick and choose your facts!
Just a second ago, you were a pillar of strength, but now you're all weak and weepy...
Stop it! It makes me sick!!

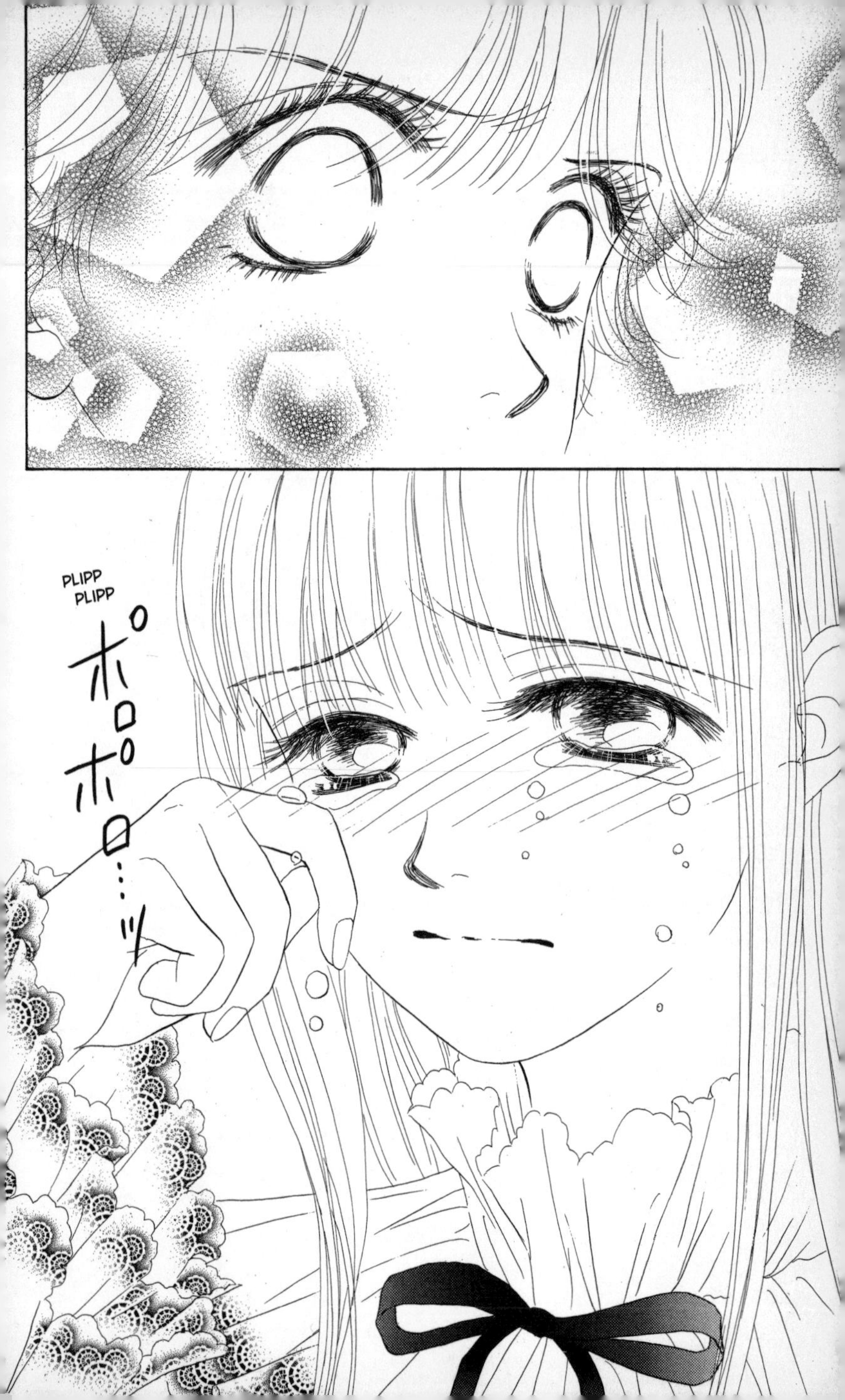
PLIPP
PLIPP
ポロポロ…ッ

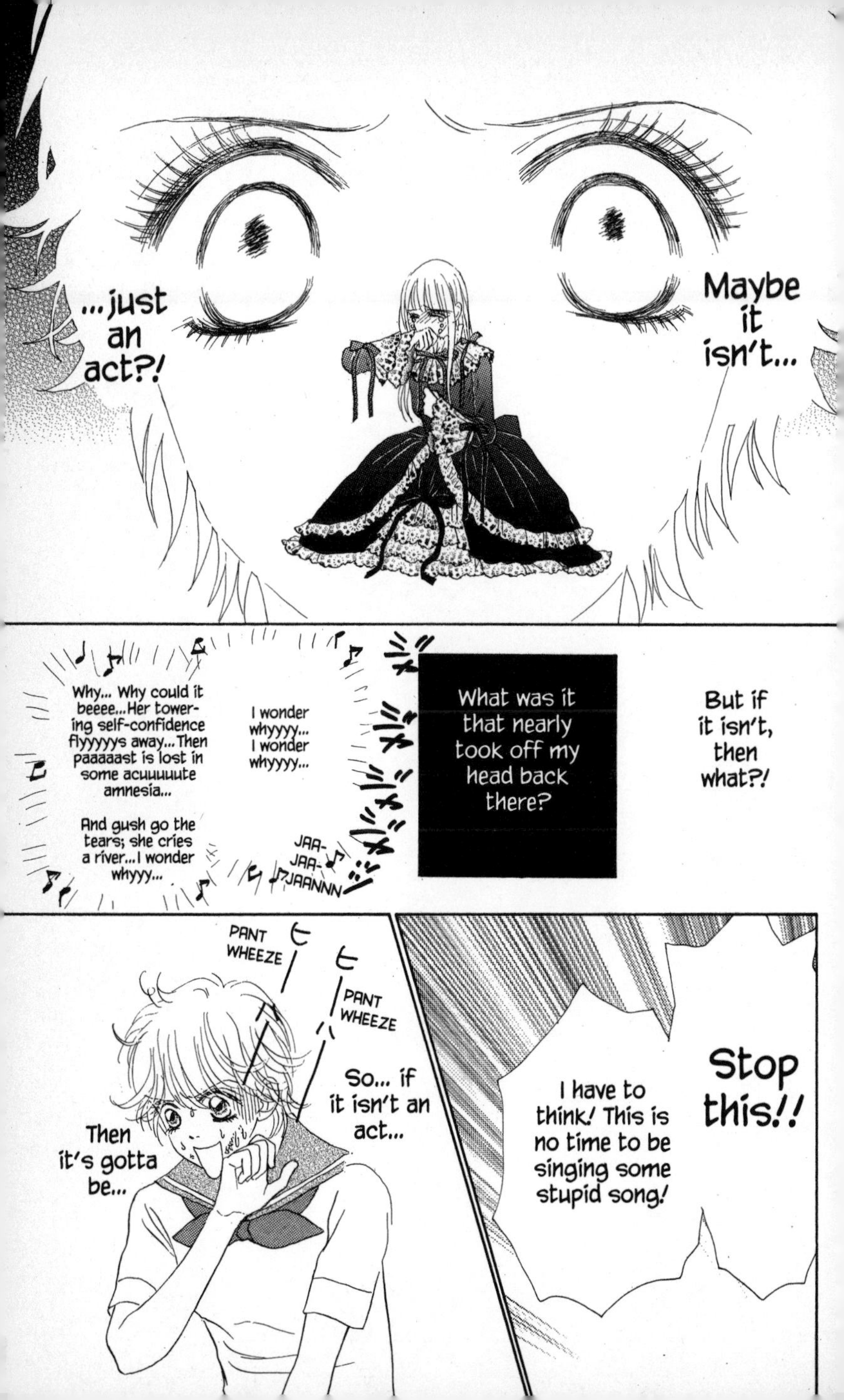
Maybe it isn't...
...just an act?!
But if it isn't, then what?!
What was it that nearly took off my head back there?
Why... Why could it beeee...Her towering self-confidence flyyyyys away...Then paaaaast is lost in some acuuuuute amnesia...
And gush go the tears; she cries a river...I wonder whyyy...
I wonder whyyyy... I wonder whyyyy...
JAA-JAA-JAANNN
Stop this!!
I have to think! This is no time to be singing some stupid song!
PANT WHEEZE
PANT WHEEZE
So... if it isn't an act...
Then it's gotta be...

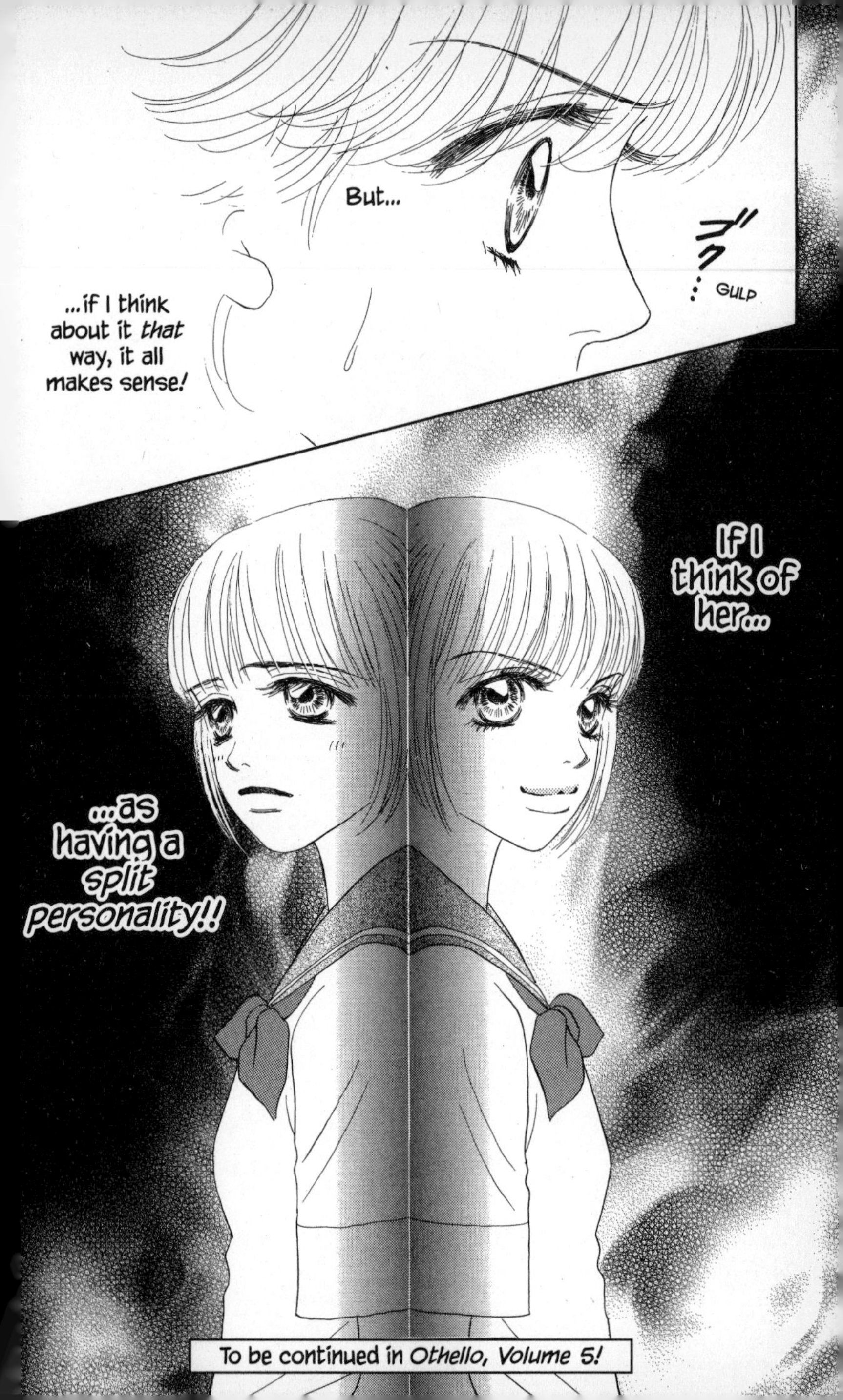
But...
...if I think about it *that* way, it all makes sense!
GULP
If I think of her...
...as having a split personality!!
To be continued in *Othello, Volume 5!*

Staff

THANK YOU ALL!!

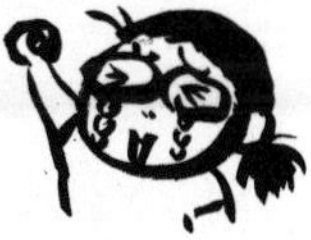

vol. 9 ~ 16 (~2003.4)

Emi-Nishi

Michiyo-Kobori

Mitsuyo-Anzai

Rie-Amano (Just married)

Rie-Takeuchi

Eiko-Kobayashi

Ema-Ezumida

++++++

Editor

Satoru-Matsumoto (New Editor in Chief)

Izumi-Morisada (New Editor)

+Home Page+

http://home.f02.itscom.net/ikezawa/

About the Author

Satomi Ikezawa's previous work before *Othello* is *Guru Guru Pon-chan*. She currently continues to work on *Othello,* which is being serialized in the Kodansha weekly manga magazine, *Bessatsu Friend.*

Ikezawa won the 24th Kodansha Manga Prize in 2000 for *Guru Guru Pon-chan.*

She has two Labradors, named Guts and Ponta.

Translation Notes

Japanese is a tricky language for most Westerners, and translation is often more art than science. For your edification and reading pleasure, here are notes on some of the places where we could have gone in a different direction in our translation of the work, or where a Japanese cultural reference is used.

"H" Manga, Page 17

"H" is short for "hentai," which means lecher or pervert, and "H" manga, anime, or other productions can be as innocent as sex-farce or as disturbing as some of the worst fetishist illegal pornographic material. But usually when someone says "H" (pronounced "eichi"), they are referring to people with a greater than normal interest in sex or sexually charged material.

S-Stop it! Othello isn't an "H" manga!

Aru-Aru (Hakkutsu! Aru-Aru Daijiten), Page 40

Aru-Aru was a game show that seemed doomed to be just another standard Japanese quiz show where several minor celebrities guess at foreign or domestic trivia. However, after its first set of shows, Aru-Aru shifted its focus to health issues and advice on proper behavior, and that's when the show's popularity truly took off.

"For 7", Page 54

In the same way the words "first" and "second" mean pretty much the same thing as the words "one" and "two" (without sounding the same any way), the numbers in Japanese also have various ways of being pronounced. The number 7, for example, can be pronounced "shichi," but it can also be pronounced "nana."

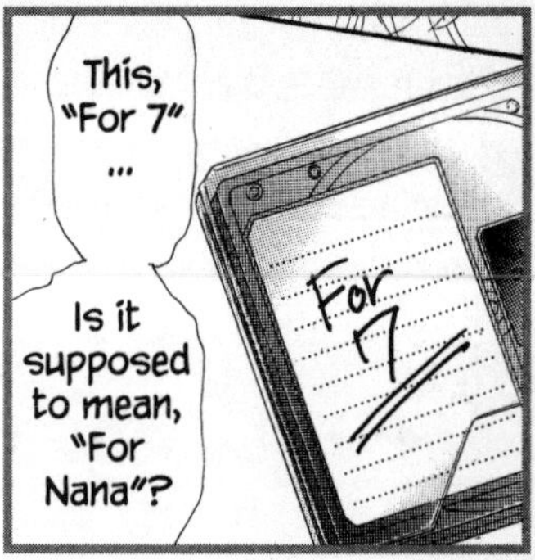
This, "For 7" ...
Is it supposed to mean, "For Nana"?
For 7

Becoming "Talent", Page 61

Japan has a pervasive "Idol" system for generating new stars out of pretty-but-talentless teenage girls. The debut of the ironically named "Talent" is usually accompanied by a pop-single, a small part on a nighttime TV drama, endorsements and commercials, and other marketing-hype techniques. The shelf life of these idols can be counted in weeks, and then they are quickly forgotten. Rumors fly about what can happen to new idols ranging from, at best, exhaustive schedules to, at worst, sexual and physical abuse. The agency run by Hano-chan's father seems to be one of the idol factories that produce these disposable stars.

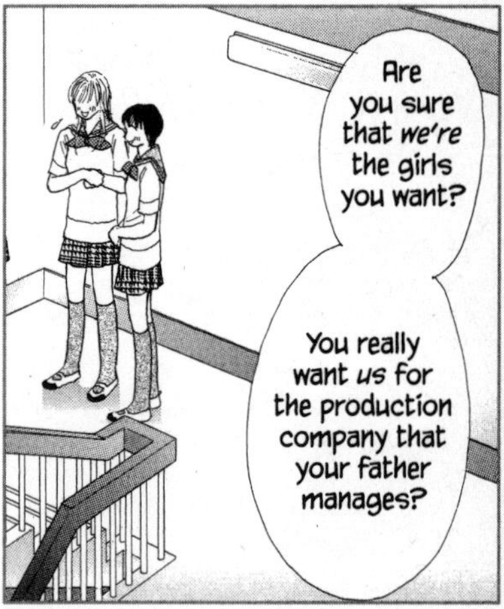
Are you sure that *we're* the girls you want?
You really want *us* for the production company that your father manages?

Costs of the agency, Page 62

A good rule of thumb for approximating yen costs to dollars
is to divide the yen cost by 100. So Hano-chan's stated costs
come out to approximately $1000.00 admission fee and
$250.00 per month tuition, which Hano-chan "bargains down"
to a $500.00 admission fee and $200.00 per month.

He also agreed to reduce the monthly tuition from 25,000 to only 20,000 yen!

The school entrance fees are usually 100,000 yen, but I talked to my Papa and got it reduced to only 50,000!

Here. The contracts are all made out!

Wing Talent Agency: Talent School Admission Form

The stamp (hanko), Page 72

If non-Japanese peo-
ple go to Japan, their
signature is all that
is needed to endorse
legal documents. But
Japanese nationals
also have a wooden,
hand-made stamp
called a hanko, which
is registered at the
local city hall, to affix
their seal to contracts
and other legal work.
Sharp-eyed fans of
Japanese cinema will

All it needs is your signature and stamp.

I'll fill in all of the boring contract details! I even brought our

Wing Talent Agency: Talent School Admission Form

WINGタレント養成所入学申込書

remember the climax of *A Taxing Woman* when hundreds of hanko
are discovered in the criminal's house. Each of these stamps rep-
resented a different bank account.

Bob Sapp, Page 92

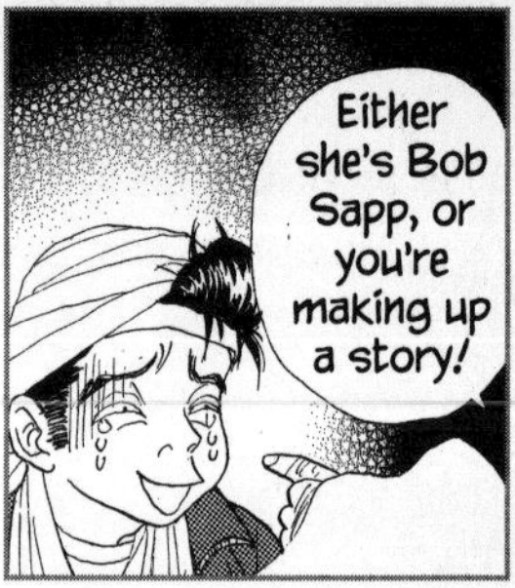
Either she's Bob Sapp, or you're making up a story!

One of the stars of the mixed martial-arts tournament league, K-1, and the IWGP Heavyweight Champion for 2004 is Bob "The Beast" Sapp, a 342 lb. hulk of muscle, bone, and not an ounce of fat. Reported to bench-press more than 650 lbs., lifting Detchan and a sofa would be a breeze for him.

Ayaya, Page 99

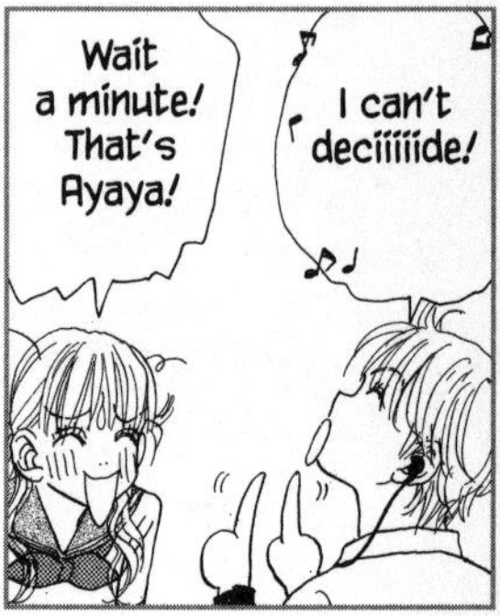
I can't deciiiiide!
Wait a minute! That's Ayaya!

Because it was a popular commercial on television, the song "Ne~e" by Aya Matsuura (nicknamed Ayaya) became a tune (and lyrics) that nearly the entire nation of Japan could sing in 2002.

Image Club, Page 116

One of the darker sides of Japan is the thriving sex trade. This can range from hostess bars where pretty girls will talk and flirt with male customers, to peep shows, to soapland and massage parlors, and finally to unabashed prostitution. These flesh markets go by such names as Play Spots, Image Clubs, Fashion Health, and Pink Salons.

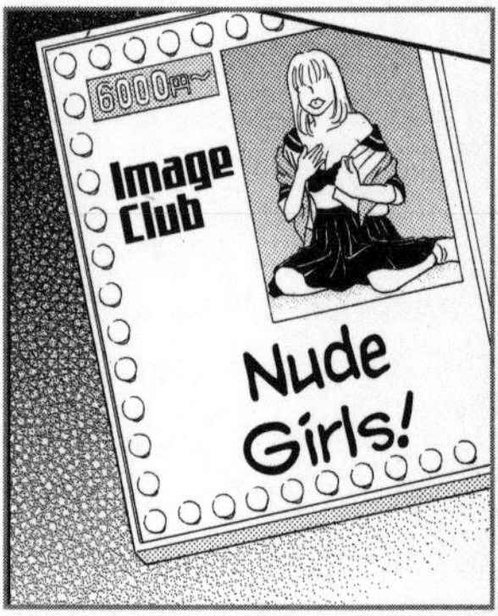
6000円~
Image Club
Nude Girls!

Payment, Page 123

Jobs in Japan can pay daily, weekly, every two weeks or monthly, but since checks are unusual in Japan, the pay is distributed either by direct bank transfer, or, more commonly, by cash in an envelope.

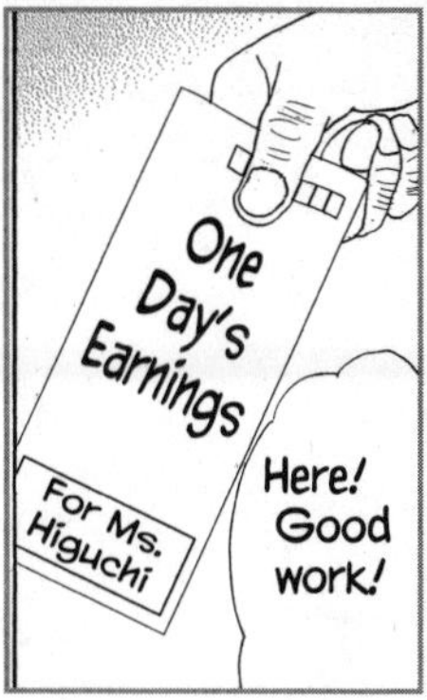
One Day's Earnings
For Ms. Higuchi
Here! Good work!

V6, Page 146

After a decade of popularity and more than fifteen albums, V6 has broken from its boy-band roots to become an established part of the Japanese popular music scene.

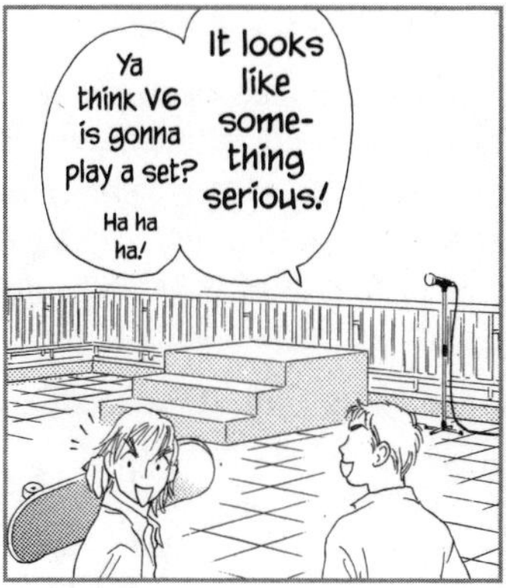
It looks like some-thing serious!
Ya think V6 is gonna play a set?
Ha ha ha!

Dear Readers,

We are delighted to present you with a preview of GURU GURU PON-CHAN by OTHELLO creator Satomi Ikezawa!

Ponta is an energetic, mischievous Labrador retriever puppy, the Koizumi family's pet. When Grandpa Koizumi, an amateur inventor, creates the Chit-chat Bone, Ponta's craving causes trouble. She eats the bone—and turns into a human girl!

Surprised but undaunted, Ponta ventures out of the house and meets Mirai Iwaki, the most popular boy at school. Soon, she's in love! Using the power of the Chit-chat Bone, Ponta switches back and forth from dog to girl—but can she win Mirai's affections?

This is a re-bark-ably original manga full of fun and romance. We hope this preview will make you drool for the first volume!

Volulmes 1-8 are available from Tanoshimi now.

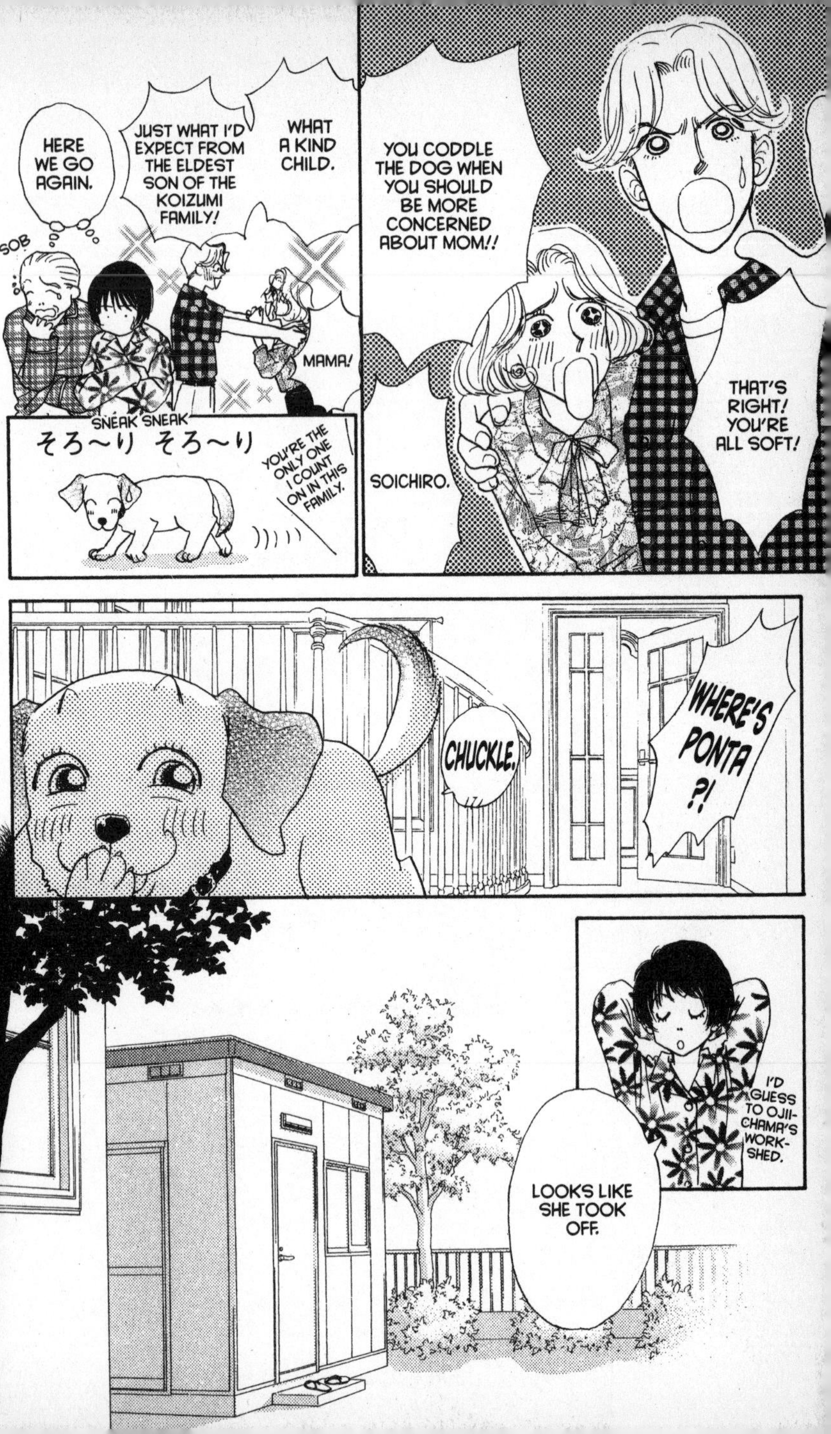
YOU CODDLE THE DOG WHEN YOU SHOULD BE MORE CONCERNED ABOUT MOM!!
THAT'S RIGHT! YOU'RE ALL SOFT!
SOICHIRO.
WHAT A KIND CHILD.
JUST WHAT I'D EXPECT FROM THE ELDEST SON OF THE KOIZUMI FAMILY!
MAMA!
HERE WE GO AGAIN.
SOB
SNEAK SNEAK
そろ～り そろ～り
YOU'RE THE ONLY ONE I COUNT ON IN THIS FAMILY.
WHERE'S PONTA?!
CHUCKLE.
I'D GUESS TO OJII-CHAMA'S WORK-SHED.
LOOKS LIKE SHE TOOK OFF.

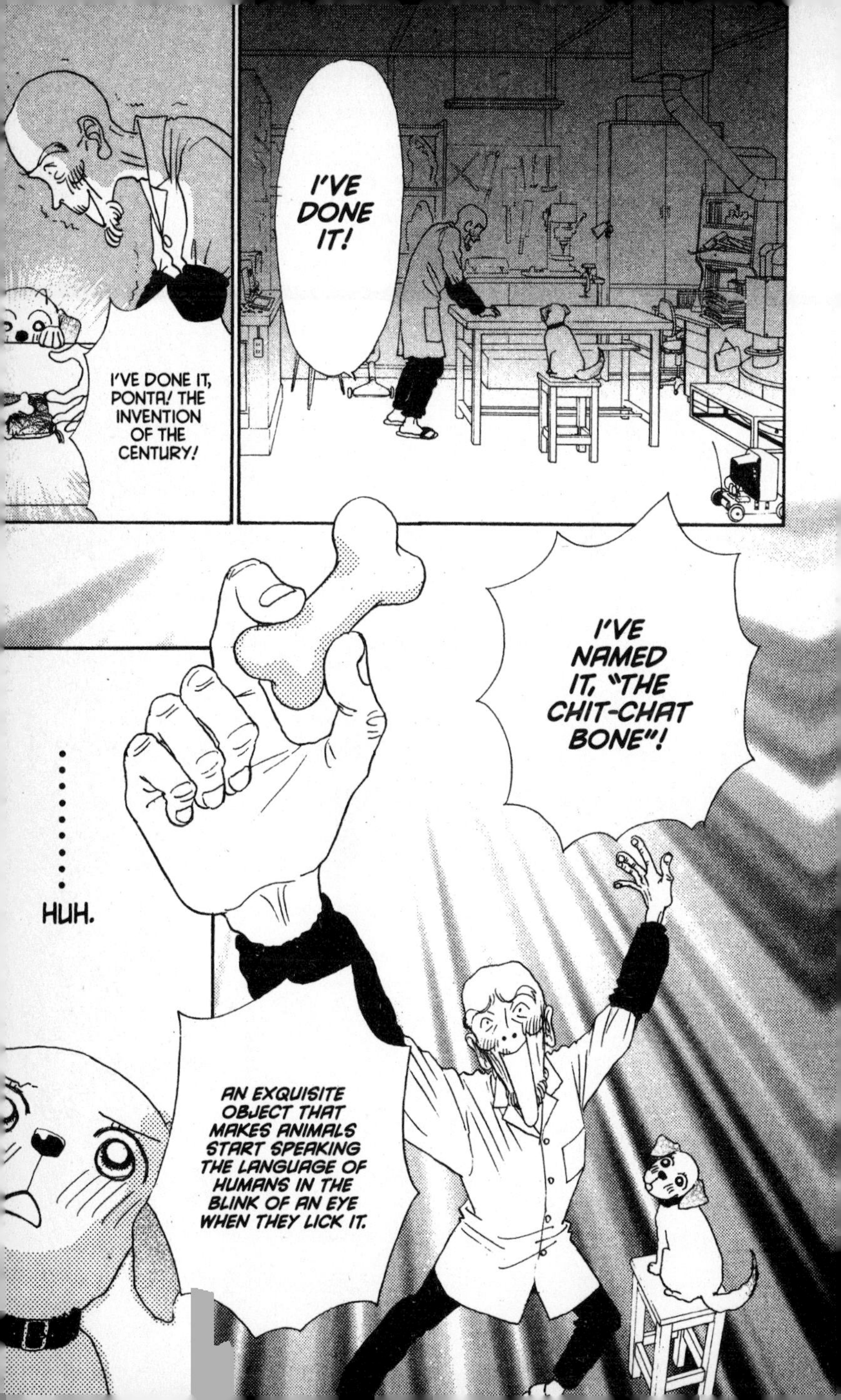
I'VE DONE IT!
I'VE DONE IT, PONTA! THE INVENTION OF THE CENTURY!
I'VE NAMED IT, "THE CHIT-CHAT BONE"!
AN EXQUISITE OBJECT THAT MAKES ANIMALS START SPEAKING THE LANGUAGE OF HUMANS IN THE BLINK OF AN EYE WHEN THEY LICK IT.
........HUH.

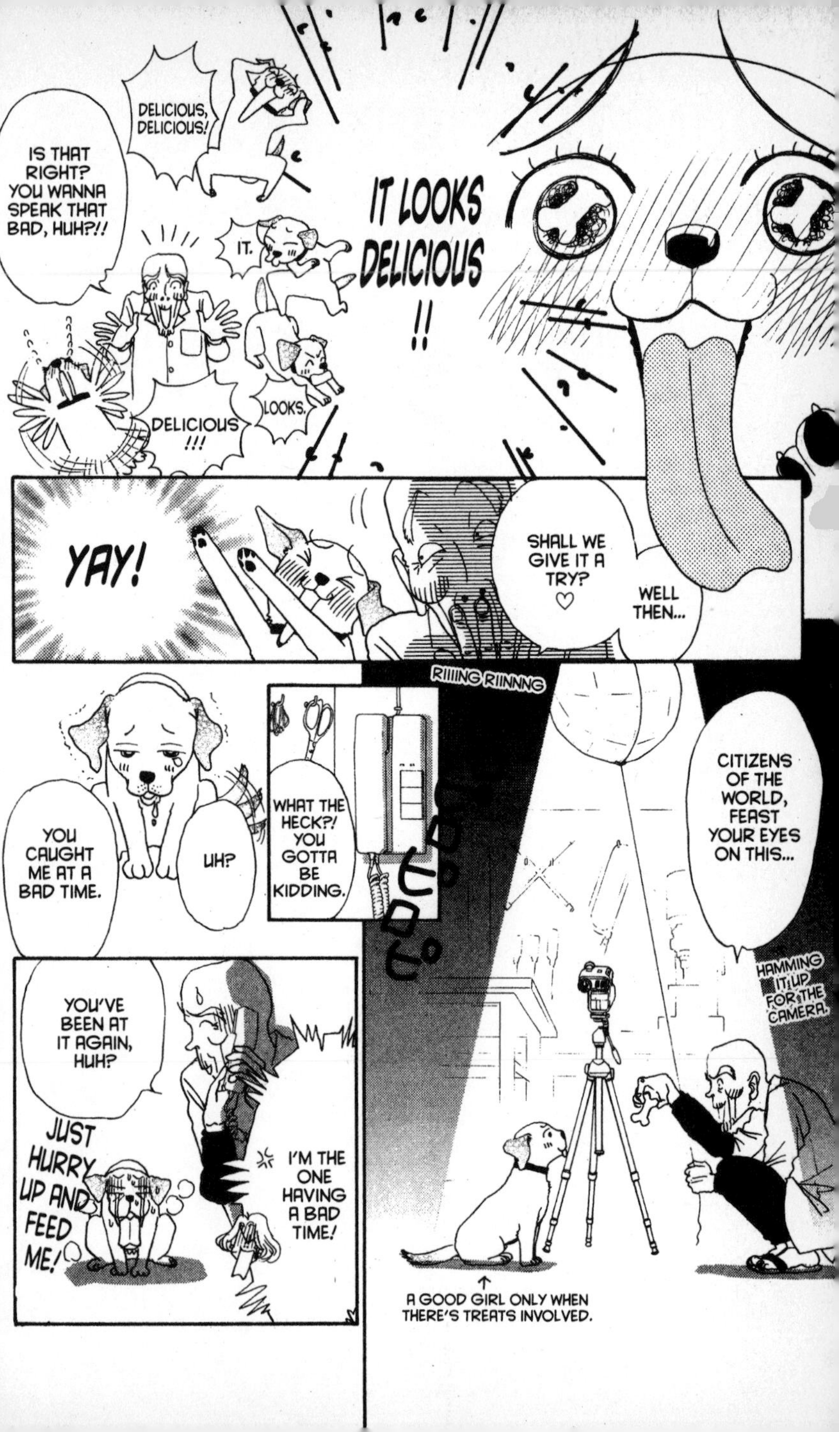
IT LOOKS DELICIOUS!!
DELICIOUS, DELICIOUS!
IS THAT RIGHT? YOU WANNA SPEAK THAT BAD, HUH?!!
IT.
LOOKS.
DELICIOUS!!!
WELL THEN...
SHALL WE GIVE IT A TRY? ♡
YAY!
CITIZENS OF THE WORLD, FEAST YOUR EYES ON THIS...
HAMMING IT UP FOR THE CAMERA.
↑ A GOOD GIRL ONLY WHEN THERE'S TREATS INVOLVED.
RIIING RIINNNG
WHAT THE HECK?! YOU GOTTA BE KIDDING.
UH?
YOU CAUGHT ME AT A BAD TIME.
YOU'VE BEEN AT IT AGAIN, HUH?
I'M THE ONE HAVING A BAD TIME!
JUST HURRY UP AND FEED ME!

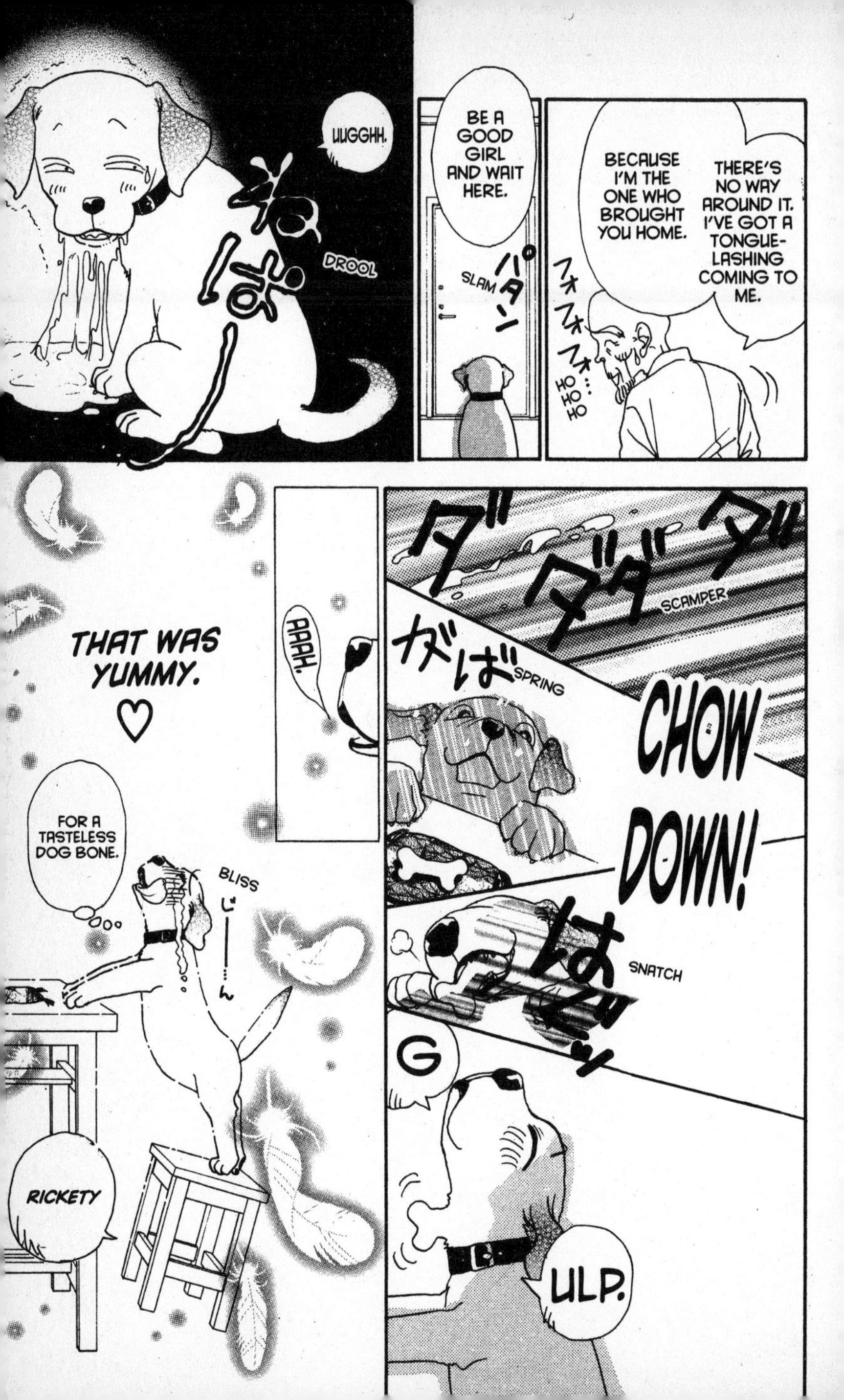

THERE'S NO WAY AROUND IT. I'VE GOT A TONGUE-LASHING COMING TO ME.
BECAUSE I'M THE ONE WHO BROUGHT YOU HOME.
フォフォフォ…
HO HO HO
BE A GOOD GIRL AND WAIT HERE.
パタン
SLAM
UUGGHH.
DROOL
SCAMPER
がば
SPRING
CHOW DOWN!
SNATCH
G
ULP.
AAAH.
THAT WAS YUMMY. ♡
FOR A TASTELESS DOG BONE.
BLISS
RICKETY

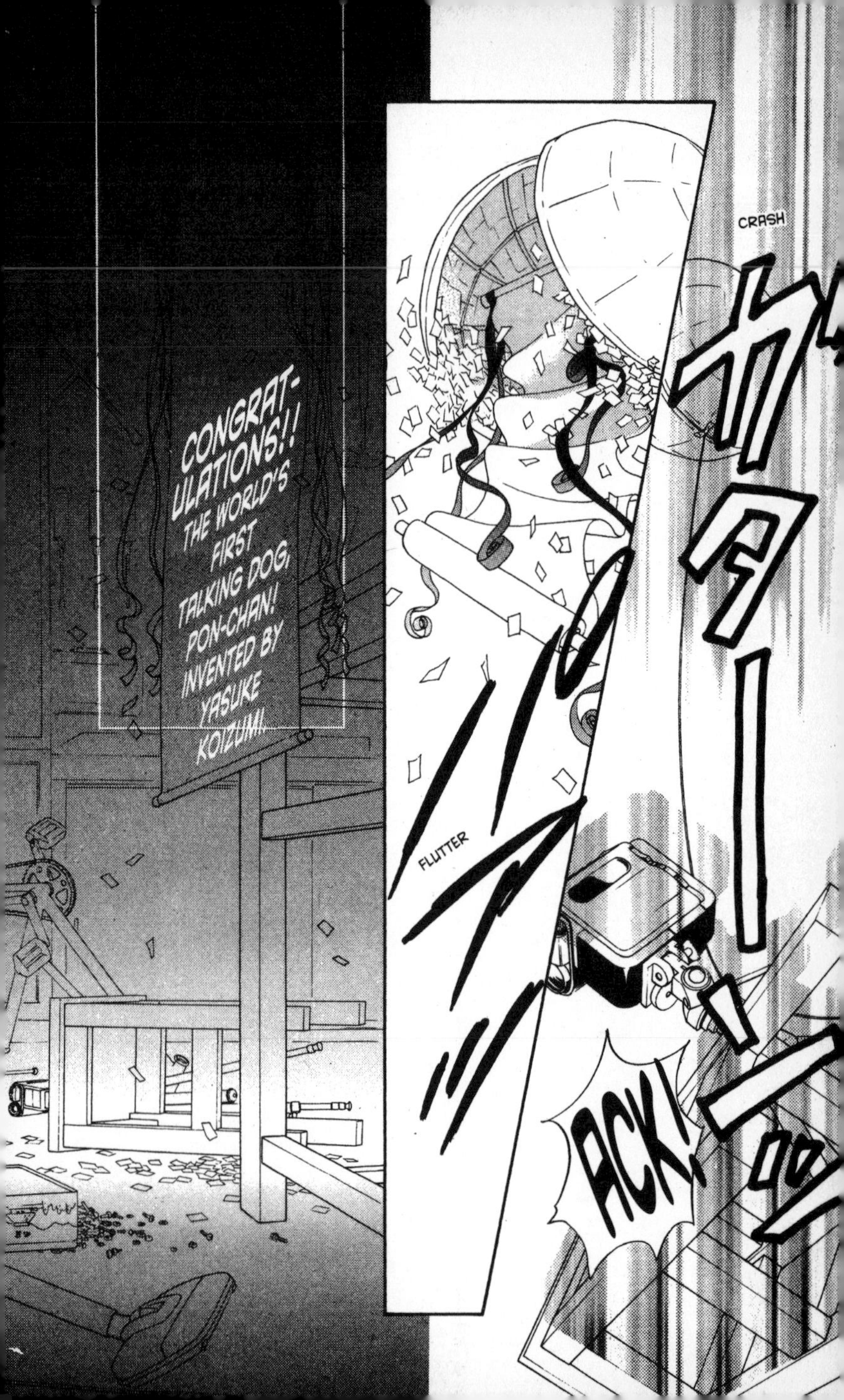
CRASH
ガタ——ン
ACK!
FLUTTER
CONGRATULATIONS!! THE WORLD'S FIRST TALKING DOG, PON-CHAN! INVENTED BY YASUKE KOIZUMI.

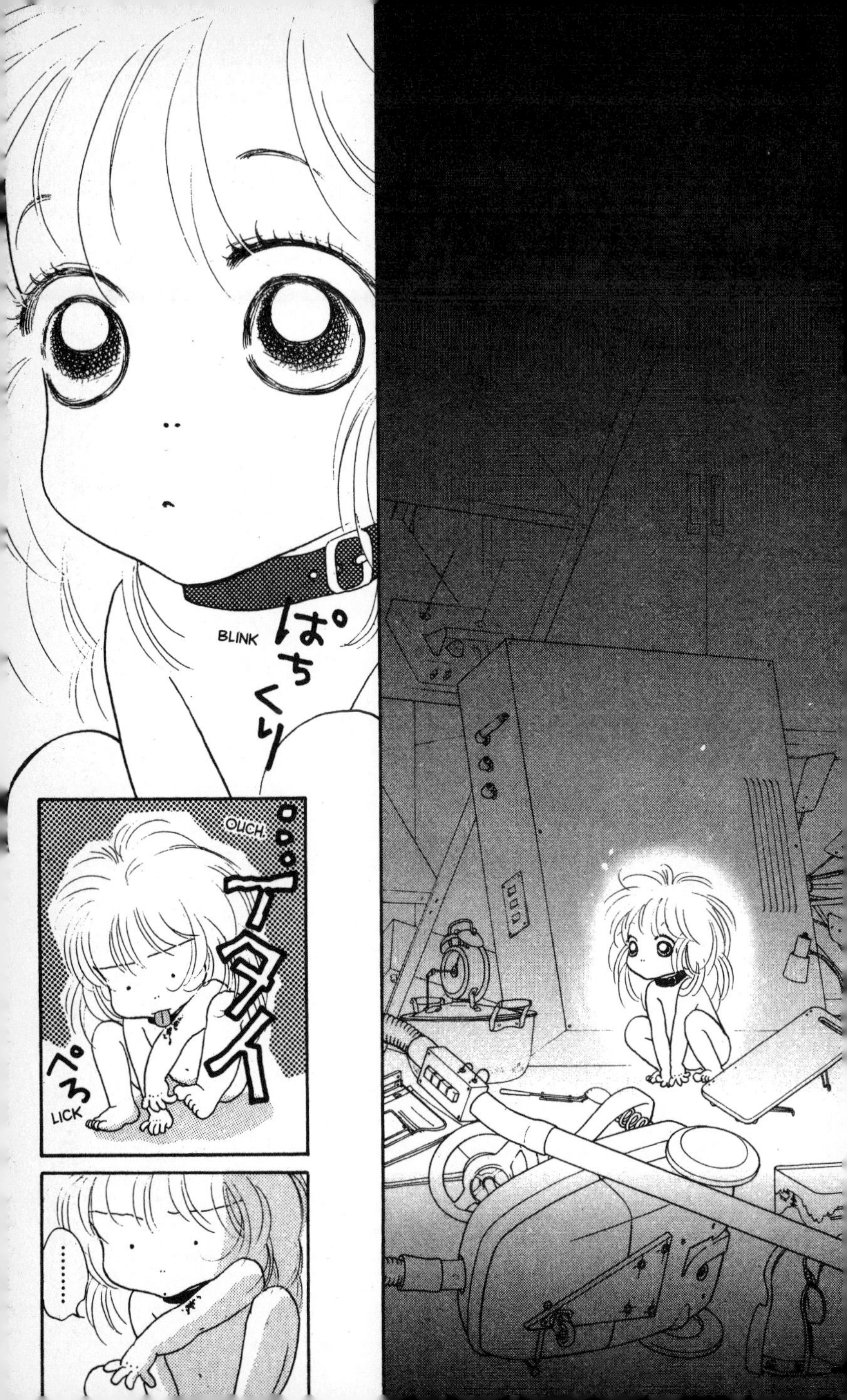
ぱちくり
BLINK
...アタイ
OUCH.
ぺろ
LICK
......

FREE COLLARS KINGDOM

フリーカラースキングダム

TAKUYA FUJIMI

THOSE FEISTY FELINES!

It's hard to resist Cyan: he's an adorable catboy, whose cute ears and tail have made him a beloved pet. But then his family abandons him, leaving the innocent Cyan to fend for himself.

Just when Cyan thinks he's all alone in the world, he meets the Free Collars, a cool gang of stray cats who believe that no feline should allow a human to imprison his Wild Spirit. They invite Cyan to join them, and the reluctant housecat has to decide fast, because a rival gang of cats is threatening the Free Collars' territory! Can Cyan learn to free his Wild Spirit—and help his new friends save their home?

1
FREE COLLARS KINGDOM
TAKUYA FUJIMA

Ages 16+

Special extras in each volume! Read them all!

tanoshimi

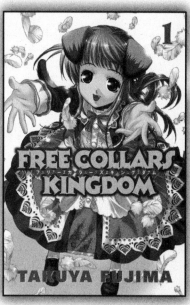

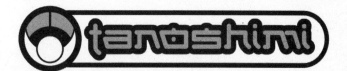

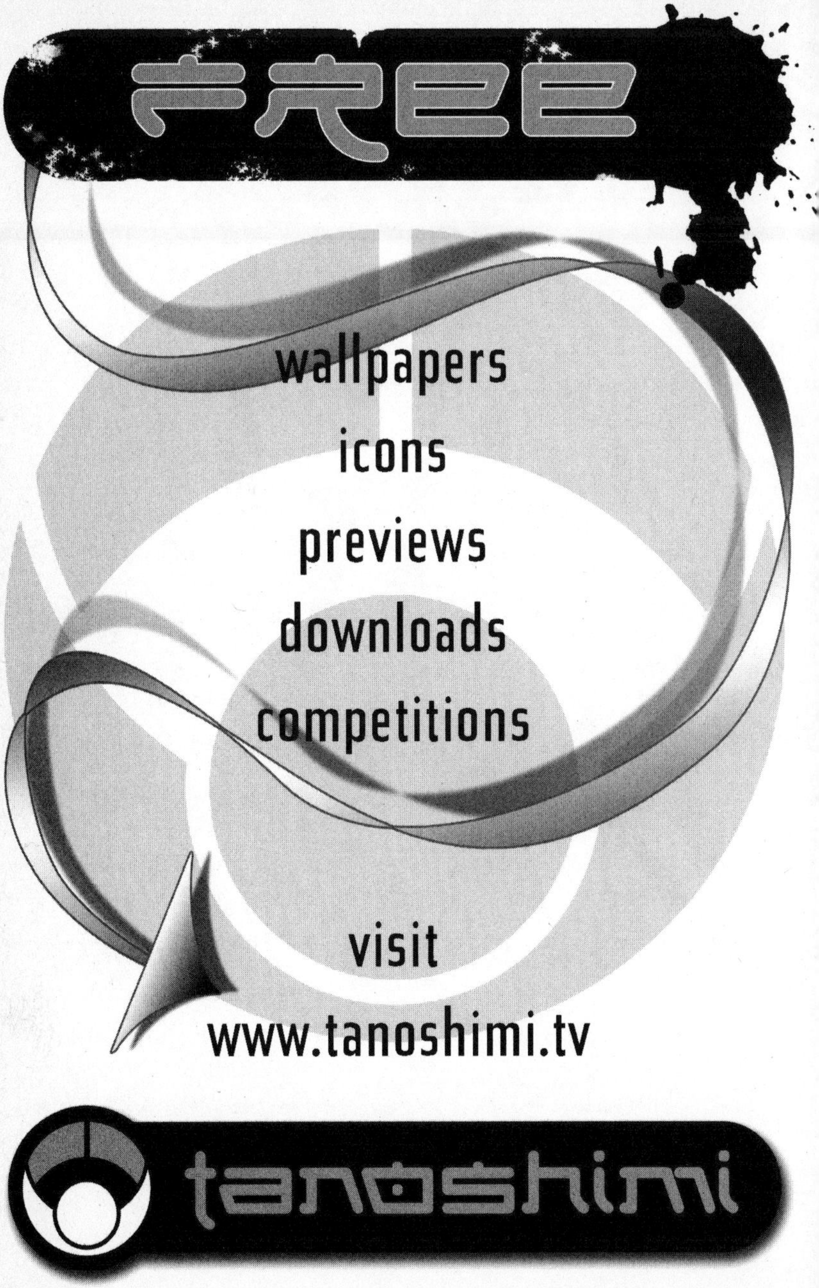
FREE
wallpapers
icons
previews
downloads
competitions
visit
www.tanoshimi.tv
tanoshimi

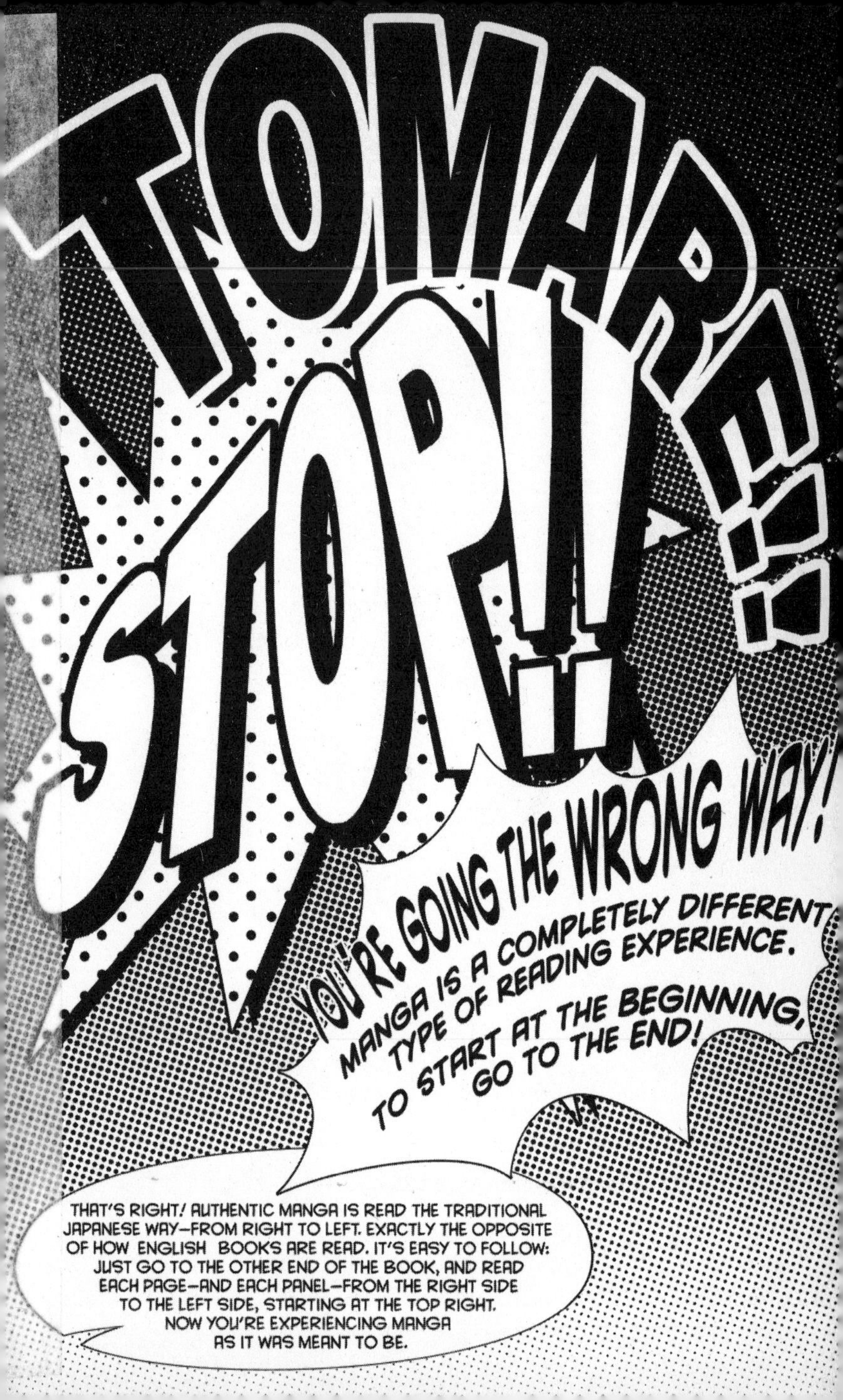
TOMARE!!
STOP!!
YOU'RE GOING THE WRONG WAY!
MANGA IS A COMPLETELY DIFFERENT TYPE OF READING EXPERIENCE.
TO START AT THE BEGINNING, GO TO THE END!
THAT'S RIGHT! AUTHENTIC MANGA IS READ THE TRADITIONAL JAPANESE WAY—FROM RIGHT TO LEFT. EXACTLY THE OPPOSITE OF HOW ENGLISH BOOKS ARE READ. IT'S EASY TO FOLLOW: JUST GO TO THE OTHER END OF THE BOOK, AND READ EACH PAGE—AND EACH PANEL—FROM THE RIGHT SIDE TO THE LEFT SIDE, STARTING AT THE TOP RIGHT. NOW YOU'RE EXPERIENCING MANGA AS IT WAS MEANT TO BE.